EDWARD SAID
A Critical Reader

B

EDWARD SAID

A Critical Reader

EDITED BY
MICHAEL SPRINKER

BLACKWELL
Oxford UK & Cambridge USA

Copyright © Blackwell Publishers, 1992

First published 1992
Reprinted 1993

Blackwell Publishers
238 Main Street
Cambridge, Massachusetts 02142
USA

108 Cowley Road
Oxford OX4 1JF
UK

Library of Congress Cataloging-in-Publication Data
Edward Said : a critical reader / edited by Michael Sprinker.
p.   cm.
Includes bibliographical references and index
ISBN 1–55786–228–1 (alk. paper). – ISBN 1–55786–229–X (pbk.: alk. paper)
1. Politics and literature.   2. Criticism–Political aspects.
3. Said, Edward W. – Influence   4. Critics – 20th century – Political
activities.   5. Intellectuals – 20th century – Political activities.
I. Sprinker, Michael.
PN51.E39   1992
801'.95'092–dc20   92–15598
CIP

British Library Cataloguing-in-Publication Data
A CIP catalogue record for this book is available from the British Library.

Typeset in 10 on 12pt Sabon
by CentraCet, Cambridge
Printed in Great Britain by T. J. Press (Padstow) Ltd., Padstow, Cornwall

This book is printed on acid-free paper

CONTENTS

CONTRIBUTORS

Tim Brennan is Assistant Professor of English at the State University of New York at Stony Brook. He is the author of numerous articles on colonial literature and culture and of *Salman Rushdie and the Third World*.

Partha Chatterjee holds an appointment in the Centre for Studies in Social Sciences, Calcutta. He is the author of *Nationalist Thought in the Colonial World*.

Richard G. Fox is Professor of Anthropology at Washington University in St Louis. His books include *Lions of the Punjab*.

Ferial J. Ghazoul teaches in the English department at the American University in Cairo.

Barbara Harlow is Associate Professor of Comparative Literature at the University of Texas at Austin. She is the author of *Resistance Literature* and of numerous articles on Third World literature and politics.

Nubar Hovsepian writes and lectures on Middle East affairs. He is co-editor of the forthcoming *A Middle East Reader* and is currently completing a doctorate in political science at the City University of New York.

Abdul R. JanMohamed is Associate Professor of English at the University of California at Berkeley. Founding editor of *Cultural Critique*, he is the author of *Manichaean Aesthetics* and is currently completing a book on Richard Wright.

Benita Parry writes and lectures on culture and imperialism. She is the author of *Delusions and Discoveries* and *Conrad and Imperialism*. She is working on a study of 'The Discourse of Imperialism'.

Bruce Robbins is Professor of English and Comparative Literature at Rutgers University. His books include *The Servant's Hand* and a forthcoming study of professionalism and the discipline of literary study.

Ella Shohat teaches Cinema and Cultural Studies at the City University of New York, and coordinates the Cinema Studies program at CUNY-Staten Island. She is the author of *Israeli Cinema: East/West and the Politics of Representation* (University of Texas Press) and co-editor with Robert Stam of *Unthinking Eurocentrism*.

Michael Sprinker is Professor of English and Comparative Literature at the State University of New York at Stony Brook, where he teaches literary theory and courses on culture and imperialism.

Jennifer Wicke is Associate Professor of Comparative Literature at New York University. She is the author of *Advertising Fictions*.

INTRODUCTION

During the melancholy and frustrating months leading up to the Persian Gulf War and even more insistently during the war and its aftermath, no voice dissenting from the Anglo-American consensus was more prominent or persuasive than Edward Said's. He was quite literally the most frequently cited, interviewed, and published oppositional figure in Britain and the United States. It bears directly upon the essays included in the present volume to inquire why this should have been the case.

About a decade ago, not long after the publication of *The Question of Palestine*, a prominent American historian acidly observed to me that he was "tired of the Said phenomenon." Putting aside the obvious professional envy that I surmise motivated the remark, one wonders why a "phenom-enon" like Edward Said would disturb an American scholar sufficiently to wish that Said would, in effect, just go away. Partly, no doubt, the irritation stemmed from political differences (as it happens, the historian was of Jewish heritage), but I think there were, as well, powerful intellectual and scholarly convictions that Said's public career directly affronted.

In the first place, Said's writing over the past quarter-century has resolutely resisted any easy disciplinary or professional pigeon-holing. Trained in comparative literature, fluent in at least three languages (English, Arabic, and French), literate in several more (Spanish, German, Italian, and Latin), Said can legitimately lay claim to the tradition of scholars like Auerbach, Curtius, and Spitzer whom he has often invoked as models for critical practice. Highly cultured, steeped in European classical music (he is an accomplished if these days strictly amateur pianist), well-travelled and at home in Cairo, Paris, London, and New York alike, he incarnates the very ideal of the cosmopolitan intellectual that remains so central to the humanities' self-image to this day.

At the same time, he has contributed to focal debates in an array of social

scientific disciplines, from history and sociology to anthropology and area
studies (particularly the Middle East). Specialists in these fields have often
been critical of his interventions, but they have on the whole not been able
to ignore or dismiss him out of hand.

Most famously, however, Said has for more than twenty years been the
most visible spokesperson for the Palestinian cause in the United States
(more recently in Britain as well). As journalist, television pundit, and
essayist, he has tirelessly contested the standard caricature of the politically
engaged Arab as terrorist, barbarian, maniac. Urbane and charming, he
presents a totally different image of Arabs to an anglophone audience
accustomed only to seeing them in the guise of gun-toting kidnappers and
hijackers. Even his Zionist opponents have begun to concede that what one
scurrilous attack dubbed the "professor of terror" scarcely fits the profile
of this particular Arab militant. The standard line now is that he is
seductive; wariness – rather than shrill denunication – is the new order of
the day for supporters of Israel.

Born in Jerusalem, Palestine, in 1935, Edward Said is the product of a
complex historical conjuncture that perhaps is unimaginable anywhere
outside the Levant. His family are members of one of the oldest Christian
communities in the world, a fact that has placed him in a curious relation
to the most volatile confessional confrontation in the region, although the
situation in Lebanon is a major exception in this regard. (Both his wife and
mother hail from Lebanon, and Said has written eloquently on this
country's tragic destruction since the mid-1970s.) Avowedly secular, Said
has never participated in – indeed, he occasionally professes scarcely to
comprehend – the murderous religious rivalries that have in part fueled the
conflict between Arabs and Jews.

Said's family fled Palestine in 1947-8 for Egypt, where Edward was
enrolled in British schools. Eventually, he was sent to the United States to
complete his secondary education and attend university. He studied English
and history at Princeton, where he fell under the spell of Richard Blackmur,
one of the most significant – and certainly the most singular – of the so-
called New Critics. Said's admiration for Blackmur has survived the years
and numerous shifts in Said's own critical focus, although he is far from
uncritical of his mentor's fellow-travelling with US Cold War policy
interests. Still, Blackmur may be said to have been a decisive influence,
notably in the attachment both he and Said felt for the essay form.

Said completed his formal academic training at Harvard, where he read
comparative literature under Harry Levin, writing a doctoral thesis on
Joseph Conrad – an enduring object of fascination about whom Said has
written some of his finest paragraphs. From this period Said seems to have
imbibed, above all, that somehwat surprising, persistent respect for the
canon of European literature which he retains to the present day.

A Christian Arab; raised in the Middle East but almost exclusively

Western-educated; a political activist who is yet broadly cultured in quite traditional, even conservative, ways – such are the tensions exhibited in Edward Said. Affected by all these currents that have rippled across his life, Said's career has been as variegated in its objects of interest and attention as the historical forces he has been compelled to negotiate. The present volume attempts to map this career in a preliminary manner, to trace some of its principal trajectories, and to confront its major, ongoing concerns.

The contributors to the present volume represent nearly the full range of interests covered in Said's published work. Only his music criticism is absent from a list that includes scholars from anthropology, politics, literature, and history. Yet, for all the diversity of his subjects and of the contributors themselves, several themes run through many of these essays. Perhaps the most frequent note sounded in them is the attention Said's work has devoted to the masters of philological and textual scholarship. Translator of Erich Auerbach, devotee of Spitzer and Vico, critic of Renan and Sir William Jones, throughout his career Said has meditated upon the disciplinary constraints imposed by closely examining the verbal intricacies of texts. As he remarks in the interview with which this volume closes, his aim has for many years been to extend the project of the great European *Philologen* who laid the foundations for contemporary literary (and other textually oriented) study in directions they themselves scarcely envisioned. However critical he may be of this legacy in books like *Orientalism* (1978) and *The World, the Text, and the Critic* (1983), he continues to honor the enormous care and respect for the European high cultural tradition their writings embody.

What separates Said from these august forebears is not only his recognition of the ethnocentrism that, covertly or overtly, underwrote their labors, but also his programmatic commitment to disseminating the fruits of his scholarship beyond the restricted audience of academic specialists and intellectual elites. A famous American literary critic once maintained, at a special session of the Modern Lanugage Association convention, that Said's access to mass print and visual media bears no relationship to his academic career. Surely this is false. Said became a prominent public intellectual and has maintained a continuous presence on television talk shows and in mass circulation newspapers and magazines in large measure because he has attained the knowledge and expertise in the Middle East and its relations to the West that only serious, sustained inquiry can provide. If most Americans and Britons know him through the *Today* show or the *Macneil-Lehrer News Hour* or the BBC, it is most unlikely that he would have appeared in these and other comparable venues without his having achieved well-deserved fame as a literary critic and humanistic scholar. During the Persian Gulf War, in fact, he was characteristically introduced as a professor of comparative literature and an authority on Islamic culture. Other commentators, particularly those whose views more

closely approximated the dominant Anglo-American view on the war, had
no need of such academic credits. Said's public visibility, I strongly believe,
depends upon them vitally.

But the politics are important as well, even if they have typically hindered,
not helped him to be more in the public eye. The cause of Palestinian
nationalism has not enjoyed significant favor in the United States, for
reasons that scarcely need rehearsing here. Said's longstanding support for
the Palestine Liberation Organization and his membership on the Palestine
National Council have been burdensome for him personally and professionally, absorbing time and energy and often putting him at risk. During
the mid-1970s, he expressed his own sense of living two lives, each almost
hermetically sealed off from the other. Since *Orientalism*, that has changed,
as his intellectual work has increasingly come to be integrated with – indeed
motivated by – his political commitments. In this way, too, he differs
markedly from those earlier humanists whose example he has honored. It
is as if his professional life over the past fifteen years has been a single,
sustained rebuttal of Julien Benda's thesis that intellectuals who hitch their
scholarly work to politics betray the principles of their vocation.

As this volume goes to press, Said is completing his *magnum opus* on
culture and imperialism, contemplating a volume of political essays, and
envisioning a long-meditated study of intellectuals. His Wellek lectures,
Musical Elaborations (1991) have recently appeared. In short, his astonishing scholarly productivity, kept up amid a flurry of articles and interviews
on the Gulf War, shows no sign of flagging. It would be foolhardy to
predict what he may write over the coming decade, but it is probably safe
to bet he will continue to follow a path laid down by the interests and
passions that have dominated his work over the past 20 years and are
discussed by the various contributors below. No single volume can do full
justice to the rich and voluminous treasure of Edward Said's intellectual
endeavor. The present collection is an interim balance sheet drawn up to
assess a career whose future may hold even more brilliant accomplishments
than those to date. We are far from having seen the end of "the Said
phenomenon."

Michael Sprinker

1

CONNECTIONS WITH PALESTINE

—

Nubar Hovsepian

On more than one occasion when I have traveled with Edward Said, I have observed that he takes a lot of luggage with him. In a reflective moment I asked him, why? His answer was connected with his experience of displacement in 1948 from Palestine. Since then, every time he travels he harbors the fear of not returning. Indeed, 1948 and the experience of permanent exile have left an indelible mark on many Palestinians. Said, who with his family went to Cairo in 1947, recalls: "I certainly did not think I was never going to return." But war and the establishment of Israel in 1948 and the continuation of the Arab-Israeli conflict have caused him and many of his compatriots to endure exile and separation from their national place. He notes that since "ancient times," exile as punishment was considered to be "the most horrible fate, a permanent fall from paradise," that an individual could endure. In his "Reflections on Exile",[1] Said views exile as a condition of permanent duality: one is only in a country, never exclusively of it. Life as an exile is less seasonal, settled, and successive than life at home. One's life, hopes and aspirations become bound to the inherent duality of being an exile. As one acquires new citizenship, interests, and affiliations, attachment to the concerns of "homeland" do not disappear.

The idea of exile, coupled with the need for connections and convergences,[2] has been central to Said's professional endeavors, as well as to his involvement with the question of Palestine. Other papers in this volume explore these connections and convergences in Said's professional work. In this essay I shall be concerned with his connection to Palestine, not only as a homeland but as an adversarial idea in both the West and the East.

In 1982–3, I worked at the United Nations in the secretariat of the International Conference on the Question of Palestine. Despite a nearly unanimous mandate from the General Assembly the convening of the conference encountered numerous obstacles. No western country wanted to risk hosting it. The subject was too "controversial." With great reluctance, the Swiss government acquiesced in holding the conference at the Palais des Nations in Geneva. I was entrusted with the production of the conference's written documents. In this connection, I worked with Said, who served as a consultant on these matters. One of the papers he commissioned was the writing of a "Profile of the Palestinian People." The paper was written by leading scholars on the Palestinians but was never officially issued.[3] It too was deemed too "controversial" by the preparatory committee, the UN body responsible for the conference. However, a photo exhibit featuring Jean Mohr's representation of life conditions of the Palestinian people was approved, with a proviso that the captions he had written be excluded. Even in this seemingly friendly environment, the Palestinians were denied the right of complete respresentation.[4]

Said asks, "Where do you stand on the question of Palestine? A shamelessly provocative question, but an interesting one against the background of theories of interpretation."[5] Given the controversy over Palestine, he wants to remove the discourse from the confines of the colonial legacy. He insists on the need for a national narrative that does not reduce the Palestinian reality to a mere function of Zionism. For him the Palestinian narrative stems directly from the Palestinian people's existence in and displacement from Palestine. The consciousness of the Palestinian self is to be reproduced by recounting their humanly produced secular history which could challenge the prevailing interpreations in the West. Therefore,

> there is no neutrality, there can be no neutrality or objectivity about Palestine . . . so ideologically saturated is the question of Palestine, so manifestly present is it to most people who come to deal with it, that even a superficial or cursory apprehension of it involves a position taken, an interest defended, a claim or right asserted. There is no indifference, no objectivity, no neutrality because there is simply no room for them in a space that is as crowded and overdetermined as this one.[6]

For those engaged with Palestine, a discourse of inclusion is essential if a future is to be assured.

Said's connection with Palestine prior to 1967 was essentially limited to his ties with family and friends. His entire family became refugees as a result of the 1948 war; all of his aunts, uncles, grandparents, and cousins were deracinated against their will. He received a solid British colonial education in Cairo, and during the 1950s his political awareness was mostly shaped by an anti-colonialism directed against the British. He also remembers harboring a deep dislike for President Truman. During his youth he was not politically active, nor did he have any organizational affiliations. By 1963 the Said family was centered in Beirut. His father was a respected businessman who had connections to the village of Dhour el-Shweir since 1942. When his father died in the early 1970s, none of the villagers would sell a piece of land in the local cemetery for his final resting place. Said observes that this experience forced him painfully to recognize that his father was an outsider, "a Palestinian, and no matter how jolly they were when he was alive, the residents wouldn't tolerate his long-term presence even after he had died."[7]

During this period he did not dwell on the idea of going back to Palestine. The conflict was seen as one between the Arabs and Israel. The issue of liberating Palestine was not really posed.[8] After the dispossession of the Palestinians in 1948, and the 1956 invasion of Egypt by Britain, France, and Israel, the Arab Middle East was imbued with a strong sense of anti-imperialism and a resurgent nationalism led by President Nasser of Egypt. To Arabs, and especially Palestinians, Nasser's promise of revived Arab nationalism seemed to provide a hope for a future that could negate the condition of permanent exile. But the hope proved elusive. In this period Said was at Harvard and Columbia. His work had little to do with Palestine and the Arabs or the Middle East. "There was no discursive formation to which one could attach oneself." For him Palestine remained an idea, and, more importantly, a historical memory.[9] The living aspect of the memory meant that "stability of geography and the continuity of land – these have completely disappeared from my life and the life of all Palestinians."[10]

He went to Amman and Beirut in 1969 and 1970, ostensibly to visit his family. While there he renewed contacts with relatives, such as Kamal Nasser, who by then was immersed in the work of the PLO. He had known him since the mid-1950s, but it was not until 1969–70 that he actually engaged Nasser in a conversation about Palestine. Kamal Nasser was an accomplished Arab poet, who also served as the official spokesperson of the PLO until 1973, when he was assassinated in Beirut by an Israeli hit team. Though Said was obviously aware of the PLO, he was not immersed in its activities, nor was he in touch with its leaders. What his compatriots did was important, but his challenge was to tell the story of Palestine from New York, the center of his exile.

On the personal level, Said's 1970 visit to Amman and Beirut ended the memories of a failed marriage as he met and later married Mariam Cortas, the daughter of a Lebanese Quaker family. In Amman he noticed that the Palestinians did not feel at home, but ironically they "could not feel more at home anywhere else now."[11] The Palestinian who had become immersed in the various guerilla organizations of the PLO, symbolized through his act of resistance the act of repatriation, hence the reversal of the condition of dispersal. For Said this meant the emergence of "Palestinianism."[12] The 1968 battle at Karameh provided the Palestinian with the opportunity to engage Israeli soldiers head-on. The Palestinian fought for himself instead of relying on the Arab armies as he had done in the past. The act of

Palestinian resistance enabled the articulation of a Palestinian identity. Thus, whereas displacement had characterized the Palestinian's life since 1948, as evidenced by his ". . . peripherality, his isolation, and his silence . . .," the battle of Karameh "presented the refugee with a new alternative, the chance to root peripherality, isolation, and silence in resisting action."[13] In short, Palestinian resurgence redefined the conflict as one between an Israeli occupier and an occupied Palestinian population engaged in resistance.

In 1980, the *New York Times* published an article by Richard Eder entitled "Edward Said: Bright Star of English Lit and P.L.O." (February 22, 1980). After the 1988 session of the Palestine National Council (PNC) which adopted the Palestinian "Declaration of Independence," the cover of *New York* magazine featured an article about Said entitled "Yasser Arafat's Man in New York."[14] After the 1967 war, Said had written "The Arab Portrayed," an essay printed in a collection on the Arab-Israeli conflict. The editor of the volume, Ibrahim Abu-Lughod, is Said's close and respected friend. In his introduction to the volume, Abu-Lughod described "The Arab Portrayed" as an essay which "powerfully and poetically probes the cultural values that surround and underlie an appreciation of the immediate issues and consequences of the Arab-Israeli confrontation of June, 1967." He added that its author was an "American humanist of Palestinian ancestry . . ."[15] How did this "American Humanist" become in a short period of time, the most recognized Palestinian in the US?

To be an Arab living in the US during the 1967 war was an experience in humiliation. One could not escape the "vulgar demotion" of the Arabs in both popular culture and in academe. In response, Said wrote what turns out to have been one of the many precursors to his *Orientalism* (1978). "The Arab Portrayed" was a sullen figure who could not face reality. He lacked culture, and his history was obscured by the fact that it was written in a language that cannot be read by Americans. In Western consciousness, the Arab was denied the most basic human attributes. For the Arab, "suffering and injustice, it seems, can never be his lot."[16] With only a few exceptions like I. F. Stone, the West could not understand or accept the irony that Palestinian Arabs in fact suffered or were victimized by the victims of the Holocaust. Said wanted (and still wants) the Arabs to gain permission to narrate their own history, and not simply to reduce it to a function of Zionism and Israel.[17] His early challenge to Orientalism was the need to restore the Arab's demand ". . . to reoccupy his place in history and in actuality."[18] With the enabling of an Arab Palestinian narrative, Said is quick to acknowledge that both Israelis and Arabs have contributed to the existing "maelstrom of [mutual] exclusion."[19]

In 1975–6, while a Fellow at the Center for Advanced Study in the Behavioral Sciences at Stanford University, Said's "The Arab Portrayed" gave way to the writing of *Orientalism*. From this book he derived the essence of both *The Question of Palestine* (1979), and *Covering Islam* (1981). The trilogy lays out Said's conceptual framework in analyzing the nature of the encounter between the West and the East. It is beyond the scope of this essay to reconstruct the central elements of Said's discourse on Orientalism. I will simply extract the elements from it that are relevant in contextualizing the basic thesis of *The Question of Palestine*.

In his book *Orientalism*, Said did not defend Islam or the Arabs. In fact he was attacking the notions of both the Orient and the Occident. Of primary concern was the delineation of the sources of Western knowledge about non-Western societies. He concluded that the function of Orientalism was to ". . . understand, in some cases to control, manipulate, even incorporate, what is manifestly a different world . . ."[20] Like a mirror, Orientalism reflects Western power and its imperial appetite. This type of knowledge developed in step with the expansion of European colonialism. "Thus the representation of other societies and peoples involved an act of power by which images of them were in a sense created by the Western observer who constructed them as peoples and societies to be ruled and dominated, not as objects to be understood passively, objectively or academically."[21] In this context, the question of representation is of central importance. To challenge colonial domination, it is imperative for the colonized to produce and create their own narratives that negate the colonial misrepresentations of their reality. A rewriting of history is required to enable liberation and to put an end to colonial suppression and domination.[22]

Said clearly associates Orientalism with Zionism. Both deal with the Arabs and Palestinians from an adversarial vantage point. *The Question of Palestine* was written mostly in 1977, in the period which coincides with Said's membership of the Palestine National Council (PNC). It was initially turned down as a manuscript by both Beacon Press and Pantheon, and was finally published in 1979 by New York Times Books. Rather than summarizing the entire book, I wish to focus on two aspects: Said's view of "Zionism From the Standpoint of Its Victims" (chapter 2); and his attempt to engage Zionists in a discourse of inclusion (a feature that was not appreciated by most reviewers). The book was in turn viewed by Palestinian radicals as having made too many concessions to Zionism.[23]

Said argues that at bottom Zionism is an "unchanging idea that expresses the yearning for Jewish political and religious self-determination – for Jewish national selfhood – to be exercised on the promised land."[24] However, what did Zionism entail for non-Jews? Said suggests that Zionism needs to be discussed in two ways: (1) "Genealogically," in the Nietzschean tradition, in order to situate and contextualize the origins of their ideas and ultimately to demonstrate the historical linkages with the dominant colonial ideas and institutions; and (2) "as practical systems for *accumulation* (of power, land, ideological legitimacy) and *displacement* (of people, other ideas, prior legitimacy)."[25] In his discussion of George Eliot's *Daniel Deronda* and Moses Hess's writings, Said identifies three ideas that served as a common denominator for them, as well as for most subsequent Zionist thinkers and ideologues. These are: "(a) the nonexistent Arab inhabitants, (b) the complementary Western-Jewish attitude to an 'empty' territory, and (c) the restorative Zionist project, which would repeat by rebuilding a vanished Jewish state and combine it with modern elements like disciplined, separate colonies, a special agency for land acquisition, etc."[26]

Furthermore, Said argues, Zionism developed in a European context of territorial acquisition in Africa and Asia. It did not define itself only as a national liberation movement, but rather "as a Jewish movement for colonial settlement in the Orient."[27] Theodor Herzl had absorbed and "internalized the imperialist perspectives on 'natives' and their 'territory'."[28] Regarding the mass expropriation of the poor, Herzl had noted: "both the expropriation and the removal of the poor must be carried out discreetly and circumspectly."[29] These views were aided by the "prior European inclination to view the natives as irrelevant to begin with."[30] From the historical record, one can conclude that the native Palestinian population was convinced as early as 1908 that the Zionist project in Palestine intended to reduce them to a minority in their historical abode.[31] Correlatively, Said's analysis leads him to conclude that "Zionism aimed to create a society that could never be anything but 'native' (with minimal ties to a metropolitan center) at the same time that it determined not to come to terms with the very natives it was replacing with new (but essentially European) 'natives.'"[32] In essence, the success of the Zionist project depended on the appropriation of land and the displacement and dispossession of the Palestinian Arabs from at least parts of Palestine; this, Said argues, is the only way Palestinians could have experienced and thus understood Zionism.

This analysis leads Said to insist on restoring the Palestinian narrative to history and public consciousness. The issue is really one of representation, which entails the process of self-definition (of a people) and the selection of the body and vehicle that represents them. In the case of the Palestinians, the representation is the process of self-definition. As Benedict Anderson illustrates in *Imagined Communities*, national self-definition is a function of asserting one's national being and nationhood as conceptually consistent with a people's collective memory. The Palestinian people have defined themselves as a people, a sovereign nation, and their sovereignty resides in and is embodied in their national representative, the PLO.

Said's and other Palestinians' criticisms of Israel's violations of Palestinian human rights and academic freedom, its closure of universities, its banning of books and censorship of the Palestinian media, are viewed as excessive by many Israelis. Instead of viewing these practices as a rejection of the Palestinian right to representation, some Israelis claim that they must be contextualized. In a study edited by an Israeli librarian, and circulated at the American Library Association conference (Atlanta, June 1991), Shmeul Sever cites a 1983 study by Meron Benvenisti which concludes that only 4 percent of all books imported into the Occupied Territories were banned. This 4 percent, however, represents 100 percent of all publications intended to express Palestinian nationalist feelings and aspirations.[33] This point serves to illustrate that what is at stake is not the tangential issues of specific violations of rights, but the prevention or the banning of the expression of the self-consciousness of the Palestinian community defined as a people. Their collective yearning is not simply to put an end to abusive practices of military occupation, but to end occupation itself. To do so would enable Palestinian representation, which in turn would enable the institutionalization of Palestinian sovereignty-statehood.

As stated earlier, the politics of representation means for Palestinians that their history and self-definition cannot be reduced to a function of Zionism. Their lives, culture, and politics have "their own dynamic and ultimately their own authenticity."[34] Thus Said notes that, for the Palestinians, the present as narrative stems directly from the story of their existence *in* and *displacement from* Palestine. To this day this Palestinian narrative has not found a place in official Israeli history. Accordingly, their presence is regarded as a nuisance that must be removed or expelled. Moreover, Palestinian nationalism is viewed more as aberrant or deviant behavior than as an expression of a national will. Said concludes that Israel's refusal to recognize this Palestinian reality is the key cause of the non-resolution of the conflict.

Despite Said's scathing critique of Zionism, *The Question of Palestine* could also be interpreted as "An Essay in Reconciliation."[35] When he wrote the book in 1977, it would be safe to say that most Palestinians did not concede that Jews had legitimate historical claims to Palestine. He has said: "I don't deny their claims, but their claim always entails Palestinian dispossession."[36] Said does not dispute the Zionist claim outright, but he wishes to remind Zionists that they are encumbered with Palestinians and Palestinian history, a fact entailed by what they have done and are doing in historical Palestine. In this context, Edward W. Said, then member of the PNC, recognized that the desired solution for the conflict must provide for the inclusion of both the Jews of Israel and the Palestinians. The problem at hand was to be resolved through a political encounter between these two antagonists, "whose past and future ties them inexorably together."[37] For Said, this encounter will necessarily prove beneficial to both peoples; moreover, it is the only hope for ending what Said disgustedly recognizes as the history of mindless violence and rejectionist politics that have hitherto characterized Israeli-Palestinian relations.

Said is often faulted by Jewish critics for misrepresenting the Zionist discourse. They strenuously object to having Zionism linked with the

dominant colonialist ideas at the turn of the century.[38] Wistrich wishes that
Said had only presented the affirmative case for the Palestinian yearning for
statehood instead of producing a scathing critique of Zionism. Halkin, on
the other hand, writes more as a committed Zionist. A New Yorker by
birth, he now lives in Jerusalem, Said's birthplace. In essence they have
"traded places," and in so doing Halkin and his people have ended their
exile, which by necessity was at "your people's expense."[39] Halkin is
opposed to the establishment of a Palestinian state, and might be willing to
consider peace with the displaced Palestinians only if they give him
assurances of their *real* peaceful intentions. Both authors fail to meet Said
on his central argument: namely, the right of Palestinian representation.
They acknowledge Said's recognition of legitimate competing claims to
Palestine, but fail to recognize that in creating Israel, Zionism also caused
Palestinian dispossession.

Said's essay in reconciliation is viewed by some radical Palestinians as
having gone too far. He is accused of frittering away Palestinian national
rights by making "unwarranted concessions to Zionism." Accordingly,
Said's key failure is in defining the conflict as one "between two peoples,"
instead of a class struggle against Zionism and imperialism. Said's failings
are a function of his "bourgeois humanistic approach," which makes him
distrustful of the power of "armed struggle;" hence, he is seen as favoring
a political solution.[40]

As will be shown later, this is not the only time that Said has been
criticized by both Zionist and Palestinian advocates. How does Said connect
his analysis for a political solution with the actualities of Palestinian
political life? Three important developments occurred in 1974. First, the
twelfth meeting of the PNC adopted a ten-point program, which in
retrospect has been viewed by most fair-minded analysts as the beginning
of a PLO-initiated two-state solution for the Israeli-Palestinian conflict.[41]
Second, in October of the same year, the Arab Heads of State at the Rabat
(Morocco) Summit recognized the PLO as the "sole legitimate representative of the Palestinian people," and affirmed Palestinians' rights to self-
determination. Third, on 13 November, Yassir Arafat was invited to
address the General Assembly of the United Nations. On 22 November the
PLO was accorded observer status at the UN, and on the same day
resolution 3236 was adopted by the General Assembly, recognizing the
Palestinian people's right to self-determination and to national independence and sovereignty.

At this juncture, Arafat's advisors were searching for someone to
translate the speech to be delivered at the General Assembly. Mostly at the
suggestion of Ibrahim Abu-Lughod, Said was persuaded to undertake the
task. In the process he met for the first time the Palestinian poet Mahmoud
Darwish and Shafiq al-Hout, a Palestinian writer and the PLO's representative to Lebanon. Al-Hout told me that he was intrigued by the choice

because he had not even heard of this Palestinian professor of English literature. Not only did he want to secure a proper translation, but he also wanted to meet this accomplished Palestinian.[42]

Once the PLO secured observer status at the United Nations, in effect, the rules of the game for achieving Palestinian self-determination had changed. Over time, "armed struggle" had to give way to politics and diplomacy. Already in the seventies President Sadat was suggesting that the Palestinians form a government in exile. Indeed, both Sadat and Arafat suggested that Edward Said could be a member of such a government. On several other occasions, Said's name was bandied around as a member of a Palestinian negotiating team. Though Said had cultivated a good relationship with Arafat and the rest of the Palestinian leadership, it is fair to say that he was never consulted about it, nor did he agree to play such an overtly political role. Nevertheless, Said did use his increasing prominence to meet with US and Arab officials to advance the goal of Palestinian self-determination. In 1977, Said was elected to the Palestine National Council (PNC) as an independent intellectual. He never tires of pointing out that he has never been a member of any political party. Why then did he join the PNC? Al-Hout suggests that the PLO was at this period consolidating the institutional framework for Palestinian reperesentation. They needed to create a PNC that represented more than the various factions. To attain legitimacy, the PNC needed independent members representing all sectors of exiled Palestinian civil society. Al-Hout adds, "when his [Said's] presence was needed he joined . . ."[43] In addition, Said views his membership in the PNC as an "act of solidarity" with his people, and ultimately as an affirmation of his Palestinian identity. The PNC enabled him to take an active role as a "partisan . . . on behalf of Palestinian self-determination."[44]

Since 1977, Said has attended only four sessions of the PNC (1977 in Cairo, 1984 in Amman, 1987 in Algiers, 1988 in Algiers). With the exception of 1988, his participation in deliberations has been scant. He usually attends the first day or two and then departs. He has not participated in the voting, nor has he had the patience or the inclination to engage in the internal struggles of the PLO and its various factions. Al-Hout told me that Said does not wait to receive orders from anyone; instead, he initiates his interventions independently, which is not unlike his everyday work as a critic.

For Said, the quest for Palestinian self-determination was restricted by the particularities of the given historical conjuncture. He notes that no liberation movement has ever been able to wage a struggle without a strategic ally, something that the Palestinians have not enjoyed. In addition, the Palestinians are not in a typical colonial situation, in which a majority fights a ruling minority. Moreover, the quality of the colonial adversary (Israel) is not similar to the *pieds noirs* in Algeria, or the US in Viet Nam, or the whites in South Africa. "It is entirely different, we are dealing with

Jews and the Holocaust ... The idea of the destruction of that society struck me as impermissible."[45] In this context Said, consistent with the genesis of the Palestinian two-state platform as articulated in the eleventh PNC (1974), ventured to pose some difficult questions. In 1979, he concluded that "armed struggle," which had been espoused in 1969 by the PNC, could no longer serve as the principal program for the Palestinians. In addition, he asked, "are we a national independence movement or a national liberation movement?" He advocated the need for a "clearer program for progress toward peace – forthright statements of a two-state solution and some indication how this might come about . . ."[46] The central aim of this approach is to arrive at a *modus vivendi* between an Israel within pre-1967 boundaries and a Palestinian state. The battle with Zionism must therefore secure recognition that the Palestinians have a genuine national identity and the right to a state in the land of historical Palestine.

In 1983, Said was unable to attend the PNC session due to his son's hospitalization with a serious bone disease. Instead, he wrote a memo addressed to Khaled al-Fahoum, chairman of the PNC, and to Yassir Arafat, Chairman of the PLO Executive Committee. The meeting was the PNC's first after the 1982 Israeli invasion of Lebanon, which had resulted in the further dispersal and dislocation of Palestinians. Said affirmed with pride that it is the victims of occupation who have provided the world with both principles and visions for peace. He pointed out that unfortunately the world "has not clearly heard what we said, partly because hostile propaganda has drowned us out, but partly also because we have neither been clear enough nor forceful enough."[47] For Said the time had come for Palestinians to state clearly what they wanted, and why they wanted it. He added, "we must be specific, and we must be the people whose voice, whose proposals, whose values are considered by the international community to provide an end to war, to unceasing violence and to endless devastation." To ensure the survival of the Palestinian people, the international community, the Arab world and the Jewish world must be addressed. Furthermore, to defend the right to self-determination, Palestinians must also be willing "to come to terms with the wishes of other communities." The Zionism of Begin and Sharon must be countered with a Palestinian vision for democracy, peace, non-violence, non-belligerency, political justice and equality. Furthermore, Said urges that, "we not delude ourselves into believing that more fighting and more destruction will help us: they will not, because we will be the people to pay the highest price."

In the same memo Said urged the PNC to adopt a clear program of non-violent but massive civil resistance in the Occupied Territories. Military or terrorist means have been too costly for the Palestinian people, and they have also undermined the moral basis of the cause. The aim of this non-violent campaign is not only to claim the territory but to also highlight

Israel's colonization of Palestinian lands. Conjuncturally, the PNC was urged to undertake a major informational campaign targeting the people and the institutions of civil society in the US, as a prerequisite for changing US policy. Finally, Said insists that the Jewish world must be addressed. The Palestinians cannot be rejectionists; instead, the world must see that the "Palestinian idea is an idea of living together, of respect for others, of mutual recognition between Palestinian and Israeli."

The outbreak of the Palestinian Intifada in 1987 enabled the PNC to adopt the Palestinian Declaration of Independence at its 1988 session in Algiers. Upon his arrival in Algiers, Said was given a draft text of the "Declaration" to adapt to English. He used the process of translation from Arabic to English to influence the re-phrasing of the Arabic text. Upon its adoption, Said made numerous representations in the American media arguing that the PNC's declaration was tantamount to a historic compromise. However, the Reagan administration wanted more. Arafat was denied a visa to address the UN General Assembly, and so the venue was changed to Geneva. After delivering his speech to the duly convened General Assembly, Arafat was essentially forced unceremoniously to read a prepared statement at a press conference in the Palais des Nations. The words he read were largely written by the State Department and faxed from Washington to the Swedish Embassy. Arafat's utterances caused the opening of a US-PLO dialogue that in retrospect seems more monologic. As I witnessed these developments from Geneva, the only excitement I could detect was among the ranks of the press corps. Said, like most Palestinians I know, was certainly not elated. He did not object to the clarifications Arafat made, but he told me, "I resented, on an emotional level, the idea that he had to say words dictated by the State Department."[48]

Despite his emotional disappointment, Said vigorously supported the Palestinian Declaratiorn of Independence in writing and through many media appearances. However, he perceives his task in the US to be more than as a propagator of the PNC's declarations. The issue for him is quite basic. He wants to bear witness to his people's condition. In 1988, he shared a platform at the *Tikkun* conference with Michael Walzer. Instead of talking about the mundane details of acceptable negotiating positions, he insisted on focusing on the meaning of occupation for the Palestinian people. Walzer wanted to evacuate history from the discussion; in contrast, Said's challenge was to remind Walzer and the audience that they are encumbered with Palestinian history. In essence Said was presenting Walzer with the Palestinian insistence on "never again."

Said does not reserve his sharply worded criticisms for supporters of Israel only. In fact, his severest criticism has been levelled at the PLO. In 1989, Said charged that the PLO did not understand the US context. Its representatives were essentially corrupt, inept or both. He considered the PLO ignorant of the workings of American society. Instead of focusing on

American civil society, they simply relied on "middlemen" to transmit their messages. The issue for Said is the need for intelligent and coordinated Palestinian intervention in the US public domain to secure support for his compatriots in the Intifada. On this score, his efforts were a total failure. Instead of responding to his appeals for reform, PLO apparatchiks denounced Said and resorted to rhetorical formulas.[49] Said's critique prompted a debate among Palestinians, but did not produce any tangible reforms. It is interesting to note that only a few months before this episode, Said was slandered in the pages of *Commentary*, in an article entitled "Professor of Terror." In neither instance could the author understand or grasp the importance of the intellectual as an oppositional force.

Said, like many exiles, lives in several worlds. In the late 1980s and until August 1990, he contributed a monthly column to *al-Majalla*. Through this column and the translation of his books into Arabic, he has engaged his compatriots in a dialogue. He has urged them to understand America on its own cultural terms. But Iraq's invasion of Kuwait put a halt to his column. In his last article he lamented the brutalization of Kuwait by the invading Iraqi army. However, like many of us, he refused to be constrained to choose between being either pro-Saddam or pro-Bush despite the fact that a position critical of both was scarcely permitted. Indeed, the Arab press did not allow for dissent. All behaved as if they had one editor-in-chief, namely King Fahd of Saudi Arabia.[50] The Arab condition is dominated by the national security state, which fears debate and dissent. But as an Arab living in America, Said urges his exiled compatriots to be critically engaged. He notes, "because we have access to this society here [US] and that one over there [Arab world] we should think of ourselves as more critically engaged with both, entitled not only to ask questions and make demands of US policy and society, but also of current policies, particularly when these policies inside almost all the Arab countries are so generally repressive."[51]

As indicated at the outset of this essay, the exile must make connections and linkages with the multi-dimensional world he or she inhabits. The Palestinian and Arab exile is urged to adopt the model of the Intifada, which entails a new sense of community woven out of the threads connecting the various domains of their distinctive life spheres. Out of these connections, new forms of cooperation can serve as the basis for living together. Empowered with this sense of inclusion, Israelis can also be engaged, even despite their exclusion of the Palestinians. Said concludes that neither the Israelis nor the Palestinians have a military option against one another. Thus, the Palestinians must remain in parts of Mandatory Palestine, and in turn must use a "variety of means to persuade Israelis that only a political settlement can relieve the mutual seige, the anguish and insecurity of both people. There is no other acceptable secular, that is, real alternative."[52] The Palestinian exile in America must not only render testimony to the plight of Palestinians under occupation, but must also be part of the struggles for human and minority rights, and women's rights, and must defend the right to free expression and self-determination both in the Arab world and in the Americas. This is a position that Edward Said has not only espoused for others, but has been willing, often at great personal risk, to act out in his own life.

Notes

1 See Edward W. Said, "Reflections on Exile", *Granta*, 13 (Winter 1984).
2 "Convergences-Inventories of the Past" is the title of the new series Said edits for Harvard University Press.
3 *A Profile of the Palestinian People*, written collectively by Edward W. Said, Ibrahim Abu-Lughod, Janet L. Abu-Lughod, Muhammad Hallaj, and Elia Zureik, was published by the Chicago-based Palestine Human Rights Campaign in 1983, and distributed unofficially to the conference participants. It was later included in Edward W. Said and Christopher Hitchens, eds., *Blaming the Victims: Spurious Scholarship and the Palestinian Question* (London: Verso, 1988).
4 This experience was one of the factors that prompted the collaborative effort between Edward W. Said and Jean Mohr in producing *After The Last Sky: Palestinian Lives* (New York: Pantheon, 1986).
5 See Edward W. Said, "The Burdens of Interpretation and the Question of Palestine", *Journal of Palestine Studies*, No. 61 (Fall 1986), p. 29.
6 Ibid., p. 30.
7 Said, "Edward Said Reflects on the Fall of Beirut", *London Review of Books* (July 4, 1985), p. 3.
8 Interview with Said, April 5, 1991.
9 Ibid.
10 See *After The Last Sky*, p. 19.
11 Edward W. Said, "The Palestinian Experience", in *Reflections on The Middle East Crisis*, ed. Herbert Mason (The Hague: Mouton and Co., 1970), p. 130.
12 Ibid., p. 132.
13 Ibid., pp. 143–4.
14 Dinitia Smith, "Arafat's Man In New York – The Divided Life of Columbia Professor Edward Said", *New York*, January 23, 1989.
15 Ibrahim Abu-Lughod (editor), *The Arab-Israeli Confrontation* (Evanston: Northwestern University Press, 1970).
16 "The Arab Portrayed", p. 4.
17 See E. Said, "Permission To Narrate: Reconstituting The Siege of Beirut," *London Review of Books* (February, 1984), pp. 16–29.
18 "The Arab Portrayed", p. 9.
19 "The Palestinian Experience", pp. 141–2. Here and in later works Said insists that a solution to this conflict requires a discourse based on inclusion. See in particular "Burdens of Interpretation", cited in n. 5 above.
20 Said, *Orientalism* (New York: Pantheon Books, 1978), p. 12.
21 Said, "Orientalism and Zionism", in *al-Majalla*, December 2–8, 1987 (Arabic). The quotation is from the original English typescript.
22 This idea has been developed by many theorists from the Third World; most

importantly, Amilcar Cabral, "The Weapon of Theory" in *Revolution in Guinea* (New York: Monthly Review Press, 1969), pp. 90–111. Feminist theorists have also made use of Said's discourse; in particular see Joan Cocks, *The Oppositional Imagination: Feminism, Critique and Political Theory* (London: Routledge, 1989).

23 For Zionist perspectives see Hillel Halkin, "Whose Palestine? An Open Letter to Edward Said", in *Commentary* (May 1990), pp. 21–30; and Robert S. Wistrich, "The Unresolved Conflict", in *Jewish Quarterly* (Spring 1980), pp. 56–8. For a radical Palestinian critique, see "The Question of Palestine According To Edward Said", in *The PFLP Bulletin*, No. 47 (February 1981).

24 *The Question of Palestine*, p. 56.

25 Ibid., p. 57.

26 Ibid., p. 68.

27 Ibid., p. 69.

28 Ibid., p. 70.

29 Quoted in ibid., pp. 70–1.

30 Ibid., p. 71.

31 See the excellent study by Muhammad Y. Muslih, *The Origins of Palestinian Nationalism* (New York: Columbia University Press, 1988).

32 *The Question of Palestine*, p. 88.

33 Shmuel Sever and Ziv Beyth, "Freedom of Speech and Intellectual Freedom in The Israeli Occupied Territories."

34 *The Question of Palestine*, p. 112.

35 See Eqbal Ahmad's review, "An Essay in Reconciliation", *The Nation* (March 22, 1980), pp. 341–3.

36 Interview, April 5, 1991.

37 *The Question of Palestine*, p. 238.

38 See articles by Robert S. Wistrich and Hillel Halkin cited in n. 23 above.

39 Halkin, p. 23.

40 See the review in *The PFLP Bulletin*, in n. 23 above.

41 For a synthetic account, see Muhammad Muslih's *Toward Coexistence: An Analysis of The Resolutions of The Palestine National Council* (Washington, DC: Institute for Palestine Studies, 1990).

42 Interview with Shafiq al-Hout, January 9, 1989 (New York). Subsequently, Said became good friends with both Darwish and al-Hout.

43 Interview with Shafiq al-Hout, January 9, 1989.

44 Interview, April 5, 1991.

45 Ibid.

46 Interviews with Mark Bruzonsky, published in *The Middle East* (April 1979), and *Worldview* (May 1979). Said's views were harshly criticized by partisans of Fateh and the PFLP. To them he was frittering away Palestinian rights. By 1988, however, these views were adopted by the PNC in Algiers.

47 Quoted from the memo to Fahoum and Arafat, February 16, 1983.

48 Interview with Said, April 5, 1991. As to the text read by Arafat, I have a copy of the fax communication between the State Department and the Swedish Embassy in Geneva.

49 See the interview with Edward Said, *Al-Qabas*, October 7–8, 1989. Yasser Abed Rabbo's response was published on October 14–15, 1989.

50 This characterization was formulated by the Lebanese novelist Elias Khoury, during a conversation with me in Beirut (August 1991).

51 From a speech by Said, delivered to the Arab Anti-Discrimination Committee's (ADC) annual convention, May 4, 1991.

52 Quoted from Said, "Reflections on Twenty Years of Palestinian History", *Journal of Palestine Studies*, XX, Number 4 (Summer 1991), p. 22.

2

OVERLAPPING TERRITORIES AND INTERTWINED HISTORIES: EDWARD SAID'S POSTCOLONIAL COSMOPOLITANISM

Benita Parry

Here really is the theme of my work, its main "figure" if you want to give it a poetic equivalent, the figure of crossing over ... The fact of migration is extraordinarily impressive to me: that movement from the precision and concreteness of one form of life transmuted or imported into the other ... I think culture has to be seen as not only excluding but also *exported*; there is this tradition which you are required to understand and learn and so on, but you cannot really be *of* it ... And that to me is a deeply interesting question and needs more study because no exclusionary practice can maintain itself for very long. Then you get the crossings over ... and then of course the whole problematic of *exile and immigration* enters into it, the people who simply don't belong in any culture; that is the great modern or, if you like, post-modern fact, the standing outside of cultures.
   "Media, Margins and Modernity", a conversation between Raymond Williams and Edward Said, Appendix to Raymond Williams, *The Politics of Modernism: Against The New Conformists*, pp. 187–8, 196
   The sense of being between cultures has been very, very strong for me. I would say that's the single strongest strand running through my life: the fact that I'm always in and out of things, and never really *of* anything for very long. "Edward Said", in Imre Salusinszky, *Criticism in Society: Interviews*, p. 123

A critique of culture and imperialism that situates itself on the borders and boundaries of knowable communities, intellectual systems, and critical practices, celebrating the unhoused and decentered counter-energies generated by the displaced critical consciousness, enacts a theoretical mode symptomatic of a postcolonial cosmopolitanism which proclaims its multiple detachments and occupancy of a hybrid discursive space.[1] It is a precarious position for a politically aligned theorist to maintain, and a demonstration of Said apparently contradicting himself, is when in the same breath he acknowledges the importance of moving from one identity to another, and affirms that "[O]ne of the virtues of being a Palestinian is that it teaches you to feel your particularity in a new way, not only as a problem but as a kind of gift" ("On Palestinian Identity", pp. 74 and 75). Said's remarks signal the dilemma for intellectuals in a climate where the militancy of anti-essentialist critiques inhibits their conceding the power of imaginary organic collectivities constructed under conditions of subjugation and conserved in the process of liberation struggles. Since Said appears more aware than most of the chasm between the "optimistic mobility of the intellectual and artist between domains, forms and languages," and the mass dislocations endured by economic migrants or expelled refugees, his project admits to a greater ambivalence on the tensions between the cognitive recognition of cultural heterogeneity and the political need for solidarity. But it also avoids the conceit of conflating the transactions with imperialism's structures effected by the elite postcolonial with the exigencies of the situations experienced by forcibly displaced populations or by unemancipated peoples.

The impurity which Said discerns as systemic in the colonial and postcolonial condition becomes the theoretical mode through which these experiences are to be apprehended; and even as attention is drawn to the absence of imperialism and the indifference to "Third World" liberationist thinking in continental theory, Western Marxism and Anglo-Saxon cultural criticism, Said's own writings negotiate an alliance among these spheres and the analyses developed within anti-imperialist movements, in the process producing elaborations that were not inherent in the metropolitan sources. Hence, when Said describes the revisionist projects of postcolonial intellectuals who "address the metropolis using the techniques, the discourses, the very weapons of scholarship and criticism once reserved exclusively for the European" as "original and creative work" which has transformed the very terrain of the disciplines ("Third World Intellectuals/ Metropolitan Culture", p. 29), this can be read as self-referential. Peter Hulme has mapped how the conceptual area we now designate Colonial Discourse came into being through a critique of continental theoretical work, in particular tracking Said's reworking of Foucault as an exemplary procedure in which Said, despite his recognizing "the scrupulously ethno-centric nature" of Foucault's undertaking, chooses to emphasize the *possi-bilities* inherent in this work, most importantly in the concept of discourse producing texts within networks of history, power, knowledge, and society ('Subversive Archipelagoes: Colonial Discourse and the Break-Up of Continental Theory", *Dispositio* (1989)).[2]

In a parallel resituation of another theoretical practice within a more extensive terrain, Said, despite his declaration of dependence on Raymond Williams's criticism, again conducts a dialogue with the borrowed mode that interrogates its privileged inclusions and calls attention to its silences.

Lodged within the handsome appreciation of Williams's pathbreaking studies is a commentary on the irrelevance of the colonial experience to his revisionist narrative of the making of English culture, the zones of exclusion staking out the ground on which Said offers an interpretation of imperialism as *constitutive* of metropolitan cultures.[3] The incommensurability between the cultural circumscription of the one, and the other's incessant crossings of thresholds, is manifest in Said's acerbic praise of Williams's "belonging-ness" and "native vision," where politesse is leavened by the addition of an inconsonant stance: "the power of Williams's work is intrinsically at one with its rootedness and even its insularity, qualities that stimulate in the variously unhoused and rootless energies of people like myself – by origin un-English, un-European, un-Western – a combination of admiring regard and puzzled envy" ("Narrative, Geography and Interpretation", p. 84). The disparity between different forms of oppositional critical consciousness brought to the same set of theoretical problems emerges in an exchange where Williams, while acknowledging that these terms have been appropri-ated by the existing social order, explains his use of "common culture" to counter notions of elitism, and of "community" to oppose competitive individualism. The gap opened up by Said's response – "As for me, though perhaps I am putting it too strongly, culture has been used as essentially not a cooperative and communal term but rather as a term of exclusion" (*The Politics of Modernism*, p. 196) – is elsewhere measured in definitions of culture as a system of normalization and legitimation, of demotions and defensive boundaries between polities designed to keep others out, but which despite its aspiration to sovereignty, is a discrete entity that includes "foreign elements and alterities."

On one level the charge of organicist assumptions made against Wil-liams's cultural criticism is invalidated by Williams's grasp of culture as a mutable process rather than a stable system or structure, an arena of struggle where in any conjuncture there is a conflict between the class interests and social meanings of contesting groups, and in which the hegemonic must always contend with the lived and practiced elements of both the residual and the emergent (see for example *Marxism and Litera-ture*, pp. 125–6). Yet this is a theoretical construct which, while fore-grounding internal division and volatility, is caught within an holistic notion of the island's histories. Paul Gilroy, in a manner less circumspect than that of Said when he dissents from Williams, has censured the latter's definition of culture as lived identities formed through long experience and actual, sustained social relations, for excluding immigrant blacks – "visibly different people . . . unfamiliar neighbours" – from this "significant social entity" (*There Ain't No Black in the Union Jack*, pp. 48–50). Certainly for all its dissociation from "the alienated superficialities of 'the nation' which are the limited functional terms of the modern ruling class," Williams's avuncular disquisition on "The Culture of Nations" in *Towards 2000* does

associate culture with fixed location and comes close to naturalizing a
conception of the nation as equivalent to the physical and cultural continuity of autochthonous peoples. For when Williams writes, albeit as a counter
to the misconstructions of elite historiography, that "the real history of the
peoples of these islands . . . goes back . . . to the remarkable societies of the
Neolithic shepherds and farmers, and back beyond them to the hunting
peoples who did not simply disappear but are also amongst *our* ancestors"
(p. 193, emphasis added), he accords a special status to the putative
descendents of an indigenous community denied to the successive waves of
immigrants that have come to constitute the present populations of Britain.
Such a privileging of lineage, directed at disputing class power in the writing
of the nation's narrative and in the process installing ethnic power, mutes
the acknowledgement of diversity and continual reconstitution, and lessens
the impact of indignation over a patriotic heritage which was pressed into
service for imperialist ends.

A vocabulary deployed with such composure by Williams is unavailable
to Said. Even when he, with exemplary graciousness, situates his own work
as an extension of Williams's, this cannot conceal that the latter's visceral
and intellectual attachment to "deeply grounded . . . formed identities of a
settled kind" is precisely a mode of "identitarian thought" mistrusted by
Said who, in discussing liberationist thinkers, commends their commitment,
sustained even in the heat of struggle, "to abandon fixed ideas of settled
identity and culturally authorized definition" ("Representing the Colonized:
Anthropology's Interlocutors," p. 225). And that which for Williams is
self-evident and attested – the successful fusion of nationalism and political
revolution (p. 183) and the necessity of the struggle for social identities (p.
193) – is for Said beset with problems. Indeed, when Williams reprimands
the doctrinaire position on identity adopted by "many minority liberals and
socialists, and especially those who by the nature of their work or formation
are themselves nationally and internationally mobile" (pp. 195–6), he is
dissenting from the very intellectual position Said occupies. What Williams's censure overlooks is that such a stance not only advances the urgent
political need for oppressed peoples to construe an insurgent subjectivity,
but it also, in anticipating how on the attainment of conditions not based
on domination and coercion this constructed collectivity will perform its
own abolition, inscribes an aspiration to a global solidarity of heteroge-
neously positioned subjects which in no way erases the diversity of culture,
gender, and sexuality.

Is what Said has called the "stubborn Anglocentrism" of Williams's work
– a restriction which is repeated in other investigations into "Englishness"
– indicative of a more pervasive provincialism that in the past has afflicted
the British intellectual left?[4] And does it give access to considering why
there has been no theorizing on culture and imperialism in the homeland of
modern empire comparable with the undertaking being pursued by Said,

where culture is grasped not as superstructure – which permits its bracketing in studies concerned with the economics and politics of imperialism – but as itself a material practice producing representations and languages that embody active forms of power and is constitutive of a social order? It is also noticeable that whereas Said is widely acknowledged as a scholar and theorist amongst the British academic community and has frequently been its honored guest – a recognition also accorded him by left-wing circles as well as the higher-browed media – the critical engagement with his work has been less sustained in Britain[5] than in the postcolonial world or the United States, where because of various conjunctures – the study of African-American and "minority" discourses, investigations into the intersections of race and gender in feminist criticism, the vastly increased presence of faculty and students from the dismantled empires, the influence of postmodern theory – his critique of imperialism has become a landmark for diverse investigations into how systems of oppression are conceptualized, exerted and contested. The importance of the location of critical discourse is displayed in the current British discussion of colonialism and the postcolonial condition, which to a notable extent developed in opposition to the authorized exclusions of Cultural Studies, and is taking place outside of established left forums. Although this work addresses many of the same problems as do Said's writings, the emphasis is significantly different. Hence, while critics inescapably use "theory" to define the recombinant or creolized social situation of diaspora Africans, Asians and Caribbeans, they are less concerned with establishing the interdependence of metropolitan and colonial cultures and histories, and more militant in affirming the subversion of western categories exerted by postcolonial cultural production – in Paul Gilroy's phrase the "counter culture of modernity" ("It Ain't Where You're From, It's Where You're At,").

Said's observation on the massive absence of imperialism from Anglo-Saxon cultural theory is repeated in his remarks on a similar oblivion in the aesthetic and cultural work of contemporary western Marxism.[6] Although Marxist scholars have of course been major producers of theoretical work on the economics and politics of imperialism, many of these studies are debilitated by an existentially impoverished perspective in which overseas empire is held as inessential to the dynamics of western capitalism, or where the trajectory of Europe's penetration into pre-capitalist societies is perceived as progressive and in the final analysis ameliorative, both analyses occluding the colonial world's experience of subjugation as well as reinstalling the West as the sole agent of world-historical change.

In bypassing the Marxist usage of imperialism as designating the relationships between competing metropolitan nation-states during the highest stage of capitalism, Said offers a definition of modern empire covering a longer time-span and focusing on the theory and practice of ruling distant territories from metropolitan centers, while still conceptualizing imperial-

ism within a problematic that places economic and political machinery at
the center. To steal a phrase he uses in connection with Williams, it is
dangerous to disagree with Said, but it should all the same be noted that
the very range of a perspective transcending the restrictions of eurocentric
interpretations, also loses sight of the changing modes of western capitalist
penetration into other worlds, hence inhibiting the study of the specific
forms of governance, the particularity of the instrumental discourses
addressed to colonial audiences, and the rearticulations of metropolitan
self-representation which attended these different styles of domination.[7] So
sweeping a redefinition also implies that imperialism is made synonymous
with colonial possessions, a common conflation Said elsewhere unpacks by
observing how, with the ending of formal overseas empires, imperialism
has shifted its power base and mode of operation.

Given that it effects such elisions in one area, Said's work on imperialism
augments another by asserting the indispensible role of culture as the vital,
enabling counterpoint to institutional practices, demonstrating how the
aggrandizement of territory through military force and the bureaucratic
exercise of power in the colonies was sustained by the ideological invasion
of cultural space, while at home the fact of empire was registered not only
in political debate and economic and foreign policy, but entered the social
fabric, intellectual discourse and the life of the imagination. The project of
thinking non-synchronous and antithetical experiences together, of recon-
ceiving the encounter between unequal partners as an area of "overlapping
territories and intertwined histories" taking place on the same cultural
terrain, is for Said distinct from "world history" as seen from the perspective of the Western meta-subject, and is an address against western
hegemony which refuses its center/margin polarity. This entails breaking
into the West's sealed representation of its history as self-generating, its
cultures as autonomous, and disposing of the asymmetry whereby overseas
empires, their destinies shaped by foreign rule, are rendered inconsequential
to the fount of meanings engendered in the metropolitan epicenters, and
relegated as extraneous incidents in a narrative deriving its momentum
wholly from European sources. The effect is to recuperate in the histories
of the colonized a "Culture of Resistance" – to which we will return – and
to initiate the rewriting of the West's story so that the export of cultural
products from Europe is interwoven with the entry of empire into its
cultures, thus bringing back home the fact of distant domination during the
centuries of imperial power and decline.

In construing this revisionist version of the symbiotic relationship
between Western imperialism and metropolitan thought and letters, Said
brings unfamiliar interpretations to a range of familiar texts in the West's
classical and modernist literary tradition, detecting inscriptions of imperialism not in content and representation, but symptomatically in narrative
structure. His re-reading of *Mansfield Park* observes a synchronicity

between domestic and colonial authority, arguing that overseas possessions underwrite the values to which Fanny Price and Jane Austen subscribe, as the wealth extracted from the West Indian plantation is converted into maintaining the propriety, order and comfort of the English country house: "What she sees more clearly than most of her readers is that to hold and rule Mansfield Park is to hold and rule an imperial estate associated with it. What assures the one, in its domestic tranquillity and attractive harmony, is the prosperity and discipline of the other" ("Jane Austen and Empire", p. 156). Or again, Camus's fiction is inserted into the centuries-old French presence in Algeria, making it possible to understand "not just the form and ideological meaning of Camus's narratives, but also the degree to which his work further inflects, refers to, and in many ways consolidates and otherwise renders more precise the nature of the French enterprise there," his novels and stories condensing a "distilled version of the by now mostly invisible traditions, idioms, discursive strategies of Algeria's appropriation by France" ("Narrative, Geography and Interpretation", pp. 87 and 96). Whereas the formal displacements of modernist culture have conventionally been attributed to the internal dynamics of western societies, Said argues that an explanation of the dislocations must include the response to external pressures, and specifically to the contending native. Most dramatically, in contrast to those who frame their explanations of why the "great narratives of emancipation and enlightenment" lost power entirely in European terms, Said points to the exposure of the western version's hypocrisy by liberationist thinking, counterposing its inclusive vision which through proposing a model for a post-imperialist world dependent on the idea of a "collective as well as a plural destiny" for humankind, constitutes "the full situation of postmodernism" ("Representing the Colonized", p. 224).

The bold strokes of Said's sketches graphically display how empire is a substantive if occluded or displaced element in metropolitan thought. However, his configuration in some of the instances cited depends on elisions: in the interest of representing the restoration of repose and concord at Mansfield Park as contiguous with the stern order maintained in the colonial plantation, the unstable economies and conflictual forms of rule in the West Indies are suppressed; and because of an insistence on the internal consistency of colonialist representation, the existential crisis registered in the Camus novel is disregarded. Such problems are compounded when Said embarks on readings of fictions which construct the imperialist experience. For despite a perception of culture as permeable, heterogeneous and internally differentiated, despite the statement that "In human history there is always something beyond the reach of dominating systems no matter how deeply they saturate society" ("Traveling Theory", *The World, The Text, and the Critic*, pp. 246–7),[8] Said allots to texts written at a time of

pervasive consensus, a centralizing, affirmative and sovereign power that
encounters no hindrance in their underwriting the authority of overseas
empire or arrogating the right to represent what is beyond Europe's
borders.[9] The outcome is readings that are indifferent to textual gaps,
indeterminacies and contradictions.[10] As a paradigm of an overmastering
narrative of imperialism that is totalizing and all-enveloping in its attitudes
and gestures, shutting out as much as it includes, compresses and asserts,
Said selects *Heart of Darkness*:

> Whatever is lost or elided or even simply made up in Marlow's narrative, is
> compensated for in the sheer historical momentum its temporal movement
> forward describes, digressions and all ... the almost oppressive force of
> Marlow's narrative leaves us with a quite accurate sense that there is no way
> out of the sovereign historical force of imperialism, and that it has the power
> of representing everything within its dominion ... Neither Conrad or Marlow
> offers us anything outside the world-conquering attitudes embodied by Kurtz,
> and Marlow and Conrad ("Intellectuals and the Postcolonial World", pp. 46,
> 48–9).

Although Said – who elsewhere has noted that Conrad's novels irradiate an
extreme unsettling anxiety and are indicative of a post-realist modernist
sensibility – does modulate his argument with the proviso that "Conrad's
self-consciously circular narrative forms encourage us to sense, if not the
actuality, then the potential of a reality that has remained inaccessible to
imperialism and which in the post-colonial world has erupted into presence" (ibid., p. 54), this view is subordinate to his concern with the fiction's
reproduction of high imperialism's aggressive contours.

His is an exceptionally skillful practice of a criticism that detects a text's
politics in its narrative form,[11] in this instance in a trajectory which mimics
Europe's aggrandizement of space, its penetration into Africa staged by the
passage of a steamboat forcing its way into the recalcitrant interior. Yet it
is a reading which underestimates the deterrents to the imperialist world
view inscribed by the novella, for even though these are marginalized and
muted, criticism can recover counter-voices that limit or contest the
discourse of mastery. One minor diversion on the narrative's apparently
unchallenged march, and one that does not significantly arrest its progress,
comes from a discourse about women, which, since women's role in the
text is ceremonial, as the incarnations of grace, sensuality and menace, is
spoken about and not by them. Both in the rhetoric about the pure and
unreal world they inhabit and in the figure of the Intended, the text ascribes
to woman the function of embodying the utopian intention which Conrad
writes into imperialism's programme as its redemptive clause, but which
because it cannot be accommodated in its triumphalist, world-conquering
narrative, is revealed as a lie.[12] The other and more effective obstacle is

exercised by a displaced African discrouse whose intimated meanings, although screened by elaborate and obfuscatory language, are disruptive of the imperialist assumptions rendered by the text. It is obvious that "Africa" in *Heart of Darkness* is flagrantly disarticulated as a speaking subject; yet by insisting on Africa's own overwhelming reality, the text intimates the presence of meanings that disturb and have the power to interrogate imperialism's knowledge, for what Marlow's obscure and ornate language articulates or conceals is a failure to achieve mastery over Africa by naming and fixing it in the vocabulary available to the narrative voices.[13]

That a critic elsewhere so demonstrably sensitive to textual silences, elisions, and displacements, should posit interpretations of fictions as the uncontested inscriptions of the hegemonic, suggests an overriding polemical interest in displaying how articulations of mastery are enabled by the power of imperialist culture and derive strength from an intertextual relationship to other discourses of domination. Thus Said reads *Kim* as a coherent and consistent transcription of Kipling's publically declared perspective on the Raj, trusting the author sufficiently to discover his beliefs reproduced in and occupying all the textual space, while overlooking the fiction's management of oppositions and contradiction:

> There is no resolution to the conflict between Kim's colonial service and loyalty to his Indian companions not because Kipling could not face it, but because for Kipling *there was no conflict* . . . That there might have been a conflict had Kipling considered India as unhappily subservient to imperialism, of this we can have no doubt. The fact is that he did not: for him it was India's destiny to be ruled by England . . . There were no appreciable deterrents to the imperialist world view held by Kipling. Hence he remained untroubled ('*Kim*: The Pleasures of Imperialism", p. 43).

As Said acknowledges, the book was written at a time when "India was already well into the dynamic of outright opposition to British rule" (ibid., p. 30); and if Kipling was unaware of and undismayed by "deterrents to the imperialist world view" in both the emergent nationalist discourses and in India's traditional systems of knowledge, then his writings were not. Because India as challenge to the Raj is absent, attention must be directed at those strategies which effect a preemptive reply to voices able to interrogate the British Empire as cultural text and political concept.

Since *parataxis* is Kipling's favoured procedure for organizing incommensurable discourses in ways that conceal their antagonism, the road, the river, and the wheel in *Kim*, which serve dual and opposing functions within the narrative, are made to appear as different but compatible. Thus, while Kim "flung himself whole-heartedly upon the next turn of the wheel," the lama strives to free himself from "the Wheel of Things"; whereas for Kim the Grand Trunk Road is a river of life, to the lama it is a hard path to be trodden in his search for a mythic river that will cleanse him from the sin of material being. But because there is no dialogue between Kim's pursuit of action, the life of the senses and personal identity, and the lama's quest for quietism, asceticism, and the annihilation of the individual self, disjunctive goals, the one valued and the other denounced by imperialist tenets, can easily cohere as a mutual venture defined by one who is fortuitously indifferent to the temporal: "he aided me in my Search, I aided him in his . . . Let him be a teacher, let him be a scribe – what matter? He will have attained Freedom in the end. The rest is illusion" (*Kim*, Penguin ed., p. 407). Through such mediation of oppositions, the text creates a consensual arena in which Kim, by now an agent in the Secret Service, can have his nirvana and eat it, and through undergoing a ritual healing of his identity, is able to accommodate the roles he must play as apprentice spy serving the British and *chela* to a holy man whose aspirations are at every point violated by what the Raj represents and maintains.[14]

My third instance of Said's overprivileging the ability of the European novel to override or resist the threat to Western hegemony posed by the colonized world's cultural alterity and political opposition is his discussion of *A Passage to India*. Said holds out against the new orthodoxy on Forster by crediting the novel with registering India's recalcitrance to Western authority and its attempt "to represent material that according to the canons of the novel form could not in fact be represented – India's vastness, the (to the Westerner) incomprehensibility of its creeds, its secret motions, histories and social forms" (Eliot Lectures). All the same, he sees the novel as retreating and recovering from the challenge by recuperating "its own formal integrity in its ending, where Forster quite deliberately and affirma- tively articulates the novel's habit of concluding with a domestic resolution (marriage and property)" (ibid.), although he does allow that neither the intimated resolution nor the union is complete. Elsewhere Said has written of this ending as "a paralyzed gesture of aestheticized powerlessness" in which "Forster notes and confirms the history behind a political conflict between Dr Aziz and Fielding – Britain's subjugation of India – and yet can neither recommend decolonization nor continued colonization. 'No, not yet, not here' [sic] is all Forster can muster by way of resolution" ("Representing the Colonized", p. 223). But cannot this finale, which speaks of "cosmic irresolution" rather than domestic resolution, be read as indeterminate, as signalling, amongst other possibilities, the hope in a deferred, post-imperialist condition towards which the novel points but has not the means to articulate – "No, not yet" – and which cannot be fulfilled in the space the novel occupies – "No, not there"? And since the novel speaks a reluctant bourgeois Englishness, a failed cosmopolitanism, a sceptical sympathy for Indian nationalism and an unequivocal distaste for the deportment of an imperial hegemony, cannot it be received as enunci- ating a confessional and destabilized liberalism which having confronted the obscenities of European empire and having suffered a further undermining of already disarrayed values through encountering India's diverse systems of meaning, can only retreat into undecidability?

If Said veers towards attributing an uncontradicted inscription of the consensual ideology in his readings of texts of imperialism, closing off both hesitancy and contingency and writing over the marks of resistance from native alterities and political contestation, the notion that the hegemonic cannot be thought without the counter-hegemonic is developed in his engagement with the protracted struggle against imperialism jointly conducted by metropolitan opponents and rebellious natives. In drawing attention to the dynamic between these distinctive articulations, he observes that until the advent of concerted defiance in the colonies, there was no effective deterrence to empire at home, and that without domestic doubts and dissent, the anti-colonial movements would not have had the character they did. Hence, for Said, an experience that was existentially connected for the divided partners produced a dialogical interaction between Europe and its imperium acting together in the process of decolonization, and is a further working out of his project to bring the discrepant entities together within the same theoretical domain and without occluding either the disparity of power or the antagonism between colonizer and colonized. The evidence for metropolitan anti-imperialism does not make for a long or inspiring story, but all the same Said's choice of Edward J. Thompson as the exemplar of such opposition in Britain is curious, given that less equivocal instances of affiliation with the colonial struggles and commitment to colonial self-determination can be cited in the manifestoes of those groups active during the nineteen-twenties, thirties and forties, and who in 1954 reformed as The Movement for Colonial Freedom.[15]

Said has on more than one occasion referred to *The Other Side of the Medal* (1925) as a powerful and impassioned statement against British rule and for Indian independence, praising it as one of the earliest attempts to understand imperialism as a cultural affliction for colonizer and colonized and for its engagement with historiographic misrepresentation. It is instructive, therefore, to consider where Thompson's writing – with its even-handed apportioning of blame to both sides in the conflict, its quirky reiterations of received British opinion about Indian manners and customs, and its commitment to the necessity of the Raj, albeit in a more benign form – is situated in the spectrum of dissident metropolitan opinion:

> It is not larger measures of self-government for which they are longing, it is the magnanimous gesture of a great nation, so great that it can afford to admit mistakes and wrong-doing, and is too proud to distort facts . . . There is no commoner word on Indian lips today than *atonement*. England, they say, has never made atonement; and she must do so before we can be friends.

The word in their minds is the Sanskrit *prayaschitta*, usually translated
atonement; but its meaning is rather a *gesture* (*The Other Side of the Medal*,
pp. 131–2).[16]

Thompson's own exhortation to a bountiful act from India's rulers is here
attributed to a category of homogenized "Indians" as *their* desire, his
invention of a litany of repentance manifesting the will to colonize another's
capacities for manifesting protest and to tame an ongoing struggle by
offering symbolic reconciliation within the existing power structure. Thus
it would appear that Said – who has invoked the notion of "atonement" in
his discussion of the Palestinian-Israeli conflict, and scrupulously includes
"a narrative of sympathy and congruence" as a chapter in imperialism's
harsh annals – has misread a dubious text as the outstanding expression of
British anti-imperialism. Furthermore, by reiterating its injunction to ceremonial expiation, prescribed by Thompson as a substitute for radical
solutions to political conflict, he in this instance departs from his commitment to secular interpretation, giving some credence to the charge of a
tendency to lapse into a sentimental humanism.

As a critique which declares its historical location and political interest,
Said's method condenses a tension between recognizing the subject as
decentered and culture as hybrid, and acknowledging the political exigencies in the process of liberation, of constructing and affirming collective
identity, with its implications of organicism and consensus – a tension
which is not displaced by Homi Bhabha's notion of a solidarity fashioned
in the intersubjectivity of dispersed subjects. This ambivalence is registered
in Said's designating nationalism as both necessary and the enemy, as
positive and problematic, and it is staged in his response to an interviewer's
question about "the risk of essence" when his reply performs the simultaneous affirmation and cancellation of an insurgent native subjectivity and
a resurgent cultural nationalism. Hence, he refuses "the insistence on the
nativist essence," while accepting that for oppressed peoples such as the
Palestinians, there is no substitute for the identity struggle, this last qualified
by invoking a further perspective "leading to liberation" ("American
Intellectuals and Middle East Politics", pp. 51–2).[17] Such equivocation on
the necessity of inscribing cultural identity before it can be transcended, of
working through attachments in order to emerge beyond them, suggests
how Said's work commutes between a position conserving specific structures of communal subjectivity invented by dominated peoples, and that
which conceptualizes the subject as split, unfixed and disseminated and is
implacably hostile to what is perceived as the essentialist claims to
perpetuate holistic cultural traditions and a transcendent native self.

    The first may be detected in the agenda for the critique of African-
American literature drawn up by Henry Louis Gates Jr, where the notion

of 'blackness' as some mythical and mystical absolute is rejected as essentialist and exclusionary and uniquely black discourses are incorporated into a practice designed to secure a political purchase on cultural life: "the challenge of black literary criticism is to derive principles of literary criticism from the black tradition itself, as defined in the idiom of critical theory, but also in the idiom that constitutes the language of blackness, the Signifyin(g) difference that makes the black tradition our very own" ("Literary Theory and the Black Tradition", p. 54).[18]

Elsewhere Gates, pointing out that the constitution of the Western male subject has enjoyed quite a different history from that of its racial or sexual others, has criticized the universalism that undergirds poststructuralist anti-universalism, making it unable "to comprehend the *ethnos* as anything other than mystification, magic, or mirage – or what would once have been called false consciousness" ("Afterword: Critical Remarks", pp. 323–4). This suggests that the problem is how to retain the usage of "black" as signifying a relational concept marking difference and cultural specificity, without reintroducing notions of an ahistorical sovereign self or intact, petrified traditions.

A countervailing stance is exemplified by Homi Bhabha, who takes his stand "on the shifting margins of cultural displacement," stipulating "the cultural and historical hybridity of the post-colonial world . . . as the paradigmatic place of departure" ("The Commitment to Theory", p. 7). His argument is that since questions of identity can never be seen "beyond representation," or outside the act of language, but as always implicated in the instability and uncertainty of "the process of 'writing and difference,'" postcoloniality is to be located in "the performance of the doubleness or splitting of 'the subject' as enacted in the writings of a postcolonial diaspora" ("Interrogating Identity," p. 7). Because he conceives of the event of theory as negotiating contradictory and antagonistic instances, overcoming "the given grounds of opposition and opening up a space of 'translation'" ("The Commitment to Theory", p. 10), he castigates "the increasingly facile adoption of the notion of an homogenized 'Other' for a celebratory, oppositional politics of 'the margins' or 'minorities,'" and "the nostalgic demand for a liberatory, non-repressed identity" ("Interrogating Identity", p. 7).

Gates speaks from a position of affiliation to an internally diverse and differentiated but discernibly oppressed minority within the powerhouse of a contemporary imperialism, whose cultural production is redynamizing an ethnos formed under conditions of enforced uprooting, slavery, and post-emancipation persecution. On the other hand, Bhabha, whose stance is marked by a diasporic habitation within what has been called multi-racist Britain, mediates and indeed articulates the emergent cultural forms enabled by the diverse and kaleidoscopic immigrant experience, finding the construct of a contadictorily positioned, dispersed subjectivity not only congenial but essential. Stuart Hall offers a somewhat different diasporic perspective, which, while conceding the end of the innocent notion of the essential black subject ("New Ethnicities"), maintains that the disjunctive, displaced, and unstable postcolonial identity as constituted in representation does relate to a real set of histories and offers a point of resistance to the solipsism of much postmodernist discourse. He thus posits an historically, culturally, and politically constructed "ethnicity" which insists on difference, "on the fact that every identity is placed, positioned in a culture, a language, a history," as defining a new space for identity ("Minimal Selves"). Indeed, Hall has braved the reprobation directed against identitarian ethnicist claims, by directing attention to the indispensible role played in all colonial struggles by a conception of " 'cultural identity' in terms of one, shared culture, a sort of collective 'one true self' . . . which people with a shared history and ancestry hold in common," and which, he added, "continues to be a very powerful and creative force in emergent forms of representation amongst hitherto marginalized peoples" ("Cultural Identity and Diaspora", p. 223). But rather than denouncing the myth of an organic, unitary communality, Hall recognizes that this is an "imaginary reunification," imposing an "imaginary coherence" on the experience of dispersal and fragmentation, acknowledging that "its other side" is rupture, discontinuity, and difference.

Writing in related terms, Paul Gilroy, who also challenges the concept of authentic blackness and homogeneous national identities and insists on the fragmentation and inescapable differentiation of the black subject, posits a fluid category of blackness as a multi-accentual sign and sees in the position occupied by postcolonials in the diaspora as the West's step-children an experience "which ties our various histories of imperialism and colonialism to each other" ("Nothing But Sweat inside my Hand", p. 45). In yet another register, Vivek Dhareshwar, drawing on the work of Edouard Glissant, addresses the necessity for a postcolonial self-fashioning that is not a search for essences or the desire to escape the hybridization effected by colonialism, but is to be achieved through narrativizing both the dislocation or "detour" and the return to "the point of entanglement" from which the colonized were forced to turn away ("Toward a Narrative Epistemology of the Postcolonial Predicament"). Whereas Dhareshwar's concern is with the "detour" or "diversion," Glissant's own aphoristic writings constantly invoke the "re-turn" or "reversion," and while rejecting any possiblity of going back to the original matrix after the rupture that was Caribbean history, these call for an effort towards rootedness, reintegration, rehousing, seeing in the practice of creolization a struggle to repossess the memory of a fragmented past: "For history is not only absence for us, it is vertigo. The time that was never ours, we must now possess" (Caribbean Discourse: Selected Essays, p. 161).

Despite very different notions of subjectivity and cultural discontinuities, these disparate practices share a common concern with theorizing the specificities of a polymorphic postcolonial condition, which more especially from the emigré vantage point foregrounds the radicalism of a contemporary "diaspora aesthetic" in which vernacular cultural practices are prominent: "Across a whole range of cultural forms there is a 'syncretic' dynamic which critically appropriates elements from the master-codes of the dominant culture and 'creolises' them, disarticulating given signs and re-articulating their symbolic meaning" (Kobena Mercer, "Diasporic Culture and the Dialogic Imagination", p. 57). Whether creolization is a property of a postcolonial dispersal or whether, as is claimed by *Public Culture* (see Vol. 1, No. 1, Fall 1988), it is the contemporary global condition effected by transnational cultural traffic, the specificities of histories and traditions remain crucial to the variable articulations of a heterogeneous postcolonial hybridity and to the discourses fashioned by those still engaged in struggles for emancipation.

Said, in his search for an oppositional critical practice that inscribes/transcends cultural identity, negotiates this thicket by asserting the genealogy of postcoloniality, not in irretrievable native origins, but in those "authentic elements" within colonized societies that were not bequeathed by their rulers, in those reserves and resources that were resistant to imperialism, withstood the violence of invasion, and were reconceived and rearticulated in the struggle over representation. In this he follows Fanon into what is becoming a no-go area for critics, even as Fanon warns against "the paradoxes and pitfalls" of "rediscovering tradition," and despite his many strictures against nationalism, he also affirms that "this absolute valorization almost in defiance of reality, objectively indefensible, assumes an incomparable and subjective importance . . . the plunge into the chasm of the past is the condition and the source of freedom" ("Racism and Culture", p. 42). Indeed, although always qualified by a grasp of the insufficiencies of retrospection and the unstable and volatile zone in which the intelligences of modern colonized peoples are being "dialectically reorganized," Fanon's espousal of rehabilitating a native past and reinvigorating a national culture in the cause of a Pan-African political mobilization will be read as an aberration by those opposed to the recovery of devalued histories and the nurturing of cultural nationalism as sites of a political solidarity.

> The claim to a national culture in the past does not only rehabilitate the nation and serve as a justification for the hope of a future national culture. In the sphere of psycho-affective equilibrium it is responsible for an important change in the native . . . The native intellectual who decides to give battle to colonial lies fights on the field of the whole continent. The past is given back its value. ("On National Culture", pp. 170, 188)

Where Said departs from Fanon's analysis, in which colonized societies before the advent of modern liberation struggles tend to be represented as rigid and stagnant, is in perceiving resistance as being coterminous with subjugation, and consequently registering the *continuous* capacity for agency exercised by colonized peoples.

Some commentators on *Orientalism* have been critical of its situating the native as passive recipient of European scrutiny,[19] a tendency subsequently iterated in "Orientalism Reconsidered," where Said wrote of the muteness imposed on the Orient as object. His more recent work marks the emergence of a differently accented project which, in pursuing the questions asked at the end of *Orientalism*, sets out to effect those "decolonizing departures and displacements" that act to reverse the position of the colonized as disarticulated by colonialism's institutional and discursive aggression: "There is by now a good deal of information that native responses to the presence of European settlers, traders, missionaries, administrators and soldiers . . . stimulated a whole series of resistances to that outside presence *from the very beginning*" ("Third World Intellectuals/ Metropolitan Culture", p. 27, emphasis added). Said's ongoing and searching analysis "The Culture of Resistance" is a model of engaging with textual struggles over representation without representing the concept of struggle as only textual:

> It has been the substantial achievement of all of the intellectuals (theoreticians, militants, and insurgent analysts of imperialism like Franz Fanon, Amilcar Cabral, C. L. R. James, Aimé Césaire, Walter Rodney) and of course of the movements they worked with, by their historical, interpretative and analytic efforts to have identified the culture of resistance as a cultural enterprise possessing a long tradition of integrity and power in its own right, one *not* simply grasped as a belated reactive response to Western imperialism. (*Yeats and Decolonization*, p. 8).

In some crucial respects, Said's mode of theorizing would seem to be incommensurable with the poststructuralist critique of colonialism and postcoloniality. Since the counter-discourse is derived from "cultural and ideological artefacts" produced by the colonized for which "the evidence is both impressive and rich" (Eliot Lectures), the native is conceived as individual and collective actor – a concept of agency which Bhabha could see as possessing mimetic immediacy and adequacy of representation, rather than as discernible in the indeterminate and disjunctive moment of narrativizing the event. Further, Said's work accommodates "the rediscovery of what had been suppressed in the natives' past by the processes of imperialism" (ibid.), is attentive to written and remembered accounts of acts of insubordination and rebellion – he refers to the San Domingo revolution, the Abdul Quader insurrection, the 1857 Mutiny, the Orabi Revolt and the Boxer Rebellion – and acknowledges the energies of the colonized's self-affirmation and insurgency. It is therefore liable to the charges of sentimentalizing a lost past and reinstalling the self-constituting subject of idealism that have been made against other critics accused of seeking to recuperate autonomous cultural traditions and originary communities, and resituate the suppressed voices silenced by imperialist and elite nationalist historiography.

Rosalind O'Hanlon's critique of the work produced by *Subaltern Studies* argues that in aiming to retrieve the subaltern – a term she finds unusable – as historical agent, the practitioners easily slip into restoring the centered, unitary self of liberal humanism ("Recovering the Subject"). Under the slogan of presence without essence, she instead proposes a strategy which would reveal "that presence to be one constituted and refracted through practice, but no less real for our having said that it does not contain its own origins within itself" (pp. 202–3). Few now working in revisionist studies of those who have been "hidden from history," including the contributors to *Subaltern Studies*, would quarrel with so sane a procedure and its outcome. Indeed, O'Hanlon's formidable powers of interrogation seem at times to be directed at arguments which substantially accord with her own, as is also the case in her disagreement with Gayatri Spivak, who shares her wariness about reintroducing the subject as individual agent and the subjectivity of a collective agency.[20] There is, however, a significant difference between their respective stances on the production of a colonial self that is directly relevant to how Said conceives discourses of resistance. For Spivak, it is axiomatic that imperialism's "epistemic violence . . . constituted/effaced the subject that was obliged to cathect . . . the space of the Imperialists' self-consolidating other" (*"Subaltern Studies*: Deconstructing Historiography", p. 18).

O'Hanlon, on the other hand, while distancing herself from the insistence on "some form of irreducible epistemological and affective independence within indigenous cultures" ("Cultures of Rule, Communities of Resistance", p. 107), detects not only the "approved selves which the colonizer attempts to produce for the native as the sole area of legitimate public reality, but the continual struggle of the colonized to resolve the paradoxes which this displacement and dehumanization of indigenous processes of identification sets up in his daily existence" ("Recovering the Subject", pp. 204–5). Furthermore, because she recognizes that the conforming power of hegemony is never total, she is sceptical of the possibility that "the subaltern may be subject to such an intensity of ideological and material pressure that his consciousness and practice are indeed completely pervaded and possessed by it" (ibid., p. 222). Having accepted that sites of resistance can be postulated, the problem for O'Hanlon is how such presences are to be configured; and in cautioning against the temptation of making "their words address our own concerns" and rendering "their figures in our own self-image" (pp. 210–11), she argues that these signs need not necessarily take "the virile form of a deliberate and violent onslaught" (p. 223), but should be sought in fields not conventionally associated with the political, and which she designates as more "feminine" forms of resistance. Whereas the acknowledgement of such unrecognized energies of self-affirmation acts to install "agency," Spivak's thesis that the over-determinations in Europe's constructions of its Others obliterated subjectivity, leaving no space from which the subaltern could "speak" (see "Can the Subaltern Speak?", 1988) appears altogether more absolutist in its effacement of the multiplicity of positions occupied by the colonized which were outside the remit of imperialism's ideological construction, and consequently closes the space for discursive self-determination. Indeed the agenda for postcolonial agency proposed by Spivak is one which, rather than address victimage by the assertion of identity or take positions in terms of the discovery of historical or philosophical grounds, tampers with "the authority of Europe's story-lines," the critic negotiating and attempting to change what s/he necessarily inhabits "by reversing, displacing and seizing the apparatus of value-coding" (see "Poststructuralism, Marginality, Postcoloniality and Value").

This lengthy digression may lead to a perception of what is yielded by the analysis of counter-hegemonic practices which, defying the interdicts of *Subaltern Studies'* critics, and at variance with a mode that would locate agency in the realm of the intersubjective act of enunciation, is conducted in the language of the subject.[21] For Said, the work of *Subaltern Studies* is intellectually insurrectionary *because* it theorizes the insurgent subjectivities of the native by providing an alternative history of colonial India rewritten "from the distinct and separate point of view of the masses, using unconventional or neglected sources in popular memory, oral discourse, previously unexamined colonial administrative documents," while recognizing the epistemological task of how to supply this missing narrative, given the difficulty of gaining access to the sources of subaltern history (Foreword to *Selected Subaltern Studies*, p. vi). Although Said's undertaking is different in that he sets out to plot a narrative of resistance from "nativist" through "nationalist" to liberationist opposition – or in Michel Pêcheux's terminology from "counter-identification" to "disidentification" (*Language, Semantics and Ideology*, pp. 157–9, 162–4)[22] – both projects share the conviction that agency is theorized as performance by conscious human subjects, that is, both conceive the rebel to be "an entity whose will and reason constituted the praxis called rebellion" (Ranajit Guha, "The Prose of Counter-Insurgency", p. 46). Thus, in Said's account, signs of the counter-hegemonic opposition are located, not within the interstices of the dominant discourses or the ruptures of imperialist representation, but in acts and articulations of native defiance.

By reconstructing in broad outline the histories of decolonization, Said produces an uncensorious critique of those histories and of their methods of struggle that is always mindful of their conditions of possibility, acknowledging the transformative energies discharged by a literature that deranged the discourses of domination ranged against the colonized. "Nativism" he specifies as the result of the dynamic of dependency, when in retort to the distortions inflicted on their identity by colonialist representation, the colonized attempt to disprove imperialism's assumptions and accusations by recovering an original and pristine past standing free of worldly time:

> Even if we leave aside the tremendous *ressentiment* often to be found in nativism . . . to accept nativism is to accept the consquences of imperialism too willingly, to accept the very radical, religious and political divisions imposed on places like Ireland, India, Lebanon, and Palestine by imperialism itself. To leave the historical world for the metaphysics of essences like negritude, Irishness, Islam and Catholicism is, in a word, to abandon history (*Yeats and Decolonization*, p. 15).

As an alternative Said surveys the struggles against imperialism conducted in the name of nationalism, a differentiated mobilizing force which in its search for authenticity recovered the signifying function usurped by imperialism and as a political movement succeeded in winning independence for many territories. Yet despite recognizing its real accomplishments in the process of decolonization, nationalism remains for Said "a deeply problematic ideological, as well as socio-political, enterprise" (ibid., p. 8), a derivative discourse whose insufficiencies are revealed in the statements of Pan-Arabism, Pan-Africanism and Negritude, and whose institutional failures are egregiously manifest in the regimes of too many Third World states.

This moment, Said maintains, although "an absolutely crucial first step" (ibid., p. 10) in resistance and decolonization, must be distinguished from liberationist thinking whose radically new perspective on the culture of imperialism was enabled by "a deeper oppositional current deriving from both the decentering doctrines of Freud, Marx and Nietzsche" and from recognition of the limitations to nationalist ideology (Eliot Lectures). By directing a theoretical insurgency against the authority and discourse of imperialism, Said argues, this opposition, as exemplified by Fanon, articulated a transformation of social consciousness beyond ethnicity, and reconceived human experience in non-imperialist terms, neither of which aspirations was embedded in nationalist enunciations.

Said's broader sweep pays insufficient attention to the internal conflicts within apparently univocal acts of defiance, and conspicuously overlooks the class allegiances of the leaderships of national movements. Also the

"stages" which he identifies are less disjunct, and liberationist theory itself
more impure, than his analysis allows, deploying as this does polyphonic
and discontinuous discourses. Thus, the writings of Aimé Césaire, which
are cited for their moving beyond "those self-imposed limitations that come
with race, moment or milieu" (*Yeats and Decolonization*, p. 17), while
rejecting any attempt to repeat the past, accommodate an impassioned
celebration of pre-colonial civilizations that could be categorized as
"nativist":

> I make a systematic defense of the non-European civilizations. They were
> communal societies, never societies of the many for the few . . . They were
> societies that were not only ante-capitalist . . . but also *anti-capitalist* . . .
> They were democratic societies, always. They were cooperative societies,
> fraternal societies. I make a systematic defense of the societies destroyed by
> imperialism (*Discourse on Colonialism*, pp. 22, 23).[23]

Similarly, Fanon's writings, which for Said delineate the shift from nationalism to liberation theory, are marked by a double enunciation, whether in
the preservation/transcendence of black identity spoken in *Black Skin,
White Masks* ("My Negro consciousness does not hold itself out as a lack.
. . . My freedom turns me back on myself. No, I do not have the right to be
a Negro," pp. 135, 229), or subsequently in *The Wretched of the Earth*,
when this is displaced into the simultaneousness and equivocal injunction
to build a revalued and reshaped national culture around the people's
struggle for sovereignty, using and reinterpreting the past in order to
construct the future, and to foster the international consciousness growing
at the heart of national consciousness ("On National Culture", p. 189).
   At this point the tensions within Said's critique become more pro-
nounced, as his affinity with postmodernism's valorizations of the dispersed
and nomadic subject can be seen to compete with the heretical value he
attaches to prefigurations of an emergent post-imperial human solidarity.
For Said, the significance of Fanon's writing is that it effects a radical break
with merely reactive opposition to imperialism by registering a sustained
confrontation of and resistance to the Empire *as West*, programmatically
seeking "to treat colonial and metropolitan societies together, as discrepant
but related entities" (Eliot Lectures), and conceptualizing imperialism as a
totalizing system pervading western humanist culture. In this Fanon is seen
to "perform an act of closure on the empire and announce a new era.
National consciousness, he says, must now be enriched and deepened by a
very rapid transformation into a consciousness of social and political needs,
in other words, into (real) humanism" (ibid.).
   This same impulse towards detecting signs of a hybrid but integrated
post-western culture is also evident in Said's reading of C. L. R. James,
when he uses James's 1962 Appendix to *Black Jacobins* to argue that here

James resolves the methodological and meta-historical aporia of writing a post-imperialist history which, given the continuing domination of the Third World, is neither naively utopian nor hopelessly pessimistic. This, Said maintains, James does by following the movement within Césaire's *Notebook of a Return to a Nativeland* from the discovery that negritude, the reactive discovery of one's identity, is not enough, to the reinscription of Marx's famous sentence, "The real history of humanity will begin" in his vision of there being a place for all "at the convocation of conquest." It is at this moment, Said suggests, that James, instead of following Césaire back into West Indian or Third World poetic, ideological, and political antecedents, juxtaposes him with his Anglo-Saxon contemporary, T. S. Eliot; and because it "crosses over from the provincialism of one strand of history, into an apprehension of other histories," all of them actualized in the "impossible union" of Eliot's poems, Said finds that James's writing incarnates "the energies of anti-imperialist liberation" (ibid.). Because this gloss posits a symmetrical synthesis between metropolitan and postcolonial sources as prefiguring the substance of a future culture, it suggests the possibility that so neat a resolution was dictated by the occasion of its delivery – the T. S. Eliot Lectures – since Said elsewhere powerfully articulates the upheaval effected by postcolonial discourses, whether in the linguistic, syntactic and narrative dislocations of imaginative fiction or the transgression of disciplinary norms.

This is corroborated by the different reading of James offered in a subsequent essay, where Said further explores discriminations within the culture of resistance in order to distinguish between C. L. R. James and George Antonius writing in the nineteen-thirties, and Ranajit Guba and S. H. Alatas writing from the nineteen-sixties onwards. For the first, "the world of discourse inhabited by the natives . . . was honourably dependent upon the West . . . There is no sense in their work of men standing *outside* the Western cultural tradition, however much they think of themselves as articulating the adversarial experience of colonial and/or non-Western peoples" ("Third World Intellectuals/Metropolitan Culture", pp. 33 and 36). By contrast, there is "no such coincidence between the West and its overseas departments" in the work of Guha and Alatas which perceives the relationship between cultures as "radically antithetical" (ibid., pp. 37 and 39). Where James and Antonius redeployed "grand and nourishingly optimistic narratives of emancipatory nationalism" (p. 43) to establish continuity between Europe and its colonies, these were not available to the later writers, whose work uncovered total conflict between the power exercised by colonial rule and the colonized societies. Hence, in their dismantlings of colonialist historiography and their search for a distinctive postcolonial method able to demystify the interests at work in the interpretations of subaltern culture, they replace narrative with irony and a "hermeneutics of suspicion" (p. 43).

This stark account of the predicament for postcolonial intellectual work rests on a problematic reading of Guha, whose method, like Said's, is a series of negotiations with western intellectual traditions, and is indeed countermanded by Said's own pursuit of an intergrative project that will adequately theorize imperialism contrapuntally as an experience of inter-dependent histories. This is not only a matter of recognizing that the postcolonial necessarily inhabits the culture of imperialism, but is a sign of the utopianism informing writings which, if they assume rather than engage with the reconceptions of socialist theory in liberationist thinking, all the same do inscribe its visionary perspectives. His repeated return to the climax of Césaire's poem – "the work has only begun/ and man still must overcome all the interdictions/ wedged in the recesses of his fervor and no race has a/ monopoly on beauty, on intelligence, on strength/ and there is room for everyone at the convocation of conquest" – registers a hope for a global solidarity not dissimilar from that spoken as "The Internationale unites the human race;" and at a time when obituaries are being written for grand narratives of liberation, Said joins C. L. R. James in reaffirming "the value of the epic struggle for human emancipation and enlightenment" ("C. L. R. James: The Artist as Revolutionary", p. 126). Such acknowledge-ment that the oppressed, the insulted, the denigrated cannot yet abandon so powerful a source of inspiration is made explicit by Paul Gilroy in contesting the claim that grand narratives are collapsing: "Some of us . . . are just beginning to formulate our own big narratives, precisely as narratives of redemption and emancipation" (*Black Film British Cinema*, p. 46).

O'Hanlon has observed "central and inescapable tensions on the ground that Said . . . seeks to occupy." This she attributes to his drawing on poststructuralist perspectives in understanding how systems of representa-tion are historically produced and endowed with authority, while on other levels his project remains "firmly rooted within a humanist discourse of freedom" ("Cultures of Rule, Communities of Resistance", p. 109). But perhaps this tension also produces a creative paradox, since he brings the theoretical insights and discursive style of poststructuralism to narrativizing the disjunctions and indeterminacies of experience and empirical events. For other of his critics, his humanism is disabling, inhibiting him from deploying deconstruction's techniques to their radical limits, and leading him to reiterate a rhetoric of authentic human reality and human com-munity that connote a banal universalism. If this censure does perceive a tendency to accommodate positions that are incommensurable with an anti-imperialist critique seeking to reconceive existential categories, it is also insensible to Said's enunciation of a postcolonial cosmopolitanism. For while his own postcolonial project is imbricated with imperialism's struc-tures, it never relinquishes the search for signs of colonial and postcolonial self-affirmation or for prefigurations of another time beyond an imperialist present when the process of transnational cross-fertilization will produce new formations.

Said has spoken of his distaste for the "badgering, hectoring authoritative tone" that has come through even in contemporary cultural studies: "The great horror I think we should all feel is towards systematic or dogmatic orthodoxies of one sort or another that are paraded as the last word of high Theory still hot from the press" (*The Politics of Modernism*, p. 182). His hope for a "more critical, engaged, even ... dialogical approach, in which alternatives are present as real forces" – a prospect that must be uncongenial to those who bring a litigious style to their accounts of alternative opinion – is already performed by the spaciousness of his own work where that theoretical generosity and enabling utopianism he has attributed to liberation writings is fully rendered.

Notes

My thanks to Homi Bhabha, Henry Finder, Henry Louis Gates Jr, Peter Hulme and Michael Sprinker for comments which saved this chapter from many solecisms. Those that remain are my very own.

1 In James Clifford's critique of Said, "cosmopolitan" values are equated with essences and human common denominators, rather than with cultural hybridity; see Clifford, "On Orientalism", *The Predicament of Culture: Twentieth-Century Ethnography, Literature, and Art* (Cambridge, Mass. and London: Harvard University Press, 1988), pp. 255–76. This first appeared as a review of *Orientalism* in *History and Theory*, XIX (1980), pp. 204–23. On cosmopolitanism and decolonization theory and postcolonial writing, see Timothy Brennan, *Salman Rushdie and the Third World: Myths of the Nation* (New York: St Martin Press, 1989), pp. 48–50. Brennan discusses Gramsci's hostility to cosmopolitanism as the "imperial-universal" and his insistence that this is to be challenged by the national-popular in the process of struggling against colonization – a stance that has influenced Third World cultural theorists and minority intellectuals in the metropolitan world. Brennan also discusses how multiply-rooted postcolonial writers, for whom "national affiliations" have lost their meaning, conceptualize the cosmopolitan: "the cosmopolis is no longer just life in the capitals of Europe and North America, nor that place of refuge for the native intellectual seeking a break from the barbarousness of underdevelopment at home. It is rather ... the *world* – polyglot and interracial" (p. 39). Fanon, examining the insufficiencies of national consciousness amongst the colonized, saw the cosmopolitan mind-set of the national middle class as a negative quantity indicative of their intellectual laziness and spiritual penury; see *The Wretched of the Earth*, pp. 121–2.

2 For more sceptical views on Said's transcriptions of Foucault, see James Clifford, op. cit., and Rashmi Bhatnagar, 'Uses and Limits of Foucault: A Study of the Theme of Origins in Edward Said's *Orientalism*", in *Social Scientist* (Trivandrum), 158 (July 1986), pp. 3–22.

3 Williams bespeaks his own insularity in his reply to his *New Left Review* interviewers who had questioned the massive absence of imperialism from *Culture and Society* – viz. "the particular experience which ought to have

enabled me to think much more closely and critically about it was for various reasons at that time very much in abeyance: the Welsh experience." *Politics and Letters: Interviews with "New Left Review"* (London: Verso, 1981), p. 118; first published 1979.

4 See, for example, *Englishness: Politics and Culture 1880–1920*, ed. Robert Colls and Philip Dodd (London: Croom Helm, 1986), where the absence of imperialism is acknowledged by the editors. Timothy Brennan remarks that when Perry Anderson wrote of the "absent centre" in English intellectual life, and when E. P. Thompson, Williams, and others went in search of hidden socialist traditions, they overlooked the leaders of the anti-colonialist independence movements resident in Britain as representatives of this tradition (Brennan, op. cit., p. x). He also notes that Terry Eagleton, in *Exiles and Emigres*, "is surprisingly reluctant to address the effects of colonialism on the concept of exile itself" (p. 25).

5 Despite a work such as V. G. Kiernan's brilliantly descriptive *The Lords of Human Kind* (Boston: Little, Brown, 1969), the neglect of imperialist culture by both the old and the new left created a vacuum that was filled in Britain by a mode of empiricist studies where inventories of attitudes and ideas about empire stood in for sustained analysis. In a contiguous area, "commonwealth literature" studies were until recently dominated by concern with content and the realism of representing the native's authentic being, a situation that has now been altered by younger critics who are bringing analyses of textual strategies to their readings of colonial and postcolonial literatures. See, for example, Bill Ashcroft, Gareth Griffiths and Helen Tiffin, *The Empire Writes Back: Theory and Practice in Post-Colonial Literatures* (London and New York: Routledge, 1989); and *After Europe: Critical Theory and Post-Colonial Writing*, ed. Stephen Slemon and Helen Tiffin (Australia/Denmark/Coventry: Dangaroo Press, 1989).

6 "Frankfurt School critical theory, whose seminal insights into the relationships between domination, modern society and the opportunities for redemption through art as critique, is stunningly silent on, for example, racist theory, anti-imperialist resistance, oppositional practice in the empire. And lest that silence be interpreted as an oversight we have today's leading Frankfurt theorist, Jürgen Habermas, reformulating the silence, in an interview in *New Left Review*, as deliberate abstention." Quoted from the draft manuscript of Said's forthcoming study on culture and imperialism, originally delivered as the T. S. Eliot Lectures at the University of Kent, December 1985.

7 It is not Said's brief to track the course and variations within imperialism's discourses; however, attention to the wide range of texts produced during the decades of imperial triumphalism – ephemeral writing such as popular fiction, text-books for use in non-elite schools, advertizing, as well as official works on colonial policy – would enable one to construct a language of ascendency in self-definitions of Englishness, valorizing masculinity, encouraging notions of "supermen", inflecting patriotism with racism, and underwriting both exercise of and deferral to authority. For discussion of what John MacKenzie describes as "Englishness presented as a complex of historical, moral and heroic values which justified the possession of empire", see John MacKenzie, *Propaganda and Empire: The Manipulation of British Public Opinion, 1880–1960* (Manchester: Manchester Univ. Press, 1984); John MacKenzie, ed., *Imperialism and Popular Culture* (Manchester: Manchester Univ. Press, 1986); J. A. Mangan, *The Games Ethic and Imperialism* (Harmondsworth: Penguin, 1986); and Michael Rosenthal, *The Character Factory: Baden-Powell and the Origins of the Boy Scout Movement* (New York: Pantheon Books, 1986).

8 As Richard Terdiman puts it, "everything that constitutes a discourse always presupposing a horizon of competing, contrary utterances against which it asserts its own energies." *Discourse/Counter Discourse: The Theory and Practice of Symbolic Resistance in Nineteenth Century France* (Ithaca and London: Cornell Univ. Press, 1985), p. 36.

9 Cf. Fredric Jameson, *Modernism and Imperialism* (Derry: Field Day, 1988), who argues that modernist representation emerges through a "strategy of representational containment . . . where the mapping of the new imperial world system becomes impossible, since the colonized who is (the First World's) essential other component or opposite number has become invisible". Thus the significant structural element of the economic system, which is located elsewhere, "beyond the metropolis, outside of the daily life and existential experience of the home countries, in colonies over the water whose own life experience and life world – very different from that of the imperial power – and which remains unknown and unimaginable for the subjects of the imperial power, whatever social class they may belong to", is displaced into metropolitan spatial representations; p. 11.

10 Clifford has criticized *Orientalism* as lacking in "any developed theory of culture as a differentiating and expressive ensemble rather than as simply hegemonic and disciplinary"; "On *Orientalism*", op. cit., p. 263. Although this designation is inappropriate to Said's critique of imperialism and culture, it does seem relevant to his interpretations of imperialist fictions. See also Dennis Porter, "*Orientalism* and Its Problems", where the book is criticized for its failure to reflect on hegemony as process and its inattention to counter-hegemonic voices. Porter's essay appears in *The Politics of Theory: Proceedings of the Essex Conference on the Sociology of Literature, July 1982* (ed. Francis Barker, Peter Hulme, Margaret Iversen and Diana Loxley, Colchester: University of Essex, 1983).

11 Said has put forward the claim both in "American 'Left' Literary Criticism", in *The World, The Text and the Critic*, and in his Eliot Lectures, that the *form* of the European realist novel inscribes a cultural mode consolidating an authority directed towards social power and governance and therefore underwriting the status quo and consent for overseas empire. But as Michael Sprinker points out, this argument on the coercive power of literary form is not developed by Said, nor can it be sustained, since realism has been redeployed by colonial and postcolonial writing to combat imperialist representation and to repossess the signifying function usurped by imperialism.

12 A different reading of the woman in the text is offered by Bette London, "Reading Race and Gender in Conrad's Dark Continent", *Criticism*, xxxi, No. 3 (Summer 1989), pp. 235–52, who argues that by relegating women to "a world of their own", "Marlow writes them out of the narrative, out of existence itself; the ultimate embodiment of marginality, they frame masculine truth and reality" (pp. 236–7).

13 For an essay disputing Said's attribution of a totalizing power to the narrative, see Vivek Dhareshwan, "The Song of the Sirens in *Heart of Darkness*: The Enigma of Récit", *boundary* 2, XV, 1/2 (1986), pp. 69–84. See also Homi Bhabha, "Signs Taken for Wonders", *Critical Inquiry*, 12, No. 1 (Autumn 1985), pp. 144–65; and Graham Huggan, "Voyages Towards an Absent Centre: Landscape, Interpretation and Textual Strategy in Joseph Conrad's *Heart of Darkness* and Jules Verne's *Voyage Au Centre de la Terre*", *The Conradian*, 14, 1/2 (1989), pp. 19–46. See also Laura Chrisman, who in "The Imperial Unconscious? Representations of Imperial Discourse", *Critical Quar-*

terly, 32, No. 3 (1990), argues that attention must be directed at the specificities of the complex, heterogeneous and contradictory strategies of imperialist representation.

14 For a discussion of strategies to contain or displace conflict in Kipling's writings, see Benita Parry, "The Content and Discontents of Kipling's Imperialism", *New Formations*, 5 (1988), pp. 49–63.

15 See David Goldsworthy, *Colonial Issues in British Politics 1945–1961* (Oxford: Oxford Univ. Press, 1971); and Partha Sarathi Gupta, *Imperialism and the British Labour Movement 1914–1964* (London: Macmillan, 1975). The charter published in 1948 by the *Congress of Peoples Against Imperialism*, a regrouping of previous organizations and the precursor to the Movement for Colonial Freedom, reads: "We reject any theories about the 'cultural and political unfitness' of any people for full immediate independence and equally the imposition of schemes like 'Dominion Status, Indirect Rule' etc., as a substitute for self-determination and genuine self-government. These schemes are merely replacements of the earlier naked and open exploitation of the colonies, utilising the methods of collaboration with the native bourgeoisie who themselves fear mass movements. By this alliance for the joint exploitation of the colonial peoples the imperialists are seeking to safeguard the dominance of finance-capital in these countries" (quoted in Goldsworthy, p. 150). During this same period, the Communist Party of Great Britain was producing analytical and propaganda material on colonialism; see for example the writings of R. Palme Dutt.

16 His faith in such gestures is reiterated in a play, *Atonement*, written at the same time as the tract. Thompson, who died in 1946, was in the last years of his life to give unqualified support to the Indian independence movement.

17 R. Radhakrishnan has proposed a strategy for reconciling "present ethnicity" within "post-ethnicity"; see "Ethnic Identity and Poststructuralist Difference", *Cultural Critique*, 6 (1986); and "Poststructuralist Politics: Towards a Theory of Coalition" in *Postmodernism/Jameson/Critique* (ed. Douglas Kellner, Washington: Maisonneuve Press, 1989).

18 The chapter "'Race' Under Erasure? Poststructuralist Afro-American Literary Theory" in Diana Fuss, *Essentially Speaking: Feminism, Nature and Difference* (New York and London: Routledge, 1989), gives a thoughtful overview of the issues engaged by such criticism. Accusations such as those made by Elliott Butler-Evans, "Beyond Essentialism: Rethinking Afro-American Cultural Theory", *Inscriptions*, 5 (1989), pp. 121–34, that the identification of an ethnic identity wipes out differences of class, gender, etc., is an instance of what Fuss calls the tendency in current theory to conflate identity with essence. Consider, too, the specious assumption made by Butler-Evans in asserting that the concept of an African-American literature implies a unified, ideologically coherent and homogeneous body of discourses reflecting an extra-textual black culture and indifferent to texts as the site of conflicting inscriptions – an assumption coutermanded by the work of the very critics he criticizes.

19 See Lata Mani and Ruth Frankenberg, "The Challenge of *Orientalism*", *Economy and Society*, 14, 20 (1985), pp. 174–92; Homi Bhabha, "Difference, Discrimination and the Discourse of Colonialism", *The Politics of Theory* (Colchester, University of Essex, 1983), ed. Francis Barker, Peter Hulme, Margaret Iversen, Diana Loxley, pp. 194–211; and Rosalind O'Hanlon, "Cultures of Rule, Communities of Resistance", pp. 94–114.

20 O'Hanlon's dissent from Spivak's interpretation of the *Subaltern Studies* project to recuperate subaltern subjectivity as "a strategic use of positivist essentialism

in a scrupulously visible political interest", appears to be unaware that Spivak is being scrupulously courteous in her criticism of work which she sees as falling back "upon notions of consciousness-as-agent, totality, and upon a culturalism, that are discontinuous with the critique of humanism", since she visibly reads the work "against the grain", re-presenting the "retrieval of subaltern consciousness as the charting of what in poststructuralist language would be called the subaltern subject-effect" (*Subaltern Studies*: Deconstructing Historiography" in *Selected Subaltern Studies*, pp. 10 and 12).

21 See K. A. Appiah, "Tolerable Falsehoods: Agency and the Interests of Theory" in *Consequences of Theory* (ed. Jonathan Arac and Barbara Johnson, Baltimore: Johns Hopkins University Press, 1990), on arguments against the hyperbolic claim that we cannot escape the demands of our ideological construction: "Humanist criticism overplayed the self-reflexive actor, the autonomous individual, the subject. Structuralism and then poststructuralism responded by overplaying structure (alias: totality, systematicity, even 'discourse') ... What I want to suggest ... is that we should see the relations between structural explanation and the logic of the subject as a competition not for causal space but for narrative space: as different levels of theory, with different constitutive assumptions, whose relations make them neither competitive, nor mutually constitutive; but quite contingently complementary ... the understanding of agents and texts through the language of the subject is guided by different interests from the understanding that operates in the language of social structure, ... these different interests make different idealizations appropriate, different falsehoods tolerable" (pp. 70, 74–5, 79). See also Diana Fuss, *Essentially Speaking*, who follows Andreas Huyssen in pointing out the need to develop "alternative and different notions of subjectivity" that question current ethnocentric theories of the subject as male, white and middle-class.

22 Cf. Terdiman, op. cit., who stresses that counter-discourses are always interlocked with the domination they contest, opposing their dominant antagonists without effacing them, inhabiting and struggling with the dominant which inhabits them.

23 Amilcar Cabral, also cited by Said as an instance of a liberationist theorist, in "Cultural Resistance", *Unity and Struggle* (London: Heinemann, 1980), both anticipates the emergence of a "universal culture", and calls for a re-Africanization that will aim at the development of a people's culture and "of all aboriginal and positive values" (p. 153).

Works Cited

Bhabha, Homi, "Interrogating Identity", in *The Real Me: Postmodernism and the Question of Identity* (London: ICA Document 6, 1987), pp. 5–11.

Bhabha, Homi, "The Commitment to Theory", *New Formations*, 5 (Summer 1988), pp. 5–23.

Césaire, Aimé, *Discourse on Colonialism* (1955; New York: Monthly Review Press, 1972).

Dhareshwar, Vivek, "Toward a Narrative Epistemology of the Postcolonial Predicament", in *Inscriptions*, 5 (1989): *Traveling Theories, Traveling Theorists*, pp. 135–57.

Fanon, Frantz, *Black Skin, White Masks* (1952, London: Pluto Press, 1986).

Fanon, Frantz, "Racism and Culture" (1956), in *Toward the African Revolution* (New York: Grove Press, 1967).

Fanon, Frantz, "On National Culture" (1959), in *The Wretched of the Earth* (London: MacGibbon and Gee, 1965).

Gates, Henry Louis Jr, "Literary Theory and the Black Tradition", in *Figures in Black* (New York and Oxford: Oxford University Press, 1989).

Gates, Henry Louis Jr, "Afterword: Critical Remarks", in *Anatomy of Racism* (ed. David Goldberg, Minneapolis: University of Minnesota Press, 1990).

Gilroy, Paul, *There Ain't No Black in the Union Jack* (London: Hutchinson, 1987).

Gilroy, Paul, "Nothing But Sweat inside my Hand: Diaspora Aesthetics and Black Arts in Britain", *Black Film British Cinema* (London: ICA Document 7, 1988), pp. 44–6.

Gilroy, Paul, "It Ain't Where You're From, Its Where You're At . . . The Dialectics of Diasporic Identification" in *Third Text*, 13 (Winter 1990/1), pp. 3–16.

Glissant, Edouard, *Caribbean Discourse: Selected Essays* (translated and with an Introduction by J. Michael Dash, Charlottesville: University of Virginia Press, 1989; first published 1981).

Guha, Ranajit, "The Prose of Counter-Insurgency", in *Selected Subaltern Studies* (ed. Ranajit Guha and Gayatri Chakravorty Spivak, New York and Oxford: Oxford University Press, 1988).

Hall, Stuart, "Minimal Selves", in *The Real Me: Postmodernism and the Question of Identity* (London: ICA Document 6, 1987), pp. 44–6.

Hall, Stuart, "New Ethnicities", in *Black Film British Cinema* (London: ICA Document 7, 1988), pp. 27–31.

Hall, Stuart, "Cultural Identity and Diaspora", *Identity, Community, Culture, Difference* (ed. Jonathan Rutherford, London: Lawrence and Wishart, 1990).

Hulme, Peter, "Subversive Archipelagoes: Colonial Discourse and the Break-up of Continental Theory", *Dispositio*, xiv: 36–38, (Autumn 1989), pp. 1–23.

Mercer, Kobena, "Diasporic Culture and the Dialogic Imagination: The Aesthetics of Black Independent Film in Britain", in *BlackFrames: Critical Perspectives on Black Independent Film* (ed. Mbye Cham and Claire A. Watkins, Boston: Celebration of Black Film/MIT, 1988).

O'Hanlon, Rosalind, "Recovering the Subject: *Subaltern Studies* and Histories of Resistance in Colonial South Asia", in *Modern Asian Studies*, 22, 1 (1988), pp. 189–224.

O'Hanlon, Rosalind, "Cultures of Rule, Communities of Resistance: Gender, discourse and tradition in recent South Asian historiographies", *Social Analysis*, 25 (1989), pp. 94–114.

Pêcheux, Michel, *Language, Semantics and Ideology* (London: Macmillan, 1983).

Said, Edward, *The World, the Text and the Critic* (Cambridge, Mass.: Harvard University Press, 1983).

Said, Edward, "Orientalism Reconsidered", in *Europe and Its Others*, Vol. 1 (ed. Francis Barker, Peter Hulme, Margaret Iversen, Diana Loxley, Colchester: University of Essex, 1985).

Said, Edward, *Culture and Imperialism*: The T. S. Eliot Lectures, 1985/Messenger Lectures 1986: forthcoming; references in text are to the pagination of Lectures I to IV in typescript.

Said, Edward, "On Palestinian Identity: A Conversation with Salman Rushdie", *New Left Review*, 160, pp. 63–80.

Said, Edward, "Intellectuals and the Postcolonial World", *Salmagundi*, 70–1 (1986), pp. 44–80.

Said, Edward, "*Kim*: The Pleasures of Imperialism", *Raritan*, VII, 2 (1987), pp.

27–64. This essay also appears as the Introduction to *Kim* (Harmondsworth: Penguin, 1987).

Said, Edward, "American Intellectuals and Middle East Politics: An Interview with Edward Said" by Bruce Robbins, *Social Text*, 7: 1 and 2 (1988), pp. 37–53.

Said, Edward, *Yeats and Decolonization*, in series *Nationalism, Colonialism and Literature* (Derry: Field Day, 1988).

Said, Edward, Foreword to *Selected Subaltern Studies* (ed. Ranajit Guha and Gayatri Chakravorty Spivak, New York and Oxford: Oxford University Press, 1988).

Said, Edward, "C. L. R. James: The Artist as Revolutionary", *New Left Review*, 175 (1989), pp. 126–8.

Said, Edward, "Jane Austen and Empire", in *Raymond Williams: Critical Perspectives* (Cambridge: Polity Press, 1989).

Said, Edward, "Representing the Colonized: Anthropology's Interlocutors", *Critical Inquiry*, 15, 2 (1989), pp.. 205–25.

Said, Edward, "Third World Intellectuals/Metropolitan Culture", *Raritan*, IX, 3 (1990), pp. 29–50.

Said, Edward, "Narrative, Geography and Interpretation", the Raymond Williams Memorial Lecture, London, October 1989, *New Left Review*, 180 (1990), pp. 81–97.

Salusinszky, Imre, "Edward Said", *Criticism in Society: Interviews* (London and New York: Methuen, 1987).

Spivak, Gayatri Chakravorty, "*Subaltern Studies*: Deconstructing Historiography", in *Selected Subaltern Studies* (ed. Ranajit Guha and Gayatri Chakravorty Spivak, New York and Oxford: Oxford University Press, 1988).

Spivak, Gayatri Chakravorty, "Can the Subaltern Speak?" in *Marxism and the Interpretation of Culture* (ed. Cary Nelson and Lawrence Gossberg, London: Macmillan, 1988).

Spivak, Gayatri Chakravorty, "Poststructuralism, Marginality, Postcoloniality and Value", in *Literary Theory Today* (ed. Peter Collier and Helga Ryan, Cambridge: Polity Press, 1990).

Thompson, Edward, *The Other Side of the Medal* (London: L. and V. Woolf, 1925).

Williams, Raymond, *Marxism and Literature* (Oxford: Oxford University Press, 1977).

Williams, Raymond, *Towards 2000* (1983; Harmondsworth: Penguin, 1985).

Williams, Raymond, *The Politics of Modernism: Against the New Conformists* (ed. and introduced by Tony Pinkney, London: Verso, 1989).

3

THE EAST IS A CAREER: EDWARD SAID AND THE LOGICS OF PROFESSIONALISM

Bruce Robbins

"The East is a career." The quotation, from Disraeli's 1847 novel, *Tancred*, is briefly and brilliantly offensive. Activating the convention by which an empty, immobile point on the compass is held capable of condensing millions of undescribed personal destinies, the sentence equates these missing millions with a single individual's rising curve of professional accomplishment. The individual who is to enjoy the career is elided, as if in pretense of equal exchange for the elision of the colossal human diversity that is to be its raw material; in the space of symmetrical impersonality thus cleared, the static East can be spurred into movement, metamorphosed into the kinesis of a (Western) "pursuit." In this outrageous incongruity of scale, the quotation mimics the almost unimaginable overriding of the reality of "the East" by the self-interested systems of Western "experts" that Edward Said exposes in *Orientalism* (1978), to which it serves as acutely ironic epigraph.[1]

But today we must add to this sentence another, further irony, newly and eccentrically literal. Thanks largely to the path-breaking work of Edward Said, it is now possible for intellectuals from what used to be called "the East," as well as from the metropolis, to make a metropolitan academic career out of transmitting, interpreting, and debating representations of what is now called (with no more precision) the "Third World." Giving due weight to the fact that such careers are most often visibly contestatory – though rarely as much so as Said's own – it is now almost possible to say, in the flip shorthand of academic fields, that "the Third World is a career."

There are good reasons why this sentence remains not quite sayable. But there is also at least one bad reason – which is of some significance for the politics of intellectual work. This is the assumption that success in professional career-making is at best an embarrassment to any scholar who, like Said, makes a career while, and by, maintaining a commitment to radical social change. Careers, that is, are suitable for more or less irreverent *ad hominem* or *feminam* gossip; they may be strip-mined for easy ethical inconsistency or psychological insight, but their dynamics are not subject to properly social or political analysis. Few thinkers – Said himself and Perry Anderson are among the exceptions – have sought to generalize with political seriousness from the individual trajectories of scholarship. But now, when so much of the Left's intellectual work is carried on in universities and within an ideological context of professionalism, there is intense need to revitalize the genre of scholarly biography (which accounts for much of Said's own most animated prose) and to examine our highest examples of politicized scholarship on the principled level they deserve. To bring the perspective of professionalism to bear on the work of Edward Said is not to diminish in any way his achievement but rather, following his own Foucauldian insistence on the social structuring that constrains but also enables individual achievement, to show that his success reflects meaningfully both on him and on the profession which he has helped to change.

Orientalism's other, equally ironic, epigraph comes from Marx's description of petty landowners in *The Eighteenth Brumaire of Louis Bonaparte*: "They cannot represent themselves; they must be represented." This sentence has become a touchstone of the new anti-representational "common sense" that – until quite recently at least – has helped bind together the poststructuralist Left's otherwise divergent moral and epistemological impulses. Between "theory," asserting that there is no escape from representations which can never coincide faithfully with their objects, and the "new social movements," which have shaken the claims to representativeness of those false universalities that had silenced and excluded them, but have done so in the name of their own capacity to represent themselves, the common ground has been an almost uncontested ethico-epistemological denial of anyone's right or ability to represent *others*. As a result, it is widely believed (in Derrida's pithy phrase) that "representation is bad," and that the disciplines most directly based on it, like anthropology, are merely persisting in a ghostly afterlife after their vital principle has disappeared.[2] There has been little desire to face the contradictions of this position for those most likely to hold it: oppositional scholars whose *raison d'être* and daily business inescapably involve (however mediated through texts and concepts) the representation of others.[3]

As the outstanding representative of the poststructuralist Left in the US today, Edward Said is often identified as a source or center both of this modified anti-representational common sense and, more specifically, of the position on professionalism that seems to result from it. *Orientalism*'s two epigraphs help explain why. Taken together, they seem to form a parable of professionalism-as-domination. The West projects on to those it has subjugated degrading stereotypes that naturalize the West's rule as well as its monopoly on representing them, and – once the field is cleared of their protest or self-expression – representing and ruling them can become a career for enterprising Westerners. This logic, like *Orientalism* itself, has had an enormous effect – perhaps its greatest effect – outside the field of Middle Eastern area specialists and policy intellectuals, on those for whom it is only a "case" of a larger principle to be applied to very different topics, especially the arguably different issues of representation for women, people or color, gays and lesbians, and so on.[4] What is perhaps the most absolute case of non-representation, that of the Arabs of the Middle East, is taken as definitive and generalized accordingly. In its broadest extension, the logic of Orientalism is thus often held to illustrate the view that *all* professional scholarship, inherently elite and undemocratic, is similarly based on a denial of self-representation to oppressed groups, making possible a monopoly of uncontested and degrading representations of them by authoritative, self-accredited professionals, in the service of more conveniently ruling those groups. Professional careers are made, the logic goes, by representing those whom the career-maker keeps from representing themselves.

Once this version of common sense is in place, however, the way is open for the same accusation to be levelled even at those professionals, like Said, whose professional success has depended on drawing legitimacy and authority from previously unrepresented others, and who are thus charged with disciplinary self-promotion (for example, by Paul Bové). Or else, on the same basis, Said and others like him can be charged, symmetrically (for example, by Benita Parry) with *keeping* the unrepresented from representing themselves, substituting their own elite intellectual work for the voices of the oppressed even as they claim to represent those voices.[5] These accusations would evaporate, however, if the accusers could acknowledge that they characteristically share the same professional base of operations with the accused. As Jim Merod comments, "Lamentably, everything Bové says about Said's self-promotion can be turned against Bové also."[6] This professional base draws on the same resources of authority and legitimacy. The critic who accuses another of speaking for the subaltern by denying that subalterns can speak for themselves, for example, is of course also claiming to speak for them. In professional context, the belief that the subaltern can speak becomes a belief that they can speak *through us*, through our mediatory interpretations of their texts. However pure, self-effacing, and anti-representational we may try (mistakenly) to appear, we are thereby assigning ourselves a job of work – work that is justified by public interests but is also something added on to the mere existence of any constituency, and that must be accepted in its specific weight, concreteness, and supplementarity. We can neither deny representation nor self-effacingly make ourselves transparent so that others can fully and immediately represent themselves. While working toward greater democracy of representation, we can only affirm the value of one mode of representation over another. As Jonathan Arac concludes, "People do it all the time, and the crucial issue is by what means, to what purpose, with what effect."[7] The one satisfactory answer, in other words, is to strike down the assumption that a representational logic linking "the East" to a "career" is inherently and absolutely unacceptable.

Before pressing this argument further, it is important to say that the identification of professionalism with domination by means of representation is not in fact Said's own position on the matter. To begin with, it is not his position on representation; this makes sense for various reasons. In the struggle over the aspirations of the Palestinians to self-determination, the position that treats the link between the Palestinians and their representatives as illegitimate has been one major means of denying them representation, thus prolonging "the fate of every Palestinian, which is both to be *there*, and yet not to be accounted for politically."[8] Said describes the strategy of being "for Palestinian rights in general but against Palestinians and their representatives in particular." So Walzer and Howe, for instance, "speak openly against Begin – excellent – but simultaneously speak cold-bloodedly . . . of *destroying* the only authentic representatives of Palestinian nationalism."[9] In questioning the political motives of a critique whose sole determination is to pry open some gap, *any* gap, between representer and represented, making no distinctions in the doubt it casts on the legitimacy of all representation, Said insists that representation *can* be "authentic" and legitimate. He stands apart from certain trends in poststructuralist theory.

But this position is by no means a matter of practical political expediency alone. It is also entirely consistent with his theoretical stance toward professional work. In this respect he rejoins the Marxist tradition, which assumes neither that the only acceptable representation is self-representation nor that the ability to represent oneself can be taken for granted. (In the epigraph from *The Eighteenth Brumaire*, for example, Marx's irony is clearly complex; it includes some scorn at the *incapacity* of the petty landowners to represent themselves.) Said writes, for example: "if you believe with Gramsci that an intellectual vocation is socially possible as well as desirable, it is an inadmissable contradiction at the same time to build analyses of historical experience around exclusions, exclusions that stipulate, for instance, only women can understand feminine experience, only Jews can understand Jewish suffering, only formerly colonial subjects can understand colonial experience."[10] Any sense of "intellectual vocation," then, will *require* accepting the task of analyzing, understanding, representing the experience of others.

The only problem with this statement is that, by not specifying who if anyone might historically exemplify such a vocation, it permits itself to be taken exclusively as exhortation, as an ideal of how things *should* be rather than a fact about how things already are. Thus it is possible to ignore the senses in which representation is not merely potentially and desirably but *necessarily* part of the job of professional scholarship, and therefore already part – if not a sufficiently large part – of its present. A useful example is Said's well-known account of literary theory. That literary theory "has turned its back" on "the social world," Said writes in *The World, the Text, and the Critic*, "can be considered, I think, the triumph of the ethic of professionalism."[11] Along with "guild consciousness, consensus, collegiality, professional respect" (p. 20), he targets "a cult of professional expertise whose effect in general is pernicious" because it accepts "the principle of noninterference" (pp. 2–3), a neglect of "connections between texts and the existential actualities of human life, politics, societies, and events" (p. 5).[12] One can agree conjuncturally and still want to insist that literary theory would not have enjoyed the professional success it has, indeed would not exist at all, if it were as cut off from "the social world" as Said suggests – if it did not somehow accomplish, however unsatisfactorily, a task of representation.

If this point has yet to become common sense, the cause is perhaps, ironically, theory itself and its effect on the conceptualizing of professionalism. Said's description of literary theory is remarkably and unexpectedly similar to his description of Orientalism, a discipline one would have thought more closely connected – in the service of the wrong interests, of course – to the actualities of "politics, societies, and events." It is almost as if the image of theory had both controlled the definition of professionalism (as isolated and self-enclosed "system," like representation itself) and had been projected on to Orientalism, so that the actual existence of "the East" makes no difference to the professional authority, legitimacy, or procedures either of the literary theorist or of the Orientalist scholar – and need not therefore become part of even the *critique* of Orientalist scholarship. But where, then, does the critic of Orientalism stand? Trying to work his way around this problem – appropriately enough, in the passage where he explains the "East is a career" epigraph – Said allows the (negative) notion of the profession as totally hermetic, self-contained, protected from any accountability, to reproduce itself in or on the critic's own (affirmative) premises:

> it would be wrong to conclude that the Orient was *essentially* an idea, or a creation with no corresponding reality. When Disraeli said in his novel *Tancred* that the East was a career, he meant that to be interested in the East was something bright young Westerners would find to be an all-consuming passion; he should not be interpreted as saying that the East was *only* a career for Westerners. There were – and are – cultures and nations whose location is in the East, and their lives, histories, and customs have a brute reality obviously greater than anything that could be said about them in the West.

About that fact this study of Orientalism has very little to contribute, except to acknowledge it tacitly. But the phenomenon of Orientalism as I study it here deals principally, not with the correspondence between Orientalism and Orient, but with the internal consistency of Orientalism and its ideas about the Orient (the East as a career) despite or beyond any correspondence, or lack thereof, with a "real" Orient. My point is that Disraeli's statement about the East refers mainly to that created consistency, that regular constellation of ideas as the preeminent thing about the Orient, and not to its mere being, as Wallace Stevens puts it (p. 5).

Both at the beginning and at the end of this passage, there is a surprising eagerness to discuss what *Disraeli* meant by his statement – as if Disraeli's opinions about the Orient, rather than the premises and procedures of his own book, were what Said had been explaining or what the reader wanted to know. The momentary uncertainty as to who is speaking here, Disraeli or Said or Disraeli for Said, will be familiar to literary critics, who are used to playing with the possibilities for indeterminacy and multi-voicedness created by the convention of commentary on an author. But here the convention covers an unlikely complicity: the duplication by the critic of the object criticized. If Disraeli and Oriental scholarship treat the East as a "career," so does Said's *Orientalism*, which analyzes (and refuses to go beyond) "internal" and "created consistency," "regular constellation," in short, formal coherence in isolation from the reality of the Orient.

Said knows very well, of course – and it is thanks to him that many of us know it – that Orientalist scholarship most often in fact "represented" extra-professional interests and constituencies, notably those of the colonial powers, and took authority and legitimacy in part from its usefulness to colonial and neo-colonial projects. Why then should he seem to present the discipline as if – like literary theory in his view – its authority and legitimacy were based on nothing more than guild loyalty and formal coherence? Why make it seem totally arbitrary that the Orientalists said what they said and not some other thing, that in misrepresenting the East, the West was constrained by nothing but the formal or aesthetic coherence of its own created system?

The obvious answer is that it is only in this way that *literary critics*, who specialize in formal or aesthetic coherence, can claim the subject-matter of Orientalism as an appropriate object of study and commentary. Against the claims of other, more obviously pertinent disciplines like Middle Eastern studies, political economy, or history to isolate, explain, and criticize the abuses of Orientalism, and *mutatis mutandis* of other fields, an imperiously expansive literary criticism has marshalled poststructuralist theory's asser- tion that "everything is" (the terms are not interchangeable, but close enough) language, textuality, discourse, rhetoric or representation. Thus could it expose the cultural (linguistic, textual, discursive, etc.) constructedness of apparently "natural," "empirical" knowledges. In this (surely unconscious) tactic of disciplinary aggrandizement, there was a substantial political gain, and not just for the members of one discipline. Still, if we do not adopt that one discipline's perspective, the political value of asserting that knowledge is *only* representation is no longer self-evident. For if *everything* is representation, then representation is not a scandal. Or if *all* representation is a scandal, then no particular representation is especially scandalous – and in protesting Orientalism's "coherence," we are not protesting in the most useful direction.

This would explain why Said's two epigraphs might conceivably be read, removed from his own unmistakably indignant voice, as strangely, structurally *lacking* in indignation – as an uninflected account of how things are rather than a protest. No, they *cannot* represent themselves. Yes, the East *is* a career. So? Sadik Jalal al-Azm writes:

> Said himself admits readily that it is impossible for a culture, be it Eastern or Western or South American, to grasp much about the reality of another, alien culture without resort to categorisation, classification, schematisation and reduction – with the necessarily accompanying distortions and misrepresentations. If, as Said insists, the unfamiliar, exotic and alien is always apprehended, domesticated, assimilated and represented in terms of the already familiar, then such distortions and misrepresentations become unavoidable ... He even finds "nothing especially controversial or reprehensible" about the domestication of an exotic and alien culture ... If, as the author keeps repeating (by way of censure and castigation), the Orient studied by Orientalism is no more than an image and a representation in the mind and culture of the Occident (the representer in this case) then it is also true that the Occident in so doing is behaving perfectly naturally and in accordance with the general rule – as stated by Said himself – governing the dynamics of the reception of one culture by another.[13]

One can conclude, therefore, that literary critics confuse colonial and neo-colonial injustice with epistemology or "internal coherence" in order to give criticism – with its predisposition to believe, as al-Azm puts it, "in the magical efficacy of words" (p. 14) – a particular or privileged grasp over its diagnosis and exposure. This is how the subject-matter of (post)colonialism is assimilated into a new sub-discipline, very much under the sway of criticism and poststructuralist theory, called "colonial discourse" – that is, grasped specifically *as* discourse.

My point here is not to argue that Said's own critique corresponds to a particular professional logic and is shaped by (even as it reshapes) the professional exigencies of a particular discipline. This can be taken for granted about anyone, however innovative and transgressive, working within a scholarly discipline or disciplines. Since it can be taken for granted, it is not in itself a critique. Critique might begin, for example, by pointing

out how a "colonial discourse" sub-field with so much of the aesthetic in
its constitution might tend, at worst, to repeat a Romantic respect for
particulars for their own sake, recoding a discredited Arnoldian "culture"
as Third World "difference" and thus renewing it while neglecting, say,
capitalism as a world system and the common elements of struggle against
it around the world, whether First, Third, or (already upon us) Second. But
any such criticism would also have to weigh the political *benefits* of this
particular professional logic. It could not walk away once the contaminat-
ing presence of the professional had been identified, assuming that professionalism by definition precludes public or political benefits and
encourages only private gains at the public's expense.

Formal coherence is, it seems, one foundation for professional authority.
Indeed, it can even support such authority in a negative and backhanded
way. To the extent that any critic draws authority in proportion to the
magnitude and significance of the object treated, whether that treatment
involves praise or blame, even oppositional critics may well be tempted to
exaggerate, for professional reasons, the systematic, totalizing coherence of
what they oppose, tempted to exclude from it any untidy discrepancies or
counter-hegemonic utterances that, in mitigating its gravity or systematicity,
also compromise the critic's authority. But careers do not rest on "internal
consistency" alone. I open up a sizable digression here in order to make
this case with regard to Claude Lévi-Strauss. Famous for his extreme
formalization of the study of myth, from which the formalist current in
theory and the interdisciplinary imperialism I have been discussing in large
part descend, Lévi-Strauss is a far less political figure than Said, both in his
writing and outside it. To suggest the limits of "internal consistency" in
explaining *his* career, therefore, is to suggest something quite general about
the politics of career-making.

   In *Reinventing Anthropology*, edited by Dell Hymes in 1972, a collection
that served as the major expression of 1960s protest on the part of radical
anthropologists against their field, a passage from Lévi-Strauss is quoted
twice. The first time is in the introduction:

> Anthropology . . . is the outcome of a historical process which has made the
> larger part of mankind subservient to the other, and during which millions of
> innocent human beings have had their resources plundered and their insti-
> tutions and beliefs destroyed, while they themselves were ruthlessly killed,
> thrown into bondage, and contaminated by diseases they were unable to
> resist. Anthropology is the daughter to this era of violence.

A powerful indictment of an entire discipline, the passage is an important
precedent for Said's *Orientalism*. However, in the penultimate chapter,
written by Stanley Diamond, the same quotation prefaces an attack on

Lévi-Strauss as the quintessential "professional" – an "alien" whose ultimate values are "academic and ethnocentric" (pp. 403–5).

This is the charge – with some geographical allowance – that Lévi-Strauss has made the East a career. This point has been made too often not to contain an important truth. Any reader of Lévi-Strauss will be aware that the level of intelligibility of myth, in his view, has little to do with the conscious "experience" or opinions of the native informant. On the contrary, he defined myth in such a way that it could be comprehended only by the expertise of a European professional like himself, far removed from face-to-face contact with the "primitive." Indeed, he makes no secret of the self-serving vocational motives behind his research. As Clifford Geertz writes in "The Cerebral Savage," "no anthropologist has been more insistent on the fact that the practice of his profession has consisted of a personal quest, driven by a personal vision, and directed toward a personal salvation."[14] In *Tristes Tropiques*, Lévi-Strauss himself is unusually frank about his own desire, in setting sail for Brazil, not to intervene against colonial injustice but to resolve a vocational crisis, a crisis of a sort that was to become familiar to the students of the 1960s. He has never studied anthropology, but other subjects (including philosophy, which he is supposed to be teaching) leave him cold, and he doesn't quite know what to do with himself. The Indians of Brazil solve his problem.

For Geertz, as for other commentators, Lévi-Strauss' anthropology is first and foremost, or perhaps exclusively, a professional solution to this personal search for satisfying work. The characteristic imagery of this low-key satire of hyper-professionalism is that of *enclosure*. It is only the assumption that the "primitive" universe is closed, Geertz says, which permits the closure of myth, hence the definition of (enclosed) "system" or "structure" that is the true object of narrative analysis, hence the satisfying sovereign enclosure of professional territoriality. What makes anthropology, in Lévi-Strauss' words, "one of the few true vocations" (p. 354) is that, like music and mathematics, it detaches itself from the messiness of history in order to reach a high degree of order, which it identifies with reality itself. "To reach reality we must first repudiate experience" (p. 356) – in particular the experience of contact with the Other. The retreat from contact with the outside is not so much the price Lévi-Strauss pays in order to achieve professionalism's internal coherence as the formulation of the professional project itself.

In 1981, after Sartre's death, Lévi-Strauss was voted the most influential French intellectual alive. According to David Pace, this preeminence should be interpreted as the replacement of the "philosophe" by the "academic" and by "the ideology of the university."[15] Perhaps. But to the extent that this story – like Geertz's narrative of professionalization, or like the sad, familiar tale of the academicization of the 1960s – presumes that a new tendency in the academy can make its way, or an older one can sustain itself, by means of a politically self-indulgent withdrawal into self-enclosure, it seems to mistake both Lévi-Strauss and professionalism in general. It is true, as Geertz says, that objectivity and "coherence" are major vocational desiderata for Lévi-Strauss. He dislikes law, another vocational option, because "it seems unable to find any basis for itself that is at once solid and objective" (p. 45). On the other hand, Lévi-Strauss tells us that he rejects philosophy, for which he didn't have a "genuine vocation" (p. 42), because its results were judged in terms of "technical perfection or internal coherence" (p. 43) – that is, because "Expertise replaced the truth" (p. 44). His life's work, then, must be able to claim a professional authority *higher* than mere "coherence."

What authority? This question can be rephrased as the question of why structuralism struck when and as it did. The ideas of Saussure and Russian formalism came considerably earlier. Why the lag? A mechanical explanation – by chance Lévi-Strauss meets Jakobson in New York City during the war, thus acquiring the linguistic paradigm for his redefinition of "myth" – still leaves us with another more than fifteen-year lag before the phenomenon picks up any real interdisciplinary momentum. What is specific to the 1960s, on the other hand, is the context of global decolonization. While Lévi-Strauss was writing the works that won him his preeminence, France was losing wars of national liberation in Indochina and Algeria: *Tristes Tropiques* was published in 1955, the year after Dien Bien Phu; *La Pensée Sauvage* in 1962, the year Algeria finally won its independence. These events are of course part of a global pattern of self-assertion and independence by former colonies in the post-war period, beginning with the independence of India in 1947 and the victory of the Chinese Red Army in 1949 (the year Lévi-Strauss published *The Elementary Structures of Kinship*).[16]

This pattern has its analogue, in the intellectual domain, in a growing critique of Eurocentrism and an openness to Third World voices – one example of which is, precisely, Lévi-Strauss' effort to break down the loaded opposition between the rationality of "history," which supposedly belongs to Europe, and the irrationality of "myth," which supposedly characterizes "the savage mind." "Myth," in his polemical redefinition, follows cognitive laws that do not differ in essence from those of European rationality; the term "myth" applies with equal precision to the European notion of history (this is the point he made about Sartre in the famous chapter 9 of *La Pensée Sauvage*), and for that matter to his own anthropological discourse *about* myth. In short, Lévi-Strauss' effort is to define and extend an intellectual common ground between Europe and its "others," to generate a conceptual vocabulary that mediates between "us" and "them" on terms that – unlike any of the terms of cultural analysis then in circulation – would be preferential to neither. "Myth" and its successor "narrative" downplay consciousness (which could be enlisted in the service of hierarchical opposition) in favor of structure, whose very abstractness made it democratically inclusive, equally appropriate when applied to so-called "primitive" or so-called "civilized" discourse. Within the limits of scholarly discourse, "structure" creates a level playing field where the self-representations of the supposed "peoples without history" can be afforded greater respect, and the positivist truth claims of European interpreters of those representations can be relativized. In a two-step redistribution of authority, the special claims of "the West" (tied to science) are lowered, while the unacknowledged claims of "the rest" (tied to the literary or "non-scientific") become, at the least, available for recognition.

I have ignored the manifest political difficulties posed by Lévi-Strauss in order to bring out the less visible work of conceptual mediation that he accomplishes, with its oblique but real claim to improve the political conditions of representation according to the interests of colonialism's victims. In so doing, I am less interested in measuring the scope of endurance of his achievement than in illuminating its principle: his discovery of a professional authority higher than mere coherence. I want to suggest, in other words, that the appeal to this emergent constituency is part of his revitalizing of the anthropological profession, as appeals like it are part of professionalism in general. What permitted him to speak for and help produce an anthropological renaissance – the epigraph to *Reinventing Anthropology* cites his proposition that "Anthropology will survive in a changing world by allowing itself to perish in order to be born again under a new guise" – was reaching outside the discipline, to the constituencies revealed by decolonization, and to the wider public in whose eyes anthropology had to win its new social legitimacy. In this sense *Tristes Tropiques* itself is a quintessentially professional book: a book written for non-professionals, but written in order to legitimate the profession in their eyes.

This tactic of furthering his discipline's interests by demonstrating that it is neither self-enclosed nor self-sustaining is not confined to the rhetoric of his best-seller. In the classic exposé of structuralism, "The Structural Study of Myth," we find the same provocative indeterminacy about the line separating the profession's inside and outside.[17] In the essay's first paragraph it is clear Lévi-Strauss is defending its interests against "amateurs," whether from other disciplines or not: "because the interest of professional anthropologists has withdrawn from primitive religion, all kinds of amateurs who claim to belong to other disciplines have seized this opportunity to move in, thereby turning into their private playground what we had left as a wasteland" (p. 206). Later in the essay, however, his own central exhibit, a reading of the Oedipus myth, makes no claim to be "an explanation acceptable to the specialist" (p. 213). Is myth confined within disciplinary boundaries or not? Do disciplines *have* boundaries? "French sociology," he declares elsewhere, "does not consider itself as an isolated discipline, working in its own specific field, but rather as a method, or as a specific attitude toward human phenomena. Therefore, one does not need to be a sociologist in order to do sociology."[18] In explaining the attack on Sartre in *La Pensée Sauvage*, however, he writes, "I was simply obliged to clarify certain things, when Sartre, leaving his own domain, proposed to reveal to ethnologists the deep nature of their profession."[19] Is thought tamed by its "domain" or "profession," or does it roam wild? To judge from Lévi-Strauss, one would have to conclude that the opposition is a false one; the profession and its outside have no firm boundary but are mutually interdependent.

Again, the example can be generalized. Commenting on the circuitous careers of four scholars of myth (Lévi-Strauss, Cassirer, Eliade, and Malinowski), Ivan Strenski explains the apparent anomalies by declaring that history in the first half of the twentieth century "made normal professional life impossible. Professionals engaged in the study of myth might want to ponder the historical fact that perhaps the most creative thinkers in the field were nurtured intellectually – at least, for significant parts of their lives – *outside* their professions."[20] This leads him to note

> a great irony. As soon as they succeeded in re-establishing themselves professionally, they did so with a certain "vengeance"; all, except Cassirer, founded the major "schools" in their respective fields; as a result, they became responsible for entirely new enterprises of professionalization in those field ... In each case the result was the production of "professionals" who developed and disseminated the concepts of myth associated with their great mentors. Small wonder that the discourse in this field is as imperialistic as it is (pp. 198–9).

Strenski observes better than he interprets. Yes, these scholars made their breakthroughs by bringing into their professions something of what they had learned from twentieth-century history. But there is no "irony" in the fact that the result was "new enterprises of professionalization" so forceful in their impact as to be described as "imperialistic." For better or worse, this is how "normal" professions work. Those who have the vision to retool professional procedures and protocols in response to or anticipation of great historical shifts and newly emergent versions of the public interest – by no means a mechanical feat, of course – are vastly more likely to set the professional agendas of the future, force professional paradigm shifts, re-align the competing disciplines among themselves and (in so doing) in new relation to worldly power. For professions – even the notoriously unworldly literary theory – are not self-enclosed and self-sustaining, however much they would sometimes like to believe it. The outside constitutes the inside, and (limitedly) vice versa.

Presiding over the resuscitation of an endangered discipline by speaking, with exceptional force, both inside and outside it, Lévi-Strauss set an influential example. Foucault, his biographer tells us, often stated his admiration for the way in which Lévi-Strauss "was able to explode the boundary separating academic work's specialized public and the broad educated public."[21] Foucault's own example is of course significant both for Said's thinking about careers and the institutions in which they take place and for his own career. His effort to articulate a left-wing critique of Foucault that would not reject all Foucault's premises in favor of Marxist doxa, a sort of critique of poststructuralism from within, is another of his essential contributions to the formation of a poststructuralist left that would obviously include but not be restricted to the academy. The public question of common ground and common sense is therefore crucial.

Unlike Foucault and poststructuralist orthodoxy, Said has dissented from any over-totalizing system that threatens to leave insufficient room for the assertion of human will. Unlike most Marxists, he has never found much use for "capitalism" as an explanatory term (except indirectly, through "reification," about which more below). The term he shares with both, however – and through which, perhaps, he has managed so well to draw both groups together – is "work." From *Beginnings* (1975) onward, it is "work" that offers a version of "will" that need not deny "system." Even Orientalism must be seen, he says, "as a kind of *willed human work* – not of mere unconditioned ratiocination" (p. 15). But if the workplace is where will can uniquely be exercised, then the implicit social model would seem to be the relative autonomy of a *professional* workplace, and professional autonomy would seem to be the socially specific target of appeals for change.

In this respect Said and Foucault are perhaps closer than they otherwise seem. The readers addressed by Foucault, Jim Merod writes, are "the professionals who own the disruptive potential on which his strategy depends" (p. 158). "In effect the centerless power [Foucault] opposes resides precisely here, among those he calls on to disrupt a system they hold by expertise that circulates outside political inspection and political accountability" (p. 159). For Merod, who takes Said's side in the debate between them over will and "autonomy," this strategy is a mistake: "by restricting political struggle to professional combats, Foucault enhances divisions between experts and nonexperts" (p. 189). But he points us toward a Foucault with whom Said has less reason to disagree. The aim of Foucault's concept of the "specific intellectual" is to invigorate local and professional action that was disabled and downgraded by the burden of universality. For Foucault, the fact that such action may be restricted to the university, that it may deal with "a specialist matter which doesn't concern the masses" or (even) that it "serves the interests of State or Capital" is no longer decisive in itself. Thus "the question of the professionalism of intellectuals ... can be envisaged in a new way."[22] Each point holds for Said as well.

As Colin Gordon comments, a crucial step in Foucault's analysis is his provisional but powerful amoralism:

> His object is not to arrive at a priori moral or intellectual judgments on the features of our society produced by such forms of power, but to render possible an analysis of production itself. It turns out that in fact this scrutiny of power in terms of knowledge and of knowledge in terms of power becomes all the more radical ... through its rigorous insistence on this particular brand of neutrality (p. 237).

The shock of reading Foucault is partly the shock of his neutrality in unexpected places, a neutrality which distinguishes him at once from the garden-variety breeds of anti-bureaucratic thought in current circulation. And if it makes sense to consider Edward Said – in spite of their disagreements – as a Foucauldian critic, it is because he produces a similar shock and sustains a similar discrepancy: the shock of positing institutional modernity as the non-negotiable terms in which modern action must be carried out, and the discrepancy of this position for someone who cannot forget the absolute urgency of intervention.

The jolt of unexpected neutrality makes itself felt from time to time in a slight lexical estrangement. Certain key words, such as "affiliation," "worldly," and "career," seem peculiarly and inexplicably *inoffensive* as weapons with which to attack the ethic of professionalism. For example, in *The World, the Text, and the Critic*, the term "affiliation" defines the endpoint of a narrative in which modernist exile is institutionalized in the academy. In the careers of modernist writers like Joyce, Eliot, Freud, and Lukács, Said plots a three-step pattern: (1) an initial break with natural filiation – the unchosen, almost biological relationships enmeshing the individual in a given culture – leads to (2) a "pressure to produce new and different ways of conceiving human relationships," artificial and compensatory social bonds – for example, Eliot's turn from *The Waste Land* to the community of the Anglican church, or Lukács' championing of class consciousness and vanguard party as answers to alienation – which now, however, assume (3) all the authority of the old filiative order, becoming "no less orthodox and dominant than culture itself" (pp. 16–20). But does "affiliation" become oppressive with a tragically rapid and universal inevitability? In places it is a synonym for "system," a word that is never used with approval. Yet the coinage itself is a move in the direction of neutrality, and in other places "affiliation" seems entirely neutral – for example, as the realm of "social and political conviction, economic and historical circumstances, voluntary effort and willed deliberation" (p. 25). Or it is presented in such a way that it *need not* end in dominating system:

"The second alternative for the critic is . . . to show how affiliation sometimes reproduces filiation, sometimes makes its own forms" (p. 24). Are all "new forms" as oppressive as filiation, or only some? Since modernism's new affiliation is with the university, the main force of this equivocation falls on the profession of literary criticism.

In *Beginnings*, the term "career" sets the writing life apart from ordinary life as a form of modernist expatriation. Yet it weights this neo-romantic exile down with heavy semantic baggage: the homeliness of the beaten track (the grooves of the carriage road, the circled limits of the race-course) where achievement is circumscribed by a pre-established framework, a path traced in advance. It is very much a professional term, and it grants the modern writer exactly the measured "dehumanization" and the consequent freedom of action that professionalism grants. In "The Limits of Professionalism," Samuel Weber argues that the career replaces "the lateral ties of earlier local communities" with its "progressive initiation, mastery, and exercise of a profession," thus both permitting and producing "individual performance within an institutionally defined framework."[23] Defending members cut off from "earlier local communities" against the cold winds of the market, the profession offers them (in limited supply) use values instead of exchange values. Thus, on a minor scale, it could be said to overcome reification. Like modernism, in other words, the professional career substitutes for a lost or broken filiative order a new set of affiliative bonds that are both constraining and enabling. This is to say that in refusing the immediacy of inspiration and restoring the multiple mediations, the trans-personal determinants that make any literary achievement possible, Said is not setting modern writing against the bureaucratic modern world but, on the contrary, defining it as an instance of post-entrepreneurial modern labor.

Like "affiliation" and "career," "worldliness" seems slightly and provocatively out of control. In introducing the term, Said's intention is clearly to break open the hermetic, inward self-enclosure of the profession (his vocabulary for the profession, as for modernism, suggests an activity that is incestuous or sterile) and to send criticism forth into what he calls in *The World, the Text, and the Critic* "circumstantial reality" (p. 34). But it is equally clear that the force of "worldliness," and its hint of Foucauldian amorality, come from closing off, not opening up. In the context of a polemic against critical otherworldliness, one can still hear in it the sense of "devotion to worldly affairs to the neglect of religious duties or spiritual needs" (OED). To recast this definition in the affirmative is to approve a tabling of spiritual or existential questions in the interest of getting on with mortal business, a suspension of paralyzing ultimates in favor of less dramatic daily activity. In effect, it is to call for a version of professionalism. On the secular plane, the same stress on what is taken for granted within a closed system, on the enabling exclusion of outside concerns, is conveyed by Peter Brooks in *The Novel of Worldliness*: "By 'worldliness' I mean an ethos and personal manner which indicate that one attaches primary or even exclusive importance to ordered social existence, to life within a public system of values and gestures, to the social techniques that further this life and one's position in it." The emphasis falls on exclusiveness, on "the one world that counts" and on "man's way of being within its limits and in its terms: what we may call man's worldliness, or *mondanité*."[24] Parsimonious, local solidarity and strategically localized action bring worldliness back together with the professionalism against which it was marshalled.

Despite its apparent expansiveness, then, which permits Said to identify the worldly with the homeless, worldliness leads to a new investment in the local, a word Said uses frequently and approvingly. For example, again in *The World, the Text, and the Critic*, Swift's "fairly strict, not to say uninteresting conservative philosophy" (p. 74) is declared immaterial and replaced by an exhibition of "Swift the activist": "too many claims are made for Swift as a moralist and a thinker who peddled one or another final view of human nature, whereas not enough claims are made for Swift as a kind of local activist, a columnist, a pamphleteer, a caricaturist" (p. 77). Considered as a "kind of marginal, sporty political fighter" whose writing is almost entirely "occasional" and "parasitic on what it responds to" (pp. 77–8), Swift is liberated from retrospective judgement in terms of ideological universality. In the same way, the concept of the professional career, by incorporating an institutional framework that both limits and shapes possible actions, saves the individual's accomplishments from being immobilized by the crushing standards of universal justice or truth.

The homology with professionalism is clear, but incomplete. In using the local to free an activist Swift from the Tory Swift (though one might have thought Swift was an activist *because* he was a Tory), Said does what professionals do: by a willed, selective blindness to socio-moral universals, to the aims and consequences of action as they would appear to a hypothetically global perspective, he makes a place where action can be accomplished. In this sense the professional, like the local, can be described as a position that, falling short of the ideological purity of homelessness, receives in exchange a purchase on the world. The barter of a rationed amoralism for rational agency is certainly part of Said's own professional worldliness. Yet this localism is also an *affront* to professionalism. Said disengages Swift from the trans-historical content of his ideas by re-engaging him in the "particular struggles of a very limited sort" (p. 83) in his own time that have now disappeared or lost their significance. He thus associates Swift with "the scandal . . . that what is being said is being said at that moment, for that moment, by a creature of that moment" (p. 87). As an exemplar of pure localism, Swift becomes "perhaps the most worldly" of writers (p. 88), abandoned to secular interventions that will not survive their occasions, from which we can wring no transcendence.

The scandal of worldly-ascetic writing that in submitting itself entirely to
action would be entirely subsumed by the past, leaving no residue for the
reader of the present, is also the scandal of writing on which the profession
of literary criticism could no longer be based. For criticism's persistent
professional rationale has stressed the import of transcendent or trans-
historically valued writing from an over-supplied past into a needy present.

Thus the local both underwrites and undermines professional logic. Or
rather, it is inscribed in contradictory professional logics. For writing that
dissolves ascetically into its local occasion without residue becomes, by
Said's mediation, itself the residue, supplement, or transcendence of its
occasion, an instance of trans-historical transmission, an allegory of vocation. Swift the local activist emerges from the past to function as a model
for the intellectuals of the present. Swift is what the emergent professional
critic of today might look like, according to Said's allegory, if the profession
could stop imagining its vocation as the guardianship of the cultural
archives – but it is only thanks to his own residual guardianship of the
archives that we can benefit from the example.

If only because it circumvents the issue of representation, it is clear that
"the local" cannot simply or exhaustively stand for the professional. As
Said presents it, professionalism's local logic calls out for a complement –
if not necessarily for universality, then for some "express" logic that
valorizes discontinuity and distance. But in thinking through the disparity
or apparent inconsistency of these logics, we must bear in mind the value
of the initial leap. "Thinking local" helps account for Said's ability to curb
his otherwise powerful impatience with professionalism and to generate
terms and concepts that are uniquely serviceable under modern, professionalized conditions of intellectual work. Whether these conditions are ineluct-
able or open to contestation and change remains a politically significant
question. But the provocative notion of an oppositional thought that in
being local would be in *harmony* with its conditions of production deserves
separate and serious reflection. For such a notion exposes something about
our professional logics that has not been much noticed: how often
oppositional thought has in fact been defined specifically by opposition to
its conditions of production *rather than to anything else*. What would a
criticism look like that did *not* take its opposition to its own social
circumstances as the central, definitive, and exhaustive fact of its oppositionality? In telling professional critics to be paradoxically both "local,"
on the one hand, and "wordly" or "universal" or "humanistic," on the
other, this is perhaps the question Said is posing.

It is the holding together of contradictory professional logics under the
heading "Traveling Theory" that has made that essay and title so widely
influential.[25] The central voyage in question is a fall: the fall of theory from
direct, authentic politics – exemplified by Lukács' theory of reification in

History and Class Consciousness (1923) – into professional routine, illustrated in the reworking of Lukács' ideas by academics Lucien Goldmann and Raymond Williams. The difference between Lukács' theory of reification (produced as a weapon in the heat of battle) and Goldmann's application of it (in homologies between seventeenth-century literature and theology) is academicization: "Lukács writes as a participant in a struggle (the Hungarian Soviet Republic of 1919), Goldmann as an expatriate historian at the Sorbonne." Theory has been domesticated "to the exigencies of a doctoral dissertation in Paris" (pp. 235–7). After a relatively rapid passage from the ideal immediacy of revolutionary action to the predictable over-mediations of habitual scholarly practice, it works only "to shake up a few professors of literature" (p. 238).[26]

Yet for all its political bravado, this anti-academic narrative also duplicates an enabling academic myth – the myth, precisely, of the trans-local guardianship of the archives. Though he begins with the *theory* of reification rather than with the thing itself (so to speak), Said's second-degree version follows the same structure as Lukács' original. Like Weber's "rationalization" (which was a major influence on it), Lukács' "reification" depicts the transition to modernity as institutional mechanism, instrumental rationality, and cultural sterility, a horror unrelieved except by the highly theoretical prospect of the proletariat's eventual arrival at universal consciousness. In so doing, it sets off from, and sets off, a past comparatively rich in genuine relationships, organic community, cultural vitality. That is, it offers a more politicized version of what is still the strongest professional logic that the humanities possess: the narrative of "culture" dying in a modern wasteland where only a few select misfits still recall and preserve its fast-fading glories. However oppositional, this narrative obviously lends itself to a self-serving rationale for professional humanists.[27] As I have argued elsewhere, a narrative of decline that indicts the status quo for multifariously neglecting the cultural truths, beauties, and values of the past, now best known to the guardians of the archives, is a rather well-chosen means of shaming society into paying for the maintenance of those archives. If to be oppositional is to propagate such a narrative, then to be oppositional is not only not opposed to being professional, it is nearly a requirement for professional activity.

This is one logic, in fact, that makes "careers" out of "the East." When Lévi-Strauss laments the disappearance of native cultures, in part because of the activities of anthropologists themselves, he is both accusing his discipline and providing it with a version of legitimizing vocation. As James Clifford writes: "Traditions are constantly being lost. But the persistent and repetitious 'disappearance' of social forms at the moment of their ethnographic representation demands analysis as a narrative structure . . . Ethnography's disappearing object is, . . . in significant degree, a rhetorical construct."[28] The profession is sustained by protest against this repetitious disappearance, which it thus has an interest in sustaining or constructing. The continuity with the humanist decline narratives of Arnold and Eliot is clear. The logic that links professionals to the disappearance of their objects is even manifest in the poststructuralist premise that, in Said's innocuous words, "the written statement is a presence to the reader by virtue of its having excluded, displaced, made supererogatory any such *real thing* as 'the Orient.'"[29] Here, in a rarified, textualized form of Lévi-Strauss' position, "representation" as such replaces the primal act of violence that makes the cultural object disappear, thus calling for the politically ambiguous but nonetheless necessary services of those who interpret representations, and ensuring the value of those services. One reason for the relative success of the sub-field of "colonial discourse" is the ease with which geographical displacement ("the East") can substitute for temporal displacement (the past) in the professionally foundational narrative of disappearing culture(s).

At the same time, of course, Said is well and justly known for his uncompromising refusal of "culture" as an enclosed, exclusionary concept and his courageous, controversial embrace of "the great modern or, if you like, post-modern fact, the standing outside of cultures."[30] If the titular argument of "Traveling Theory" is that travel – here, the wrenching of theory out of its European context and its recontextualization in the US academy – is dangerous, travel also belongs to Said's continuing polemic against cultural rootedness and defines the uprooted critic as an oppositional figure. Nothing could be less characteristic of Said than a secure, comfortable, stick-in-the-mud localism that would restrict interpretation to its context of origin. He is manifestly uninterested, for example, in reporting at any length on the original French context of Foucault. One has the sense that he would be more engaged by the eccentric, defamiliarizing fact that in Tunis, where Foucault taught from 1966 to 1968 while working on *The Archaeology of Knowledge*, Foucault seemed a pure "représentant du technocratisme gaulliste."[31] Such facts, unavailable to the scholarly stay-at-home, nourish the roving appetite for risk and disorientation that Said celebrates as "criticism."

What follows for the imagining of academic work? It hardly needs to be said that the ideal homelessness of "criticism" does not exclude, and indeed encourages, the critic to be "placed" in the university. In the name of "travel," the academy can either be condemned as a place of drowsy rootedness and inactive belatedness, or, on the contrary, it can be defended as the one place – really a non-place – where criticism can be truly itself: non-totalizing, perpetually alert and self-critical, pure. This is the twist that Said gives to the academicizing narrative of "Traveling Theory" when, after seeming to idealize the revolutionary intensity of Lukács' reification at the expense of later scholarly apathy, he ends by censuring the over-totalized oppressiveness of reification and by crediting the critique to

Raymond Williams – in particular to the "virtue" of Williams' academic "distance."[32] As a place of "critical distance," the academy illustrates the merits of "travel" rather than either its perils or the perils of situatedness.

This revisionary move is neither complacent nor uncomplicated. Though Said criticizes the theory of reification for its inability to account for its own (oppositional) existence, he is committed to applying that same theory of reification to describe the institution in which his critique of it comes into existence. In the conclusion of "Orientalism Reconsidered," for example, academic reification seems the inescapable diagnosis, as much for well-established fields like criticism as for emergent sub-fields like colonial discourse:

> But there remains the one problem haunting all intense, self-convicted, and local intellectual work, the problem of the division of labor, which is a necessary consequence of that reification and commodification first and most powerfully analyzed in this century by Georg Lukács . . . This is where we are now, at the threshold of fragmentation and specialization, which impose their own parochial dominations and defensiveness.[33]

On the other hand, in the course of complaining about the current fragmentation of the disciplines – our "professionalized particularism" (p. 103) – he also complains that "world history as a discipline" is "essentialist universalism" (p. 102), and he praises the work of "fragmenting, dissociating, dislocating, and decentering the experiential terrain covered at present by universalizing historicism" (p. 102). Here the desideratum is "plurality of terrains, multiple experiences, and different constituencies" (p. 105). The apparent inconsistency (is totality what we have to get rid of or what we are lacking? is fragmentation a problem or the solution to a problem?) makes an invaluable point. Reification, it appears, is not something universally to be opposed. For it can open up the academy as well as enclose it. From the point of view of a Third World constituency, what might otherwise look like the reification of the humanities – their further specialization or fragmentation – is more correctly seen as *representation*. One might expect Said to challenge reification's Eurocentric assumptions, thereby reserving the non-European world as that "world of human agency outside the reach of reification"[34] which Lukács overlooks. Instead, his local, exclusive concentration on the academy exposes the hidden representational links between academic careers and "the East." If "fragmentation" can be desirable when it liberates a Third World constituency, say, from the false universality that had represented it, it can be desirable *in much the same way* when it permits a given discipline or sub-discipline to break free from given scholarly assumptions and realign itself both in regard to other disciplines and – most pertinently – to a previously under-represented

constituency. "Feminism," "Afro-American studies," and "colonial discourse" might all be taken as cases in point.

To set limits to opposing reification is in effect to overthrow the entire
fall-narrative of literary professionalization. For as I noted above, reification
is one version of the profession's enabling myth; it defines "culture" as a
perfect professional object, both missing and indispensable. In so doing, it
has been a good provider of professional legitimacy to intellectuals.
Reification is capitalism for those who do not suffer economically from
capitalism; it makes their non-economic suffering – the fragmentation of
life without the wholeness of "culture" – the representative and determining
instance. "The problematic of culture," Richard Johnson writes, "expressed
the dilemmas of some English intellectuals sufficiently removed from
industrial capital, in situation or sympathies, to distance themselves from
its morality and purposes." In other words, it was itself a product of "the
increasingly differentiated functions of intellectual labor" to which it
seemed the antithesis. "Culture" was the claim, on the part of a social
group that was already and increasingly marginal, that the privileged
knowledge that group possessed was what all society needed. The very
indistinctness of culture – like "language" and "discourse," it could not
easily be *opposed* to anything – made it more easily universalizable.[35]

But the profession's basis in "culture" also restricts its oppositionality to
whatever political value the resupplying of this object might have. If the
past proximities of "culture" are the foundation of the humanities in a time
of inhuman distances, then criticism remains a stay-at-home, grounded in
but also by its single founding gesture, unable to make the distant
connections that Said prescribes for worldliness. It is also set in contradiction with its conditions of production, that is, the intellectual division of
labor that defines it as a discipline. To the extent that it *is* a discipline –
divided from other disciplines, and dividing territory with them – in calling
out for the wholeness of "culture" it is calling for its self-destruction. Few
of our professional narratives are as successful as the narrative of "Traveling Theory" in fighting off their impulses to do precisely that.

One might conclude that because professionals *must* present themselves
as representative, there is no alternative to the sort of inconsistencies and
self-hatred that surround the professional imagery of culture and reification.
One of the many interests of Said's writing, in the moment-by-moment
richness of its undaunted textual energies, is the assurance that alternatives
exist, even when they manifest themselves only as a mode of inhabiting
contradictions that for the moment remain unsolvable. For further and
final contrast with the narrative of professionalization-as-decline, consider
the narrative of "Third World Intellectuals and Metropolitan Culture"
(1990). In this essay, the map of ironies is filled in: "the East" is again a
career, but this time for its own intellectuals.

Said's subject is

the work of intellectuals from the colonial or peripheral regions of the world, intellectuals who wrote not in a native language but in an "imperial" language, who felt themselves to be organically tied to a mass effort at resisting imperial rule ... These figures address the metropolis using the techniques, the discourses, the very weapons of scholarship and criticism once reserved exclusively for the European.[36]

Taken together, such figures form a "culture of resistance" (p. 27). Beneath this relatively straightfoward exposition, the deeper problematic would seem to be how to define the originality, resistance, and independence of intellectuals who are "apparently dependent (some would say parasitic) on a mainstream discourse like history, political science, economics, or cultural criticism" (p. 29), that is, on European scholarly disciplines. But a still deeper structure appears when we break up the last phrase. Insisting on the need for ex-colonials to counter *Europe* is one thing; it is less evident that "resistance" should or even can happen *within scholarly disciplines*.

The allegory of vocation emerges from the essay's narrative structure. In an ambitious periodization of Third World intellectuals from the 1930s to the 1960s and 70s, Said passes from C. L. R. James and George Antonius, writing "works of scholarship and advocacy" in the 1930s "from within a national movement for independence" (p. 32), to Ranajit Guha and S. H. Alatas, writing in the 1960s and 1970s "postcolonial and specialist works ... that address a smaller audience" (p. 32). Again, as in "Traveling Theory," we move away from direct (anti-colonial) politics and toward greater submission to the specialization of the academy. Through Guha, this endpoint is even associated with poststructuralist theory. But this is not a narrative of decline.

> The contrast between James and Antonius on the one hand, and Guha and Alatas on the other, is not that the earlier writers were more immediately involved in contemporary politics whereas the later two are involved mainly in scholarly disputation in newly independent states, but that history itself has changed the terms and, indeed, the very nature of the argument (p. 33).

What is this change? It is not a new separatism, though James and Antonius claim "Western" culture as their own, while Alatas and Guha see colonized and metropolitan cultures as "radically antithetical." What defines the new stage, rather, is the recognition that the intellectual's own class has been formed by and within metropolitan culture, and that it is this very class which must be opposed – from within, so to speak, and with its own tools. The project of rescuing "the suppressed native voice" is now aimed specifically at the "nationalist elite," at the intellectual's own class. To be both of this class and critically detached from it is, it seems, what it means to be "academic specialists" like Guha and Alatas (p. 39).

According to Johannes Fabian, Lévi-Strauss' anti-experiential structuralism corresponds historically to "the demise of direct colonization demanding personal and direct involvement in the *oeuvre civilisatrice*" and to the
rise of neo-colonialism's more indirect hegemony.[37] Neo-colonialism, which
is to say capitalism as a world system, also seems to underlie Said's
revalorization of the academy, which takes its cue from the confusion in
which natives can be enemies and foreigners allies. This interiority of the
struggle, within the class of the Third World intellectual, as opposed to the
dramatic exteriority of earlier nationalist struggles, produces the interme-
diate position, the embattled margin of detachment, that Said defines and
defends for "academic specialists." If ex-colonial scholarship seems secondary and belated in relation to European scholarship, it seems still more
secondary when narrativized against the predecessors' immediate solidarity
with anti-colonial struggle. In confronting the first figure of originary
authority, Said is also confronting the second. Aligning the academic and
the colonized, he defends both forms of secondariness together. The hero
of his narrative is the anti-colonial intellectual as academic, the academic
as anti-colonial intellectual.

The space thus cleared for the dignity of scholarship is open to all. The
avant-garde metropolitan formations of twentieth-century modernism, Said
suggests, have to be considered "an extension into the metropolis of large-
scale mass movements . . . The contest over decolonization has moved from
the peripheries to the center" (p. 30). His example is the Algerian war of
independence – an example that suits admirably the argument above about
Lévi-Strauss' highly mediated (indeed, high modernist) career-making intervention in global and disciplinary representation.[38] Like the metropolis
which gives them a local habitation, the scholarly disciplines are a place of
"overlap and interdependence" rather than "the reactive assertion of a
separate colonial or native identity" (pp. 30–1). In a striking phrase, Said
describes the process that produces this new kind of place as "adversarial
internationalization" (p. 31). The phrase describes what might otherwise
be called "professionalization" – the substitution of dispersed professional
community, joined only by "method," for the tight, mobilized unity of
given "culture" or nationalist conflict: "if the grand and nourishingly
optimistic narratives of emancipatory nationalism no longer serve in the
1960s and 1970s to confirm a community of culture as they did for James
and Antonius in the 1930s, a new community of method – more difficult
and exigent in its demands – arises instead" (p. 43).[39] Whether or not such
a "community of method" has already come to pass, it is surely one of the
most useful of images for students and scholars currently seeking a sense of
their own vocation.[40]

The last words of "Third World Intellectuals and Metropolitan Culture"
are "toward community." In his debate with Michael Walzer as in his
critiques of professional enclosure, Said has always publicly insisted on the

terrible injustices that are ratified daily in the name of even the most modest or progressive local solidarity. It has been harder to see that, in so doing, he has also been helping to define new "affiliations," new means and modes of community that can live and work with this knowledge. Yet his unflagging commitment to a scholarly and critical vocation – to "the belief that the study of literature has a crucial role to play in the contemporary world"[41] – and the superb power of both his commitment and his achievement to inspire so many fellow professionals must remain entirely mysterious unless we understand how the big world of East and West, North and South, is always already inscribed in, and is sometimes contested by, the making of academic careers.

Notes

1 I am grateful to Aijaz Ahmad, Gerald Graff, John McClure, Andrew Parker, Michael Sprinker, and Elsa Stamatopoulou for helpful comments on earlier drafts of this essay. For an enlightening counterpoint, see Deirdre David, "The East as Profession," paper delivered at CUNY conference on "The Professionalization of Victorian Life," May 4, 1990.

2 Jacques Derrida, "Sending: On Representation" (trans. Peter Caws and Mary Ann Caws), *Social Research* 49 (1982), p. 304.

3 A notable exception is Jonathan Arac's "Introduction" to *Postmodernism and Politics* (Minneapolis: University of Minnesota Press, 1986), from which the Derrida quotation is taken. Arac argues persuasively that "the received belief that 'advanced' theorists are 'against' representation" is both mistaken and damaging, especially given that "in the world . . . the power of representation is something sought, indeed passionately struggled for, by groups that consider themselves dominated by alien and alienating representations" (p. xxi).

4 Said himself does not claim that the peoples of the Middle East have had the same relation to dominant discourse as, say, aristocratic women in Europe.

5 The first position is articulated with far greater refinement in Paul Bové, *Intellectuals in Power: A Genealogy of Critical Humanism* (NY: Columbia University Press, 1986). The second figures, with significant variations, in Benita Parry (who is more centrally concerned with Gayatri Spivak and her supposed "deliberate deafness to the native voice where it is to be heard" [p. 39], in Dennis Porter, "*Orientalism* and its Problems," and in Homi Bhabha, "Difference, Discrimination and the Discourse of Colonialism." Benita Parry, "Problems in Current Theories of Colonial Discourse," *Oxford Literary Review* 9 (1987), pp. 27–58. The Porter and Bhabha essays are in *The Politics of Theory, Proceedings of the Essex Conference on the Sociology of Literature, July 1982*, ed. Francis Barker et al. (Colchester: University of Essex, 1983).

6 Jim Merod, *The Political Responsibility of the Critic* (Ithaca: Cornell University Press, 1987), p. 185. The *tu quoque* does not, however, apply to Benita Parry, who is an independent scholar and has never held a permanent teaching post in higher education.

7 Arac, *Postmodernism and Politics*, p. xxi.

8 Edward W. Said, *After the Last Sky: Palestinian Lives*; photographs by Jean Mohr (New York: Pantheon, 1986), p. 158.

9 "An Ideology of Difference," *Critical Inquiry*, 12:1 (Autumn 1985), p. 51. See also *After the Last Sky*: Mohr's photography "enables us to see Palestinians in the process of sustaining themselves, perhaps even of re-presenting themselves" (p. 145).

10 "The Post-Colonial Intellectual," *Salmagundi*, 70–1 (Spring-Summer 1986), p. 49. See also the discussion following, e.g., p. 55.

11 Edward W. Said, *The World, the Text, and the Critic* (Cambridge, Mass.: Harvard University Press, 1983), p. 9.

12 Here and at some later points I draw on my review of that book and *The Question of Palestine*, "Homelessness and Worldliness," *Diacritics*, 13:3 (Fall 1983), pp. 69–77. For a critique see Catherine Gallagher, "Politics, the Profession, and the Critic," *Diacritics*, 15:2 (1986), pp. 37–43. The controversy continues in "Deformed Professions, Empty Politics," *Diacritics*, 16:3 (1986), pp. 67–72.

13 Sadik Jalal al-Azm, "Orientalism and Orientalism in Reverse," *Khamsin*, 8 (1980), pp. 9–10. For a related view, see S. P. Mohanty, "Us and Them: On the Philosophical Bases of Political Criticism," *Yale Journal of Criticism*, 2:2 (Spring 1989), pp. 1–31.

14 Clifford Geertz, *The Interpretation of Cultures* (New York: Basic Books, 1973), p. 346.

15 David Pace, *Claude Lévi-Strauss: The Bearer of Ashes* (London: Routledge and Kegan Paul, 1983), p. 4.

16 Fredric Jameson makes a similar argument in "Periodizing the Sixties," *The Sixties Without Apology*, ed. Sohnya Sayres et al. (Minneapolis: University of Minnesota Press in cooperation with *Social Text*, 1984). For Jameson's key role in the fortunes of "narrative," see my "Death and Vocation: Narrativizing Narrative Theory," *PMLA* 107, 1 (January 1992) pp. 38–50.

17 Claude Lévi-Strauss, "The Structural Study of Myth," *Structural Anthropology*, trans. Claire Jacobson and Brooke Grundfest Schoepf (Harmondsworth: Penguin, 1963).

18 Quoted in Charles C. Lemert, *French Sociology: Rupture and Renewal Since 1968* (New York: Columbia University Press, 1981), p. 11.

19 Quoted in Pace, p. 12.

20 Ivan Strenski, *Four Theories of Myth in 20th Century History* (Houndmills, Basingstoke: Macmillan, 1987).

21 Didier Eribon, *Michel Foucault* (Paris: Flammarion, 1989), p. 131.

22 Michel Foucault, *Power/Knowledge: Selected Interviews and Other Writings, 1972–1977*, ed. Colin Gordon (New York: Pantheon, 1980), pp. 131–2.

23 Samuel Weber, "The Limits of Professionalism," *Oxford Literary Review*, 5:1–2 (1982), p. 72.

24 Peter Brooks, *The Novel of Worldliness* (Princeton UP, 1969), p. 4.

25 *The World, the Text, and the Critic*, pp. 226–47.

26 One might also describe this narrative as the slow fall from revolutionary Marxism (Lukács) to academic Marxism (Goldmann) to self-critical academic Marxism (Williams) and, finally, to self-critical academic anti-Marxism (Foucault), or anti-Marxist academic self-criticism, or poststructuralism. In this version, some would see a rise rather than a fall.

27 It might be objected that there is a more restrictive sense of reification in Lukács, closer to Marx on commodity fetishism, which does not lend itself to the assumptions of the humanities as easily as does Jameson's Weberian version.

28 James Clifford and George Marcus, eds., *Writing Culture: The Poetics and Politics of Ethnography* (Berkeley: University of California Press, 1986), p. 112.

29 *Orientalism*, pp. 21–2.
30 Edward W. Said, "Media, Margins, and Modernity," in Raymond Williams, *The Politics of Modernism: Against the New Conformists*, ed. Tony Pinkney (London: Verso, 1989), p. 196.
31 Eribon, op. cit., p. 201.
32 "Traveling Theory," p. 240. Ironically, "distance" is Williams's own preferred word for what is *wrong* with professionalism: its rejection of communal, experiential proximity.
33 "Orientalism Reconsidered," *Cultural Critique*, 1 (1985), pp. 106–7.
34 *The World, the Text, and the Critic*, p. 232.
35 Richard Johnson, "Culture and the Historians", *Working-Class Culture: Studies in History and Theory*, ed. John Clarke, Chas Critcher, and Richard Johnson (London: Hutchinson, in association with the Centre for Contemporary Cultural Studies, University of Birmingham, 1979). See also, in the same volume, Johnson's "Three Problematics: Elements of a Theory of Working-Class Culture," p. 212, from which the direct quotations in this paragraph are taken.
36 "Third World Intellectuals and Metropolitan Culture," *Raritan* 9:3 (Winter 1990), p. 29.
37 Johannes Fabian, *Time and the Other: How Anthropology Makes Its Object* (New York: Columbia University Press, 1983), p. 69.
38 More will have to be written on the North African context for Derrida, Lyotard, Foucault, Cixous, Althusser. The influence of Mao's China is better known but not necessarily better understood. How does Maoist populism assort with high poststructuralism?
39 This also means, as in *Orientalism*, "preferring to analyze the verbal symptoms of power rather than its brute exercise, its processes and tactics rather than its sources; to analyze its intellectual methods, its enunciative techniques rather than the morality of its holders" (p. 48). As mediated autobiographical allegory, this narrative can be contrasted with the unmediated, directly autobiographical version – specialization as forced abandonment of the wholeness of personal background, experience, culture – that Said offers in *The Politics of Modernism*, pp. 179–80.
40 As Gerald Graff suggests, the "method" that holds such communities together includes their controversies and self-contestations.
41 *The World, the Text, and the Critic*, p. 126.

4

PLACES OF MIND, OCCUPIED LANDS: EDWARD SAID AND PHILOLOGY

—

Tim Brennan

There is a startling moment in James Clifford's justifiably well-known essay on *Orientalism* where, with a sense almost of dismissal, he writes: "In a French context the kinds of critical questions posed by Said have been familiar since the Algerian war and may be found strongly expressed well before 1950."[1] The facts are almost certainly true. But how far does the comment take us? What sense is there here, finally, of discussions like those Said conducts in *Orientalism* about Ernest Renan, whose books (Said excitedly tells us) had attained "mass density and referential power"? Why, in other words, was it *Orientalism* rather than its French predecessors that changed the drift of scholarship in several disciplines, found readers in a number of languages, crept into the most unlikely footnotes, and inspired a feature-length film?

For some time Said has been creating the model of a distinctive kind of writing and speaking, what he called in relation to Raymond Schwab "a gradually developing exemplary discourse." With criticism of his work steeped in commentary about post-colonial identity, "affiliation," and his supposed neglect of German scholarship, almost no attention has gone to his deliberately repetitive elaboration of *how* to write and speak as a public person: that is, not simply his view that being a public intellectual is a good thing, but his prolonged inquiry into the mechanics of being so.

One of many such moments occurs in Said's treatment of Renan, where Said, with a mixture of hatred and love, observes: "what matters is not only the things that Renan said but also how he said them, what . . . he chose to use as his subject matter, what to combine with what . . ."[2] Embedded in the hortatory opening chapters of *Orientalism* – where the larger goal is to expose Renan – this attention to style and manner has usually been passed over by Said's critics as a simple matter of personal color.

On the contrary, between 1966 and 1975, Said was applying himself to the ways that people like Renan and Schwab had achieved a threshold of public influence. This was his major preoccupation in these years, and his conclusions fill his career-launching books of the immediate aftermath. More than to reveal new knowledges, the whole point of these books is to find ways to articulate what needed to be done – the object, for example, even of a very early essay like "Vico: Humanist and Autodidact" (1967). The goals were necessarily elusive and abstract. He was providing an outline of what one should be studying, what texts could best confront narrow scientism and the cultures of war and commerce, what manner of approaching them was most appropriate to the task. Appearing in 1975, *Beginnings*, one might say, was about intentions and interests in the sense that one speaks of "interested" parties. The book in fact records that broad-ranging but also limited list of motifs that occupy Said for the better part of his career, and that first are mentioned as a whole in an interview for *Diacritics* in the Fall of 1976 – an issue entirely dedicated to reviewing and presenting *Beginnings* itself.

Reading that interview today offers surprises in many respects.[3] All of the interests associated with a much later period of his writing are there, fully formed: the key conceptual tool of *Orientalism*, for example, or the invocation and elaboration of Fanon's centrality as an anti-colonial thinker, the necessary analytic category of "geography" in any study of imperialism, the very slogan of "worldliness," the inversion of Benda's *La Trahison des clercs* in which treason became the act of *not* messing oneself up in political struggle, the hostility towards professionalism, and the angry repudiation of literary critical textuality. The interview is like a compendium of which the rest of his career is a patient and deliberate elaboration.

It seemed that the act of mapping out *Orientalism* (which the interview indicates had been largely conceived by the publication of *Beginnings* in 1975) was itself responsible for his arriving at these research interests. His prescience in a relatively dead time in North American politics at the very moment of the official end of the Vietnam war, before the bitter assaults of the Reagan team and the new round of imperial invasions – a period that produced the high comedy of Gerald Ford and the pallid liberalism of a pre-fundamentalist popular culture (best symbolized, perhaps, by *Saturday Night Live*), a period also of relative quiescence in the Palestinian struggle – this prescience had something to do with an avid attachment, against all expectations, to a humanist legacy that made the political lull of that time appear, to him at least, temporary.

For the same book that many took to be one of "theory's" more convincing entry cards into the English department (by virtue of Said's long, admiring chapter on Foucault) actually placed Said in a curiously antagonistic posture towards "theory." It is hard to read this interview today without being struck by its (apparently lonely) enthusiasm. *Orientalism*, it should be remembered, is part of a trilogy that includes *The Question of Palestine* and *Covering Islam*. The one is an historical primer written for a major commercial publisher, the other a media study before the "media" had become a high-profile area of dissident intellectual concern. The point is not simply that Said got there first but rather that he had been able to predict (and in some ways even to help define) movements with an apparently anachronistic attachment to "humanism." That the obvious attempt to reach out to the different sectors of the intellectuals (academic, political, and media) represented by the target audiences of each volume was throughout informed by the literary and humanistic evocations of the first volume – that is, *Orientalism*. Why should this be so?

Said did not simply inherit humanism from his years at Princeton and Harvard, nor did he later trump up and glorify its "politics" simply because the European classics were what he already knew. Anyone who knows Said's early book on Conrad, or is familiar with the pantheon that emerges in the opening chapters of *Beginnings* has for a long time wrongly imagined that he once lived in a vaguely naive state of humanities euphoria, which under the pressure of Middle East developments perhaps, or the Reagan years, pushed him into critical "worldliness." This is not, on his account, what happened.

> When I was beginning to teach at Columbia . . . I was really considered two people – there was the person who was the teacher of literature and there was this other person, like Dorian Grey, who did these quite unspeakable, unmentionable things . . . I was very friendly with Lionel Trilling . . . but we never once, in the fifteen years that we were friendly, let these other matters come up; *and I trained myself to live that way*.[4]

From at least the early 1980s, this closing comment no longer described either his conduct in the classroom or his manner of dealing with the growing number of like-minded students and fellow teachers at Columbia, where his political openness and frank engagement were the very qualities that seemed to define him.[5]

Still, despite his sense of being thought dangerous at so early a time, it is surprising in retrospect to find Said writing about Arabic poetry already in 1976, about Naguib Mahfouz in 1975 (long before he was Nobel laureate), about Joyce as a colonial writer in the same year, and, also at that time, about the abstractions and political evasions of the contemporary American novel – none of them interests one would associate even with the English department trendsetters in this period.[6] Most of us, I think, would associate these interests only with Said's relatively recent work. The same person invited in the 1980s to give the Eliot lectures or to the *MacNeil Lehrer*

News Hour, the one cited in the footnotes of Cuban scholars and Chinese historians, the one about whom the very image of respectable Left commitment in literature became inseparable from *Orientalism* – this was a person essentially assured of his directions a decade before the profession at large recognized them as important. One notices only belatedly that many of the essay selections he made for *The World, the Text, and the Critic* in the early 1980s were originally written as much as a decade earlier.

So, while many frown on the politics of "humanism" and are quick to point out areas of apparent weakness in Said's range – especially the supposed absence in his work of studies of popular culture and postmodernism – few have tried to answer simply how this humanism in the mid-1970s could have helped set up Said's evident political leadership at that time – a leadership that continues today.[7]

Beginnings, then, was showing its excitement for philology at the very moment that French theory was becoming for many anxious reformers the thing that really mattered. It is odd that more has not been made of Said's debt to philology. From "Vico: Humanist and Autodidact" to his Eliot Lectures on the imperial attitudes of everyday life, philology has been the great constant of Said's career – not the ponderous discipline itself so much as the bracing example of its practitioners, now dead and gone, never to rise again.[8] One could even say that most of Said's essays, poised on either side of the watershed year of *Beginnings* in 1975, were efforts to look at these now-vanished masters by way of sketching a portrait of the intellectual he was (in those essays) forcing himself to become. And this always meant being in some elusive sense *like* a philolog.

At the time of the *Diacritics* interview, this curious interest was already a provocation. In a typical reaction, Hayden White found the focus there on Vico "baffling," Said's readings of him "eccentric," and the gist of the early chapters consequently "imperialistic" and "metaphyscial."[9] That Said dedicated the last hundred pages of the book to explaining the conflictual understanding of the term "humanism" ushered in by French theory is lost on White. He misses, as many others did, Said's almost desperate efforts to portray the framework of philology (even more in the nineteenth century than with its late twentieth-century standard-bearers) as a model of intellectual adventure.

This is why I finally have to disagree with James Clifford's otherwise brilliant, and widely praised, reading of *Orientalism* in *The Predicament of Culture.*[10] For his assertion that Said's book is a "general attempt to extend Foucault's conception of discourse into the area of cultural constructions of the exotic" is quite wrong in its exclusive emphasis on Foucault. Foucault is finally a rather minor player in Said's book, and Said has stated publicly that it was the Raymond Williams of *The Country and the City* who provided the initial motivation and, in part, the model for *Orientalism.* Not only is the specific fabric of philology within the study ignored, but there is nothing of the quirkiness in Said's humanism that, for example, Ellen Rooney has shown so well in *Seductive Reasoning*, or that Paul Bové discusses perspicuously in arguing that Said has been public enemy number one for the humanist old-guard – the ones Bové memorably calls a "priggish, belletristic apparatus."[11] That he would be so is surprising in many ways since he shares with that apparatus a dislike for the obscure, technical professionalism of the theory wave.

These distinctions are absent from Clifford's critique, although his argument shrewdly focuses on the centrality of method to Said's work:

> Said's methodological catholicity repeatedly blurs his analysis . . .[his] descriptions of Orientalist discourse are frequently sidetracked by humanist fables of suppressed authenticity . . . his critical manner sometimes appears to mimic the essentializing discourse it attacks . . . The privilege . . . of aspiring to the universalist power that speaks for humanity . . . is a privilege invented by a totalizing Western liberalism.[12]

Apart from ascribing to Said wrong sources (and so operating in a realm of expectation that is bound to be frustrated), Clifford is unable to take his criticism a needed step forward. It is not, after all, simply that these qualities exist in Said's writing, but that they are intentional: that they are insisted upon polemically as a way to stave off the pretentions of theoretical rigor.

Such rigor – shorn of humanist vagaries and "mere" opinion – is a methodological attitude with a traceable and not entirely reputable history, as Said painstakingly shows. In Clifford's case, the "discursive reading" is given attributes of crystalline purity and the full-bodied accuracy of system. It replaces the fuzziness of unwarranted generalizations with what Said would think of as the suspect consistency of a merely local knowledge. Said long ago was aware of the implications that his generalities, his "totalities" and his eclecticism held for those with Clifford's concerns, and has spent many pages justifying his own persistence in following the practice anyway. Clifford's critique does not meet Said where he stands, but appeals outwards to a theoretical community whose training and assumptions leave it unequipped to understand Said's central (I would even say defining) emphasis on the contradictory legacy of high nineteenth-century grandiosity and idealism, so out of fashion today. What is persistently neglected in Said's writing is his attentions to the *how* of empire – and to the "how" of those intellectuals like himself who set out to oppose it. His point is often that one learns from the imperialist intellectuals of the past not simply by warding them off like demons, but by assuming their outward forms.

With this caution in mind, a reader of Said can appreciate why he characteristically treats literature, not as a receptacle of damaging images or a place where stereotypes and prejudices creep into the minds of unsuspecting readers (that is, as a matter of substantive ideology), but rather as an imperial mood created by form – what he calls in a revealing passage "agreed-upon codes of understanding . . . images, rhythms, and motifs" – the evanescent stuff of style and presentation (*Orientalism*, p. 22). One sees, especially by dwelling on the history of philology, how literary intellectuals with the big gestures and the large appetites, unconfined by cultural or disciplinary systems, assume their place as the makers of ideology with some responsibility and self-consciousness, although in an excessively mediated way appropriate to cultural politics: that is, only by giving authority to certain "agreed-upon codes of understanding." The whole point is that "theory" as it is currently practiced came from that legacy, even though it is, by default, more minimalist and detached than it need be. In its efforts at conceptual purity, it has lost a vision of the social panorama.

Not only repetition is at work, then, when Said continually returns to the chore of sketching out a portrait of philology, and finding his own features within it. For even though Said has done so for fifteen years, most of his critics ignore what he has taken from philology. "Raymond Schwab and the Romance of Ideas," for instance, is filled with the traces of an exemplary but unfulfilled promise, and (more to the point) of a direct, if ambiguous, confrontation between humanism and imperialism.[13] In the essay one gets a vivid sense of Said's pure thrill in the mind and in ideas ("we are now dealing with a mind altogether of another sort of magnitude," he says of Massignon), and therefore Schwab captivates him first and foremost as a personality – a point that suggests something of the stylistic and formal resources that philology became for him. Schwab's life as poet and translator before publishing his monumental study, *La Renaissance orientale*, his death in Paris in 1956, the glowing reminiscences of his life in a special issue of *Mercure de France* – all fill the opening paragraphs of Said's essay as an important prelude to its apparently more pressing substance: to look at the "endless detail" that was "the mark of Schwab's major scholarly work," a work that "observed no national boundaries" and that took for itself "an almost ingenuously obvious motif" – the influence of the Orient in the West (*Orientalism*, pp. 248–9).

The pattern of enthusiasm is already well-marked. He wants to asborb the lessons of the emulatable career, on the one hand; on the other, he wishes to pay respect to the intangible matters of intellectual conduct that together assemble themselves into a material force. Formally and methodologically, Said observes that Schwab's philological training nudged him into that revelatory investigation of "enormous unities" such as "the Latin cultural *imperium*" and a tracing of their effects as they took textual body in subsequent ages. This, one might say, is the disturbance of the essay. It battles back and forth between the "vertiginous minuteness" of Schwab's patient chronicles and the "large movements of ideas" in Schwab's archival recovery of an immense "cultural drama."

Of course, the cultural drama in Schwab's case is nothing less than the "Orientalism" Schwab both catalogued and himself embodied, and which Said was in the act of diagnosing as a Western imperial disease. Why, then, do we keep reading phrases in the essay describing the kind of practice Said has always emulated and lobbied for, as in Schwab's "generous awareness," his "rare type of unhurried scholarship," his "epigrammatic flair" – the kind of thing Said has done so well himself? The answer is obviously that positive values can be found in negative sources, and that what some call contradiction others, in an earlier era, called "dialectics."

In Said's 1967 essay on Vico, philology had already represented a "topical" as distinct from a "geometric" method of inquiry, a "wideness of scope," the use of "broad comparisons," and the exhibiting of a "gradually developing, exemplary discourse."[14] Once again, we have a full-bodied focus on the nebulous way that the humanities help make history – a way that derives, nevertheless, from a conscious practice by scholars to avoid all pretense to "science" and to appeal instead to the genius of imperfection.

The same ideas are found in his short introduction to a 1952 essay by Erich Auerbach entitled "Philology and *Weltliteratur*," which Said co-translated only two years after the Vico essay.[15] One is struck by its preposterous, but also compelling, use of Goethe's notion of "world literature" (similar to that of a somewhat later essay by Fredric Jameson, who has decribed Auerbach as "my teacher") as a prefiguring of canonical reform. Despite the suggetsion of some critics to the contrary, Said is perfectly aware (even at this early date) that Goethe's triumphalist vision relied on a model of intellectual possession, of a universal spiritual history linking all the works of "man," and that this view was at odds with the necessarily conflictive, often differentiating thrust of colonial literary emergence, not to mention feminism. But Said also noticed that Goethe's position was that of a committed comparatist distraught by the parochialism of Europe's champions, and so was for canonical reform before his time.

Drawing on this history, Said's larger point in these writings, however, is that theory simply cannot claim the exemption from Eurocentrism that figured so largely in the humanistic legacy theory attacks. In the opening movement of *Beginnings*, Said sets out clearly what might be called philology's career, beginning in earlier centuries with an authoritative position of humbling and mind-boggling technical expertise in a vast array of languages and devolving gradually upon the fractured and individualized talents of "criticism" and later "theory." The thesis of these chapters is often not recognized for what it is – that theory, in the contentious sense of being an "intruder" into the modest competence of English departments in the mid-1970s, deserved more respect and also had to be less sure of its claims to be an abrupt and radical break. It deserved respect from dismissive

New Critics, since it had evolved from an impressive humanistic lineage nearly idolized by the old guard. On the other hand, theory bore a closer functional relationship to the sweeping claims of humanism than its own radical critique of that legacy suggested. What philology once was, in other words, theory had become, with an immense loss of vision, character, and expertise, but with a gain, too, in its taste for self-questioning and scrupulous modesty.

That gain, for Said, might be expressed in another way as theory's emphasis on "the irregularity and discontinuity of knowledge . . . its lack of a single, central *Logos*" (*Beginnings*, p. 378). But the evolution of philology into theory was never simply a trading of methodological fashions. It was one small component in a larger worldly transformation. The conditions under which theory came into its own were those of the unsavory pressures of specialization and ideological professionalism – themselves part of a climate of an expansive, creepingly technological, and progressively less free social system. Critics, in Said's view, had been driven down into an abyss; they were "uselessly transfixed by pure form and often gullibly enraptured with an uncircumstanced structural poetics" (*World*, p. 267). This is what one must keep in mind when looking at Said's emphasis on philology. In the arena of a localized formalism – or more properly, a "scientism" – Said felt that somebody like Schwab was an "antidote."

The "scientism" of theory in its contemporary variants was what Said was talking about in the story he tells about Ernest Renan in *Orientalism*. What separated Renan from Schwab and Massignon were his attempts to join philology with religion and his pretentious claims to "an exact science of the mental object," his misuse of language through specious analogies to the chemist and naturalist Cuvier. Renan's effort to "prove" European superiority was a direct outcome of his attempt to turn linguistics into a "science" of cultural differentiation. He was, in other words, a kind of Auerbach gone wrong.[16]

However much Renan's aim in philology was "designed to place [him] as an intellectual in a clearly perceptible relation to the great social issues" (p. 133) – a role Said obviously admired – he also represented an attempt to make philology stand in for "received religion." By contrast, for Said philology had to be an excited linguistic grounding in a "present, accessible reality" (*World*, p. 278).

"I AM NOT AN ARTIST"

As an opera critic, pianist, TV celebrity, professor, frequent UN presence, popular esayist, and public lecturer, Said seems to rival the impressive sweep of some of his nineteenth-century heroes, and one would expect that versatility would be among the first things emphasized in his career. In a special sense, though, "range" here is not just a matter of large appetites and abilities, nor is it only about emulating the exemplary careers of his philological forebears. One way of being like a philolog is to be non-specialized – even arrogantly general. In the United States today, such a gesture is a calculated rebuke to technological panaceas and professionalist poses in the academy and in official public culture. The often intense (and not often discussed) pressures to conform in the 1980s and 1990s have called for what Said describes as a politics of "indirection."

The career Said has constructed for himself, then, and the vast energy he has expended in theorizing his career's emulatable politics, directly face the intellectual climate of the post-war period. Some have rightly noticed a recent and subtle shift in the US from an official educational stress on the applied sciences and narrow technical training to one in which a general humanities background has been recognized as enticing to corporate employers (a shift that the war with Iraq, with its unspeakable displays of "cost-free" technological killing, is beginning to divert). But even at its height, the shift tended to conceal the merely functional role the humanities were still being asked to play, especially in the form that college curricular debates were taking at the state level. There, training in "our" history and traditions was always cited as necessary for patriotic allegiances and class-bonding in a newly threatening, multicultural, America: an America of a new and growing "guest-worker" system. Although most reformers have discussed curricular conservatism in terms of ethnocentrism, it is also a matter of the infinitely variable conservatism that arises from *method* – from an up-tight, scientistic manner; from a failure to excite people with general ideas and far-flung connections.

Said's manifest discomfort with specialization is aimed more or less consciously at these developments, and not only these. He also has in mind the sad and unnecesssary way that the humanities have mimicked these political trends, a mimicry seen in the values endorsed by professional apprenticeship. The typical questions asked of graduate students and job candidates tend to be: what is your speciality? what century (or half-century) have you mastered? What is "your" genre?

This mentality of narrow intellectual rigor (often just a camouflaged desire to have a manageable job description and to avoid retooling – in this sense quite unlike the "rigor" of theory discussed above) conveniently ignores the fact that most of the profession's stars are hopelessly unspecific: people like Renaissance scholar, modernist and Biblical hermeneut, Frank Kermode; feminist, post-colonial, deconstructionist, Gayatri Spivak; or Milton scholar, "professionalism" theorist, and professor of law, Stanley Fish. Nevertheless, for most hiring committees, being "general" remains a form of dabbling; it lacks purpose, sidesteps "serious" scholarship. Being general – despite some advertisements in the MLA Joblist for cost-saving, dead-end "generalist" positions – is vigorously praised in the past, but is abjured at faculty meetings and vilified in tenure reports.

Here is where Said's focus on presentation becomes especially interesting, since it runs up against both the disciplinary "mainstream" and that supposedly dissident wing vaguely dubbed "theory". Although as poststructuralism, theory is concerned less with scholarly competence than with an overbearing political and humanistic center, and although theory draws its metaphors not from the world of technocratic efficiency but from an anarchist political economy, the goal it sets for itself is in some ways similar to the humanities department mainstream: it attacks the act of being general – what it thinks of as a pretense to global knowledge.

The constant judging of others' work that goes on in an academic setting always puts one in the practical position of evaluating method: in tenure reports, in evaluating work for publication, and so on. Methods that rely on synthesizing vast amounts of material, reaching plausible generalizations, or tackling entire regions and peoples – all are suspect among many intellectuals today in an era of the New Historical "anecdote" and Geertzian "local knowledge." But this currently unfashionable striving towards ever-widening horizons of intellectual work is exactly what Said stands for. His extraordinary influence and impact today arise in part from his exuberant willingness to generalize.

Taking the long view, a reader of Said will see just how many of the recurrent stress-points in his writing address (and embrace) the art of being general. Over and over again we find him talking about the virtues of the roving intelligence, the need for comparatist studies, the totality that is not "totalizing," the inquiry that is "free" in the necessarily ambiguous sense of that term. But this is far from his only stylistic and methodological departure from the strange bedfellows of "theory" and the critical mainstream.

For example, one of his conclusions has been that originality is not the most important demand made of an intellectual. *Beginnings* (a title that inevitably raises this issue by way of making it a ruse) was less a refashioning of current critical views of literary modernism than a rallying-point for future work. Said played down the qualities of uniqueness or revelation, on which most professional fame is based, in pursuit of something more basic: finding one's priorities, clearing the decks of diversions, establishing the contextual field within which simple things might come to be known through cumulative informational renderings and patient explanation (some of what Clifford seems to object to when he speaks of Said's "numbingly repetitive method"). In a sense, *Beginnings* is a book-length reflection on "presentation." The entire method is a patient but agonizing attempt to capture what people in an act of literary acquisition "feel" – atmospherically as it were – but which remains intellectually elusive. As he argues there, every intellectual venture demands that one create the grounds to enable what follows.

Said's is a project in the first instance of naming – of making the invisible seen by giving it a name. Terms like "authority," "worldly," "filiation" are some of these names, and they work in part because they seem to arise out of a communal need. They are terms that bespeak the ability or the courage to state the obvious (Schwab's "ingenuously obvious motif"), to say what others have forgotten or not been able to bring themselves to say.

When in a short essay for *Harpers*, he begins to speak of "contrapuntal criticism," Said once again is approaching the politics of "how." He elaborates the idea in his latest book where he urges us to "read texts from the metropolitan center and from the peripheries contrapuntally, neither acording to the privilege of objectivity to our side nor the encumbrance of subjectivity to theirs" (Eliot Lectures). Said is questioning here not only the predictable Eurocentrism that sees all non-Western culture in terms of more or less successful *reactions* to or appropriations of the West, but also those more subtle forms of essentialism, now rampant in university hiring practices, by which scholars with "Third World" ethnic backgrounds are considered automatic authorities on non-Western literatures and cultures. The principle of mutual sympathy is, by contrast, the decisive rhetorical departure for Said – not exactly like Homi Bhabha's notion of postcolonial "hybridity," but instead a sense of one's place being a matter of position-as-belief-system (or political stance) rather than filiative belonging.

And yet Said's point here is not only rhetorical. One could discuss his writing exclusively in this way – for example, by looking at the unusual balance of his critical prose, which (with the exception of well-known polemics against Michael Walzer, Robert Griffin, Bernard Lewis, and others) is noteworthy for its basic generosity, its candid and unguarded self-criticism. Said sees contradictions everywhere, and therefore urges us to internalize them by projecting, in good philological fashion, into the full experiences of others; to take what we can and leave the rest. Said himself puts it clearly: "the persistence and durability of saturating hegemonic systems like culture [are due to the fact that] their internal constraints upon writers and thinkers [are] *productive* not unilaterally inhibiting" (*Orientalism*, p. 14).

This is why it is not surprising (although it might first appear so) that he is drawn to writers and thinkers whose politics are so unlike his. Why, for example, does he dwell on Swift rather than, say, Blake, or why Conrad when there are writers like Paul Nizan around? For every grandiose Schwab in his pantheon, there is a (splintering and intensely personal) Benjamin. All of his intellectual influences seem to be split up this way between "wholes" and "fragments" – between Auerbach, Lukács, Schwab, Vico and Fanon, on the one hand, and Adorno, Swift, Gramsci and Nietzsche, on the other.

His is a style of give-and-take, but as I have been saying, it is not only a style. We have a model for work that acts as though the specialization inherent in organizing knowledge into disciplines prevents understanding; knowledge is whole, the mind must roam, one studies one thing rather than another because it is more "interesting"; credentials (if they are worth anything) do not come from degrees or awards but speak for themselves; authority is homegrown; one speaks out of an urgent need to communicate what one knows from a general (as distinct from localized or scientific) knowledge. Although obsessed with presentation, Said is not interested in sculpting prose. The point is the attitude one has towards knowlege and communication, of one's constituencies and how to reach them. In contrast to the laboriously honed writing of critics like Harold Bloom, Mary Daly, and Frank Kermode, for example, Said has proclaimed that he is "not an artist."[17]

But his is no philistine attachment simply to "what works." We have to keep in mind the idea of what is appropriate to the national and imperial reality within which one writes. It makes sense here to contrast his rhetorical strategy to that of Raymond Williams, who in books like *The Sociology of Culture* and *Television: Technology and Cultural Form* left behind the stuffy reverence of *Culture and Society* for a businesslike, technical, and empirical rhetoric. Those later books, as though through a conversion, evoked the mind-frame of the social sciences. It was as if Williams were trying to slap the face of Cambridge by reminding it that culture was actually being formed in their society by media intellectuals, not Cambridge dons. In England, of course, the hegemonic center of higher learning is precisely literature – not the applied sciences (or their mimics in the social sciences), as it is in the United States. For that reason, the striking and appropriate thing about Said is that he almost never leaves the literary high road with its attendant languages of "irony," "criticism," and "narrative" – even in his books on media and current events.

OCCUPIED LANDS

If the scope and focus of Said's writing offer a clear way forward for intellectuals with a commitment to social responsibility, a nagging question remains: how much can one hope to change with a commitment that rejects group political identities on principle, which H. Aram Veeser has shown to be a recurrent subject of Said's writing?[18] This seems to me the decisive question to pose – not the bygone issue of Said's supposed "totalizing Western liberalism."

It is only fair to begin by mentioning Gramsci, a constant touchstone for Said. So many have been influenced by Gramsci that it seems almost in bad taste to point out how often his supporters have resisted drawing conclusions about Gramsci's membership of, and dedication to, the Italian Communist Party. Clearly, much more than the drift or framework of Gramsci's reflections were related to this experience of organizational belonging. This specific kind of belonging, instead of being (as it usually is) an occasion for marking his betrayal of its limitations, should also be given credit for *enabling* his insights. Discounting Gramsci the organizational activist has led to many, many misunderstandings and even absurdities.

For example, little commentary today has come to grips with Gramsci's attitude (developed continuously throughout the *Notebooks* and evident in numerous passages) towards the European literary classics, literary criticism, and middle-brow entertainment literature – an attitude characterized both by enthusiastic support for literature's uplifting or "humanizing" function, and a dismissive disregard for what he called "quality" literature. The latter category extended from everything we associate with the *avant garde* to the more stuffy realms of the overly venerated bourgeois canon (some of whose representatives Gramsci respected, although not for the reasons the literati did). To the aesthetic tastes and theoretical positions of Gramsci's most ardent partisans today in the field of a "decentered" politics (Ernesto Laclau and Chantal Mouffe are still the worst offenders), this attitude must appear populist and philistine.

Said is among the few who are not guilty of this kind of misreading. He has always been attentive to Gramsci's respect for philology and fully understands his emphasis on the ecstatic communities of knowledge made possible by the human "spirit" as it is depicted in literature. On the other hand, it is significant that Said rarely addresses himself to the Gramsci who liked to talk about a "conformism from below" – for which Williams seems to have had a feeling from his early work in adult education, or (in a much more mediated and aesthetic sense) that one finds in Mikhail Bakhtin's writing on transgressive laughter and "grotesque realism," the glories of swearing and bodily dirt, the raucous power and grace of ugly, lower-class *humanity*.

Conforming "from below" is basically a socialist or communist notion – the act of identifying with the "spirit" of a class, of losing oneself in its historical movement, of sacrificing on its behalf, of taking the measures necessary to achieve freedom for it and in it.

I bring up this division in Said's thinking to draw a distinction. It has always been striking to me that he has had little good to say about Bakhtin. For Bakhtin was one of the last great exemplars of European philology, and he lived under conditions of exile and alienation with the same irrespressible confidence and scope that one finds in Auerbach. Bakhtin is one whose theoretical and political drift (in concepts like "dialogism" and in ideas about language as a relationship between people rather than a machine of meaning) exist in comradeship with Said's, given the points the latter was making in the 1980s when Bakhtin was being acclaimed from all quarters of the critical community.[19] One expected Said's approach to be similar to that he had taken towards John Berger, whose emotive photo/text productions in books like *The Seventh Man* proved so influential on Said's *After the Last Sky* (even to the point of his collaborating with the same photographer, Jean Mohr). But perhaps Berger was useful because the "how" of his work was enabling. The open-ended intellectual inquiry, the honest and unfinished love of looking, was the thing that a person could think for himself *with* and *through*.

It would be convenient, but unfair, to pretend that Said's dismissive attitude towards Bakhtin came from a patrician scorn for the plebeian sensuousness in which Bakhtin revels at the aesthetic level. And yet there is a side to Bakhtin (just as there is a side to Gramsci) not discussed in Said's writing. Said's great suspicion of organizational entanglements is situated, of course, in the sense that he is both a prominent Palestinian in exile and a Left intellectual in a country where red-baiting is a national pastime and he is one, let it be said, who has made great organizational sacrifices. As I argued above, there is nevertheless a shrewd politics that comes with a rejection of party entanglements as a matter of principle, while doing one's duty in practice. What, though, do we make of his suspicion of organizational politics?

Is Said's point, for example, that intellectuals cannot be intellectuals if they are members of parties, or only that there are dangers in adhering to group identities? This is a decisive question which his major books before the late 1980s (including *Orientalism*) leave unanswered. The avoidance of Bakhtin in his work provides interesting clues, however. Looking at the "how" of Bakhtin's writing, there is a kind of excessive confidence – either derived from Bakhtin's style of Marxism or (if one follows the, in my view dubious, arguments of Michael Holquist and Caryl Emerson) his religious mysticism – that runs up against the values Said has promoted via the humanist/philological legacy: "human interpretation, vagaries, willfulness, biases, grounding in personality, radically human circumstantiality, worldliness" (*World*, p. 178).[20] What Bakhtin seemed to stand for, at least in the way people were using him, recalled what Said had found earlier in Foucault and Derrida – what was labelled "system."[21]

> The great horror I think we should all feel is towards systematic or dogmatic orthodoxies of one sort or another that are paraded as the last word of high Theory still hot from the press. I mention for instance the interest in Bakhtin, but it could equally have been the interest in many varieties of theory in the past two or three decades.[22]

What I am calling (after Gramsci) a "conformism from below" is related to "system" in a contradictory way. For the crucial idea of intellectual "freedom" – seen in Said's repeated refusal to belong, or to accept the paradox of thinking as a group in order to achieve the *conditions* of freedom for others – runs hard up against the thinking of those who have informed the values of resistance to empire, and upon whom Said has drawn heavily. Perhaps this is not so much a contradiction in Said's work as a gradual shift in emphasis. Said has been among the few to promote and explain the writing of people like Ghassan Kanafani and C. L. R. James, for whom freedom is a quest for social transformation; for whom intellectual life typically involves decisions that are wholly distasteful to many intellectuals – voluntary restraint, suppression of individual agendas and personalized mental itineraries. Can we avoid concluding that what is precious in the intellectual end products of Cabral and Fanon is also deeply related to their lived positions of "solidarity in (rather than 'before') criticism"? Fanon thought the way he did because he was, in the last analysis, part of a movement – an organization. He was not only, as a black man, involved in "combat breathing." He was in combat with others, formally and collectively.

This brings us back to the theme of intellectual conduct, and we are then appropriately led to Said's Eliot Lectures, which have begun to trade in an earlier style of literary reverence for the language of strategic global politics. Written in response to his own earlier challenge that "there is still a general essay to be written on imperialism and culture," (*Orientalism*, p. 24), these lectures mark a new departure in many ways; hence my concluding with them. There are several things to notice here. We have, even by Said's standards, an extraordinarily politicized piece of criticism. They are, among other things, a long and deliberate naming of names, as though the mood of *Blaming the Victims* had finally been spliced on to *Conrad and the Fiction of Autobiography*. The whole idea of "commitment" is re-addressed and glossed differently. While Said does not wholly resolve the question of his attitude towards organizational belonging, he creates an atmosphere in which the organizers against empire are given a very high place.

The point of reference for the lectures is a trope Said had isolated, as I pointed out above, already in 1975, but that has since signified an important tendency in literary confrontations with imperialism: the trope of geography.[23] Said had earlier brought together Matthew Arnold's ideal of the "nomadic critic" with (in a characteristically dissonant coupling) Georg Lukács' idea of "transcendental homelessness." Both images of place and space served the same purpose: to translate the elusive language of the literary spirit into an urgent and contemporary issue of intellectual method. Arnold's notion of the roving, uncommitted intellect and Lukács' idea of the utopian longing created by aesthetic illusion (very different concepts!) were both translated into Said's imperative: the need to be general, to study things comparatively, to avoid a dogmatic fixation on absolute origins and rigid teleologies. In the Eliot Lectures, though, Said gives the idea a more homely referent. He begins with a baldly historical recital of the scale of territorial accumulation by the imperial powers at their apogee (240,000 square miles of overseas territory per year). Space here is, quite simply, land.

Much of the logic of this emphasis is left implicit, but a few words are necessary here to explain that what I am arguing is his departure in these lectures. Why space? This entails an emphasis on lateral movement, on the simultaneity of life in the separate but coeval cultures of a world that exists in the present. The potency of an imperial term like "civilization," Said implies, grew out of a meeting (a confrontation *in space*) between cultures supposedly at different *moments* of development. The time that separated "their" savagery from "our" civilization was both decisive and, conveniently, unbridgeable. To focus on space paradoxically eliminates distance between West and South, since space at present has been rendered insignificant by communications and transportation technologies. Such a thesis can develop with equal force both with reference to the world and to the empowering and disabling metaphors of thinking about "civilization" – including (in Said's usage) the conception of territory as it arose in English fiction of the nineteenth century. To put it provocatively, as Said does, one role of the critic is to "liberate as much territory for criticism as possible."

There is something definite and "hard" about space, moreover, that gives this book a different feel from his others. In this sense also, it constitutes a departure. It is a "hardness," however, that is alien to that of theory's scientific pretensions. The effort is not that imperious one of creating a mental straightjacket or impasse (a perpetual self-deconstructing), but to provide a material backdrop for an argument that, in the foreground, explores the indefinite contours of a "mood created by a form." Hardness as an explicit reference to the imperial plunder of third-world geographical spaces is, in this sense, a foil to the horribly real outcome of ideas created by literary men and women. Although at one remove, space is purposely kept from playing the metaphorical role it has in some examples assembled by Caren Kaplan recently, where the materiality of space is used in bad faith to prop up a basic idealism.[24]

The Eliot Lectures suggest that this will be the first of Said's books to position non-European intellectuals center stage; it is the first time he speaks of Europe (after Fanon) as being "literally the creation of the Third World." While still talking in the persuasive, coaxing tones of a professional literary person, he keeps declaring himself in a way he knows will trouble many of his more traditional readers. The words are exceptionally unyielding. At one point he goes so far as to argue that art itself (not just specialist machineries of interpretation) helped create imperialism:

> The power to represent what is beyond metropolitan borders derives putatively and actually from the power of an imperial society and . . . that power

takes the discursive form of a re-ordering of "raw" or primitive data which
are shaped into the continuities of narrative or the systemacities of disciplinary
order . . . It will not do to ignore those tendencies found in narrative . . . that
enable, encourage and otherwise assure the readiness of the West during the
19th century to assume and enjoy the experience of empire.

The excitement of art evident in Said's writing – particularly in his opera
criticism – is intentionally suppressed here in favor of a close look at
cultural complicity. The extremity of this move, while not unknown in his
earlier work, constitutes the core of the lectures, and comes as a deliberate
shock. This perhaps explains why he avoids some of the literary acclaim he
had called on in earlier studies: "my subject," he says, is in need "neither
of simply chronological nor of simply anecdotal narrative. What it needs is
an attempt at a general, as opposed to a total, description." The emphasis
here not only pits "general" against "total," but "description" against
"narrative," thereby calling the alluring coherence of narrative itself into
question.

As the lectures unfold, with an extended reading of Jane Austen's
Mansfield Park, warming up to a long theoretical elaboration of what Said
calls the "moral order of space" within narrative, as they make distinctions
between types of resistance intellectuals (those involved in the "grand
narratives of enlightenment and emancipation" and more recent practitioners of the "hermeneutics of suspicion") – as they do all this, one
recognizes a different mood, noticeably less at ease with the high-ceilinged
portrait rooms of the Ivy League lecture hall. There it would be out of place
to describe, as Said does approvingly, Fanon's re-reading of Western art
history – the almost gleeful description of the "large hectoring bolus of 'the
Greco-Latin pedestal' bodily [transported] to the colonial wasteland where
'this artificial sentinel is turned into dust.'" Art is suddenly and radically
suspect: it is something to be "demystified," whereas the idea that art
"mystifies" (that is, misleads) is not at all common in his earlier work.

If in *Covering Islam* Said had implicitly made the point that any politics
of representation was incomplete if one wasn't also analyzing the "news,"
here he pushes that point much further. Citing an array of institutional
studies, he focuses on "an over-all pattern of domination" in our corporate
economy and our "centralizing culture" in which literature no longer plays
the leading role – where it has been dislodged from its previous place in the
unsoiled heights of the cultural hierarchy: "We have today an international
media presence that insinuates itself, frequently at a level below conscious
awareness, over a fantastically wide range."

Said is careful to cut off the allure of the popular cultural reading that
these observations tend to offer intellectuals professionally trained in art
criticism – the ones who want to acknowledge the media's power and scope

but who want to refine their discussions of this vulgar terrain by transforming it back into:

> I don't think it's the case that you can "deconstruct," as the word has it,
> *Dynasty* or *Dallas* in the same way that you would, say, *Bleak House* . . . It
> seems to me that a much more interesting approach would be to look at the
> sociology of the form itself, to look at the construction of the media
> conglomerates, the industry, and the formal tools used which make up, as
> you know, an extremely sophisticated apparatus reduced to rather simple
> ends: pacification, the depoliticization of ordinary life, as well as the
> encouragement and refinement of consumer appetites . . . I wonder whether
> that isn't best dealt with allusively, and whether the effort of looking at this
> kind of stuff shouldn't really come from a quite serious study of the history
> and sociology of literature . . .[25]

In this passage, we can find the rationale for his departures from
Williams, the communiations critic, and an extraordinarily clear statement
of his politics of "indirection." To "deal allusively" is not bad advice in
what is, after all, a country of increasing paranoia, intolerance, and
censorship. But we have here both a call for doing more media work, and
also for not abandoning literature, whose specific brand of cultural authority allows for interpretations seemingly above crude institutional constraints
– the very delusion that allows one's deciphering of its meanings to seem
compelling, unlike the mass media which wear their ideology on their
sleeve.

What goes on in the Eliot Lectures, then, is a direct interrogation of
literary means. As we have been pointing out, this tactic is not particularly
new. The institutional focus of the lectures, their awareness of and
commentary on decisive Third-World resistance intellectuals, their painful
negotiation of media imagery and literary knowledge – all of these are
already in place in Said's writing from at least 1975. What does seem to be
new is the obsessive focus on specifically militant and embattled intellectuals
like Cabral, whose ideas in another mood would (one expects) be relegated
by Said to the dangerous outposts of "system." Also novel is the serious
deflating of the rhetoric of reverence and exaltation in the presence of the
open-ended literary life. On both counts, the book is both extraordinarily
interesting and brave; it represents a welcome extension of the solidarity
and integrity Said had established earlier.

The Eliot Lectures are a culmination of many of the ideas traced out in
this chapter. What appears as a departure from the motifs and styles of the
philological legacy is at once its continuation. For the lectures testify to the
power of simplicity by asking questions so big, so imposing, and so
universally felt that they are often not dealt with at all, or are overlooked
as "ingenuously obvious." The big swagger of philology, understandably

challenged by critics of humanism, does provide the instruments for describing an "immense cultural drama," which in certain areas of the world (the Third World, let us say) is more appropriate than in other, "postmodern" ones.

If we forget for a moment the slightly new directions represented by these lectures, the thing to notice is that (however strange this may seem) philology is what has helped Said matter to political life in this country in a way that many Left theorists and academic Marxists do not. In the opinion of the public and the media intellectuals, a non-technical, broadly available rhetoric of the "human" is perhaps the only acceptable expertise that literary intellectuals can manifest in order to be taken as public authorities. This is not to say that Said adopts it opportunistically. As I have been arguing, "generalism" as a mode of intellectual conduct is as much an epistemological conviction as a way of mattering publicly. Nevertheless, by assuming the nineteenth-century mantle of progress and enlightenment, Said is able to reach people who are not reached by "theory," whose antiseptic verities remind most of a poorer version of unintelligible math. At the same time, the literary aura allows him to temper his role as political advocate on American television – a tempering that, I suppose, can be thought of as a conscious rhetorical mitigation of unpopular views, but in the end is not that. For, as I have been trying to show, range is finally a matter of intellectual integrity. Shifting between many arenas strengthens Said's conduct in all of them.

Said's insight, then, is a profound and simple one: in the United States – which likes to think of itself as not having classes – one can effectively be an organic intellectual of the poor and the disenfranchised by taking the traditional intellectual's high road.[26] Of course, Said has been extraordinarily effective in positive ways on the issues of public policy, curricular change, and intellectual conduct, making many (although by no means all) of the more obviously "radical" theorists seem weak by comparison. We should, like him, be asking "how."

Notes

1 James Clifford, "On *Orientalism*," *The Predicament of Culture: Twentieth-century Ethnography, Literature, and Art* (Cambridge, Mass.: Harvard University Press, 1988), p. 267.
2 Edward W. Said, *Orientalism* (New York: Vintage, 1979), p. 131. Further references to this book will appear in the text.
3 Said, "Interview," *Diacritics*, 6, 3 (Fall 1976), pp. 30–47.
4 Raymond Williams and Edward W. Said, "Media, Margins, and Modernity," in Raymond Williams, *The Politics of Modernism: Against the New Conformists* (New York and London: Verso, 1989), p. 187. Emphasis added.
5 I base these comments on personal experience. I began studying with Said in 1980, and remained at Columbia for most of the decade. Some of the statements

I attribute to Said in this essay were made in seminars, lectures, or in conversation.

6 See Said, "Insider and Outsider," *Times Literary Supplement* (December 10, 1976); and "Contemporary Fiction and Criticism," *Tri-Quarterly* 33 (Spring 1975), pp. 247, 250, 255.

7 Although he has not emphasized such work, Said has in fact written prominently on popular culture. See, for example, his essay on the Tarzan films of Johnny Weismuller, "Jungle Calling," *Interview*, 19, 6 (June 1989), pp. 61–6, 112; or his essay on the great Egyptian belly dancer, Tahia Carioca, "Homage to a Belly-Dancer," *London Review of Books* (September 13, 1990), pp. 6–7.

8 Said, "Vico: Humanist and Autodidact," *The Centennial Review*, 11, 3, (1967) and his T. S. Eliot lectures, delivered at Kent in December 1985, on culture and imperialism. These lectures will appear in book form in 1992; I cite them from the typescript available at the time of writing.

It will be noticed that my argument here entails a notion of philology very different from Paul de Man's in the essay "Return to Philology" in his *The Resistance to Theory* (Minneapolis: University of Minnesota Press, 1986), pp. 21–6. I suspect that it is a mark of de Man's cleverness that he noticed the drift of Said's efforts before others did and, not at all sharing Said's goal of engagement, wanted to head those efforts off by claiming philology for the "science" of theory. De Man, in fact, identifies theory with what he sees as philology's "analytical rigor," its "precision" as distinct from "generality," the "tidiness" of its philosophical investigations. Philology for him is the "examination of the structure of language prior to the meaning it produces." On these matters, see note 16 below.

9 Hayden White, "Criticism as Cultural Politics," *Diacritics*, 6, 3 (Fall 1976), pp. 8–13.

10 For an example of this essay's influence, see Gayatri Spivak in the interview, "The New Historicism: Political Commitment and the Postmodern Critic" in H. Aram Veeser, ed., *The New Historicism* (New York and London: Routledge, 1989).

11 Ellen Rooney, *Seductive Reasoning: Pluralism as the Problematic of Contemporary Literary Theory* (Ithaca and London: Cornell University Press, 1989). This excellent book is dedicated to exposing the tendentious notion of "pluralism" lying at the core of much of the false, male-centered, and politically conservative "consensus" routinely assumed by the humanities mainstream. She pointedly does not place Said in this company. See also Paul Bové, "Closing up the Ranks: Xerxes' Hordes are at the Pass," *Contemporary Literature*, 26 (Spring 1985), pp. 91–106. Both Rooney and Bové mention different, although one would think related, people as belonging to the humanist old-guard – in Bové, Walter Jackson Bate, Wiliam H. Pritchard, and Hilton Kramer; in Rooney, E. D. Hirsch and Wayne Booth.

12 James Clifford, *The Predicament of Culture*, pp. 271, 270, 262, 263.

13 Said, "Raymond Schwab and the Romance of Ideas," *The World, the Text, and the Critic* (Cambridge, Mass.: Harvard University Press, 1983). pp. 248–67. Further references to this book will appear in the text, indicated by *World*.

14 Said, *Beginnings: Intention and Method* (Baltimore and London: Johns Hopkins University Press, 1975), pp. 368–70. Further references to this book will appear in the text.

15 Erich Auerbach, "Philology and *Weltliteratur*," translated with an introduction by Maire and Edward Said, *The Centennial Review*, 13, 1 (Winter 1969), pp. 1–17.

16 Philology as a discipline always had a side that wanted to present itself as a "science" of language, very much in concert with the positivistic euphoria of nineteenth-century scholarship. Its tools were perceived as unassailable by the non-specialist – closed off to the relativistic quibbles of loose interpretation – for it dealt with the hard stuff of etymology, semantic and morphological shifts, "dead" classical languages, which allowed those who mastered them to silence the uninitiated. But Said notices sufficient good beneath this positivist crust. The bogus "universal spirit" sought in its voracious learning, after all – however much defined by male European norms – entailed a progressive method; it gave dignity to the serious study of modern (as distinct from classical) languages in an approach that was comparative on principle; it discovered the life and language of the people and the vernacular.

17 Conversation with the author, Spring 1982.

18 Most recently, at the Midwest Modern Language Association conference in Kansas City, November 3, 1990. Veeser looked particularly at Said's essay on Jean Genet, where Said ostensibly praises the virtues of "betraying" one's own group in the name of intellectual integrity. Veeser is currently writing a book on Said.

19 Said's avoidance of Bakhtin is odd in other respects as well. Like Said, Bakhtin was a theorist of the novel. The latter's idea of the "chronotope" closely resembles Said's "moral order of space" in the English novel (Eliot Lectures), and Bakhtin's well-known (although largely mangled) idea of the "dialogic" nature of language is reflected in Said's idea of the "overlapping territories" of intellectual life. It is interesting that Said's rejection found no parallels in Williams, who in his last book, in a section entitled "the Road from Vitebsk," heralds Bakhtin as one who defined an era.

20 For a capsule, and not widely known, example of Said's views on Marxism, see Edward W. Said, "Between Chance and Determinism" (a review of Bela Kiralyfalvi's *The Aesthetics of György Lukács*) in the *Times Literary Supplement*, February 6, 1976, p. 126. It is outside the scope of this essay to look more closely at Said's relationship to Marxism, but it is a subject that demands close attention. The obvious issue is his careful negotiation of its many legacies – a brave stand in the current climate, and one he has stood much to lose by taking. Said, for example, has done much to give Marxists their due in print – not only the safe ones (Gramsci and Adorno, for example) but the later Lukács, Emile Habiby, Joseph Needham, C. L. R. James, and others. But just as important are the implications of his occasional hostility. The question needs to be asked: however much invoking Marxism today is rhetorically doomed (and in this essay, *that* is the type of question at hand), is it true that the actual *record* of Marxists is the same as the fictions concocted about what that record is? Is Said reacting to what, say, Marx himself said and did, or what most scholars today agree to believe he said and did? On at least three separate occasions, for example, Said has accused Marx of elitist scorn with reference to *The Eighteenth Brumaire*, where Marx says of the French peasantry in 1848: "They could not represent themselves, they must be represented." Cited in passages of his own writing where the Eurocentrism of the Western Left is the basic issue, Said's point (even in regard to Marx) is quite valid. However, the claim that Marx was being high-handed and even hypocritical is wrong. Note the following passage from Yvonne Kaplan's biography of Eleanor Marx. These are Marx's words, directed precisely at the events of 1848, and written at the same time as *The Eighteenth Brumaire*: "We cannot associate ourselves with people who openly state that the workers are too uneducated to emancipate

themselves and must be freed from above by philanthropic big bourgeois and petty bourgeois . . . for which purpose the working class must place itself under the leadership of 'educated and propertied' bourgeois, who alone possess the 'time and opportunity' to acquaint themselves with what is good for the workers" *Eleanor Marx*, vol. I (New York: Pantheon, 1972), pp. 208–9. As always, Marx is a much more interesting (and useful) figure than he is typically given credit for.

21 Gary Hentzi and Ann McClintock, "An Interview with Edward W. Said," *Critical Texts* (Spring 1987), p. 11: "I think that the unevenness and the heterogeneity of the territory that one is looking at has to be the main point of assertion . . . All of these systems that confirm themselves over and over again so that every shred of evidence becomes an instance of the system as a whole – these systems are really the enemies." Said's elaboration of this charge in relation to Foucault and Derrida occurs in "Criticism between Culture and System," *World*, pp. 178–225. It seems significant that "Criticism between Culture and System" was the title Said had originally proposed for the volume as a whole.

22 "Media, Margins, and Modernity," in Raymond Williams, *The Politics of Modernism*, p. 182.

23 See Caren Kaplan, "Reconfigurations of Geography and Historical Narrative: A Review Essay," *Public Culture*, 3, 1 (Fall 1990), pp. 25–32.

24 Ibid.

25 Hentzi and McClintock, "An Interview with Edward W. Said," pp. 10–11.

26 Wide disagreement persists about what these terms mean. I think it is clear (despite much writing to the contrary) that Gramsci meant by "organic intellectuals" those who openly identified with a class, shared its interests, and worked on its behalf – particularly (for him) members of "The Modern Prince," the Communist Party. Organic intellectuals did not necessarily mean those who were allied with the working (or, in the euphemism he was forced to use, "subaltern") classes, since Gramsci speaks of organic intellectuals of the bourgeoisie (time/motion study experts in the factory are one of his examples). Traditional intellectuals, on the other hand – allied historically to a now-vanished aristocratic clerisy – hid their *de facto* allegiances to class interests under the guise of transcendence, either unconsciously or in bad faith. What I am referring to here, then, is Said's occasional evocations of "transcendence" in the pursuit of a specific and localized commitment. And I am saying that this is a good thing.

5

WORLDLINESS-WITHOUT-WORLD, HOMELESSNESS-AS-HOME: TOWARD A DEFINITION OF THE SPECULAR BORDER INTELLECTUAL

—

Abdul R. JanMohamed

[Because Conrad] had an extraordinarily persistent residual sense of his own exilic marginality, he instinctively protected his vision with the aesthetic restraint of someone who stood forever at the very juncture of *this* [i.e., the colonial] world with another, always unspecified but different, one.[1]

How did exile become converted from a challenge or a risk, or even from an active impingement on his [Auerbach's] European selfhood, into a positive mission, whose success would be a cultural act of great importance?

SC, pp. 6–7

I

What "cannot be said" in *Beginnings*, without making the production of the book impossible, is just those latent aporias about the self and its intentions, about history, and about beginnings, out of which the book constantly goes on producing itself, like a mushroom out of its mycelium. *Beginnings* constantly recognizes these contradictions, without quite recognizing them, in passages which are like slips of the tongue or the pen . . .[2]

This remark by J. Hillis Miller, while specifically commenting on *Beginnings*, is, I believe, applicable to Edward W. Said's entire corpus, or indeed to that of any author who has produced a significant and innovative body of criticism. Among all the productive aporias that could be located in Said's work, this essay will be confined to that which surrounds the "self and its intentions," the self to be understood not as the individual, Edward W. Said, but as the authorial subject-position implicit in Said's work, a position I shall categorize as that of "the *specular border intellectual*."

While this paper will not fully elaborate a typology of border intellectuals, it may be useful to distinguish at the outset between the *specular border intellectual*, the focus here, and the *syncretic border intellectual*, to be explored in detail elsewhere. Said describes the awareness of intellectuals situated on cultural borders as "contrapuntal." This musical metaphor, while aptly defining a structural symmetry and tension that characterize the border intellectual's subject position, tends to obscure the border intellectual's agency as well as the orientation of his or her intentionality toward the two cultures. While both syncretic and specular border intellectuals find themselves located between two (or more) groups or cultures, with which they are more or less familiar, one can draw a distinction between them based on the *intentionality of their intellectual orientation* (as opposed to a categorical epistemic differentiation).

The syncretic intellectual, more "at home" in both cultures than his or her specular counterpart, is able to combine elements of the two cultures in order to articulate new syncretic forms and experiences. An apposite example of such syncretic intellectuals can be found in Third World artists such as Wole Soyinka, whose plays often combine Greek tragedy with Yoruba mythology, or Salman Rushdie, whose "English" novels are often articulated in Urdu syntax, or Chinua Achebe, whose "English" fiction is structured by Igbo oral narrative patterns, and so forth. Anton Shammas's novel *Arabesques*, written in Hebrew by a Christian Arab, brilliantly problematizes the positionality of specular and syncretic intellectuals.[3]

By contrast, the specular border intellectual, while perhaps equally familiar with two cultures, finds himself or herself unable or unwilling to be "at home" in these societies. Caught between several cultures or groups, none of which are deemed sufficiently enabling or productive, the specular intellectual subjects the cultures to analytic scrutiny rather than combining them; he or she utilizes his or her interstitial cultural space as a vantage point from which to define, implicitly or explicitly, other, utopian possibilities of group formation. Intellectuals like Edward W. Said, W. E. B. DuBois, Richard Wright, and Zora Neale Hurston occupy the specular site, each in a distinctive way.

II

Perhaps the best place to begin an exploration of Said as a specular border intellectual is with his statements on exile. With his usual insight and eloquence, Said reminds us in his essay, "The Mind of Winter: Reflections on Life in Exile" (MW, pp. 49–55), that we should not romanticize the exile's predicament; that we must avoid a redemptive, i.e., a primarily religious, view of exile; that the "interplay between nationalism and exile is like Hegel's dialectic of servant and master," wherein opposites inform and constitute each other; and, finally, that we must not allow the aura of isolation and spirituality surrounding exile to displace our awareness of "refugees" who are often politically disenfranchised groups of innocent and bewildered people. Those who are exiles, he argues, know "that in a secular and contingent world, homes are always provisional. Borders and barriers, which enclose us within the safety of familiar territory, can also become prisons, and are often defended beyond reason or necessity. Exiles cross borders, break barriers of thought and experience" (MW, p. 54). While this is surely true, the exile's manner of border-crossing can be usefully distinguished from those of the immigrant, the colonialist, the scholar, etc. The salient question is how, precisely, do exiles cross borders; what are their intentions and goals in crossing borders, and how do these in turn affect the kinds of barriers they are inclined to break?

Said's concern with exile manifests itself, among other instances, in his preoccupation with intellectuals who cross borders in various ways: most notably T. E. Lawrence, Joseph Conrad, Eric Auerbach, and Louis Massignon. The last two clearly occupy privileged, albeit distinct, positions in Said's canon of border intellectuals, and I shall be scrutinizing Said's treatment of both. But it must be noted in passing, as both the epigraphs to this essay indicate, that Said's fascination with all these individuals is in some sense specular. Like Conrad, these intellectuals are located at the juncture of the world that formed them, and, like Auerbach, they transform their border-crossing into positive missions that lead to significant cultural acts. Said's relation to them is specular because, from his very different location on the same border between European and non-European cultures, he faces these Western intellectuals across that border, so to speak, and crosses over into the West only to re-cross the border with them in order to map the politics of their forays into other cultures. Thus Said's commentaries on these individuals constitute a series of specular crossing and re-crossing of cultural borders.

Yet Said's appropriations and rearticulations of these intellectuals are often ambiguous about positionality and borders, a characteristic best exemplified by his treatment of Auerbach. In discussing the instrumentality of Auerbach's exile in the production of *Mimesis*, Said ascribes the "existence [of the book] to the very fact of Oriental, non-Occidental exile and homelessness," and the "conditions and circumstances" of the book's existence not to European culture but to "an agonizing distance from it" (SC, p. 8). While Auerbach's exile is clearly "non-Occidental" in terms of specific location, it seems confusing to characterize it as "Oriental" exile, since there is no evidence that Auerbach's views were modified by any aspect of "Oriental" cultures: the book could have been written in any other part of the non-Occidental world without significant difference. I am teasing semantics here in order to ascertain the nature of Auerbach's allegiance to the culture that formed him and to ask whether that allegiance is modified significantly by the influence of an alien culture. If such were the case, then one could characterize the transformation as "agonizing," since it would call the very formation of the intellectual into question. If not, then the distance is sufficiently enabling rather than agonizingly debilitating. Auerbach seems inclined to see it as enabling: "The most priceless and indispensable part of a philologist's heritage is still his own nation's culture and heritage. Only when he is first separated from this heritage, however, and then transcends it does it become truly effective" (cited in SC, p. 7). The ambiguity and slippage in Auerbach's use of "heritage" – a slippage from a professional, methodological inheritance to a national patrimony, which after being "transcended" returns in a more effective guise because it is now simultaneously professional and cultural, the latter having been subsumed by the former – emphasize that an enabling distance leads ultimately to a more profound suture between the subject and the culture that formed her or him. And this, it seems to me, is the central issue in defining exile: how that particular mode of crossing a border elucidates the politics of cultural construction of subjects and how the latter can begin to break free from their indigenous formation by crossing borders.

Said's specular appropriation of Auerbach for defining the value of exile seems to overlook some fundamental differences betwen the two men. While Auerbach writes about and for Western cultures, Said does not write principally for or about Middle Eastern cultures; he writes in the main for and about the West. Even *The Question of Palestine* is addressed, at least in part, as Said explicitly acknowledges, to a Euro-American audience. Thus, while Auerbach is an exile in the weak sense, that is, a subject who always belongs to his home culture in spite of, indeed because of, a circumstantial and temporary alienation, Said, who is neither quite an exile nor quite an immigrant, is able to develop, out of his more complicated border status, an enabling theory of "exile" as an "ascetic ode of *willed* homelessness" (SC, p. 7, emphasis added). However, the discomfort caused by this complicated status inhibits a systematic and clear articulation of the code, which remains embedded in the ambiguities and aporias of Said's entire *oeuvre*.

Said's ambivalence toward defining the nature of border-crossings is most dramatically revealed in his article on "Traveling Theory," the influence of which is amply illustrated by the special issue of *Inscriptions* devoted to this topic.[4] Said's essay, designed to demonstrate how ideas and theories are transformed when they cross borders, provocatively diagnoses the nature and the dangers of transformations that have taken place either in mutations of a given theoretical position or between concrete historical analysis and general theory related to that analysis; however, his argument about the causes of these transformations remains vague. Hence, the essay offers an apposite instance of the combined insight and blindness that characterizes Said's thinking about border-crossings.

After a rather general reference to ideas moving from West to East (and vice versa) in the nineteenth century, Said focuses on the transformation of Georg Lukács' theory of reification as it is later taken up by Lucien Goldmann and turned into the theory of "homologies." This transmutation of a complex theory into a vague, formulaic metaphor is rightly character-ized by Said as a "degradation." Yet he seems unwilling to consider the possibility that this change may be produced by the failure of individual understanding or imagination; instead, he argues, it is "just that the situation has changed sufficiently for the degradation to have occurred." One waits to see what specific modifications in the situation are responsible for this, what kind of border has in fact been crossed, what are the socio-political differences between the two locations that can bring about such changes. Perhaps because he senses the reader's expectations, Said insists several times that relocation *in itself* precipitates the transformation. The tension caused by the contradiction between the insistence that change in location produces transformations and the refusal to specify the nature of that cause reaches its climax in the following statement:

> In measuring Lukács and Goldmann against each other, then, we are also recognizing the extent to which theory is a response to a specific social and historical situation of which an intellectual occasion is a part. Thus what is insurrectionary consciousness in one instance becomes tragic vision in another, for reasons that are elucidated when the situations in Budapest and Paris are *seriously compared*. I do not wish to suggets that Budapest and Paris determined the kinds of theories produced by Lukács and Goldmann. I do mean that "Budapest" and "Paris" are irreducibly first conditions, and they provide limits and apply pressures to which each writer, given his own gifts, predilections, and interests, responds. (TT, p. 237).

One is no closer to understanding what kind of border has been crossed and how that might have contributed to the change. Said's equivocation about the relations between a subject and the determining socio-political situation has reached an infinitely periphrastic refusal to come to terms with the issue.

By the time he moves to Raymond Williams's meditation on Lukács' and Goldmann's ideas, the problem of crossing cultural borders has been displaced by epistemological questions. When Said turns to Michel Fou-cault, the last theoretician considered in the essay, his concern has shifted to the discrepancy between the value of Foucault's detailed historical work and the weaknesses in his theoretical pronouncements about power/

knowledge. By the end, "travel" has become a general metaphor covering a series of diverse theoretical transformations, but the effects of crossing borders have not been illuminated. Said has a strong awareness of situations and borders, yet he declines to specify the precise causes and effects of such crossings. Instead, he produces criticism that emanates from and reflects the difficult predicament of border intellectuals in two ways: first, his criticism is a "reflection," an indirect meditation, on the predicament; and, second, it occupies a specular position in relation to Western culture.

III

Before proceeding to examine further Said's meditations on the nature of borders and the relation of these meditations to his own location, a few clarifications about different modes of border-crossing may be useful. A systematic scrutiny must avoid a metaphoric use of the term "exile," which tends to be shrouded in the emotionally-charged connotations of the exile's plight. One can schematically identify four different modes of border-crossings: those used by the exile, the immigrant, the colonialist, and the scholar, the last typified by the anthropologist studying other cultures (one might add the tourist and the traveler as subcategories of the scholar/ anthropologist). While both the exile and the immigrant cross the border between one social or national group and another, the exile's stance toward the new host culture is negative, the immigrant's positive. That is, the notion of exile always emphasizes the absence of "home," of the cultural matrix that formed the indivudal subject; hence, it implies an involuntary or enforced rupture between the collective subject of the original culture and the individual subject. The nostalgia associated with exile (a nostalgia that is structural rather than idiosyncratic) often makes the individual indifferent to the values and characteristics of the host culture; the exile chooses, if indeed s/he has any choice, to live in a context that is least inhospitable, most like "home." The immigrant, on the other hand, is not troubled by structural nostalgia because his or her status implies a purposive directedness toward the host culture, which has been deliberately chosen as the new home. Most importantly, his or her status implies a voluntary desire to become a full-fledged subject of the new society. Thus the immigrant is often eager to discard with deliberate speed the formative influences of his or her own culture and to take on the values of the new culture; indeed, his or her success as an immigrant depends on what Said calls "uncritical gregariousness," that is, on an ability to identify rapidly and to merge with the structure of the new culture's collective subjectivity.[5]

Unlike the exile and the immigrant, for both of whom the problematic consists in a rupture between and a re-suturing of individual and collective subjectivities, the colonialist and the anthropologist, who also cross cultural borders, are not troubled by this problem.[6] Colonial and anthropological projects are both characterized by a deliberate denial and often an explicit, militant repression of the indivudal's desire to become a subject of the host culture. Both must apprehend the new culture, not as a field of subjectivity, but rather as an object of and for their gaze. For the colonialist the new culture becomes an object of his military, administrative, and economic skills, which, according to colonial theory and practice, remain objective and uncontaminated so long as the administrator is prevented from "going native," i.e., from becoming a subject of the new culture.[7] For the anthropologist the situation is, of course, more complicated. While he or she is professionally obliged to "master" the language and culture of the host society, all aspects of his or her indivdual subjectivity – the fundamental epistemological structures of professional work or career, fundamental values and beliefs, even bodily well-being – remain under the discursive control of the home culture. The anthropologist, too, cannot afford to "go native," for to do so would mean the loss of an "objectivity" essential to professional status.[8] For both the colonialist and the traditional anthropologist, the host culture ultimately remains an object of attention: the gaze of the former is military, administrative, and economic; that of the latter is epistemological and organizational. Both gazes, quite unlike the perspectives of the exile and the immigrant, are panoptic and thus dominating.

IV

If we begin to scrutinize Third World intellectuals like Edward Said and American minority intellectuals like Richard Wright, it quickly becomes evident that while they fit none of my four categories, their subject-positions do share some characteristics of all but one. Obviously, neither is a colonialist, but in some sense both are simultaneously exiles *and* immigrants. Said and Wright are both descendants of people forced to leave their original cultures, and, like immigrants, both operate more or less effectively in their new culture. However, neither becomes a full-fledged subject of the latter: Said because he chooses not to, because he does not wish to rush into what he calls an "uncritical gregariousness"; Wright because racism would not permit blacks to become full members of white American culture. Somewhat like anthropologists, both are quasi-subjects who participate in the new culture yet stand on its border; however, unlike the anthropologist, neither is a full participant in any other culture. Both are subjects in a dominant culture, yet marginal to it. Hence, both are confined to the predicament of border intellectuals, neither motivated by nostalgia for some lost or abandoned culture nor at home in this or any other culture.

This predicament of the border intellectual must be carefully defined.

How can one situate oneself on the border? What kind of space characterizes it? In theory, and effectively in practice, borders are neither inside nor outside the territory they define but simply designate the difference between the two. They are not really spaces at all; as the sites of differences between interiority and exteriority, they are points of infinite regression. Thus, intellectuals located on this site are not, so to speak, "sitting" on the border; rather, they are forced *to constitute themselves as the border*, to coalesce around it as a point of infinite regression. In consciously or unconsciously constituting themselves in this manner, they have to guard themselves against the traps of specularity, for the border only functions as a mirror, as a site defining the "identity" and "homogeneity" of the group that has constructed it. Said is clearly aware of this paradox, and its resultant demand, but seems unwilling to unravel it explicitly:

I am speaking of exile, [he says] not as a privileged site for self-reflection but as an *alternative* to the mass institutions looming over much of modern life. If the exile is neither going to rush into an uncritical gregariousness [like the immigrant] nor sit on the sidelines nursing a wound [like the exile], he or she must cultivate a scrupulous (not indulgent or sulky) subjectivity (MW, p. 54).

This formulation leads to two related questions. First, is it possible to cultivate a subjectivity, especially a "scrupulous" one, without the aid of self-reflection? And second, what does "scrupulous" mean in this context? Though Said never provides direct answers to these questions, the scrupulousness that is entailed in the subject-position of the border intellectual, it seems to me, is everywhere exemplified in his work.

V

Without going into the details of Said's forced migration from Palestine to Lebanon to Egypt and then eventually to permanent settlement in the US, or into other aspects of his biography, his work shows how he occupies a subject-position that is neither quite that of an exile nor quite that of an immigrant. As a Palestinian and an advocate of his people's rights and aspirations, Said, in spite of his Western education, functions as an exile on the borders of the dominant culture. Thus, even when articulating Palestinian aspiration, as for instance in *The Question of Palestine*, Said feels obliged to address the West, whose power greatly determines Palestinian destiny.

The Question of Palestine aims, Said says in the preface, to put "before the American reader a broadly representative Palestinian position . . ." (QP, p. xi). The power of the US is more explicitly acknowledged when Said comments that "there is an important place in the question of Palestine for what Jews and Americans now think and do. It is this place to which my book addresses itself" (*QP*, p. xvi). The politics underlying such an address account for Said's position as a subject: "Every Palestinian," he says, "has no state as a Palestinian even though he is 'of,' without belonging to, a state in which at present he resides" (*QP*, p. 120). Though this is true of all Palestinians, and, I would add, of all border intellectuals, the statement defines the political position in cold, neutral terms; its affective results are exposed when Said permits himself to speak in a more subjective vein:

> My hope is to have made clear the Palestinian interpretation of Palestinian experience, and to have shown the relevance of both to the contemporary political scene. To explain one's sense of oneself as a Palestinian in this way is to feel embattled. To the West, which is where I live, to be a Palestinian is in political terms to be an outlaw of sorts, or at any rate very much an outsider. But that is reality, and I mention it only as a way of indicating the peculiar loneliness of my undertaking in this book. (*QP*, p. xviii)

This sense of being an outsider is rearticulated in a different register as the collective obligation of Palestinians to negotiate constantly a variety of borders in order to define themselves individually and collectively. Hence Said's striking description of Palestinian reality as "cubistic, all suddenly obtruding planes jutting out into one or another realm" (*QP*, p. 123).

However, Said's subject-position is only partly that of articulator and defender of Palestinian aspirations within the West; he is also an active and important producer of the evolving Palestinian identity. In the absence of an authoritative history of Palestinians, *The Question of Palestine* marks an early stage in the production of such a history, and, in the absence of an informed, sympathetic, and serious discussion of the Palestinian "problem" in the West, the book plays an important role by inserting the question into Western discourse. As Said makes clear, his book is motivated not only by the current plight of Palestinians, but also by a utopian vision of Palestine, a "nonplace," an idea that galvanizes Palestinians everywhere. In relation to this utopian potential, as in relation to the American audience for whom Said articulates Palestine, he is a border intellectual, and this just because "Palestine" is a most unusual "place":

> If we think of Palestine as having a function of both a place to *return to* and of an *entirely new* place, a vision partially of a restored past and of a novel future, perhaps even of a historical disaster transformed into a hope for a different future, we will understand the word's meaning better. (*QP*, p. 125).

In the context of such a "Palestine" and the US, where he is professionally located, Said can be seen as at once an "exile" and an "immigrant." He is an exile from the land of his birth who has become an eminent member of the American academy but who refuses, unlike most immigrants, what he calls an "uncritical gregariousness," that is, an anxious desire to become an uncritical subject of the new culture. Yet in relation to "Palestine" he is an exile waiting across the historical, temporal border for the establishment of a utopian state.[9]

Thus Said is enmeshed in a complicated border space, which is by no means the single source of his work but which does leave a singular trace throughout his writing. Quite often his position, which allows a kind of distance from Western literature and discursive practices, permits Said a specular role – that is, he is able to provide in his writing a set of mirrors allowing Western cultures to see their own structures and functions.

Said's most famous book, *Orientalism*, is just such a specular performance. It mirrors analytically a Western mode of discursive control that Said labels "orientalist": he reveals to Orientalists (those few who are willing to listen) their own hidden ideological procedures and programs. *Orientalism* is clearly not the product of a "traditional" intellectual in Gramsci's sense, that is, of one who produces the ideology of the dominant class while believing that her or his work is neutral and unbiased. In fact, the book is a stringent critique of the traditional orientalist intellectuals who are blind to their ideological formation. On the other hand, *Orientalism* is not the product of an "organic" intellectual either, since in producing his deconstruction of "orientalism," Said does not speak for any *particular* organic group outside the West; the book is not in the service of a *specific* counter-hegemonic formation,[10] though many Third World and American minority intellectuals have found it sympathetic. *Orientalism* is, instead, the work of a border intellectual: one who is the subject neither of the host culture or the dominant class, as are the immigrant and the traditional intellectual, respectively, nor of the "home" culture or the subaltern class, as are the exile and the organic intellectual, respectively. Said's critique is articulated from the neutrality of the border: *Orientalism* is deeply "interested" in unmasking the underlying, organizational structure of the discourse that masquerades as truth, but Said is not motivated to offer an alternate positivity, whether in the guise of a truth or a set of alternative group "interests."

While the border status of *Orientalism* is virtually self-evident, that of Said's earlier book, *Beginnings*, is more complicated and intriguing. This work is clearly an important part of the structuralist and poststructuralist debate, a debate that it scrutinizes in the fifth chapter. However, *Beginnings* itself implicitly challenges one to look for the enabling and creative "beginning" contradictions that make this very book possible.

Said's definition of "beginnings" and "intentionality," the work's key concepts, is circular. "*The Beginning*," he tells us, "*is the first step in the intentional production of meaning*" (B, p. 5). By intention, he "mean[s] an appetite at the beginning intellectually to do something in a characteristic language – either consciously or unconsciously, but at any rate in a language that always (or nearly always) shows signs of the beginning intention in some form and is always engaged purposefully in the production of meaning" (B, p. 12). The term "intention" also has two other important implications for Said. First, "intention is the link between idiosyncratic view and the communal concern" (B, p. 13); second, it "is a notion that includes everything that later develops out of it, no matter how eccentric the development or inconsistent the result" (B, p. 12). What is implicit in these tautological definitions is made more explicit when Said argues that for "the great modern rethinkers," like Marx and Freud, "beginning is a way of grasping the whole project" (B, p. 41). That is to say, a study of beginnings implies a scrutiny of the entire project of a given culture or a given historical period. Since the choice of any given intention, implied in the concept of beginning, involves the rejection or bracketing of other intentions, one is obliged to examine the axiology according to which intentions are prioritized; hence, one has to study the entire cultural *gestalt*. Similarly, if intentions must be studied teleologically, and if they link the individual and collective cultural subjects (i.e., the idiosyncratic view and the communal concern), then a thorough scrutiny of beginnings necessarily involves an analysis of economic, political, social, ideological, and psychological relations.

However, Said explicitly refuses an analysis of the socio-political circumstances of beginnings, and he avoids any sustained comparisons of beginnings in Western and non-Western cultures. (It would be fascinating, for instance, to compare, as Said does not, the phenomenology of beginnings in oral-mythic cultures, on the one hand, with that in chirographic-historical cultures, on the other.) Said *does* make a brief reference to the long shadow cast by the Koran on the development of modern Arabic fiction, which, from the viewpoint of the authorial subject-position, serves to define the nature of Said's attention. Having ruled out other cultures, as well as a socio-political examination of beginnings, Said can confine himself to a scrutiny of the literary, critical, and philosophical texts of Western high culture. The problem here is not that the field is artifically demarcated, but that, having limited himself to a field where writers are consciously concerned with the problem of beginnings, Said is then able to undertake an analysis that, to use his own terms, is neither quite intransitive nor quite transitive: it is an uneasy, though illuminating and stimulating, mixture.

Transitive and intransitive analyses of beginnings are, Said tells us, "two styles of thought, and imagination, one projective and descriptive, the other tautological and endlessly self-mimetic." The former leads to a "beginning with (or for) an anticipated end, or at least expected continuity"; the latter "retains for the beginning its identity as *radical* starting point: the intransitive and conceptual aspect, that which has no object but its own constant clarification." Said's work is clearly not a systemic and rigorous intransitive analysis similar to those of Husserl and Heidegger. Nor is it quite a transitive one, for its *telos* is never entirely clear. The intentionality of Said's book, it seems to me, is ambivalently caught between an attempt at a rigorous phenomenological reduction of the concept and experience of "beginnings," on the one hand, and a non-phenomenological, historical survey of the same topic, on the other. In effect, Said ends up with what one might call a "transitive phenomenology" of "beginnings."

This particular form of analysis is privileged for various reasons. The one of greatest interest here stems from the structural position of the exile or immigrant in the new culture. In defining exteriority, Said links it with the feeling of what Lukács, echoing Novalis, call "transcendental homelessness," which Said says "is the result of discovering an absolute incompatibility between the realm of totality and the realm of personal interiority, of subjectivity" (*B*, p. 312). This is precisely the incongruity experienced by the exile and, in a less problematic manner, by the immigrant. The subjectivity or interiority of the immigrant or exile is formed and informed by the "totality" of her or his "home" culture. When individuals go to a new society, they experience a major gap between the alien culture and the self (in)formed elsewhere: collective and individual subjects no longer coincide. The immigrant who wishes to integrate himself into this new social structure will be forced to contemplate, first and foremost, how and where he must begin. How to enter the host culture and where to begin will become a transitive phenomenological problem for him. For the indigenous subject, who is a part of the prevailing cultural discourse, intentions and beginnings will at best be mundane problems. It is no accident, then, that a border intellectual like Said "happens" to produce a massive, scholarly study of beginnings and that this study takes the form of a transitive phenomenology that Said repeatedly classifies as a "meditation" about beginnings, nor, indeed, that Said "begins" his own scholarly career with a study of Joseph Conrad, whose life and work exemplify the challenges and problems of exile and immigration.

One might reasonably expect a scholarly meditation on beginnings to scrutinize its own beginnings and intentionality, and one might assume that, for it to be rigorous and hence productive, such an endeavour would ultimately have to be either intransitive, thereby pushing the beginning of *Beginnings* to its fundamental epistemological and ontological ground, or specifically transitive, thereby providing a concrete socio-political and biographical account of the origin and *telos* of the task. Said not only avoids each alternative, he also evades biographical reflexivity about his project. Instead, he provides us with the most passive and impersonal account of the book's genesis. In discussing the circumstances that led to this meditation, Said promises to tell us "why such a study proposed itself to its author, why it is pursued in this way in particular, and how a rationale for such a study is arrived at" (*B*, p. 5). Further, the argument of the book is based on "what the subject of 'beginning' *authorizes*" (*B*, pp. 16–17). Thus the agency of the writer is almost totally repressed, and the writing subject is implicitly split between the active scribe and the passive meditator. Indeed, the meditating mind turns itself into a reflecting mirror: "constructing the tautology that says one begins at the beginning depends on the ability of both mind and language to reverse themselves, and thus to move from present to past and back again, from a complex situation to an anterior simplicity and back again, or from one point to another as if in a circle" (*B*, pp. 29–30).

The mind not only becomes a reflecting surface, but also adopts a paradoxically passive form of volition – it elects to be passive: "The form of writing I chose," Said says, "was the meditative essay – first, because I believed myself to be trying for a form of unity as I write; and second, *because I want to let beginnings generate in my mind the type of relationships and figures most suitable to them*" (*B*, p. 16, emphasis added). The meditating mind becomes a (relatively genial) host to the problematic of beginnings revealed in the canonical literature of the (relatively genial) host culture.

That specular meditation produces a transitive phenomenology of beginnings that is not particularly goal-oriented. Unlike the immigrant, whose life and well-being depend on a concrete transitive comprehension of the host culture's intentionalities, on his or her mastery of where and how to begin in this new milieu, Said, precisely because he is not motivated by the desire to become a full, uncritical subject, can embark on a teleologically "neutral" transitive phenomenology of beginnings in Western societies. In so doing he once again constructs an analytic mirror that reflects and refracts the structures of the host culture.

These considerations of the authorial subject-position manifested in *Beginnings* lead to several conclusions. The first is an aporia that I will take up again in discussing Said's method. As Hayden White has noted, one of the cures that *Beginnings* seems to propose for the contemporary crisis in Western cultures is "the revitalization of the will."[11] Yet in Said's account of the origins of *Beginnings*, the authorial will seems to be subordinated drastically to the "authority" of (others') beginnings, to the object of contemplation. (Said thereby raises, but does not pursue, the question of the extent to which and in what manner the meditating mind is active, as he later insists it is.) The aporia, however, revolves around the relation between the quieting of the authorial will and the advocacy, direct or indirect, of a revitalized will. It is the very same aporia Said subsequently explores in Louis Massignon's study of Islamic religious mysticism.

Of more immediate interest is the fact that, via his transitive phenomenology, Said has produced a new methodological emphasis. The procedure of *Beginnings* implies that phenomenological investigation need not be torn between the polar opposites of pure, idealist meditations or starkly materialist studies of worldly determinations. His transitive phenomenology points towards the possibility of a "political phenomenology," analogous to Alfred Schutz's social phenomenology, a procedure devoted to mapping the dynamic structures of the intentionality and teleology of power and of relations of domination, a typology of these structures from their macroscopic – the politics of group and cultural formations – to their microscopic manifestations – the politics of discursive constructions of "individual" subjects.

Finally, the procedure of *Beginnings* sheds interesting light on the relations among the apparently discrete works within Said's critical corpus. As J. Hillis Miller observes,

> [t]here is, in both Said and his work, that discontinuity which is one of the central themes of *Beginnings*: the difficult concept of production or assemblage which is not disorder or heterogeneity, and yet not assimilable to the familiar models of order – organic unity, dialectical progression, or genealogical series – in which origin fathers forth a sequence leading without break to some foreordained end.[12]

This "discontinuity" is informed, if not produced, by the position of the border intellectual and the very concern with beginnings. Each of Said's major works begins anew, striking out in a different direction from the previous studies; each opens up novel fields and provides different angles of vision. His work as a whole can be described, to borrow his own metaphor about Palestinian experience, as "cubistic." The cement holding the different planes and fields together is the fundamental procedures and attitudes of his never explicitly articulated method.

VI

Hayden White has perspicuously described the core of Said's method. *Beginnings*, he argues, does not "authorize" either the logic of identity and contradiction ("the hypotactical principles of subordination and reductive inclusion") or the principle of analogy ("the paratactical principle of similitude or resemblance"). Said's method, rather, is based on "notions of adjacency, complementarity, discontinuity – in other words, *contiguity*, which serves as both an ontological principle and a method of exposition. In Said's world-view, things exist side-by-side with one another, not in hierarchies of relative reality or ordered series of dynastically related groups. But the principle of contiguity here embraced is not a mechanistic one."[13]

Examples of this method can be found throughout Said's work. "Intellectuals in the Post-Colonial World" provides a striking instance:

The comparative or, better, the contrapuntal perspective then proposes itself and with it, Ernst Bloch's notion of non-synchronous experience. That is we must be able to think through and interpret together discrepant experiences, each with its particular agendas and pace of development, its own formations, its own natural coherence and its system of external relationships. (IPW, p. 56)

This is followed by a fascinating comparison between Fournier's *Description de l'Egypte* and Abd al Rahman al Jabarti's *Journal*, both of which date from the 1820s, and by a sketch for an analysis of other texts that follow each of these writers on either side of the divide. The language of Said's articulation – "contrapuntal," "non-synchronous," "discrepant," etc. – stresses separation rather than continuity, implicitly emphasizing the interpreting will of the critic who compares the two sides. Such a method, while obviously productive in Said's hands, raises questions about the nature of the critical will and Said's subsequent deep valorization of the term "criticism." To use this method productively, a critic must attain a certain "neutrality"; he or she must transcend those deep ideological allegiances to "group," "nation," "race," "gender," or "class" that lead to the manichean valorization of one side and reciprocal devaluation of the other that *Orientalism* and a variety of feminist texts have criticized in their respective fields. The critic, in short, must be able to transcend the ideological boundaries that are imposed upon him or her by "home."

"Secular Criticism" takes up the discussion of "home" in terms of its binary opposite, "homelessness." These definitions ultimately remain metaphoric and generate an ambiguous proliferation of meanings. Thus, "home" comes to be associated with "culture" as an environment, process, and hegemony that determine individuals through complicated mechanisms. Culture is productive of the necessary sense of belonging, of "home"; it attempts to suture, in as complete a manner as possible, collective and individual subjectivity. But culture is also divisive, producing boundaries that distinguish the collectivity and what lies outside it and define hierarchic organizations within the collectivity. "Homelessness," on the other hand, is first defined negatively via Matthew Arnold as the opposite of "home": "anarchy, the culturally disfranchised, those elements opposed to culture and State." More positively, "homelessness" as an enabling concept is associated, via Raymond Williams's rearticulation of Gramsci, with the civil and political space that hegemony cannot suture, a space in which "alternative acts and alternative intentions which are not yet articulated as a social institution or even project" can survive. "Homelessness," then, is a situation wherein utopian potentiality can endure.

"Criticism," which denotes an oppositional socio-political attitude as well as a method and procedure in this essay, can be seen to emanate from this space of "homelessness." Said, it seems, is deliberately employing and redefining "criticism", an over-determined, emotionally charged term already over-used in literary and cultural studies, in order to shock critics into re-examining their practices and assumptions and into abandoning their "home," that is, the ideological attitudes constraining a freer, more "neutral" pursuit of knowledge. Yet precisely in this forceful attempt to redirect our use of that term, "Secular Criticism" produces a certain ambiguity: "In its suspicion of totalizing concepts, in its discontent with reified objects, in its impatience with guilds, special interests, imperialized fiefdoms, and orthodox habits of mind, criticism is most itself and, if the paradox can be tolerated, most unlike itself at the moment it starts turning into organized dogma" (SC, p. 29). In this paradoxical formulation, criticism functions to define that which is simultaneously to be affirmed and denied. The same effect is produced by statements like the following: ". . . contemporary criticism is an institution for publicly affirming the values of ours, that is, European, dominant elite culture . . ." (SC, p. 25); "Criticism in short is always situated, skeptical, secular, reflectively open to its own failings" (SC, p. 26). Such contradictions not only lead to the kind of debate on Said's work, essentially over terminology, that took place in *Diacritics*;[14] they also draw our attention away from a clarification of "homelessness' that is crucial to Said's privileging of "criticism."

"Secular Criticism" hints at two crucial aspects of this border space that Said calls "homelessness." The first concerns the critic's location. After noting that intellectuals can collaborate with as well as oppose a dominant order, Said remarks: "All this, then, shows us the individual consciousness placed at a sensitive nodal point, and it is this consciousness at that critical point which this book attempts to explore in the form of what I call *criticism*" (SC, p. 15). "Criticism" here designates the distance, made possible by self-reflexivity, between a given hegemonic order and the individual critic. The "sensitive nodal point," then, in effect defines the location of the border intellectual, as Said's fascination with various individuals who cross borders indicates. The second concerns the nature of criticism itself: "For in the main – and here I shall be explicit – criticism must think of itself as life-enhancing and constitutively opposed to every form of tyranny, domination and abuse; its social goals are non-coercive knowledge produced in the interest of human freedom" (SC, p. 29). The nature of this criticism will of course depend on how one defines "human freedom," about which there will surely be much disagreement. What seems beyond dispute, however, is the valorization of "non-coercive knowledge." "Secular Criticism," in keeping with its introductory function in the anthology, does not further articulate either the location of the border intellectual or the nature of non-coercive knowledge. That task is left to Said's commentary on Massignon.

Although Said's essay, "Islam, Philology, and French Culture: Renan and Massignon," sets out to demonstrate that humanistic fields, based not on criticism or discipline but on cultural prestige, are incapable of self-criticism, one is struck less by this purpose than by Said's warmth, generosity, and respect for Massignon; and one soon discovers beneath these sentiments an even finer appreciation of Massignon's method and style. Massignon's "epistemological attitude" toward the Arab cultures he studied, characterized by Said as one of "sympathetic assumption and rapprochement," is ultimately responsible for his method. In Massignon's work, Said explains,

> the problem of language and of the philological vocation are considered within a *spatial* perspective, as aspects of a topography of distances, of geographical differentiation, of spirits of place separated from each other by a territory whose function for the scholar is that it must be charted as exactly as possible, and then in one way or another overcome. (IPFC, p. 284)

The imperative to chart cultural differences with exactitude in order to overcome them begins to define non-coercive knowledge. Clearly, Said values both Massignon's refusal to subordinate Islam and Arab cultures to Christianity and European cultures and the resultant analysis that is non-manichean, non-agonistic, and non-polemical. In Said's view, Massignon goes well beyond freeing himself from the negative, confining ideology of European superiority that is typical of orientalist thinking. He even seems to have based his method on a certain dialectical notion of relation between self and other in Arabic grammar and rhetoric:

> For language is both a "pilgrimage" and a "spiritual displacement," since we only elaborate language in order to be able to go out from ourselves toward another, and also to evoke with this other an absent One, the third person, *al-Gha'ib*, as He is called by Arab grammarians. And we do this so as to discover and identify all these entities with each other. (cited in IPFC, p. 286).

Every aspect of Massignon's endeavour – his epistemology, his view of language, his approach to Arab cultures, even his view of the orientalist's vocation – is informed by a "spiritual displacement" that permits him to understand the Arab in the latter's own terms. This open and generous approach, unfettered by the powerful ideological forces of his "home" culture, is what I believe Said has in mind by "non-coercive knowledge." Massignon thus stands as Said's prime example of an intellectual who manages to overcome the powerful ideological confinements of "home"; his capacity for "spiritual displacement" symbolizes Said's valorization of "homelessness."

But "homelessness" cannot be achieved without multiple border crossings, indeed, without a constant, keen awareness of the politics of borders. Such an awareness permeates Massignon's work and style, which Said characterizes as discontinuous and abrupt, "as if it wishes constantly to embody distance and the alternation of presence and absence, the paradox of sympathy and alienation, the motif of inclusion and exclusion, grace and disgrace, apotropaic prayer and compassionate love" (IPFC, p. 287). Said aptly characterizes this constant oscillation in spatial terms, that is, not only as co-equivalence but also as repeated border crossings. Massignon, Said implies, was perfectly comfortable as a subject in his host culture and elsewhere; he was quite "at home" without having to subordinate himself to the ideological constraints of any particular national or cultural group. The paradox of "homelessness-as-home" is best captured by the ambiguity of the following statement: for Massignon, says Said, the Arabic language "is a closed world with a certain number of stars in it; entering it, the scholar is both at home and repatriated from his own world" (IPFC, p. 286). Massignon is "at home" in this tension, in the play between Arabic and European cultures. Said here transforms the border into "homelessness-as-home" by turning a negative determination, i.e., the status of an outsider or marginalized border intellectual, into a positive vocation, mining that site for its political and epistemological wealth.

Bruce Robbins succinctly captures an aspect of this paradox:

> If criticism is not to be subsumed by the interest of the homeland, Said suggests, it can only be located in dislocation itself, in the always shifting, always empty space "between culture and system." But he also argues that if criticism is not to withdraw into harmless seclusion, it must accept the taint and constraint of placement in the world – and even, perhaps, make a home for itself there. Homelessness or worldliness? Between them there is nothing so satisfying as a choice or a contradiction, but there is a lively project of critical self-discovery.[15]

Robbins's characterization is generally accurate, except for the negative connotation that he attaches to worldliness and the potential opposition he perceives between it and homelessness. It seems to me that the opposition between "secular" and "religious" criticism implies that Said sees a certain kind of worldliness as being free precisely of the "taint and constraint" produced by the attachment of "religious" criticism to the "parochial" interests of *particular* worlds. Worldliness represents in Said's criticism, for example in his analysis of Massignon, the critic's achieved freedom from loyalty and subordination to specific ideologies, cultures, systems, worlds. Seen in this way, worldliness is not opposed to homelessness, but is its complement. "Worldliness-without-world" and "homelessness-as-home" are different formulations privileging the same subject position: that of the specular border intellectual.

Borders, as implied earlier, are articulations of epistemic and socio-political differences; indeed, borders are digital punctuations of analog differences, that is, highly valorized, stylized, and formulaic punctuations of infinite, continuous, and heterotopic differences that fill a given continuum. In contrast to the analog differences, borders, digitalized articulations of differences, introduce categorial gaps in a continuum. In a sociopolitical register, borders that articulate or impose categorial "differences" between groups – demarcated in terms of "nations," "cultures," "classes," "genders," "races," etc. – tend to reify analog relations into imaginary identities and oppositions. In the context of such charged gaps, *syncretic* border intellectuals are those whose work fills the gaps – for instance, between two cultures. (I have in mind here particularly the artistic production of authors such as Soyinka, Rushdie, etc., who bridge the gaps between different cultures.) By contrast, *specular* border intellectuals produce work that reflects (on) the gaps and that articulates their nature and structures. Indeed, "worldliness-without-world/homelessness-as-home," the paradoxical formulation that is embedded in Said's corpus, elucidates the relation between the task and the location of the specular border intellectual. "Worldliness-without-world" represents a sophisticated awareness of the politics produced by socio-cultural-classed-gendered locations, an awareness, however, that does not subjugate itself to that politics. It represents a freedom, or at least an attempt to achieve freedom, from the politics of imaginary identification and opposition, from conflation of identity and location, and so on – in short, from the varied and powerful forms of suturing that are represented by and instrumental in the construction of "home." While "worldliness-without-world" emphasizes the specular border intellectual's awareness of his or her location outside the group in question, "homelessness-as-home" accentuates a *jouissance* derived from transitoriness, from privileging process and relationship over allegiance to groups or to objects representing reified relationships; it privileges the pleasure of border-crossing and transgression.

VII

The power of this formulation informs a large part of Said's work, but he never explicitly privileges either the "identity" of the border intellectual or the productive site occupied by that intellectual, in part, perhaps, because to do so risks essentialism. On the other hand, not to generalize at all, to argue, for instance, that there are as many types of border intellectuals as there are individuals situated on borders, risks the chaos of infinite monadic specificity. This is not the place to attempt an encompassing or complete definition of the border intellectual that would systematically negotiate the twin dangers of essentialism and infinite heterogeneity, or to provide a typology of border intellectuals; yet it may be useful to essay *some* general statements about the circumstances of border intellectuals. Said is obviously not the only intellectual who speaks from the border. While his work provokes serious thought about the border as a site of intellectual work, other individuals, for example, W. E. B. DuBois, Zora Neale Hurston, or Richard Wright, have also written from that subject-position and yet articulated it differently because of their various historical, political, class, and gender determinations. Thus, while the specific *foci* and strategies of border intellectuals can vary considerably, the position that they find themselves in has certain common features.

To the extent that groups – whether organized around culture, nation, class, gender, or race – tend to define their identities, their "homogeneity," by differentiating themselves from others, and to the extent that the inscription of difference tends to be valorized in a more or less manichean fashion, border intellectuals, who are caught between various group formations, are often forced to internalize the manichean dichotomies. If a group defines itself, as all groups finally do, as "human" in contrast to others who are classified as "sub-human," then the intellectual situated on the border of that group, that is, an intellectual who does not have (or chooses not to utilize) access to another group that will adequately and confidently empower him or her according to its alternate definition of itself as "human," will be torn between his or her aspiration for "humanity" and the actual socio-historical experience of being treated as sub-human.

In the case of border intellectuals, the rupture between aspiration or ego-ideal valorized by the dominant culture and the experience of actual social devaluation cuts through the very center of subjectivity. This rupture, we must remember, is not inflicted on an already formed "individual" or subject but is involved in the very process of formation.[16] Thus, not only are images of self-as-human and other-as-sub-human related in a binary opposition, but the very process of *suturing* a "homogeneity," which seems crucial to the cultural necessity of the group's "identity," is simultaneously the process of rupturing the subject on the border: the border subject becomes the site on which a group defines its identity. Among the many implications of this predicament, I can only touch on some of the more salient:

**If the border is the site of infinite regression and if the border subject is the site on which the group defines its identity, then the ruptured body of that subject becomes the text on which the structure of group identity is written in inverted form – the *in*-formation of the group is inscribed on the body of the border subject. The border intellectual willing to read his or her own body, his or her own formation, has ready access to the structures and values of the group in question as well as to alternate possibilities of individual and collective subject formation.

**If the border subject is a deeply ruptured one, then a contemplation of how that subject was formed can, given a certain utopian impulse, lead to a desire to purge all the manichean valences, all the negative inscriptions that the group projected in its formation. In its most radical instance, such as that of Richard Wright, such a desire to deconstruct the received, manichean subjectivity becomes a prolonged project, which in turn paradoxically constitutes the core around which a new subjectivity begins to coalesce. Caught between a white racist society that would not accept him and a black culture that he repudiated for complex (and ultimately mistaken) reasons, Wright dedicated his life to investigating the border space between the two. In his bifurcated *oeuvre*, his utopian, communitarian urge is almost totally relegated to his journalistic writing. By contrast, his fiction – which explores different facets of the question "What quality of will must a Negro possess to live and die with dignity in a country that denied his humanity?" – is dedicated to excavating the individual subjectivity that has been formed by the struggle between black and white cultures. Each of Wright's novels successively probes and reveals a deeper stratum of the political, ideological, and cultural processes of subject formation on the racial border. In so doing, Wright in effect becomes an archaeologist of the site of his own formaiton, devoting most of his energies to deconstructing the black subject's formation, thereby re-forming his (Wright's) own subjectivity as a writer around the project of excavating the border. In short, Wright's work constitutes a systematic reading of the border subject's body.

**The site of the border subject is clearly one mode of what Foucault identifies as "heterotopia," even though he does not have this kind of subjectivity in mind.[17] Utopias and heterotopias are, according to Foucault, the two sites that "have the curious property of being in relation with all other sites, but in such a way as *to suspect, neutralize, or invert the set of relations that they happen to designate, mirror, or reflect*" (emphasis added). These two sites are linked with all others, but primarily by a relation of contradiction. Heterotopias, like boundaries, established "in the very founding of society," are "counter-sites" in which all the other real sites that can be found within a culture "are simultaneously represented, contested, and inverted." Foucault's subsequent elaboration of the specular nature of heterotopias and the principles according to which they function, while very suggestive for a more extended exploration of the border intellectual as a heterotopic site, cannot be taken up here. It is crucial, however, to make one distinction. While Foucault's heterotopic sites are all *social* and *institutional* spaces – cemeteries, fairs, libraries, prisons, etc. – the border intellectual, as I have defined that concept, is simultaneously a "space" and a subject, is, indeed, a subject-as-space. Unlike Foucault's sites, which are inherently heterotopic, the transformation of the border subject, who is always constituted as a *potential* heterotopic site, into an *actual* heterotopic, specular border intellectual depends upon his or her own agency: only by directly or indirectly reading himself or herself as a heterotopic border constructed as such by society can the intellectual articulate his or her specular potentiality. In their own very different ways, both Said and Wright investigate this shifting site.

**If a constructive appropriation of the heterotopic site by the border intellectual depends on articulations of specularity, then one must guard against the varied traps of auto-affection, the most important of which is a disguised, if not open, desire for an "authentic identity," a self-presence that is somehow thought to lie beyond the politics of specularity. The self-reflection of the border intellectual privileges less a transitive search for what Said call "origins" than an intransitive hermeneutics of socio-cultural structuration, a political phenomenology attentive to the rhetorical construction of all discursive formations and subject-positions.

**In many ways the specular border intellectual is homologous with what Donna Haraway has defined as the "Cyborg." "There is no drive in cyborgs to produce total theory," she argues, "but there is an intimate experience of boundaries, their constructions and deconstructions"; "Cyborg imagery can suggest a way out of the maze of dualisms in which we have explained our bodies and our tools to ourselves. This is a dream not of a common language, but of a powerful infidel heteroglossia."[18] Said's valorization of "affiliation" over "filiation" can be read as form of "infidel heteroglossia." While the life of Joseph Conrad (with whose border crossings Said "begins" his professional career) also exemplifies a certain type of heteroglossia, Conrad's discomfort with and desire to overcome the dilemma of the border intellectual is marked by a dual desire: to belong to a select group, to become an insider – "one of us" – as Marlow puts it in *Lord Jim* and to value "fidelity" above all else. Unlike Conrad and like the Cyborg, the border intellectual must affirm the value of infidelity to cultures, nations, groups, institutions, etc., to the extent that these are defined in monologic, essentialist terms.

**For border intellectuals in the academy the political phenomenology founded on their positionality necessarily leads to two major consequences, both easily visible today. First, to what Aronowitz and Giroux call "border pedagogy," which urges students to scrutinize knowledge from the position of "border-crossers, as people moving in and out of borders constructed around coordinates of difference and power." This pedagogy encourages students "to develop a relationship of non-identity with their own subject positions and the multiple cultural, political, and social codes that constitute established boundaries of power, dependency, and possibility."[19]

Second, to the enormous amount of theoretical and archival work, begun during the 1960s and 70s and currently gathering greater momentum, by feminist and minority intellectuals, who have had to function on and against the borders of a Eurocentric and patriarchal cultural canon. Within this area, a great deal of criticism on the positionality of feminist and minority intellectuals – for instance, by Gayatri Spivak and bell hooks on minority/"Third World" feminist intellectuals, and by Harold Cruse and

Cornel West on African-American intellectuals – has explored in diverse ways the power and limitations inherent in the border status of such intellectuals. A recent anthology of essays on Chicano literature and culture, *Criticism in the Borderlands*, foregrounds more deliberately the politics of border crossing.[20]

Yet for minority and feminist intellectuals, the valorization of heterogeneity and a heterotopic site, of "homelessness," poses severe problems, for it tends to complicate the demands of and desire for identification and solidarity with the group from which the intellectual draws some of her or his power.

**The position of the border subject, complicated and precarious, can generate, when appropriately cultivated, as it is by intellectuals like Said and Wright, a tense productivity that resists stability and the coercive tendencies of fixed, indigenous identities. Such an appropriation can transform the predicament of the border intellectual into a fruitful and powerful asset.

Notes

I would like to thank the following for commenting on earlier drafts of this essay: Nancy Armstrong, David Lloyd, Alicia Ostriker, Donna Przybylowicz, Mark Rose, Jochen Schulte-Sasse, Muhammad Siddiq, Michael Sprinker, and Leonard Tennenhouse; The Humanities Research Institute at UC, Irvine provided a fellowship that allowed me to begin the essay; the Literary Criticism conference at Georgetown University afforded an opportunity to present a part of it as a talk.

 1 Edward W. Said, "Intellectuals in the Post-Colonial World," *Salmagundi*, no. 70–1 (Summer 1986), p. 49. Henceforth, citations from Edward Said's works will be included in the text and abbreviated as follows: *B* – *Beginnings: Intention and Method* (New York: Basic Books, 1979); IPFC – "Islam, Philology, and French Culture," *The World, the Text, and the Critic* (Cambridge, Mass.: Harvard University Press, 1983); IPW – "Intellectuals in the Post-Colonial World"; MW – "The Mind in Winter: Reflections on Life in Exile," *Harper's*, no. 269 (September 1984); QP – *The Question of Palestine* (New York: Times Books, 1979); SC – "Secular Criticism," *The World, the Text, and the Critic*; TT – "Travelling Theory," *The World, the Text, and the Critic*.
 2 J. Hillis Miller, 'Beginning with a Text," *Diacritics*, 4, no. 3 (1976), p. 4.
 3 Anton Shammas, *Arabesques*, trans. Vivian Eden (New York: Harper and Row, 1983).
 4 See *Inscriptions*, no. 5 (1989), which is devoted to a consideration of "Traveling Theories, *Traveling Theorists*."
 5 Robert A. Burt's book, *Two Jewish Justices: Outcasts in the Promised Land* (Berkeley: University of California Press, 1988), provides a fascinating study of the manner in which the stances of the exile and the immigrant taken up, respectively, by Justices Louis Brandeis and Felix Frankfurter, affected their legal opinions and attitudes and, in the long run, the Supreme Court itself. According to Burt, Brandeis "found a place to stand both in and apart from his

society. He was neither insider nor outsider. He found a unique place for himself, poised always at the boundary." By contrast, "to become a full-fledged American . . . Frankfurter had to separate himself from his immigrant past – as it were, by *force majeure*, by corporal . . . punishment" (citations come from pp. 13 and 39 respectively).

6 I have in mind here the nineteenth- and twentieth-century European colonialist's relation to Third World colonies, which defined the European as the controller and administrator. Settler colonialism, of the kind that was practiced in the US, Canada, Australia, and for a time in Kenya and southern Africa, is significantly different. This difference is marked precisely by the fact that at a given historical point (i.e., after the natives are sufficiently subjugated, if not destroyed) the designation used for Europeans coming to these countries changes from "colonialist" to "immigrant" or "settler."

7 For an excellent analysis of the appropriating colonialist gaze, see Mary Louise Pratt, "Scratches on the Face of the Country; or, What Mr Barrows Saw in the Land of the Bushmen," in *"Race," Writing, and Difference* (Chicago: University of Chicago Press, 1985), pp. 138–62.

8 I have in mind here, of course, a traditional, non-reflexive anthropological practice. James Clifford's analyses of the narrative structures of ethnographic accounts as well as what one might characterize, for the sake of brevity, as self-reflexive enthnography have successfully challenged the "objectivist" model. See, for example, Paul Rabinow, *Reflections on Fieldwork in Morocco* (Berkeley: University of California Press, 1977) and, more recently, Michael Jackson, *Path Toward a Clearing: Radical Empiricism and Ethnographic Inquiry* (Bloomington: Indiana Univ. Press, 1989); Kirin Narayan, *Storytellers, Saints, and Scoundrels: Folk Narratives in Hindu Religious Teaching* (Philadelphia: University of Pennsylvania Press, 1989); Ted Swedenburg, "Occupational Hazards: Palestine Ethnography," *Cultural Anthropology*, vol. 4, no. 3 (1989), pp. 265–72; Dorinne Kondo, *Crafting Selves: Power, Gender, and Discourse of Identity in a Japanese Workplace* (Chicago: University of Chicago Press, 1990); Smadar Lavie, *The Poetics of Military Occupation: Mzeina Allegories of Bedouin Identity Under Israeli and Egyptian Rule* (Los Angeles: University of California Press, 1990); Brackette Williams, *Stains on My Name, War in My Veins: Guyana and the Politics of Cultural Struggle* (Durham: Duke University Press, 1991).

Of particular relevance here are the meditations on border crossings and "relational knowledge" by Renato Rosaldo in *Culture and Truth: The Remaking of Social Analysis* (Boston: Beacon Press, 1989), and, in a different register, by Gloria Anzaldua, *Borderlands/La Frontera: The New Mestiza* (San Francisco: Spinsters/Aunt Lute, 1987).

9 Said's refusal to become an uncritically gregarious member of the US community and his utopian use of "Palestine" find fascinating parallels in (and invite a fuller comparison to) the stance of Justice Louis Brandeis, which is characterized by Robert Burt as follows: "The only homeland that Brandeis wholeheartedly embraced was thus an imaginary place – not America as it was, but only a romanticized Jeffersonian vision of a past America, and not Palestine as it was, but this same romantic vision of a Zion" (*Two Jewish Justices*, p. 17). However, Said's vision, it seems to me, is not really romantic, as Brandeis' might have been.

10 I am thinking here of various non-Western cultures as potentially counterhegemonic ones, for none of which Said speaks directly. Said is, of course, a

specific intellectual in the Foucauldian sense, but then by definition he does not represent others.

11 Hayden White, "Criticism as Cultural Politics," *Diacritics*, 4, no. 3 (1976), p. 13.
12 Miller, "Beginning with a Text," p. 2.
13 White, "Criticism as Cultural Politics," p. 12.
14 See the exchange between Bruce Robbins and Catherine Gallagher, *Diacritics*, 13, no. 3 (Fall 1983), pp. 69–77; 15, no. 2 (Summer 1985), pp. 37–43; 16, no. 3 (Fall 1986), pp. 67–72.
15 Bruce Robbins, "Homelessness and Worldliness," *Diacritics*, 13, no. 3 (Fall 1983), p. 69.
16 The most dramatic and penetrating representation of this rupture I know of appears in Zora Neale Hurston's *Their Eyes Were Watching God*, where the young Janie, the protagonist, is initially unable to recognize her black self in a photograph with other white children.
17 Michael Foucault, "Of Other Spaces,"*Diacritics*, 16, no. 1 (Spring 1986), pp. 22–7.
18 Donna Haraway, "A Manifesto for Cyborgs: Science, Technology, and Socialist Feminism in the 1980s," in *Coming to Terms: Feminism, Theory, Politics*, ed. Elizabeth Weed (New York: Routledge, 1989), p. 204.
19 Stanley Aronowitz and Henry A. Giroux, *Postmodern Education: Politics, Culture, and Social Criticism* (Minneapolis: University of Minnesota Press, 1991), pp. 199 and 200.
20 Hector Calderón and José David Saldívar, eds., *Criticism in the Borderlands: Studies in Chicano Literature, Culture, and Ideology* (Durham: Duke University Press, 1991). According to the editors, this book is in part "an invitation . . . for readers . . . to remap the borderlands of theory and theorists. Our work in the eighties and nineties, along with that of other postcolonial intellectuals, moves, travels, as they say, between first and third worlds, between cores and peripheries, centers and margins. The theorists in this book see their texts always "written for" in our local and global borderlands."

6

ANTINOMIES OF EXILE: SAID AT THE FRONTIERS OF NATIONAL NARRATIONS

——

Ella Shohat

In a situation where critical academics are marginalized, their power visible mainly in debates about the canon, Edward Said has managed to break the conventional public-sphere boundaries which keep critical intellectuals out of the establishment-linked mass media. In Said's case, academic vocation has not been divorced from political activism. At a time when the academic Left often fails to engage sufficiently with "crude" political matters, Said constitutes a contemporary exemplar of precisely the kind of "worldly" intellectual that he has himself described with such acuity.

Whenever an academic/political activity requires a "Palestinian speaker," Edward Said's name emerges; he is forever "burdened" with the glorious weight of that representation. Said's intervention has above all attempted to break the assymetrical representations between Israel and Palestine within the United States, where Zionism has undertaken "to speak for Palestine and the Palestinians," resulting in "a blocking operation, by which the Palestinian cannot be heard from (or represent himself) directly from the world stage."[1]

Said has negotiated a discursive space for a suppressed national narrative within a specific intellectual and political conjuncture. His project of introducing an alternative to the Zionist master-narrative must be understood within the context of the symbiotic geopolitical and cultural-discursive links between Israel and the US. A discussion of these symbiotic links, I will argue, helps us comprehend the exact nature of Said's political and intellectual intervention, and suggests a continuity between Said's scholarship on the imperial imagination, particularly in *Orientalism*, and his more explicitly polemical and political work. Rather than perform an exegesis of his writings on worlds, texts, and critics, I will focus on Edward Said the critic "in" the world, and on his impact and reception in debates about Zionism. I will explore Said's role as a representative figure of "Palestine"

(*Filastin*) in the US seen in his academic writings as well as in his myraid activities, lectures, journalistic writings, media engagements – a representative figure, in short, whose praxis of representation transgresses the rigid codes of Israeli national narration.

Edward Said's work is situated on the fragile borders separating cultures, nationalities and discourses. He writes on the "West" and in the West from the perspective of intimate familiarity with Western culture, and yet still as an Arab, an outsider, whose historical identity was formed on the colonized margins of the British Empire (Palestine and Egypt). Similarly, he writes on the "East" as someone who has lived *fil kharij* (in the exterior) for years, a fact which again testifies to his positioning along an almost invisible dialectical line of insider/outsider: "My background is a series of displacements and expatriations which cannot ever be recuperated . . . I am always in and out of things, and never really of anything for very long."[2] Writing in exile is not here merely a metaphor for the "postmodern condition," but also an actual experience of the impossibility of returning to a millenial locus of community. Said in this sense brings to the often amorphous postmodernist sense of exile a telling material and historical edge. A displaced member of a displaced community, Said does not resort to a metaphysical contemplation of home and exile, nor to an aesthetic romantic-elegiac reflection on lost origins. Rather, his work brings these dimensions to an acutely political engagement, where the intellectual is at all times called upon to examine "word politics." Edward Said writes his position as an Arab-Palestinian into his work, refusing the illusory transparency of much academic work. "In many ways," Said writes, "my study of Orientalism has been an attempt to inventory the traces upon me, the Oriental subject, of the culture whose domination has been so powerful a factor in the life of all Orientals."[3]

This is one of the ways in which this chapter will engage in a kind of dialogue with Said's work, for I too write as an "Oriental,"[4] as an Arab Jew, or more specifically as an Iraqi-Israeli who cannot go back to my parents' native Baghdad despite the fact that Jews have been there since at least the Babylonian exile, and as a member of a marginalized majority in Israel that has experienced the systematic discrimination and institutional suppression of their Middle Eastern history and culture, and as an academic who now lives in the US and writes in English as a third language, I am therefore vitally implicated in the dialogue with Edward Said's work. This chapter continues for me an attempt to ponder Said's position and positioning, his status as a Palestinian in exile (even if by now he is in many ways at home in this exile). My engagement with Said's work goes hand in hand with an attempt to understand the historical, political and cultural links between the suppressed narrative of the Jews of the Muslim Arab world and that of Palestinians in its implications for our complex Oriental Jewish-Arab identity and our uprooted and displaced condition in the wake of the Israeli/Arab conflict.

The unmasking of the intellectual's "transparency" in Said's work is linked to a recognition of the intellectual's communitarian "affiliations," and the interplay of a multiplicity of communities and identities, particularly in circumstances of direct conflict: "No one would deny that critics belong to a community, work in a sphere, are connected to a people." Yet, Said continues, "there is a considerable moral difference between the critic whose connection is to an oppressing society, and a critic whose connection is to an *oppressed* one."[5] More specifically, "Which takes more confidence for a Jew today, to denounce Palestinian terrorism along with Reagan and Schultz, or to denounce Israeli state terrorism with Chomsky and Shahak?"[6] Edward Said's task has thus been multi-dimensional. He reassesses the role of the intellectual as critic, combatting the tradition of liberal and even leftist intellectuals in the US who, on the whole, have had difficulty sustaining a progressive and critical stance in relation to the Middle East.

It is perhaps not a coincidence that critical debate around the question of "national culture" has tended to avoid the "delicate" question of Israel/ Palestine, betraying a feeling of discomfort with applying anti-colonialist discourse to that region. The still-burning memory of the Holocaust, as well as fears of stigmatization as "self-hating" or "anti-Semitic" malcontents, compounded by a kind of ideological bewilderment in the face of Zionism, have blocked a coherent alternative approach to the issues, and have placed Said's work at the razor's edge of national contestations. Israeli national existence (and as a consequence the encounter between it and Palestinian national existence) is in some ways anomalous. And this anomalous character is itself inseparable from the particular European Jewish historical experience as that of a dispersed, cosmopolitan, and syncretic people with an ambivalent relation to the very idea of the East. On the one hand, the Jews of the diaspora have been inextricably mingled with the life of the West, yet Jews are also linked to the East. As an *ethnos* with historical roots in Palestine, speaking (in Israel) a Semitic language, whose religious idiom is intimately linked with the topography of the Middle East, European Jews are connected by tradition to the East, and have often been seen as an alien "Eastern" people within the West. In the case of Sephardic Oriental Jews – largely from Asia and North Africa – the balance shifts even further to the Eastern side of the dichotomy, for here we find a people historically and culturally rooted, in some instances for millennia, in the societies of the Orient. The paradox of Israel, however, is that it ended a diaspora, characterized by Jewish ritualistic nostalgia for the East, only to found a state whose ideological and geopolitical orientation has been almost exclusively toward the West. Although Jews have historically been the victims of anti-Semitic orientalism, Israel as a state has become the perpetrator of orientalist attitudes and actions.

The Israel/Palestine national conflict, as a result, does not fit neatly into any standard categorizations. Just as Israel partakes of both "East" and "West," it also constitutes both a "First World" and a "Third World" country. Israel can be considered "Third World" in a strangely double and even paradoxical sense: first, in terms of the analogies between the struggle for Jewish liberation and Third World struggles against colonialism (Jews, it might be suggested, formed Europe's internal "other" long before the nations in Latin America, Africa and Asia became its external "other"); and secondly, in terms of Israel's structural analogies to the Third World. In purely demographic terms, an overwhelming majority of the Israeli population is of Third World origin: Palestinians make up about 20 percent of the population in Israel proper, and Sephardic Jews, most of whom came within very recent memory from Third World countries such as Iraq, Morocco, Egypt, Turkey, Iran, and India, constitute another 50 percent of the population. Thus, a total of 70 percent of the population is Third World or Third World-derived (above 80 percent if one includes the West Bank and Gaza Strip). In political, economic, and cultural terms, Palestinians and Sephardic-Oriental Jews in Israel have been marginalized and denied access to virtually all power. And if Palestinians form a captive nation, Sephardim, as a Jewish Third-World people, form a semi-colonized nation-within-the-nation. In Israel, then, European Ashkenazic Jews, a distinct numerical minority, constitute a First-World elite dominating, in different ways, both Palestinians and Oriental-Sephardic Jews.

Israel's anomolous character, then, makes anti-colonialist discourse at once applicable and non-applicable to it. On the one hand the ideological roots of Zionism can be traced to the conditions of nineteenth- and early twentieth-century Europe, as a reaction not only against anti-Semitism but also to the rapid expansion of capitalism and of European empire-building. Israel, in this sense, has clearly been allied to Western colonial and neo-colonial interests, has deployed colonialist-inflected discourse, and has exercised colonialist policies toward Palestinian land and people. Hebrew texts portray pre-Zionist Palestine as an unproductive desert awaiting Western penetration and fecundation. The question is further complicated by the socialist pretensions, and at times the socialist achievements, of Zionism. In the nationalist discourse, the conflict between the socialist ideology of Zionism and the real praxis of Euro-Jewish domination in Palestine was resolved in the inviting thesis that the Arab masses, subjected to feudalism and exploited by their own countrymen, could only benefit from Zionist praxis. This presentation embodies the historically positive self-image of Israelis as involved in a non-colonial enterprise and therefore morally superior in their aspirations.

At the same time, Zionism cannot be simplistically equated with colonialism or imperialism. Unlike colonialism, Zionism constituted a response to millennial oppression and, in contradistinction to the classical paradigm, metropolis and colony in this case were located in the self-same place. The colonial mind-set which regarded non-European continents as "lands without people" here becomes inseparable from the Zionist concept of a Jewish people in need of land. *Eretz Israel* (the Land of Israel), furthermore, had always been the symbolic locus of Jewish cultural identity. Israel does not represent a repetition of the classical colonial case of European expeditions into America, Africa and Asia, since the ideology of Return to the Motherland (a view of the land as belonging to the Jews, with the Palestinians merely "guests"), in some ways constitutes a departure from traditional colonial discourse.

These anomalous aspects of Zionist colonization inform the attacks on Edward Said's work, including those from liberal and at times leftist Americans (Jews and non-Jews). Criticism of Said – the debates published in *Social Text*, *Grand Street*, *Critical Inquiry*, and *Tikkun* – reveals the discursive struggle of a Palestinian representative working for national recognition within a left/liberal American context. The kind of argument that can be taken for granted in leftist circles in relation to other Third World regions provokes serious resistance in the case of the Israeli/Arab conflict. Said has had to operate, furthermore, in an ambiance where the Arab has been portrayed with negative colonialist imagery, particularly so in the mass-mediated evocations of the terrorist. As a consequence, Said has been compelled to interrogate the very word "terrorism," challenging its political uses, for example in *The Question of Palestine*, *Covering Islam* and *Blaming the Victims*[7] without necessarily endorsing the activities that are made to fall under that term. Rather, He points, rather, to the disproportionate massacre of Palestinians by Israelis, thereby raising a question relevant to other regions such as those in Latin America: the question of state terrorism. But above all, Said has striven not so much to justify these acts, as to root them in a history of desperation and denial.

CIVILITY, TERRORISM, RAGE

It is perhaps not surprising, therefore, that one of the favored strategies used to discredit Edward Said has been systematically to associate him with the presumably irrational rage of the terrorist. This has been particularly true since the beginning of the *intifada*, precisely when the Palestinian image began to acquire more sympathetic resonances. As is typical of mainstream denunciations of anti-colonial critics, Edward Said has been accused of a presumably irresponsible anger. Edward Alexander linked Said directly to terrorism in his infamous *Commentary* article, "Professor of Terror," foregrounding Said's supposed "double career as literary scholar and ideologue of terrorism."[8] Alexander calls Said's language the "verbal equivalent of the weapons wielded by his colleagues on the Palestinian National Council." "Said," he argues, "spills ink to justify their spilling blood."[9] Having thus "detected" the terrorist behind the academic, Alexander forecloses any dialogue with a conflicting perspective, delegitimizing it through *ad hominem* character assassination.

William Phillips, in his *Partisan Review* comment on the debate in *Critical Inquiry*,[10] claims Said's "rough attacks on Israel and on three professors who argued with him . . . sounded more like the work of a street fighter than a scholar."[11] In the context of the *intifada*, it is difficult not to associate the image of a street fighter with that of the *shabab*, the young people fighting in the streets against Israeli occupation. But Said's words in the corridors of the American academy appear to Phillips in some ways more efficacious than the stones in the streets of Gaza and the West Bank. He is shocked to see Said in *Critical Inquiry* ("that journal of staid, abstruse literary criticism"), assaulting "them [the three professors] with abuse and savage irony."[12] (Can the adjectives be accidental when applied to a spokesperson for anti-colonial critique?) Phillips also notes, with typical liberal concern for "civility," that "I have not agreed with Said's deconstructionist and marxist thinking, but to my knowledge, in his literary and cultural criticism Said usually has followed the rules and courtesies of academic discourse. Yet apparently here he is acting in his other, political role, that of a Palestinian spokesman – indeed, as I understand, then member of the PLO Central Committee." Said's official Palestinian position as a member not of the Palestine Liberation Organization but of the Palestinian National Council (the Palestinian parliament in exile) is distorted and invoked here to discredit his struggle to narrate Palestinian experience within an academic framework. Phillips' eagerness to imagine an official PLO position for Said forms part of a systematic effort to associate him with terrorism, for the PLO has characteristically been portrayed as a terrorist organization by Western media. Said is thus presented as a professional with an agenda, whose intellectual judgement, as a result, inevitably lacks "objectivity." Certain kinds of political activist discourses, it is implied, are incompatible with intellectual honesty. At the same time, academics who are not officially linked to a political organization, it is generally assumed, somehow possess an olympian objectivity "above" narrow partisan perspectives.

More important are the assumptions underlying such criticism, assumptions much cultivated by the upper classes, permeated by imperial ideology, which the ideal of a "civilized politeness elevate" implying the control of emotions, since emotions are viewed, in direct opposition to rationality. If the academic intellectual, in other words, expresses emotions, he or she is incoherent, irrational, and consequently his or her analysis does not pass the "objectivity" test. (There is of course here an implicit gender and national-ethnic bias concerning how one is to dress, speak, and write properly, in order to pass the test of "rational argument.") The mind/body dichotomy that still holds sway in the academy is based on the binary thinking that cannot imagine a passionate or angry and still coherent argument. For Phillips, who asks, "Could it be that his [Said's] anger breaks into his prose?,"[13] a taboo has been clearly violated. The words "rage" and "anger" cast suspicion on Said's work. Similarly, Micahel Walzer writes: "For Jewish supporters of Israel, there is only one politics, and we cannot design it for ourselves; Said designs it for us in the image of his rage."[14] And Mark Krupnick, in his *Tikkun* article, significantly entitled "Edward Said: Discourse and Palestinian Rage," criticizes Said for the "tone," for the "kind of language" which is "by no means unusual in Said's political writing."[15]

Why is rage necessarily wrong? The debate over tone and manner is not in fact what it seems. It makes possible a diversion from the heart of Said's political critique. Phillips dimissively summarizes Said's *Critical Inquiry* article as "a familiar anti-Israel position," while Krupnick does not address Said's major critique of the Exodus narrative, i.e. its oppressive dimensions. Rather than simplistically applauding the liberatory aspects of Exodus, Said "revisits" the pre-figuring colonial aspects of conquest from an imagined Canaanite perspective. The censure of "rage" implies that the intellectuals involved in these exchanges speak from positions of equality as community representatives, thus obscuring the basic question of asymmetrical power relations and the history of Palestinian dispossession caused by the very establishment of the state of Israel. The idea that we do not live on the West Bank and therefore should not excuse the presumed "manifest incivility,"[16] furthermore, is a form of literal-mindedness, a refusal to appreciate the underlying pain of seeing one's people being systematically dispossessed, exiled and massacred.

Through a poignant historical irony, the Jews, who have themselves been oppressed in the name of "civility," end up using this same discourse to attack a critic of oppression. John Murray Cuddihy in *The Ordeal of Civility* attributes certain conflicts within modern Jewish identity to the Enlightenment ideal of "civilized" behavior, arguing that modern Jewish identity is largely a result of the drive to accept "civilized" behavior and the need to reject "uncivilized behavior."[17] The crucial question, to my mind, concerns the tone an intellectual is expected to adopt, particularly when that intellectual is constantly forced to defend his people's right to exist, to articulate repeatedly what has been denied, to explain repeatedly the basic principle, the refusal of a people to cease to exist. And this in a situation where Said's very existence in exile, as he so eloquently testifies to in *After the Last Sky*, is a direct consequence of that brutality.[18] What is most striking in this aesthetic critique of Said's tone is the refusal to see that a "civilized" tone and manner might itself be seen as offensive, aggressive and even violent, when it serves to mask the thousands of brutalities peformed against dominated people. Such is the case when the elision of the Palestinian narrative is written into an antiseptic "civilized" analysis, for example the elision of a Palestinian perspective in the Zionist usages of the Exodus biblical narrative. Furthermore, is it not usually the relatively privileged who enjoy the luxury of controlling their emotions? Don't we see here a repetition of the perennial association of the oppressed (women, Third World peoples) with violence, possession, hysteria?

It would be amusing, were it not so tragic, to observe the clear annoyance on the part of a certain Jewish establishment at Edward Said's emergence into academic and media prominence. That Said is singled out for attack is revealing, since there are many other legitimate Palestinian (and non-Palestinian, including Israeli) academics and scholars who take a position similar to his. But Said, unlike most Palestinian intellectuals, is not academically confined to "Middle East studies." He is also a celebrated authority on Western culture. In its sense of the worldly, his writing shares certain features with the work of the (mainly Jewish) New York intellectuals who contributed to the same journals, Commentary and Partisan Review, during a happier period of their history.[19] An interesting division separates the response to Said's academic scholarship from his more explicitly political writing. Whereas his academic writing constitutes a relatively rational "good object," his political writings, inseparable from his intellectual-academic achievements, are branded with rage and terrorism. Despite Said's intimacy with Western culture, then, the mere fact of his Arabness is used to disqualify his writing. Edward Alexander's personal attack, commenting on what Said might have whispered in Arafat's ear during the PNC meeting in Algiers ("Who can forget . . . television images of this intellectual-in-ordinary to the king of terror, whispering [who knows what?] into his master's ear . . .?"),[20] operates on the same continuum as the physical harassment Said has had to endure, reaching its apogee when he was put on the Jewish Defense League hit-list after Meir Kahane's murder.

ORIENTALIST IMAGES AND THE POLITICS OF STYLE

What is it about the figure of Edward Said that has become so threatening from a Zionist perspective? On one level, it is a question of the imagery of nations, of how they are represented and self-represented, particularly in the West. In this sense, it is instructive to look into Said's image and reception in the delicate context of the Israeli/Palestinian question. One thing that has haunted the Israeli and American reports on the recent wave of Palestinian spokespersons is not simply the content of their arguments, but their *style* of presentation and representation; in other words, the politics of style. Spokespersons such as Said, Ibrahim Abu-Lughod, James Zogby, and Rashid Khalidi defy the stereotype Arab look of thick mustaches, hooked noses, or halting English and heavy Arab accent. They can also speak within the American media's discursive norms. Said, whose area of academic specialization is not Middle Eastern studies but English and Comparative Literature, presents an entirely "mainstream" image. Since Arabs have been consistently represented as antithetical to all things Western, the idea of a spokesperson on Palestinian-Arab rights intimately aware of Western culture is extremely disturbing, particularly for the Israelo-centric politics of representation. The point is a sensitive one for Israel's self-image and for official Israeli propaganda, which, along the lines of the culture of Empire, portrays "Arabs" as ignorant of Western civilization. Historical encounters between Arabs and the West, for example during the "Golden Age" in Iberia and during the two hundred years of colonial rule, are minimized.[21] Such a representation has been especially crucial for a nation-state that is geographically situated in the Middle East but whose imaginary constantly revolves around the "West." Geopolitically, furthermore, Israel has been "marketed" as suitable for Western interests in the region. During the *intifada* the official Israeli tourist advertisement on American television, for example, appealed to that geopolitical friendship by proclaiming "Come to Israel, come be with friends," visually emphasizing the camaraderie of an "all American" Waspish-looking family, and its counterpart in Israel, an Euro-Israeli (Ashkenazic) family.

The full creation of that image entailed playing down the presence and cultural impact of the West on the Arab world. It is precisely Said's expert knowledge of the West's "high" culture, articulated in such books as *Beginnings* and *The World, The Text, and the Critic*, that is as at least subliminally threatening for Zionist discourse.[22] Israeli journalistic accounts of Said, routinely stress his impeccable English, as though it formed part of a manipulative scheme; if the "Americans" could see the "essential truth" behind the images and sounds of his fluent English, they would not grant the Palestinian spokesperson any sympathy. Since the trope of language has been central to the ideology of civility, Said's "Englishness" disturbs and disorients the Enlightenment binarism of Zionist discourse. The exclusion of Jews from "civilization" in anti-Semitic and in particular Nazi racism, ironically, also had a linguistic dimension. The Jews, even when fluent in the German language, could never really possess it since they had their own hidden tongue, the true tongue that articulates their Jewish Otherness.[23] The perennial mark of exile and diaspora, bilingualism, is quite similarly raised by Zionists towards the Easterners of the American continent, the Arab-Americans, whose English, it is insinuated, masks Arab conspiracies.

These symptoms are acutely present in a long Hebrew-language article entitled "Ashafei ha'Tikshoret" ("The media experts," ashafei/experts being a pun on the Hebrew acronym for the PLO, "Ashaf"), published amidst the *intifada* in Israel's most widely circulated daily, *Yedioth Ahronoth*.[24] The first page shows a large photo of Edward Said and Ibrahim Abu-Lughod after their meeting with George Schultz (the same photo was also published

in a JDL newsletter calling them the "PLO professors"). The Hebrew article
was concerned with the "conquest of the American media" by the Palestinians, focusing on the fact that among the "advocates of the PLO in the US
are a number of Palestinian intellectuals, polished, articulate, knowledgable
about the issues, and fluent in English. All of them speak and look like
Americans – and indeed they are after twenty or thirty years in the US." The
article verifies this observation through interviews with Israeli Orientalists:

> The American media today host Palestinian spokespersons who look more
> and more like Palestinian versions of Bibi [Benjamin] Netanyahu. "They are
> superstars," Dr Yossi Ulmart, an Orientalist on sabbatical in the US,
> expressed his amazement. "Impressive people, with senior academic positions,
> who without inhibition exploit their status in order to defend their national
> case. And I do not say it as a condemnation. They are polished, slick.
> Sometimes it seems as if they were filed with sand paper."
>
> "Their style is professional," says professor Eli Reches, an Orientalist who
> is also on sabbatical in the US. "You won't find the emotional propaganda
> that characterized PLO spokespersons in the past. You don't hear from them
> unreasonable accusations such as 'you want to destroy the Arabs.' This style
> has gone. Their message sounds much more moderate than the Israeli
> message."

Although they occupy opposite ends of the political spectrum, Palestinian
spokespersons such as Edward Said are compared to Benjamin Netanyahu;
this should not come as a surprise. Netanyahu's reactionary discourse (he
often speaks of and in the name of the "civilized world," i.e. Israel and the
West as opposed to the uncivilized Arab East) perfectly enacts the American
professional manner: he speaks with very little accent, presumably offering
a reasonable outlook. Netanyahu represents precisely the dominant Israeli
phantasy of Americanization, and reinforces the image of Israel as a
Western entity, not only for the world but also for itself. Said's knowledge
of the West and his professional style disturb this binarism.

Although the article concerned several leading Arab-American spokespersons, it began with Said, focusing throughout on his "propagandistic"
methods:

> Edward Said knows how to do it. His article on Yassir Arafat in the New
> York magazine *Interview* was excellent. Everything was there: Arafat in
> slippers, Arafat as freedomfighter, as politician, as loyal friend, as victim, as
> philosopher. Prof. Said arrived with Arafat's portrait for *Interview* as part of
> the Palestinian propaganda effort in the United States. A sophisticated effort,
> wise, ramified, successful. Edward Said is a favorite, frequent visitor in the
> American media.
>
> *Interview* . . . is not exactly made for the Arafat-type . . . the combination
> of Arafat and *Interview* proves that the Palestinian propaganda is shrewd and

sharp, and effective. It understands that it must push Arafat's image into media domains which are not explicitly political or news items. Said presented a human, determined, humorous Arafat. The Israeli who appeared this year in a long portrait-article in *Interview* is Amos Oz. And here is Arafat! The roadblock was broken: Arafat the terrorist is a legitimate subject for an elite magazine which is not political but cultural, somewhat eccentric, very stylized.

But, perhaps without Edward Said, Arafat would not have reached this magazine.

In other words, Edward Said is perhaps the real story. Said and Prof. Ibrahim Abu-Lughod. And with them another dozen American-Palestinians, professors and intellectuals, who constitute the army of Palestinian advocates in the US. *Interview* bought Arafat because Said, a Professor of Literature at Columbia, sold him to the magazine . . . Edward Said is the combination of an intellectual, a friend of Arafat, an American, photogenic, and relevant. It is not possible to bypass or to ignore him. He won't model tomorrow for men's perfume or for Subaro. He is not the 60's boys, Jerry Rubin or Abbie Hoffman who ended up as a kind of caricature ten years after the Hippy struggle. Said is made of solid material . . .

This image of efficiency and professionalism is therefore read as disturbing the binarism between "us" (the West, presumably including Israel) and "them" (Palestinians, Arab terrorists), a redrawing of boundaries that is alarming for Israel in this battle over images.

He is the best known of the Palestinian advocates in the US, a "superstar" in the words of Dr Yossi Ulmart. Yet Ulmart argues that the man does not loathe lies, twisting facts, dirty tricks and blows under the belt. He does not have a command of the facts like some of his colleagues, but he has everything required for a media star in the US: his English is perfect . . . and without a foreign accent. He looks excellent, charismatic, polished, brilliant. You will never catch him without an answer.

The article goes on to describe the work of Palestinian spokespersons as a process in which "the PLO is taking control of the American screen. The screen is the American consciousness. And they are taking control of the consciousness . . ." It also observes that "in Israel it is understood what's going on." Even when Palestinians like Said express their wish for dialogue, the gesture is interpreted as an Arab scheme. To be a Palestinian intellectual, photogenic and fluent in English, the article implies, is just another trompe-l'oeil meant to lure the naive image-captive Americans. The pun in the title, "Ashafei ha'Tikshoret," which alludes to both experts and the PLO, is symptomatic of this cynical tone and attitude. The Hebrew word used for "expert," "Ashaf" also signifies "magician," "sorcerer."

The question of style, in other words, threatens the long-established paradigm of East versus West with regard to the Israeli/Palestinian conflict, particularly within the Western media context. The issue bears on which

nation belongs on this side of the meta-narrative of progress and the
"civilized world." At the same time, the attacks on Said suggest that his
writings on the Palestinian question have touched another deeply held
narrative, that of the Jew as victim. Said has often lamented the difficulty
of narrating the Palestinian national experience vis-a-vis the Jewish history
of victimization in Europe. Said's major task as a representative of an
oppressed community has been to combat the dominant discourse of
another community – the (European) Jewish – whose self representation
has become virtually synonymous with its history of repression. Even the
English terminology regarding the Palestinian/Israeli conflict tends to be
borrowed from official Israeli language, for example referring to the 1948
war also as the Israeli "Independence War" (*milkhemet ha'atzmaut*) and to
the 1967 war as the "Six Day War" (*milkhemet sheshet hayamim*), without
acknowledging the Arab perspective, which refers to 1948 as "*al nakba*"
(the catastrophe) and to 1967 as "*al naksa*" (the setback.)

EXILE, DIASPORA, AND THE DISCOURSE OF VICTIMIZATION

The assertion of a Palestinian nation not simply subsumable under the
category of "Arabs" has become crucial in the work of Palestinian
intellectuals, for only this distinction could permit the narration of Palestinian victimization. The events of 1967, a turning-point in Palestinian history,
encouraged Palestinian self-assertion in the face of corrupt Arab regimes.
The occupied territories, no longer under Egyptian and Jordanian control,
came under the responsibility of Palestinians themselves. The image of the
Palestinians as "passive" refugees was transformed into that of active but
sinister "terrorists" in the Western media, and the *fidayeen*, or liberation
fighters of "non-aligned" discourse. The Jewish image in the American
media, meanwhile, altered after the establishment of Israel from that of
diaspora victim and refugee to the heroic and overpowering Israeli *sabra*,
the fighter for Jewish liberation. "Israel" thus made possible the media
transmogrification of the passive "Diaspora victim" into the heroic Jew,
best exemplified in Paul Newman's incarnation of the Israeli in *Exodus*.[25]
But if the Jews, the "Easterners" of anti-Semitic European discourse, could
be re-admitted into the West via their grand act of physical rupture from
Europe and simultaneous "spiritual" reintegration with it (a Western-style
state serving as evidence for the Jewish metamorphosis into "normal"
people), the Arab-Palestinians, because of their "inherent Easternness,"
could not be celebrated as enlightened Westerners, nor as heroic nationalist
fighters. For the Palestinian version of nationalism has been formulated in
the tradition of anti-colonial, anti-Western struggles. The "New Jew," the
Israeli, came to be seen as an extension of the West due to Western

identification with its Middle Eastern representative, Israel, whose own ideologues have insisted on its Western soul despite its geographical location in the East, and despite the fact that the majority of the Jewish Israelis are not of European but of Asian and African origins. (An ironic example of Israel's Western image is its participation, despite its location in Asia, in the annually televised European popular music contest, the Eurovision Song Contest. Israel has based its positive image in the West on a moral argument linking the Jewish history of victimization with the colonial ideals of enlightenment. Official Israeli representatives, such as David Ben Gurion, Golda Meir, Abba Eban, and more recently Benjamin Netanyahu, have appeared in the American media insistently portraying Israel as an integral part of the "civilized world," a phrase buttressed by its claim to be "the only democracy in the Middle East." Jewish and Zionist institutions in the US have made great efforts to incorporate Jewish history into the consciousness and conscience of America. Jewishness has been equated with Zionism and "Israeliness" to the point that the two terms have become virtually synonymous. Until the late 1940s, however, Zionism was a minority movement among world Jewry. The implementation of institutions and discourses meant above all the understanding of basic experiences – diaspora, exile, and return to the motherland – as a uniquely Jewish narrative. Jewish institutions have managed in the post-Holocaust era to bring to center-stage the horrible experience of the Jews of Europe. Palestinian national discourse therefore threatens the central Jewish role on the privileged margins of Europe and Euro-America. Subtle and not-so-subtle forms of censorship have been directed towards any articulation of such concepts as exile when used in a non-Jewish context. (Reportedly, even the journal *Diaspora* was pressurized for applying its titular concept to other non-Jewish nations such as the Armenians and Palestinians.) The Holocaust, written with a capital "H," is seen as uniquely Jewish; formidable resistance bars usage of the term for other histories of genocide, for example that of Native Americans.

In the Israeli/Palestinian context, the terms of exile and return have led some of Said's critics to accuse him of narrative envy of Zionism. Often with little apparent knowledge of Palestinian culture, they ethnocentrically define that culture's national discourse as lack, as devoid of distinct icons and symbols, acting as if Jews have a monopoly over the concepts of exile and return. This penchant for seeing Said's work as an attempt to create "imitations of Jewish stories,"[26] must be viewed, I suggest, in relation to the growing Arab-American institutional presence in the US. Although the Arab-American organizations were established in the mid-1950s partly to fight the pro-Israeli policy of the American government, they were enabled to speak and fight for Arab issues in the US and in the Middle East only after the 1967 war. The same Hebrew language article discussed earlier explicitly states this anxiety over Palestinian institutional mimicry and latently manifests what I would term subaltern envy:

> The American-Jewish society serves as a model of imitation for the Arabs. Since 1967, scores of Palestinian Arab organizations, which resembled very much the Jewish ones, appeared. The national union of Palestinians in the US resembles in its function the Jewish lobby of AIPAC. The Palestinian organization for aid was established on the pattern of the JOINT in Detroit in 1978. The United Palestinian appeal was established in 1980. Even the abbreviation, UPA, resembles that of UJA.
>
> At the end of 1980 the organization of the Arab-American Anti-Discrimination Committee which resembles the Jewish Anti-defamation League was established. And in 1982 the organization of Arab women in the US, which resembles Wizo organization, was established.
>
> The First American Palestinian Congress took place at the Biltmore in New York. In the same hall where Ben Gurion called for the establishment of the State of Israel in 1946, Samia Parson, the chairman of the Arab Congress, called for the establishment of an independent Palestinian State. The world, he hoped, will already understand the hint.[27]

Edward Said, more specifically, is seen as inheriting the place of that distinguished representative of "civilized Jews," Abba Eban,[28] whose native language is English: "In a certain sense, Said inherited the place of Abba Eban in the American media. Through the years, Abba Eban represented a small Israel, courageous, intelligent, sane."[29]

The question of victimization is crucial for the representation of Jewish experience and identity and for the liberationist Zionist project. The suggestion that a history of other victims might be told, that there might be victims of Jewish nationalism, leads to violent opposition, or, in the case of liberals, to epistemological vertigo. Zionist discourse betrays the symptoms of acute discomfort with the very idea of a Jewish victimizer, since Jewish popular tradition characteristically narrates its suffering at the hands of oppressors. Jewish holidays recount tales of persecution by a host of historical enemies, and Jewish rituals relay the collective lore of an interminable series of victimizations and near-victimizations.

But Jewish history provides no basis for viewing Jews as *collective* oppressors. Nothing in the historical culture of Judaism prepares its intellectuals for such a tale. When after 1967, Israelis found themselves, in the clear position of an occupying power, what were intellectuals, primed historically to know themselves only as victims in relation to neighboring collectivities, to do? How were they to deal with the inversion of the traditional imagery of David and Goliath when Palestinian children, armed only with slings, were confronting Israeli soldiers armed to the teeth? The liberal-Zionist peace movements in Israel and in the West embody the diverse compromise solutions encountered in response to this challenge, solutions involving half-way confrontations, partial focalizations and problematic displacements, obvious in the debates with Said in *Social Text*, *Critical Inquiry*, *Grand Street*, and *Tikkun*. A predisposition to a discourse of victimization leads to arguments that ultimately present the Israeli "peacenik" as the principal victim of the Israeli/Arab conflict. The bewildered question, "where is the Palestinian equivalent to Peace Now?", distracts attention from the national oppression of the Palestinian people toward the supposed absence of an interlocutor for the peace-loving Israeli liberals. Ignoring the crucial question of asymmetries in power relations between Israelis and Palestinians, the liberal-Zionist lament has focused attention on the *sabras'* own torment as those caught between the Israeli right wing and the Palestinians. The *sabra* liberal is thus represented as an innocent Isaac sacrificed on the altar of peace.

Edward Said's writings, particularly as encapsulated in such titles as "Zionism from the Standpoint of its Victims," and "Blaming the Victims," touched the paradoxical core nature of Israeli-Jewish-Zionist identity.[30] Said's work, furthermore, testifies to a historical irony by which the cultural signifiers of Jewishness – exile, diaspora, wandering, homelessness – have become applicable to Palestinians themselves. Israel has very rarely had to confront "civilized" Palestinians who speak from within the West, yet who deconstruct the myth of the "civilized world." The Israeli obsession with Said and with Palestinian intellectuals in the West results partly from fear of a blockage to Israel's own self-presentation in the West. Said's critique of Walzer, for example, focuses precisely on this question of address: "Walzer's political and moral study is addressed to us 'in the West' and his prose is dotted with *us*'s and *ours*, the net result of which is to mobilize a community of interpretation . . ."[31]

Correlated with the issue of victimization are the concepts of exile and diaspora that permeate the Jewish-Zionist debates with Said. Hitherto "diaspora" and "exile" have largely been monopolized on the American intellectual scene to refer to the Jewish experience. Zionism often saw its role as a transformer of "abnormal" Jewish existence in the *gola* (diaspora) into that of a normal nation. Its Hebrew motto was *migola legeula*, 'from diaspora to redemption'. For Zionism, it was necessary to create a rupture with the *shtetel* Jews, and to incorporate the "extraterritorial Jews" into "history." Exile (*galut* in Hebrew) from the promised land, the ingathering from the four corners of the globe, constitutes in Zionist discourse a mark of ethnic-national uniqueness. Said's explicit evocation of the displacements experienced by Palestinians became, from a Zionist perspective, a haunting mirror-image. The imagination of the territory – the Land of Israel or Palestine – attempts to recuperate identities, to construct them in relation to a Motherland, indeed the same homeland for both national imaginations. Said's narration of Palestinian people in exile (*manfa* in Arabic) from the very same "Promised Land," and the dream of return (*awdah*), raises

questions about a history that simultaneously genereted the ingathering of
the Jewish diaspora in Israel and the exile of Palestinians to the four corners
of the globe. The bombing of the Palestinian boat destined to travel from
Cyprus to Palestine in 1988 was an attempt to crush the intended symbolic
act of Return.

For a political culture that adopts a righteous stance toward the world,
the very image of its victims entails a kind of epistemological violence. The
idea of Zionism from the perspective of its victims (including its Sephardic
Jewish victims, as I have argued elsewhere)[32] suggests that even movements
established as a response to dispossession are not necessarily immune to the
disease of dispossessing others. Ronald Aronson's riposte to Said's essay,
"Zionism from the Standpoint of its Victims," symptomatically focused on
the Holocaust in order to center the debate on Jewish victimization.[33]
Aronson's argument fails to see the uses and abuses of the Holocaust in a
Middle Eastern context, where this single tragic event often becomes a
rhetorical device designed to block not only Palestinian national rights, but
also Sephardic-Oriental self-assertion. The instant invocations of the genocide of the Jews in Europe results in the silencing of any criticism of Israeli
policies of aggression. It was thus always necessary for Zionist discourse
metaphorically and metonymically to associate Arabs with Nazis, as is
often seen in Zionist rhetoric, evident in popular films like *Exodus* (1960)
and *Raiders of the Lost Ark* (1981), as well as in the recent comparison of
Saddam Hussein to Hitler.[34]

Stressing the victimization of the Jews and linking Arabs with anti-
Semitism has repressed the emergence in the US of discourses sympathetic
to Palestinians. Zionism, on one level the answer to exile, has created its
own exiles. Said's personal exile has thus become a paradigm of the
Palestinian diaspora. The "threat" he represents is related to the interest he
provokes in the situation he embodies. Perhaps more than any other
Palestinian writer, however, Edward Said has qualified his anti-colonial
critique of Israel, pointing out all the complex entanglements the place
entails:

> [Palestine is] the place where religions were manufactured and all kinds of
> revelations are alleged to have occured. And it has a kind of density and
> resonance that virtually no other place in the world has. And it is also a very
> small place and crowded. And that criss-crossing, that fabric of claims and
> counter claims interests me a great deal. The political and even philosophical
> question is, why is it that visions of community in a land that is as dense as
> this have tended not to triumph, and what has triumphed instead are visions
> of exclusiveness?
>
> It has been very important to me to try to understand the tremendous
> appeal of Zionism to the European mind ... Zionism appears to be a
> movement and ideology that gathered together the remnants and remains of
> a shattered community of people who has historically been oppressed, abused,

discriminated against and persecuted in the West, and gathered them together
into a very powerful movement which created a new country. It had all the
elements of a kind of phoenix rising from the ashes.[35]

Together with a consistent effort to present a Palestinian perspective in
relation to Israel, Said reflexively articulates the difficulty for a Palestinian
intellectual in the West to offer a Palestinian vision of Israel. Said's work is
thus strikingly dialogical in its effort to study, imagine, and empathize with
Jewish history, while also pointing out the paradoxes and even absurdities
resulting from the Palestinian understanding of the Jewish experience in
Europe:

> It's very hard for the Palestinian who feels himself or herself to have been the
> victim of injustice by the Jews, Israeli Jews, to sympathize or imaginatively
> incorporate the history of the Holocaust and say: well, we forgive them for
> what they did because after all they have suffered this enormous, this colossal
> historical tragedy, and the fact that they are evicting us from our territory,
> that they are placing us under occupation, that they are treating us like third-
> class citizens, that they are killing our people, that they are confining us to
> camps, etc., etc., we understand. Look, nobody can understand that. You can
> grasp the first fact, the fact of the Holocaust, but you can't translate that into
> your own doom, I mean as another person, the doom that is visited on you
> by those people. It's very very hard to do that. On the other hand I really
> genuinely believe that it is incredibly important for the Palestinians to try to
> understand what force it is that we are dealing with. I made a great effort to
> see *Shoa* . . . It's nine-and-a-half to ten hours, and I am certain that my wife
> and I were the only two Arabs in the audience. I could feel it and understood
> the enormous horror, and I was devastated because I understood as a kind of
> European or Westerner the Holocaust for what it was. But then, when I came
> to the point of saying what does this mean to me, it means that this is the
> legitimisation of what has happened to us as a people, the Palestinians. And
> then it's a paradox. You can call it an antinomy, you can call it a tragedy, but
> it doesn't lessen one's will, it doesn't lessen your will to struggle against it.[36]

Ironically, Said is often denounced as the most demagogic of the Palestinian
spokespersons in the US, when in fact he so often acknowledges the
European Jewish experience of anti-Semitism. He attempts to present a
multiplicity of perspectives, including Jewish perspectives, without losing
the basic conviction in the necessity of creating a Palestinian state. Said's
sensitivity to these multiple positions constitutes what he himself calls the
"privilege of exile," which entails having "not just one set of eyes but half
a dozen, each of them corresponding to the places you have been."[37]

That the predisposition to Jewish victimization selectively emphasizes
certain points in Jewish history and privileges them over other powerful
moments (e.g. the Judeo-Muslim culture in Iberia prior to the Christian
Inquisition), as well as over people victimized by a Jewish state apparatus,

preeminently the Palestinians, is pointedly argued in Said's critique of
Walzer:

> Walzer spends no time at all on what brought the Jews to Egypt (in Genesis)
> nor on the great degree of wealth and power which because of Joseph they
> achieved there. It is quite misleading to refer to them as an oppressed people
> when Genesis 46 and 47 tell in some detail of how "they had a possession
> therein, and grew, and multiplied exceedingly."[38]

And Genesis clearly suggests further that the Pharaoh welcomed the family
of Joseph, the Israelites.

Here Said calls attention to a structuring absence in Walzer's writing,
one characteristic, I would suggest, of Zionist historiography generally, and
a crucial omission in that it implies a refusal to evaluate later points in
Jewish histories. Most of the Jews expelled from Spain in 1492, along with
the Muslims, returned to their region of origin in North Africa and the
Middle East, and in fact were *invited* by the Turks to live there. Indeed
Sephardic Jews lived thereafter in all sections of the Ottoman Empire
(including its European sections), joining the Jews in North Africa and the
Middle East who never left the region. In the Arab Muslim world, Jews
were integral to economic, political and cultural life. It is only his Eurocentric perspective on Jewish history that allows Walzer to give the example
of the Jews of the Arab world as one of the "groups marginal to the nation"
for whom the situation "can only be smoothed by helping people to leave
who have to leave."[39] Such a suggestion internalizes a hegemonic Zionist
discourse, according to which Jews in Arab and Muslim countries simply
wanted to leave their millenial homelands. In fact, Middle Eastern and
North African Jews have constituted just one minority among many
religious and ethnic minorities in the Arab Muslim world. That Walzer
singles them out, and not any other minority, as examples of those who
have to leave when the new mold of a nation is established, reproduces the
Zionist inability to allow any conceptual space for Arab Jews, and elides
the fact that Zionism was at least partially responsible for the dislocation
of Jews from the Arab Muslim World.[40] Here the corollary to the denial of
Palestinian victimization is the projection of European Jewish experience
on to the very different history of Middle Eastern and North African Jews.

For Said, the Exodus narrative becomes the site of contestation between
Palestinian and Zionist perspectives, in which "exodus politics" represents a
Zionist reading that undermines the question of occupation and conquest of
Canaan. Said narrates that forbidden territory: "How can one exit Egypt for
an already inhabited promised land, take that land over, exclude the natives
from moral concern . . . kill or drive them out, and call the whole thing
'liberation'?"[41] This point is elided by Zionist ideologues, who limit Jewish
teleology to Zionist liberation. The retroactive Zionist allegorical reading of

Exodus sees only redemption, liberation from slavery and "national" independence, while denying the costs to others of that liberation. Rereading the Exodus story within the contemporary context becomes inevitable; if liberal Zionists typically undermine the Canaanite perspective, Said voices that muteness of ". . . two million Palestinian refugees, those people (with their recent descendants) who like the Canaanite were originally driven out of their native land by Israel on the premise that they were 'explicitly excluded from the world of moral concern.' "[42]

Even the perspective offered by the Canaanite intellectuals in Israel (*cna'anim*), I would argue, is problematic. The Israeli Canaanites have called for breaking cultural and historical links with diaspora Jews, based on much of the anti-Jewish diaspora arguments of Zionist discourse, envisioning a solidarity among all the inhabitants of contemporary Canaan on the basis of their continuation of the Canaanite past.[43] Their rebellion against the culture of the Jewish diaspora focuses on intellectual and aesthetic attempts to revive the ancient, pre-biblical Hebraic culture, as well as on other pagan myths and rituals, Canaanite and Assyrian. (The Canaanites even spoke of giving "minorities," i.e. Palestinians, Hebrew education.) The so-called rebellion of the Canaanite movement in Palestine/ Israel has been best encapsulated in Yitzhak Dantzinger's sculpture, 'Nimrod', the ancient Assyrian hunter whose name literally means "we will rebel." Yet the Canaanite Israeli discourse has also ignored the Arabness of Palestinians. While establishing a romantic link themselves with a non-existent people and past, it elides the Arabs of Palestine and their Arab culture.

A major difference separates Said's use of the Canaanite idea from that of Hebrew-Israeli Canaanites. Whereas Said proposes a Canaanite reading in order to problematize the Zionist Exodus master-narrative, the Israeli Canaanites emphasize a return to a non-Jewish (or anti-Jewish) culture in the region represented by the Canaanites, while denying the very culture of the contemporary Canaanites, the Palestinians. Their romantic return to the pre-biblical origins of Hebraic tribes ironically reflects a desperate attempt to negate their own diasporic origins, encapsulated in the virtually anti-Semitic disgust with the *shtetel* Jew, and to construct, in fact, a new Hebrew culture. While a minority movement, "Canaanism" has inflected much of *sabra* culture, leaving traces in the writing of Amos Kenan, A. B. Yehoshua, and Amos Oz.[44] The Oriental touches of *sabra* folklore, then, have signified its rootedness in the area, while simultaneously maintaining a Western geopolitical imagination. Said's Canaanite reading, in contrast, is supplemented by linking all oppressed groups, including oppressed Jews, to Palestinians: "If Jews were still stateless, and being held in ghettos, I do not believe that Walzer would take the positions he has been taking. I cannot believe that he would say, for example, that communities have the right to restrict land ownership or immigration so that Jews (or Blacks, or

Indians) couldn't participate equally in an absolute sense."[45] Said, then, has consistently historicized the Israeli/Palestinian dispute in a truly anti-essentialist mode. Communities are presented in shifting dialectical positions in relation to one another.

VIRGIN LANDS: ISRAEL/PALESTINE AND "AMERICA"

If Zionism saw itself on a nineteenth-century continuum of nationalist renaissance in Europe – although the establishment of its state had to await the post-World War II dissolution of Empire – Palestinian nationalism has naturally tended to define itself in the name of Third Worldness. Apart from their obvious Middle Eastern context, the debates swirling around Said must be seen as also having specific echoes in the US. The *intifada*, with its anti-colonial overtones, and the Israeli/Palestinian conflict as a whole, touch on some sensitive historical nerves within "America" itself. As a product of schizophrenic master-narratives, colonial-settler state on the one hand and anti-colonial republic on the other, "America" has been subliminally more ready for Zionist nationalist discourse than for Palestinian nationalist discourse. The image of the *sabra* as a new (Jewish) man evokes the American Adam. The American hero has been celebrated as prelapsarian Adam, as a New Man emancipated from (European) history before whom all the world and time lay available, much as the *sabra* was conceived as the antithesis of the "old world" European Jew. The rupture with the "old world" in both Israeli and American official discourses was similarly premised on the absent "parent." The American Adam and the *sabra* archetypes implied not only their status as creators, blessed with the divine prerogative of naming the elements of the world about them, but also their fundamental innocence. The notions of an American Adam and an Israeli *sabra* elided a number of crucial facts, notably that there were other civilizations in the Promised Land; that the settlers were not creating "being from nothingness," and that the settlers, in both cases, had scarcely jettisoned all their Old World cultural baggage, their deeply ingrained attitudes and discourses. Here the gendered metaphor of the "virgin land," present both in Zionist and American pioneer discourses, must be seen in diacritical relation to the metaphor of the (European) "motherland."[46] A "virgin" land is implicitly available for defloration and fecundation. (Said has referred to the feminization of the Orient in *Orientalism*.) Assumed to lack owners, it therefore becomes the property of its "discoverers" and cultivators. The "purity" of the terminology masks the dispossession of the land and its resources. A land already fecund, already producing for the indigenous peoples, and thus a "mother," is metaphorically projected as virgin, "untouched nature," and therefore as available and awaiting a master.

In the case of Zionist discourse, the concept of "return to the mother land," however, suggests a double relation to the land, having to do with an ambivalent relation to the "East" as the place of Jewish origins as well as the locus for implementing the "West." The *sabra* embodied the humanitarian and liberationist project of Zionism, carrying the same banner of the "civilizing mission" that European powers proclaimed during their surge into "found lands." The classical images of *sabra* pioneers as settlers on the Middle Eastern frontiers, fighting Indian-like Arabs, coupled with reverberations of the early American biblical discourse encapsulated in such notions as "Adam", "(New) Canaan," and "Promised Land," facilitated the sympathetic reception of Zionist nationalism in the US. Furthermore, both the US and Israel fought against British colonialism, while also practicing colonial policies towards the indigenous people. Finally, one could argue for a triangular structural analogy by which the Palestinians represent the aboriginal "Indians" of Euro-Israeli discourse, while the Sephardim constitute the "Blacks" of Israel. The Palestinians' manifest refusal to play the assigned role of the presumably doomed "Indians" of the (far) Western narrative has generated both suppression of and identification with the Palestinian national narrative.

It is impossible, in sum, to discuss the Israeli/Palestinian conflict without addressing the paradoxes, anomalies and antinomies entailed in applying colonial and anti-colonial discourses to that region. Edward Said's effort to dialogize the Israeli/Palestinian conflict shows the way out of the current intolerable impasse. His indispensable contribution to the critique of imperialism, furthermore, won considerable academic prestige for this area of knowledge, indirectly helping to lift the veil of censorship too often shrouding this fundamental political and intellectual issue.

Notes

1 Edward W. Said, *The Question of Palestine* (New York: New York Times Books, 1979), p. 39.
2 Said in an interview with Imre Salusinsky (ed.), *Criticism in Society* (New York: Routledge, 1987), pp. 122–48.
3 Said, *Orientalism*, p. 25.
4 I should make it clear that the term "Orientals" is used here not simply to evoke the colonialist naming of all peoples of the East, but also in its liberatory critical sense. "Oriental," or *Mizrakhim* in Hebrew, is used by militant Middle Eastern and North African Jewish intellectuals and activists in Israel to express resistance to the conception of Israel as a Western country, and to re-link themselves with the history and culture of the Arab and Muslim world, after the brutal rupture experienced since the foundation of Israel. This vision is obvious in the names of such leftist movements as "East for Peace" and "The Oriental Front" in Israel, and "Perspective Judéo-Arabes" in France.
5 Said, "An Exchange: Michael Walzer & Edward W. Said," *Grand Street*, 5, no. 4, p. 253.

6 Ibid., p. 258.

7 Said, *Covering Islam: How the Media and the Experts Determine How to See the Rest of the World* (New York: Pantheon Books, 1981); Said and Christopher Hitchens, (eds.), *Blaming the Victims: Spurious Scholarship and the Palestinian Question* (London & New York: Verso, 1988).

8 Edward Alexander, "Professor of Terror," *Commentary*, 88, no. 2 (August 1989). See also "'Professor of Terror': An Exchange/Edward Alexander & Critics," *Commentary*, 88, No. 6 (December 1989).

9 Alexander, "Professor of Terror," p. 49.

10 See "An Exchange on Edward Said and Difference," which includes Robert J. Griffin, "Ideology and Misrepresentation: A Response to Edward Said"; Daniel Boyarin and Jonathan Boyarin, "Toward a Dialogue with Edward Said," and Said, "Response," *Critical Inquiry*, 15, No. 3 (Spring 1989). See also Said's earlier essay, "An Ideology of Difference," *Critical Inquiry*, 12, No. 1 (Autumn 1985), to which Griffin and the Boyarins were responding.

11 William Phillips, "Comment: Intellectuals, Academics, and Politics," *Partisan Review*, LVI, No. 3 (1989) p. 343.

12 Ibid., p. 344.

13 Ibid.

14 Walzer, "An Exchange: Michael Walzer and Edward Said," p. 249.

15 Mark Krupnick, "Edward Said: Discourse and Palestinian Rage," *Tikkun*, 4, No. 6 (November/December 1989), p. 21.

16 Mark Krupnick, a response to letters, "Said and Walzer," *Tikkun*, 5, no. 3 (May/June 1990), p. 91.

17 John Murray Cuddihy, *The Ordeal of Civiliy: Freud, Marx, Lévi-Strauss, and the Jewish Struggle with Modernity* (New York: Basic Books, 1974).

18 Said, *After the Last Sky: Palestinian Lives* (New York: Pantheon Books, 1985).

19 For more on the New York intellectuals, see Vincent B. Leitch, *American Literary Criticism from the Thirties to the Eighties* (New York: Columbia University Press, 1988).

20 Alexander, "Professor of Terror," p. 50.

21 Even the commemorations of the quincentenary of the expulsion from Spain tend retroactively to rewrite history by refusing to address the expulsion of *both* Jews and Muslims.

22 Said, *Beginnings: Intention & Method* (New York Basic Books, 1975); idem, *The World, the Text, and the Critic* (Cambridge, Mass.: Harvard University Press, 1983).

23 See Sander L. Gilman, *Jewish Self-hatred: Anti-Semitism and the Hidden Language of the Jews* (Baltimore & London: Johns Hopkins University Press, 1986).

24 Arel Ginai, Tzadok Yehezkeli, and Roni Shaked, "Ashafei ha'Tikshoret," *Yedioth Ahronoth* (February 17, 1989); translations from the Hebrew are my own.

25 *Exodus* reinforces the *Sabra*/Waspish cultural and geopolitical links. Casting an archetypical Anglo-American star in the role of the *sabra* undoes the largely negative connotations of the stereotypes of the Jew in the Western-Christian popular mind and equates him with the desired hero of American dreams. Newman embodies the virility of both *sabra* soldier and the American fighter, merging both into one myth, reinforced and parallelled by the close Israeli-American political and cultural links since the sixties. The film suggests that the Israeli experience has "normalized" the Jew, so that now even the English anti-Semitic officer cannot spot him. The *Sabra*-Wasp link is further reinforced on a

linguistic level. While the weak Jewish immigrants to Israel generally speak Yiddish-accented English, the *sabra* hero and his heroine sister speak with the hegemonic American accent.

26 Although Mark Krupnick acknowledges Palestinian national rights, he argues that Palestinian national culture, when compared with Zionism, lacks narratives and symbols. He even goes so far as to suggest that "Said's rage . . . derives in part from his perception that the stories of his people have tended to be imitations of Jewish stories" ("Edward Said," p. 23).

27 Ginai, Yehezkeli, Shaked, loc. cit.

28 Not accidentally, Abba Eban was a major narrator for the PBS series *Civilization and the Jews*.

29 Ginai, Yehezkeli, Shaked, *loc. cit.*

30 Said, "Zionism from the Standpoint of its Victims," *Social Text* 1 (Winter 1979); also published as a chapter in Said's *The Question of Palestine*.

31 Said, "Michael Walzer's 'Exodus and Revolution;' A Canaanite Reading," *Grand Street*, 5, No. 2 (Winter 1986), p. 90. Arab-Americans in Western media, it must be pointed out, have now begun to use the rhetoric of "we." This is true of Said as well.

32 See Ella Shohat, "Sephardim in Israel: Zionism from the Standpoint of Its Jewish Victims," *Social Text*, 19–20 (Fall 1988).

33 Ronald Aronson, "Never Again? Zionism and the Holocaust," *Social Text* 3 (Fall 1980).

34 For more on the association of Hussein with Hitler, see Ella Shohat, "The Media's War," *Social Text*, 28 (1991). On the submerged geopolitics of such popular films as *Raiders of the Lost Ark*, see Ella Shohat, "Ethnicities-in-Relation: Toward a Multi-Cultural Reading of American Cinema," in Lester Friedman (ed.), *Unspeakable Images: Ethnicity and the American Cinema* (Urbana & Chicago: University of Illinois Press, 1991).

35 "Edward Said: The voice of a Palestinian in Exile," *Third Text*, 3/4 (Spring/ Summer 1988).

36 Ibid.

37 Ibid.

38 Said, "Michael Walzer's 'Exodus and Revolution'," p. 91.

39 Walzer, "An Exchange," pp. 247–8.

40 For a brilliant account of the exile of Arab Jews, see Abbas Shiblak, *The Lure of Zion* (London: Al Saqi Books, 1986). Shiblak, a Palestinian, has been extremely interested in the situation of Arab Jews, precisely because of its implications for Palestinian dispossession. He was one of the Palestinian intellectuals to attend the first meeting between Sephardic Jews and Palestinians in Toledo, Spain (1989), which with its several agendas was also an effort to understand the Zionist notion of "population exchange."

41 Said, "An Exchange: Michael Walzer & Edward Said", p. 253.

42 Said, "Michael Walzer's 'Exodus and Revolution'" p. 92.

43 For a general account of the Canaanite movement in Palestine/Israel see Ya'cov Shavit, *Mi'Ivri le'Cnaani* (From Hebrew to Canaanite) (Jerusalem: Domino Press, 1985).

44 See Nurit Gertz, *Khirbet Hiz'e vehaBoker sheleMakharat* (Khirbet Khiz'e and the Morning After) (Tel Aviv: Hotza'at HaKibbutz haMeukhad, 1983), pp. 26–27.

45 Said, "Michael Walzer's 'Exodus and Revolution'," p. 103.

46 For further discussion of gendered metaphors and colonial discourse, see Ella Shohat, "Imaging Terra Incognita: The Disciplinary Gaze of Empire," *Public Culture*, 3, No. 2 (Spring 1991).

7

EAST OF SAID

Richard G. Fox

The creation of geographies – the recognition and understanding of symbolic territories – is central to Edward Said's work as I understand it. He writes, for example, about the creation of places of exile, of locations where there is a protracted sense of "not yet" and "not here" and a terrain of "national incompleteness" (Said, *After the Last Sky*). In *Orientalism* (1978), he writes of lands defined by domination – the borders of the Orient mapped out by the superiority of the West's power to inscribe them.

Even when writing in the abstract, Said is moved to use geographical imagery, and his sense of intellectual movement is phrased in terms of diffusion. Thus, he mounts the notion of "traveling theories" in one of his essays (*The World, the Text, and the Critic*), which serves as a vehicle for him to consider theory as it moves from one intellectual locale to another. A theory has a point of origin, then travels a certain distance and meets new circumstances upon arrival, and finally, must undergo alterations in the contact situation.

Said's scholarly diffusionism, his own concern for traveling theories and the need to modify them in new circumstances, gives me purchase for these comments. How far can his theory of Orientalism travel? Can it travel East of Suez – where proverbially Europe stopped and Asia began – to reach as far as South Asia? Or does it founder on subcontinental history and culture? How far should anthropology (for I can only hope to judge my own discipline) travel with him? To what extent does the theory redirect anthropology along new paths in the study of culture? Or, conversely, can anthropology move the theory along in its own way?

Asking these questions, which demand measures of "how far" and "how much," rather than an invariant "yes" or "no" in our judgement of Said's Orientalism is, I believe, in itself a step in the right direction. Said's theory has gathered too many hasty fellow travelers (compare Inden, "Orientalist Constructions of India"), who condemn all South-Asian scholarship as

Orientalist – a judgement of our collective understanding that is even more stereotyping, dominating, and pejorative than the Orientalism it deplores. Said's theory, conversely, has also mobilized an unreflective opposition, who refuse to budge from the idea of a value-free scholarship, which is as mythical as any epic tale from India.

I want to move my further comments along in two different ways. The first is a journey of pilgrimage, paying my respects to Said's theory of Orientalism, and charting how far it has taken me. When I came to write about the Sikhs of northern India a few years ago (*Lions of the Punjab*), Said's Orientalism brought me to a deeper understanding. I saw how British images of what India was like in general and what the Sikhs were like specifically constituted and compelled Sikh consciousness in the late nineteenth and early twentieth century. I saw how far an unreflective Orientalism carried British policy in India. Believing that some Indian "races" were inherently martial, the British recruited an army of Sikhs, who, the military authorities made sure, not only wore the badges of British regiments, but also the marks of Sikh religious orthodoxy, as British officers understood it. Sikh religious commandments became British military commands, and Sikh identity was therefore commandeered by the colonials. Said's theory traveled well to the Punjab I knew, at least as far as it, or I, went.

Along the way, I started thinking about what Orientalism meant for the standard concept of culture in anthropology. Citing Laroui's criticism of a Kroeberian cultural approach to the Near East, Said (*Orientalism*) intimated that anthropology's concept of culture was part of the stereotyping tradition pushing Orientalism along – the approach in anthropology to the Other as "always Singular, always Capitalized," to quote Clifford Geertz ("Waddling In"), who also condemns this approach. I think Said is right. With Said's impetus, the Sikh work tried to move away from the unitary, cohesive, constituting, and coercive model of culture that materialists like me, just as much as interpretive anthropologists, have been carrying around for a good while. Going forward with Said's Orientalism gives anthropology, I believe, a much more profound sense of the fictions of ethnography, of the conventions in the culture concept, of the tropes in our scholarly travels than the recent reflexive or postmodern critique does[1] – because Orientalism shows that our fictions, conventions, and tropes are motored by inequalities in the world, not interlocutions in the field.

My second way of approaching Said's Orientalism is not a pilgrimage; it is more like a raiding trip on the theory where I think it is weakest and most in need of modification to fit different circumstances. The starting-point is: how far did Orientalism, not Said's theory of Orientalism now, but the Orientalist domination he has documented, travel to the Orient that was its object and destination? Said allows in passing that Orientalism reached the Orientals (*Orientalism*), but he does not go on with this idea. Therefore, I think Said's theory of Orientalism does not travel as far as Orientalism itself did. It remains a history of Orientalism from the West and affirms in the very way it is set out the categories of West and East it ostensibly attacks. It also does not allow the possibility that Orientals, once Orientalized by Western domination, could use Orientalism itself against that domination.

To return to the Sikhs: in the 1920s Sikh reformers believed and practiced the Orientalist stereotypes of the Sikh. Nevertheless, they used these stereotypes to lead a mass movement that eventually turned against British colonialism, although never against the British Orientalist image of the Sikh. They now commandeered British military forms and turned them into vehicles of protest. They inducted the martial and now militant Sikhs into rebellion and marched them along in anti-colonial formations. Said's theory stops before reaching this point: it does not map how far Orientalism traveled and how much Orientalism came to constitute the consciousness of the Orientals. Said's theory also stops before reaching a still more important point: that Orientalism came to enable resistance against Western domination. Such, it seems to me, was the case in India, and not just for the Sikhs.

My current project (*Gandhian Utopia, Experiments with Culture*), which concerns what I refer to as Gandhian utopia, provides another case in point. The Gandhian utopian vision was a form of resistance to capitalism, colonialism, and the West. *Hind Swaraj*, the essay from 1909 in which Gandhi passionately condemns Western civilization and equally fervidly defends traditional India, powerfully expresses cultural resistance, as I shall soon show.

Where did Gandhi's cultural resistance come from? Many scholars, including K. M. Panikkar, Louis Dumont, Partha Chatterjee, Ashis Nandy, and Lloyd and Suzanne Rudolph, see Gandhi as expressing an indigenous cultural resistance against the West and its domination. Stephen Hay argues that Gandhi's rejection of modern civilization rested on the model of the Jain path to liberation of the soul, which was "so deeply imprinted on his mind that he did not even think of it as a Jaina one" ("Jaina Goals and Discipline in Gandhi's Pursuit of Swaraj", p. 127).

The origins of Gandhian utopia are complex, as I shall indicate below. This history not only takes us far beyond what is in effect an Orientalist notion that it was indigenous resistance, but also prods us to go beyond Said's theory of Orientalism. Both Orientalism and Said's theory of it invest in Otherness. They depend on an elaboration – an exaggeration, I will now argue – of cultural differences and separate histories that certainly no longer existed by the nineteenth century.

ENGLISHTAN VS. WISDOM-LAND

Writing in the *Illustrated London News* for September 18, 1909, G. K. Chesterton exercised his wit on the Indian nationalist movement. Indian nationalism was neither very nationalist nor very Indian, Chesterton asserted. He went on to give weight to his word-play: the Indians putting forth demands for home rule (they wanted an independent, elected government for British India) belonged to an elite that did not represent Indian opinion. According to Chesterton, they were a small and decultured group that existed in a false, shadowed world – shadowed because they had been somewhat enlightened by British education and civilization, yet they were still partly darkened by India's obscure oriental traditions.

These Indian nationalists therefore did not represent the true India, and what they asked for in the way of nationalism was quite inauthentic. After all, Chesterton argued, how could their nationalism be authentic when all they wished for was their own English-style parliament, and their own English-style elections, and their own English-style liberties. Now if they asked for a truly Indian independence, Chesterton maintained, the British should naturally be required at least to listen to them seriously, but this sham nationalism hardly deserved credence.

Chesterton's fulminations profoundly convinced one reader, who wrote home about them in 1909. This reader came to repudiate the brown Englishmen who ran the nationalist movement – Macaulay's bastards, as an Indian character in Anita Desai's novel Bye-Bye Blackbird self-deprecatingly calls them, after the mid-nineteenth-century British official who wanted to produce a class of Indians British in all but their skin color – but he reproved them more gently than Chesterton. He came to repudiate the Parliament the nationalists wanted; he agreed with Chesterton that this was not authentically Indian. And he grew to believe in a people's democracy that started in the little republic of the Indian village and built up in "oceanic circles" – village added to village – to form a national government. He also, because he was thorough to a fault, repudiated modern physicians and Western medicine (except for Dr Kellogg's nut butter), trains, lawyers, printed books, telegraphy, and modern civilization in general.

Mohandas Karamchand Gandhi, not yet the Mahatma, read Chesterton's diatribe while in Britain to plead for the plight of South Africa's Indians. He wrote home excitedly, endorsing Chesterton's condemnation of an Indian nationalism that only aped the West:

> Indians must reflect over these views of Mr Chesterton and consider what they should rightly demand ... May it not be that we seek to advance our own interests in the name of the Indian people? Or, that we have been endeavoring to destroy what the Indian people have carefully nurtured through thousands of years? I ... was led by Mr Chesterton's article to all these reflections ... (Collected Works of Gandhi; hereafter, CWG 9, p. 426).

On the return voyage to South Africa, Gandhi reflected further and even more passionately embraced an Indian nationalism that claimed authenticity by declaiming against the West. In *Hind Swaraj or Indian Home Rule*, written aboard ship, Gandhi inscribed Chesterton's message as the credo for a different Indian nationalism. He went far beyond Chesterton's sarcasm and superficiality. Condemning *ersatz* Indian imitations of the West, as Chesterton had, Gandhi on the one hand broadened it into a fervid rejection of modern civilization, while on the other, he used it as an acclamation of traditional India – and thereby as an apology for contemporary India's "backwardness." Gandhi first disowned a nationalism that "would make India English. And when it becomes English, it will be called not Hindustan but *Englishtan*. This is not the Swaraj that I want" (Gandhi, *Hind Swaraj*, p. 30). True nationalism, for Gandhi, must disavow modern civilization and build on India's traditional strengths:

> The tendency of Indian civilization is to elevate the moral being, that of the Western civilization is to propagate immorality. The latter is godless, the former is based on a belief in God. So understanding and so believing, it behoves every lover of India to cling to the old Indian civilization even as a child clings to the mother's breast. (p. 63).

India needed no Parliament other than the ancient village *panchayat*; no Western enslaving machinery when the peasant's plow had served well for thousands of years; no all-consuming Western consumerism when India's wise ancients had counseled against luxuries and indulgence (pp. 61–2). British colonialists and Indian nationalists who mimicked them wanted to replace India's traditional strength with modern Western weakness, precisely because they mistook strength for weakness:

> It is a charge against India that her people are so uncivilized, ignorant and stolid that it is not possible to induce them to adopt any changes – What we have tested and found true on the anvil of experience, [however,] we dare not change. Many thrust their advice upon India, and she remains steady. This is her beauty. (p. 61).

Disowning modern civilization in 1909, Gandhi already perceived his utopian vision in broad outline. What precisely brought him to this condemnation? If long-latent beliefs – from Jainism or Indian culture in general – were important influences, why did Gandhi wait to reject modern civilization and "Englishtan" until 1909, when he was forty years old? Even Hay allows that Gandhi's disenchantment with modern, rather than Western, civilization developed as he prepared a talk on "The East and the West" for a British pacifist society ("Jaina Goals and Discipline," p. 125). Gandhi delivered this talk on October 13, 1909 (*CWG*, 9, p. 477).

Let us look into the immediately previous history to see if it throws light on what led to Gandhi's supposed realization of his Jain imprinting. Gandhi stated right after his talk to the pacificsts (*CWG*, 9, p. 478) that "the thing was brewing in my mind" and in a letter of October 14, 1909, he maintained that his ideas were not "new but they have only now assumed such a concrete form and taken a violent possession of me" (*CWG*, 9, p. 481).

Did Gandhi's "not new" condemnation in 1909 in fact go back to a Jain past brewing in his mind over many years? It does not seem so. Gandhi's condemnation of an Indian nationalism premised on modern civilization was rapid. In 1906 he thought he would rather live in London than anywhere else (Hunt, *Gandhi in London*, p. 143), but by 1909 he was of a much different mind. He suggested that it might be necessary to visit London, but "I am definitely of the view that it is altogether undesirable for anyone to . . . live here" (*CWG*, 9, p. 389). What made London deplorable in 1909 was modern civilization: "We have trains running underground; there are telegraph wires already hanging over us, and outside, on the roads, there is the deafening noise of trains. If you now have planes flying in the air, take it that people will be done to death. Looking at this land, I at any rate have grown disillusioned with Western civilization" (*CWG*, 9, p. 426).

Modern civilization had not just come to London between 1906 and 1909. What, then, had come to Gandhi over this short period that produced his disillusionment? Perhaps one precondition was the strong influence of the vegetarian and Theosophist Edward Maitland during Gandhi's early days in South Africa. Maitland corresponded with Gandhi and sent him books. In 1894, Gandhi advertised himself as an agent for Maitland's Esoteric Christian Union in Natal. This organization stood in opposition to "present-day materialism" (Hay, *Asian Ideas of East and West*, p. 278). Sometime after 1906, he re-read Tolstoy's affirmation of nonviolence in *The Kingdom of God Is Within You*, which proved much more affecting the second time (Green, *Tolstoy and Gandhi*, p. 89). Still, even as late as 1907, Gandhi continued to believe in the benefits of British rule and Western education (Swan, *Gandhi: The South African Experience*, pp. 143–5).

Then in the spring of 1908, Gandhi translated Ruskin's *Unto This Last*, which he had read for the first time some years earlier. This original reading led him to set up his first experimental community, the Phoenix settlement, in 1904. Gandhi played off Ruskin's condemnation of capitalist political economy to argue that British commercialism and industrialism were unsuitable for India (Hunt, *Gandhi in London*, p. 144). Introducing his translation of Ruskin (Spring 1908), Gandhi allowed that imitating the West in some ways might be necessary, but that "many Western ideas are wrong" (*CWG*, 8, pp. 239–41). In a talk to the Johannesburg YMCA in May 1908, Gandhi distinguished modern technology from Christian progress, declining "to believe that it is a symbol of Christian progress that we have got telephones . . . and trains" (Hunt, *Gandhi in London*, p. 144). Although he already regarded Western civilization as destructive, he also viewed India as lethargic. Eastern civilization, Gandhi argued at this late date, "should be quickened with the Western spirit," and he saw mutual advantage to the meeting of the British and Indian "races" in India (*CWG*, 8, pp. 244, 246).

His growing disbelief in the West was further confirmed and sharpened by what he read in London during 1909.[2] Gandhi absorbed Edward Carpenter's "very illuminating work," *Civilization, Its Causes and Cure*, and its condemnation of modern civilization. Carpenter, who called ancient India "the Wisdom-land" (Carpenter, *From Adam's Peak to Elephanta*, p. 355), in recognition of its spiritual superiority to the West, led Gandhi to see clearly and afresh the Indian nationalist problem. Gandhi warned his correspondent Polak in a letter of September 8, 1909 that during a previous trip to Bombay Polak saw "Westernized India and not real India." Gandhi also said that he issued this warning upon reading Carpenter's book (*CWG*, 9, p. 396). Shortly thereafter he read Chesterton's article; about a month later he wrote *Hind Swaraj* aboard ship. Chesterton and Carpenter, in different ways, clarified for Gandhi that his resistance should not be to the British people, but to modern civilization, and that a truly Indian nationalism – not the simulacrum of the West that Chesterton rightly ridiculed – had to build on ancient traditions and had to be a *swaraj* of the spirit. They helped Gandhi distinguish his nationalism from the Indian "anarchism" adopted by expatriate groups he also met during his London visit (Gandhi, *Satyagraha in South Africa*, p. 211). These other Indian nationalists disowned Gandhi for his loyalty to the British, not understanding his more profound disloyalty to modern civilization (Yajnik, *Shyamji Krishnavarma*, pp. vii–viii; also see Secretary of State for India, pp. 56–9).

Gandhi's new nationalism is compelled by Chesterton's diatribe against what Gandhi shortly thereafter labels "Englishtan" in India. Gandhi accepts the definition of an authentic Indian nationalism that Chesterton thrusts at him – and so he embraces an Indian nation without parliaments, physicians, lawyers, and trains. Chesterton's view of the authentic path for India is obviously shot through with cultural stereotypes – the notions, for example, that parliaments and elections are inherently foreign to India or that the Westernized Indian is fundamentally decultured and unrepresentative. Butting up against the domination encoded in Chesterton's stereotype, Gandhi can only achieve an authenticated Indian nationalism by rejecting "Englishtan." Chesterton also enables Gandhi, however: by saying what an authentic Indian nationalism cannot be, Chesterton gives Gandhi the space to say what it can be: if not "Englishtan," then a Wisdom-land utopia built on the ancient cultural essentials.

In positing this utopia, Gandhi is again compelled and enabled, in a reverse way, by the critics of modern capitalist civilization, Ruskin and

Carpenter. Through their resistance to Western materialism and mechani-
zation, Ruskin and Carpenter enable Gandhi's rejection of modern civilization. Carpenter, however, compels Gandhi's nationalism by stereotyping
India as a Wisdom-land of spirituality and anti-materialism. He was of
course not the first to give a positive image of India, just as Chesterton was
not the first to offer a pejorative view. Whether negative or positive, these
stereotypes are equally Orientalist, that is, they are equally products of the
cultural domination of India by the West, and they equally compel and
enable Gandhi's utopian resistance to that domination. Gandhi is compelled
against "Englishtan" by Chesterton, and further enabled in that opposition
by Carpenter and Ruskin. By Carpenter, however, Gandhi is compelled
into an Indian nationalism based on the traditional Wisdom-land, which
Chesterton enables by denouncing "Englishtan." What actualizes Gandhi's
utopian denunciation of the West is not some long-latent Jain influence,
although this latter may have entered into it. Gandhi's dream develops
early in the twentieth century as he struggles with and "bounces off" the
negative *and* positive Orientalist stereotypes of India encoded in existing
Western domination.

Gandhian cultural resistance depended on an Orientalist image of India
as inherently spiritual, consensual, and corporate. This image had a
complex authorship and a contradictory character. Pejorative stereotypes
of India, mainly portrayed by European detractors, led to one aspect of it.
In this view, India was passive, otherworldly, tradition-ridden or super-
stitious, caste-dominated, morally degraded, unfree and despotic, and
therefore weak, backward, and unchanging. Moral degradation was everywhere: in the hereditary associations dedicated to evil, like that of the
Thugs, in the so-called self-immolation of widows (*sati*), in female infanti-
cide, and in Untouchability. There were, furthermore, idolatry, indecent
ceremonies, slavery, ritual murder, and many other vile practices that all
went to show, as Southey put it, "that of all false religions, Hinduism was
the most monstrous in effect" (quoted in Bearce, *British Attitudes Towards
India*, p. 104). Politics was no less a sink of inequity, for despotism ruled
India; James Mill said in 1812 it proved India's incapacity for self-
governance (Bearce, p. 71). So foul a culture justified a harsh cleansing,
which could come, in the opinion of colonial administrators like Macaulay,
only by turning India from the Brahmans to the British, from superstition
to science, from traditional lore to European logic, from the otherworldly
to the utilitarian, and from the backward to the modern. Alexander Duff,
William Wilberforce, Charles Grant, and many others contriubuted to this
pejorative Orientalist stereotype (see Duff, *India and India Missions*; Risley,
The People of India; Müller, *India: What Can It Teach Us?*; Kopf, *British
Orientalism*, pp. 254–61; Bearce *British Attitudes*).

Affirmative stereotypes of India created another, although contradictory,
aspect of this Orientalist image. These stereotypes butted up against the

negative image of India and reversed it. What appeared in pejorative Orientalism as India's ugliness now became India's beauty; her so-called weaknesses turned out to be her strengths. Otherworldliness became spirituality, an Indian cultural essential that promised her a future cultural perfection unattained in the West. Passiveness became at first passive resistance and later nonviolent resistance – the age-old Indian character thus provided a revolutionary technique by which to bring on that future perfection. The supposed penchant of India to accept despotism led Gandhi to reject the state entirely. The backward and parochial village became the self-sufficient, consensual and harmonious center of decentralized democracy. An absent national integration turned into the oceanic circles of a people's democracy. Insufficient Indian individualism became altruistic trusteeship, and inadequate entrepreneurial spirit turned into non-possessiveness. This "affirmative Orientalism" owes much to Europeans like the vegetarian Henry Salt, the Theosophist Annie Besant, the Hindu convert Sister Nivedita, the simplifier Edward Carpenter, and the champion of spiritual nonviolence, Tolstoy, all of whom employed these positive stereotypes against a modernized, aggressive, capitalist, materialistic, and carnivorous Europe for which they bore little love. Indian nationalists, in advance of Gandhi or coterminous with him, also contribute to affirmative Orientalism: Lokmanya Tilak and his portrayal of caste as a means to organize society without class conflict; the reformers of the Arya Samaj and the Brahmo Samaj, who believed India's current progress depended on rediscovering the past, when it had been a Wisdom-land; and Veer Savarkar, who justified a modern nationalism by what he took to be an antique spiritual bond between Hindu and Hindustan, the Fatherland (for a more detailed exposition, see Fox, *Gandhian Utopia*, ch. 6).

Gandhian utopia reacts against negative Orientalism by adopting and enhancing this positive image. It therefore ends up with a new Orientalism, that is, a new stereotype, of India, but an affirmative one, leading to an effective resistance. In this transformation, Said's theory seems to be left behind.

To be sure, Said's theory started with Europe, and perhaps it was never meant to travel to the Orient itself. But it also skirts some important European history, for example, the consequences for Europe itself of affirmative Orientalism or what Raymond Schwab called the "condescending veneration" of the Orient. Orientalism did not only serve European domination. Affirmative Orientalism furthered the resistance by Europeans to Western capitalism and modern industrial society. Said's theory, because it bounds West from East, misses this world system of authorship – the ramified intellectual work group composed of European utopians, Unitarians, simplifiers, vegetarians, and sexual libertarians like Ruskin, Tolstoy, Carpenter, Salt, and Kingsford, joined by Indian cultural nationalists like Gandhi, Vivekananda, Krishnavarma, Savarkar, and Aurobindo, and linked through "Indians by persuasion" like Besant and Noble. Their affirmative Orientalism not only configured a utopian future for India but also condemned the dystopian present in the European core. If we are enjoined not to be silent about domination, we cannot use categories like West and East that may silence the dynamics of struggle against cultural domination anywhere in the world system.

Orientalism as a theory does not go far enough in recognizing that resistance to Orientalist domination proceeds from within it. In this respect, it may travel too far toward several Third-World writers who stress the autonomy of cultural resistance – for India, for instance, Ashis Nandy or the so-called subaltern scholars, some of whom argue for a peasant revolutionism or a Gandhism contingent on European domination but quite autonomous from it.

Partha Chatterjee, for example, maintains that Gandhi's was an authentic and effective indigenous resistance. It may have utilized European commentaries, but it was in essence unauthorized by British domination, although it never completely escaped its control (Chatterjee, *Nationalist Thought*, p. 42). Unlike Chatterjee, Nandy does not see Gandhi as the nearly perfect representative of deeply-rooted Indian cultural values, but he does believe that Gandhi's dream creatively used them. For Nandy, Gandhi operated outside the shared system of ideas that configured both British imperialists and many other Indian nationalists. The Mahatma was neither simply "a genuine son of the soil" nor a "totally atypical Indian" (Nandy, *At The Edge of Psychology*, p. 83). Nevertheless, Nandy agrees that Gandhi championed and transformed folk values that "had remained untamed by British rule" (Nandy, *The Intimate Enemy*, p. 100), and he thereby constructed a denial of the West that was also not of the West (ibid., pp. 100–6; Nandy, *At The Edge of Psychology*, pp. 130–1, prefigures this approach).

But here again we see a retreat to a notion of East is East and West, West, even after 150 years of British Indian colonialism and 350 years of the capitalist world system's penetration of India. Gandhian utopia occurred not in the first flush of indigenous resistance but only after nearly two centuries of the world system's penetration and domination. By the late nineteenth century, British colonialism, under whose aegis the capitalist world system gained a purchase on India, had introduced fundamental changes at all levels of Indian society and culture (for general descriptions of change under colonialism, see Fox, "Resiliency and Change", and *Lions of the Punjab*; Jones, *Arya Dharm*; Sarkar, *"Popular" Movements*; Seal, *Emergence of Indian Nationalism*; Srinivas, *Caste*; Rudolph and Rudolph, *Modernity of Tradition*; Washbrook, *Emergence of Provincial Politics*).

Are there really crannies of indigenous culture that remain proof against the world system long after its uninvited arrival, as Nandy and Chatterjee – and, by extension, Said's theory of Orientalism – maintain? Or must we speak of a world system of cultural domination, in which Orientalism – and cultural resistance to it – emerge from a complex global authorship? Orientalism in India travels far and wide – not only on Indian backs, but also in their minds. So, too, the affirmative Orientalism that led to an effective cultural resistance in India makes its way into the world stream, as Gandhi's spiritual and spirited nonviolence, well-fitted to India's traditions (he thought), comes to rest on a bus seat in Montgomery, Alabama or in a California vineyard.

Traveling theories, like any baggage, get knocked about in transit. I do not mean to mishandle Edward Said's Orientalism, but I do think our ultimate destination lies further along than it has travelled – or perhaps can travel. I suspect Said would rather see it tossed about and then reinforced for further travel than have it artificially brought along with kid-glove treatment. Certainly, Orientalism has proved very sturdy in recognizing Western cultural domination and prodding anthropologists and South Asianists to see our complicity in it. But now we have to travel further on, to see the intimacies between European Orientalism's domination and the Third World's cultural resistance. We have only reached this point, however, because Said's theory has traveled so well and because he has been so remarkable a cicerone.

Notes

1 My reference is to the textual critiques of ethnography – its treatment as a "fiction" or literary construction, as, for example, in Clifford (1983) and Clifford and Marcus (1986).
2 In 1909, Gandhi read a work that was very influential on him, Tolstoy's plea for nonviolence, Letter to a Hindu, but which is not discussed here. I deal with this work in the context of the invention of satyagraha in Gandhian Utopia, ch. 7.

References

Bearce, George D., British Attitudes Towards India, 1784–1858 (London: Oxford University Press, 1961).

Carpenter, Edward, Civilization, Its Causes and Cure (New York: Scribner's Sons, 1921 [1889]).

Carpenter, Edward, From Adam's Peak to Elephanta (London: Swan Sonnenschein, 1910).

Chatterjee, Partha, "Gandhi and the Critique of Civil Society", in Subaltern Studies III, edited by Ranajit Guha, (Delhi: Oxford University Press, 1984), pp. 153–95.

Chattergee, Partha Nationalist Thought and the Colonial World, A Derivative Discourse? (London: Zed, 1986).

Clifford, James, The Predicament of Culture: Twentieth-Century Ethnography, Literature and Art (Cambridge, Mass.: Harvard University Press, 1983).

Clifford, James and George Marcus, *Writing Culture: The Poetics and Politics of Ethnography* (Berkeley: University of California Press, 1986).

Desai, Anita, *Bye-Bye Blackbird* (Delhi: Hind Pocket Books, 1971).

Duff, Alexander, *India and India Missions* (2nd. ed. Edinburgh: John Johnstone, 1840).

Dumont, Louis, *Homo Hierarchicus* (trans. by Mark Sainsbury, Chicago: University of Chicago Press, 1970).

Fox, Richard G., "Resiliency and Change in the Indian Caste System: The Umar of U. P.", *The Journal of Asian Studies* 26 (1967), pp. 575–88.

Fox, Richard G., *Lions of the Punjab: Culture in the Making* (Berkeley and Los Angeles: University of California Press, 1985).

Fox, Richard G., *Gandhian Utopia, Experiments with Culture* (Boston: Beacon Press, 1989).

Gandhi, Mohandas Karamchand, *Hind Swaraj or Indian Home Rule* (Ahmedabad: Navajivan Publishing House, 1938 [1909]).

Gandhi, Mohandas Karamchand, *Collected Works of Mahatma Gandhi*, 89 vols. (Delhi: Publication Division, Ministry of Information and Broadcasting, Government of India, 1958–83).

Gandhi. Mohandas Karamchand, *Satyagraha in South Africa* (trans. by V. G. Desai, Ahmedabad: Navajivan Publishing House, 1972 [1928]).

Geertz, Clifford, "Waddling In," *Times Literary Supplement*, June 7, 1985, pp. 623–4.

Green, Martin, *Tolstoy and Gandhi, Men of Peace*, (New York: Basic Books, 1983).

Hay, Stephen N. *Asian Ideas of East and West, Tagore and His Critics in Japan, China, and India*, (Cambridge: Harvard University Press, 1970).

Hay, Stephen N., "Jaina Goals and Discipline in Gandhi's Pursuit of Swaraj," in *Rule, Protest, Identity, Aspects of Modern South Asia*, edited by Peter Robb and David Taylor, (London: Curzon Press, 1978), pp. 120–31.

Hunt, James D., *Gandhi in London* (New Delhi: Promilla, 1978).

Inden, Ronald, "Orientalist Constructions of India", *Modern Asian Studies* 20 (1986), 401–46.

Jones, Kenneth W., *Arya Dharm. Hindu Consciousness in 19th-Century Punjab* (Berkeley and Los Angeles: University of California Press, 1976).

Kopf, David, *British Orientalism and the Bengal Renaissance* (Berkeley and Los Angeles: University of California Press, 1969).

Müller, Max, *India: What Can It Teach Us?* (New York: Funk and Wagnalls, 1883).

Nandy, Ashis, *At The Edge of Psychology* (Delhi: Oxford University Press, 1980).

Nandy, Ashis, *The Intimate Enemy, Loss and Recovery of Self Under Colonialism* (Delhi: Oxford University Press, 1983).

Panikkar, K. M., *Hinduism and the West: A Study in Challenge and Response* (Chandigarh: Panjab University Publications, 1964).

Risley, Sir Herbert Hope, *The People of India* (London: W. Thacker and Company, 1915).

Rudolph, Lloyd I. and Suzanne Hoeber Rudolph, *The Modernity of Tradition: Political Development in India* (Chicago: University of Chicago Press, 1967).

Said, Edward W., *Orientalism* (New York: Vintage Books, 1978).

Said, Edward W., *The World, the Text, and the Critic* (New York: Vintage Books, 1983).

Said, Edward W., *After the Last Sky* (New York: Pantheon, 1986).

Sarkar, Sumit, *"Popular" Movements and "Middle Class" Leadership in Late*

Colonial India: Perspectives and Problems of a "History From Below" (Calcutta and New Delhi: K. P. Bagchi, 1983).

Schwab, Raymond, *The Oriental Renaissance, Europe's Rediscovery of India and the East 1680–1880* (trans. by Gene Patterson-Black and Victor Reinking, New York: Columbia University Press, 1984).

Seal, Anil, *The Emergence of Indian Nationalism: Competition and Collaboration in the Later Nineteenth Century* (Cambridge: Cambridge University Press, 1970).

Secretary of State for India, United Kingdom, *Report and Minutes of Evidence of the Committee Appointed by the Secretary of State for India to Inquire into the Position of Indian Students in the United Kingdom* (London: Eyre and Spottiswoode, 1907).

Srinivas, M. N., *Caste in Modern India* (Bombay: Asia, 1962).

Swan, Maureen, *Gandhi: The South African Experience* (Johannesburg: Ravan Press, 1985).

Washbrook, David, *The Emergence of Provinical Politics: The Madras Presidency, 1870–1920* (Cambridge: Cambridge University Press, 1976).

Yajnik, Indulal, *Shyamji Krishnavarma, Life and Times of an Indian Revolutionary* (Bombay: Lakshmi, 1950 [1934]).

8

THE RESONANCE OF THE ARAB-ISLAMIC HERITAGE IN THE WORK OF EDWARD SAID

—

Ferial J. Ghazoul

Whether I'm with Americans or with Arabs, I always feel incomplete. Part of myself can't be expressed.

Edward Said

Edward Said was trained as a literary critic, mostly in educational institutions located in the West, apart from his early education in Palestine and Egypt and sabbatical leave in Lebanon in the 1970s[1]. His critique of these Western institutions of learning and their discursive productions stems partly from a personal awareness that they leave him incomplete by neglecting that part of him which belongs to an alien cultural group. Said's sense of such exclusion and displacement comes from a lived experience that charges his academic speculations with urgency. As a Palestinian, Said is painfully aware that discursive deformations justify the actual dehumanization and obliteration of his Arab roots: verbal disfiguring and hegemonic overpowering are closely related and perceived with immediacy. This Western discourse, with its marvelous classics, wealth of details, experimental freedom, dynamic metamorphoses — all of which Said appreciates and revels in — has remained, in both its public and specialized forms, indifferent if not downright hostile to Said's roots. It is not surprising that the suppressed part of himself will find opportunities to break forth. This may take subtle and oblique forms when he treats another figure, Joseph Conrad, ambivalent like himself, for his doctoral thesis, or when he investigates beginnings in his subsequent research. The revolt against the unfair displacement may also take the more direct mode in confrontational essays and books whose aim is to undermine Western discourse's claims to impartiality. But the most fascinating aspect of Said's writing remains, for me at least, his embryonic efforts to bring together the two aspects of himself in a tentative project of self-fulfillment.

Said was also trained as a comparativist and is therefore armed with techniques and skills that allow for bringing together disparate facts, divorced situations and dissimilar heritages in order to uncover analogies, identities, differences, contrasts, and paradoxes. Said the literary scholar has transferred the use of such analytical tools to the fields of ideology, politics, and cultural studies.[2] In this transfer he strives also to bring together the two dimensions of his identity: American and Arab. If the American and Arab heritages have something in common, then it is this plurality, within a somewhat listless, ever-changing oneness. The plurality reveals itself neither as "melting pot" nor as "mosaic". It is made up of ever-shifting, multiple, semi-autonomous units with unequal access to power and expression. His is a context most akin to the "postmodern scene", where the multiplicity of genres, discourses, and terminologies threatens a babelization, but also promises a possible symphonic order where each instrument is heard while at the same time contributing to the overall music. It is at this intersection of the two heritages with Said's cast of mind as a critic and a comparativist, as a paradigmatic postmodernist, that we can glimpse the underlying possibilities of changing the contemporary cultural chaos into a genuinely global order, neither universal in concentrating on idealist essences, nor cosmopolitan in covering up difference under a common veneer. Said's tendency to exemplify his arguments through reference to music is an index of his inner desire to resolve tensions between points and counterpoints, to fulfill himself, to "complete it", as it were, not only as a liminal individual but as a citizen of liminal cultures. Thus, our quest to understand Said goes beyond understanding the man or the scholar. It is a quest to understand our postmodern condition with its contradictions, inconsistencies, incompleteness – and with its equally promising possibilities.

The personal element and the professional training fertilized each other in Said to produce one of the most original and controversial spokesmen of critical theory today. Situated in the center but with roots on the periphery, allowed to articulate from a privileged platform but denied an authentic voice, Said finds himself betwixt two civilizational modes. He partakes of American and Arab cultures that more often than not are at odds with each other, viewed as mutually exclusive, presented in terms of the Self versus the Other. Furthermore, Said is positioned prominently in the metropolitan arena where he systematically addresses students and readers from the United States and Europe. His audience is located essentially in the West, although he has written and been translated in the Arab world.[3] He is best known in Western popular circles for having explained the Palestinian position vis-a-vis the Zionists in the United States, and having gained a *succès de scandale* with his best-seller, *Orientalism*. But on a less flashy and perceptible level, Said has been also expanding the cultural space of the Other in the dominant Eurocentric discourse.

In this study I propose to show the strategy and tactical steps used by Said in challenging the monolithic structure of the hegemonic discourse, as well as the modes of introducing and mobilizing Arab-Islamic thought in his work, in both its manifest and latent presence. Said's use of notions and figures from Arab-Islamic culture remains marginal to the mainstream of his work; and he is by no means a specialist in Arab culture. Yet his contribution towards linking Arab-Islamic and Western cultures is, I maintain, highly relevant as a model for breaking down the normative and artificial barriers between the marginalized and the canonical without intellectual reductiveness or ideological polarization. The idea is not so much to learn from his occasional references to the Arab-Islamic legacy, but to look into his *démarche* as a possible alternative to the stale, impotent, and chaotic present scene.

Said's approach has been to start by dismantling accepted fallacies and entrenched views concerning Arab-Islamic culture in Western discourse by attacking its scholarship in *Orientalism* (1978), its mass media in *Covering Islam* (1981), and its political myths in *The Question of Palestine* (1979). This trilogy, supported by a number of other essays and articles, deconstructs the tinted glass with which everything Arab-Islamic is tainted and deformed. It flushes away, as it were, the plaque and accretions that prevent proper viewing. To what extent has Edward Said succeeded in repairing the damage that highly sophisticated false images and simulacra of the Arabs have done to Arab-Islamic culture? Clearly he has not demolished the false idols entirely: Orientalist discourse is still alive and not doing so badly. However, a dent has been made in the tight system, from which many contesting views and primal questions can now be posed publically, not only as far as Arabs and Muslims are concerned, but also for other excluded categories which could benefit from any ruptures in the tightness of the self-enclosed discursive system. A certain indeterminancy towards Orientalism, if not outright rejection of Orientalist theses, prevails in the academic air.

Moving from unmasking partiality, one-sidedness and prejudice to constructing a more viable discourse is a different and more laborious taks. Said's strategy in constructing an alternative discourse is just beginning to appear, and we can catch glimpses of it in his writing. In a sense, Said tries to go beyond Foucault, not by simply pointing out the mechanisms of hegemony and the interrelationships between power and knowledge, but by activating resistance and sketching alternatives. Thus, he not only unveils hegemony but also takes the first step towards the construction of alternative modes.[4]

Said's strategy seems to be twofold. On the one hand he develops a critical theory that links texts to their social and circumstantial origins. Thus the delinking of literature and its non-literary background that often takes place in criticism is questioned. But then the linking, as practised by

Said, is clearly not done in the traditional sociological mode of criticism (such as a conventional Marxist approach or an old-fashioned sociology of literature). He elaborates the relationship of the literary texts to the life of the author, as in *Joseph Conrad and the Fiction of Autobiography* (1966), the scholarly text to colonial policies, as in *Orientalism*, narratives to history, as in *Beginnings: Intention and Method* (1975), criticism to the socio-political scene, as in *The World, the Text, and the Critic* (1983), and the intersection of the literary with the social, as in the book of selected papers he edited entitled *Literature and Society* (1980). This linking reveals the complicity of the text with a given way of life by using and incorporating the insights of contemporary literary theory that bear on the subject. The mode is not so much to explain how the literary product expresses the ideological background of the author or dominant system, but how the *absence* in the work of art, what is not being said, what is not being articulated, is a form of suppression that foregrounds certain elements in the picture and excludes others.

In his studies of Jane Austen and Albert Camus, Said draws on Raymond Williams to show the ideological significance of incidental details and even programmed silences in literary texts. He extends Williams's method to include the semiotic connotations of global geography in addition to Williams's historical contextualization. Said shows persuasively how, in the case of Austen's *Mansfield Park*, the literary work in oblique ways contributes to justifications and rationalizations of the imperialist scheme of plunder. The novel insinuates a correspondence between order in the English mansion and order in the colonial estate, on income from which the mansion depends. Domestic morality dovetails with colonial discipline in the Caribbean. The prosperity, propriety and class morality of the English country house require a sugar plantation and slave labor overseas.[5] Geography is, therefore, charged with connotations; it figures in the literary works discussed by Said as political geography. Similarly, in Camus' short story, "The Adulterous Woman", Janine, the French Algerian protagonist, achieves a mystical union with the North African desert. This union with the land, as Said points out, contrasts with the absence of rapport with the land's native inhabitants, the Arab Algerians. Thus the story harbors an ideological message. It moves us by Janine's metaphoric union with the land, while dismissing the Arabs from such a union. This translates the wish of French colonialism: Algeria without the Algerians.[6]

The second aspect of Said's strategy operates on a different level. By introducing Arab-Islamic thought into his writing, Said brings in parallel views, and, in order to show affinities, draws insights from them to solve intellectual problems in metropolitan thought. This is not a matter, in my opinion, of noting that Said adorns his discourse with Arab-Islamic touches, the way someone may have a thoroughly modern urban house decorated with a few Bedouin cushions. Said is clearly feeling his way towards ushering in a more global comparative approach that goes beyond the cosmopolitan, essentially European approach.

Said's project is to undo the binary opposition of East/West and Self/Other, not to reverse it but to apply a different type of dialectic. Manichean oppositions such as East/West, us/them, tend to shape the worldview of Americans and Europeans as well as their victims. In the West they manifest themselves specifically towards Islam as the ultimate and dangerous Other. Said does not seek to dissolve the differences between cultures, nor to synthesize them in a totality, but to show how they coexist in a cross-fertilizing, heterogeneous global whole. He seeks to liberate Arab-Islamic culture from the view that it is fixed and threatening, demonstrating its dynamism and humanism. Furthermore, he delivers the marginalized culture from its ghetto in the isolation of area studies and shows its relevance to comparative studies. He wants Arab-Islamic culture re-admitted to the discourse of nations, in the first place by introducing and establishing hitherto unnoticed parallelisms and affinities to its Western counterpart. Using a figure from one culture to throw light on the other, Said establishes the analogies between, for example, the Irish poet W. B. Yeats and the Palestinian poet Mahmoud Darwish,[7] or Joseph Conrad and T. E. Lawrence.[8] Similarly, and without reductiveness, Said illuminates Foucault with Ibn Khaldun, and vice versa:

It is probable that Foucault's admirably un-nostalgic view of history and the almost total lack in it of metaphysical yearning, such as one finds in heirs to the Hegelian tradition, are both ascribable to his geographic bent. So marked is this in Foucault, and so deeply linked to his vision of statements as carefully fashioned extensions of institutions and instruments of governance, that it is usefully elucidated by someone who, although in a different and much earlier tradition than Foucault, resembles him in many ways, Ibn Khaldun, the great fourteenth-century Arab historiographer and philosopher. In the *Muqaddimah* Ibn Khaldun says that the science of history is unique because while related to rhetoric and civil politics it is different from both. He thus sees the historian's task as work taking place between rhetoric, on the one hand, and civil politics, on the other. This, it seems to me, describes Foucault's analytical attitude uncannily well: statements for him carry more weight than ways merely of speaking either convincingly or not, and these statements are also somewhat less in authority than the direct pronouncements of someone in governmental power.

The difference between Ibn Khaldun and Foucault is no less instructive. Both men – Ibn Khaldun more – are worldly historians who understand, and perhaps even appreciate, the dynamics of secular events, their relentless pressure, their ceaseless movement, their elusive complexity which does not permit the luxury of easy moral classification. And both are unlike Hobbes in that they respect and suspiciously admire the drive towards coherent order which characterizes human discourse as well as the historian's craft. Ibn Khaldun's vision of social order is what he calls 'asabiyah (usually translated as "group solidarity"); Foucault's is "the order of discourse", *l'ordre du discours*. Yet Ibn Khaldun's perspective is such that history for him is composed of social life cycles describing movements from origin, to ascendency, to decline, and rise again that occur within various polities, each of which is organized around the greater or lesser degree of *'asabiyah* within it. Foucault's perspective, however, is that in the modern period to which he belongs there is an unremitting and unstoppable expansion of power favouring the administrators, managers, and technocrats of what he calls disciplinary society.[9]

In many ways the similarity of Ibn Khaldun and Foucault in their concern with power structures and how they function is countered by the difference between them, which rests on their underlying metaphors: Ibn Khaldun's being essentially organic,[10] Foucault's the archive. The living organism is bound to die and its internal structure will decay, but the archive can extend indefinitely, as in a library invented by Borges.

What is the significance of mentioning Ibn Khaldun in an article for a collection of essays on Foucault written in English for a Western audience? Surely such an audience does not find Foucault easier to grasp by reference to Ibn Khaldun, who is not familiar within the Western frame of reference. The significance seems to me to lie in two areas. One is that Foucault had a precursor – and an Arab one at that! – who was equally concerned with issues of power and control. Cultures are seen here not so much as hopelessly different in time and mode, but as essentially pertaining to common human endeavor, although variable in conclusions and outlook. Secondly, the comparison offers another way of viewing power, not as extensive and tight, but as fragile and subject to decline. This view undermines and challenges the logic of power as defined by Foucault. It offers fresh ways of looking at the phenomenon of power.

Ibn Khaldun in many respects prefigures not only Foucault, but also Vico (and the Vichian view of historical cycles) – two European figures who have left their impact on Said's thought. Ibn Khaldun's resonance in Said's thought is part of his presence in a human archive or cycle, a presence that has been dismissed through the exclusion of non-Western thinkers from current debates in the West. This exclusion can be seen as an exile of non-European thought, its confinement to the prison-house of Orientalist discourse. Said thus combats marginalization by reactivating the obliterated documents, by reshuffling them, rather than replacing some by others. His endeavor has always been, not to fight for the occupation of a place, not to displace one ideology by another, not to glorify one figure at the expense of another, but to make room for cohabitation and coexistence, clearing space for the marginalized and subjected to present their case and enter into dialogue with the established (a Saidian tactic that parallels the solution that he envisages for Palestine). Resistance in this arena is a means for making one's voice heard. Said's quest is the more effective because, rather than being based on reversal or erasure, it is aimed at the dialogical and polyphonic. Errors, whether in the intellectual archives or in political geography, are not corrected by simply returning to an earlier historical moment – even if it is to the advantage of his people and constitutes the redress of their wrongs – but by looking forward to a situation where different needs, discursive and political, could live together.

Said not only evokes Ibn Khaldun on a manifest level: we also find Ibn Khaldun's method as a submerged trope elsewhere in Said's work when he sets out to reformulate issues. Said's project is to be radically corrective, to amend the lacunae and the corruptions, to revise distorted Western discourse. His tools are those of an "editor" who collates different versions and corrects misconstructions in order to establish the authenticity and the totality of a text. This very much resembles the "scientific" endeavour of Ibn Khaldun, who reflecting on human history thought it mandatory to collate and edit the available historical narratives in the light of reason and human conduct before drawing any conclusions. Thus Ibn Khaldun used anthropological observation to establish limits and varieties of human experience, by which one can correct the exaggerations and mythical presentations of historical accounts. The patterns and the lessons of history are then drawn from these "edited" accounts by use of human reasoning, not by attributing one's conclusions to a dogma or faith.[11] Now the conclusion may very well corroborate theological authority and revealed truth (as in the case of Ibn Khaldun and other Muslim philosophers); however, it was reached by human agency following human reasoning. Thus an emphasis is laid on truth reached secularly and profanely, a "worldly" truth, as it were. Said similarly collates, edits, uncovers, arranges, reflects in order to arrive at a more representative archive; his path in this endeavor is secular in the sense that it emphasizes human reasoning, possibilities of error, and progressive correction.

This centrality of the metaphor of the "text", its proper editing, transmission, and interpretation, is basic to Ibn Khaldun's historical research, and also is typical of Arab-Islamic culture as a whole, if one may so generalize. For instance, Nasr Hamid Abu Zeid, an influential Egyptian intellectual, has called Arab-Islamic culture one of the "text", in contrast to Greek culture, which revolved around the "mind", and ancient Egyptian culture, which centred on the "afterlife".[12] Arab-Islamic civilization centers on a *text*, namely, the Koran.

Said himself has been concerned with the notion of the text in several essays. Early on, he evoked the difference of the sense of the text in both the European and Arabic traditions in "The Text as Practice and as Idea":

> In the West the classics and the Bible are the most preserved, the most worked over, the most transmitted, and hence the most original texts of all. Many

institutions, including both the Church and the university, are devoted to continuing the texts, prolonging them as it were, even as a part of their preservation. Standing very near the center of intellectual life in the West is the tradition of classical scholarship . . . A probable reason for the fertility of the great classical tests is that access to them, their preservation, and their transmission is irrevocably connected to their original appearance in three different "foreign" languages. Hebrew, Greek, Latin and then the numerous vernaculars have accounted for the continuing need of translations, editors, interpreters, whose culture and institutional focus is the text . . .

Outside the Judeo-Christian textual tradition, in the Arab-Islamic for instance, rather different traditions prevail. One of them is *i'djaz*, a concept which describes the uniqueness of the Koran as rendering all others impotent by comparison. Thus since the central text is in Arabic, and since, unlike the Gospels or even the Torah, it is given as unitary and complete, textual traditions are essentially supportive, not restorative. All texts are secondary to the Koran, which is inimitable . . . there is a hierarchy of disciplines and of books in relation to the Koran. Thus two sciences above all other, jurisprudence (*fiqh*) and tradition (*hadith*), systematic textual traditions control the editor's work, and in the case of the *hadith* they are very elaborate and systematic indeed . . . When not dealing with texts associated with the Koran, Islamic editors made use of the system of *idjaza* (license to transmit), which although originally the third method of transmitting Koranic traditions in print, came to be used for all other manuscripts.[13]

It is significant that Said's comparisons move beyond the level of mere individual figures (Ibn Khaldun versus Foucault) to that of the larger issue of textuality. We tend to oppose textuality to orality, often forgetting that attitudes towards the "text" in post-literate cultures may vary. It is this variation that Said insists upon.

Western culture since Plato has emphasized the written text, with all its connotations of speculation, over the oral. More recently, ethnologists and folklorists have enriched our understanding of the mechanisms of literature and mythology through extracting the aesthetic and intellectual lessons of oral tales and ritual performances. In critical discussions today, these two modes of discourse and knowledge tend to be opposed. The Islamic attitude towards textuality combines within it, deriving from notions of Koranic revelation, both the textual and the oral, the text and the context, as Said explains. This contemporary controversy between the literate and the oral, with its implications of reflection versus memorization, on the one hand, and elitism versus populism, on the other, is resolved in the Islamic tradition, where the contextual dimension is incorporated in the text. The Koran's first revealed verse opens with the command: "Recite/Read".[14]

Islam has been characterized as a literate culture, described as obsessed with the book in all its manifestations, (whether material – binding, calligraphy, illuminations, etc. – or metaphorical – authenticity, interpretation, reception). The Koran was not only "the first best-seller" (in the words of the Islamic scholar Isma'il Raji al-Faruqi), but in it all faiths with "Books" are recognized. Their followers are known as *ahl al-kitab* (the people of the Book), in contrast to those without, to the *jahalis* (the "ignorant" ones). In fact, the Islamic critique of the other religions of the Book, Judaism and Christianity, is based on their failure to preserve the Book correctly. One of the charges, though it is not so absolute as to invalidate these religions, is that they failed "to preserve the revealed word of God and are calling 'word of God' that which redactors and editors had reworked . . . This is not to question the integrity of the Biblical text *since*, but *before*, canonization", as Faruqi puts it.[15]

Arab-Islamic culture is dominated by a ruling metaphor, that of the "text". Specifically, the textual metaphor that Said underlines is textuality within a dialogical context. This centrality of the text, as Said, along with a number of contemporary Arab intellectuals, senses, can be easily turned to serve dogmatic and reactionary purposes. At the same time, the textual corpus cannot be discarded any more than one can discard one's cultural identity. Said sees the vital necessity of the text, but not as a severed entity from the body of history where it turns into an aesthetic commodity or a sacralized fetish to be contemplated, as in a game or process that is intransitive – in the sense that it does not contribute to historical change. The only way for Said to dissolve the rigidity and the reification of texts is to look into their circumstances; how they originated and came about, how they entered human history. Hence, his emphasis is not on the final product, but on its onset, where its objective and *raison d'être* can be detected. Said is eager to discover what brings about, and what configurations permit, the insertion and perpetuation of certain texts or structures in order better to understand their significance. Said protests against allowing a text to stultify human possibilites. This can happen where the ahistorical, eternal and metaphysical epithets cover up ideological manipulations, where potential questions are displaced by high-sounding critical prose, and where the present and the future are contained by an appropriation of the past manifested in reserving the right to speak in the name of its texts. Said therefore opposes mummifying texts or rendering them impotent through elevating them or stigmatizing them – and, since that is often done in the name of scholarly order, structure or grammar, he warns about the emptiness of academic pursuits that are more concerned with proving a critical dogma, with reinforcing a known point at the price of the knowable, than with questioning the order and trying to revise and radicalize it. He seeks in his project to revive examples of resistance to fixations in both Western and Arab-Islamic cultures.

Said's text-oriented vision happens also to coincide with his profession as a commentator on texts. This intersection of cultural background and vocational training has not resulted in a blind commitment to "textualism". It has produced a critical attitude towards the "text", which preserves it as an activity and not as a cult object. Differently put, Said humanizes – or makes worldly – the texts by rendering them pertinent to human experience. Said opted to align himself with the Zahirites – who emphasized the event and context in medieval Islamic scholarship – just as he sided with scholars who emphasized human relations from Vico to Raymond Williams.

Said's opposition to "textualism" – where the text replaces human beings, where the eternal removes the present, where the structure and its perpetuation become more important than acts, where grammatical systematization takes priority over communication and dialogue – is expressed and illuminated in his reference to a linguistic debate that took place in medieval Andalusia over the *'amil* (the regent, a grammatical term indicating the governance of a word by another in syntactical regimen). The evocation of the book, entitled *Response to Grammarians*, by the minor Zahirite figure Ibn Mada' al-Qurtubi, seems odd in Said's literary works.[16] Yet it stands as a metonym for the refusal to subordinate scholarship to perfecting neat systems (of grammar, in this case). Ibn Mada's underlying objective was to contribute to understanding the mechanisms of language and so render it accessible. What attracted Said to this medieval scholar was his resistance to subordinating meaning and communication to self-styled and self-contained systematizations. For Said, meaning precedes systematization; systematization necessarily employs interpretive violence to achieve its order.

Said's decision to insert a distant grammarian in his contemporary discourse reflects a certain selective and critical attitude towards the Arab legacy. His approach neither endorses nor dismisses *in toto*, but searches the articulations of the culture to find points of "worldliness" that can be recovered and with which alliances can be established. His interest in certain exegetical practices reflects his inclination towards excavating the culture to find potential insights.

Said uses the distinction between the two interpretive schools, Zahirites and the opposed Batinists, linking them to actuality versus textuality, event versus structure, while also taking the side of the Zahirites who emphasized the contexts of revealing the Koranic message, in order to support his position that texts should be anchored in reality. The Batinists, Said maintains, turned meaning into an esoteric exercise, rather than opening it up towards communal issues. In Batinist exegesis, the circumstantial setting of the revealed verses was obliterated, and the inner speculation was privileged to arrive at the significance of the sacred message:

> Batinists held that meaning in language is concealed within the words, meaning is therefore available only as the result of an inward tending exegesis. The Zahirites – their name derives from the Arabic word for clear, apparent and phenomenal – argued that words had only a surface meaning, one that

was anchored to a particular usage, circumstance, historical and religious situation.[17]

Texts, of course, have specific locations in time and place. Yet, whether sacred or profane, they seem at times to be transported beyond their place and time. Great texts defy geography and history; everyone, especially comparatists, can attest to the potency of texts produced in different cultures and different times. Critics have argued over the issue of localism versus universalism in literature and literature's historicity or ahistoricity for centuries. Marx, for example, wondered how man in an industrial world can enjoy Greek mythology. His answer explained the pleasure as a sort of nostalgia for one's childhood, a recollection of an earlier mode of production.[18] Said's resolution of the simultaneous historicity and transhistoricity of texts is borrowed from Koranic scholarship. In exegetical works on the Koran, one factor is the "occasions of revelation" (asbab al-nuzul). Said makes use of a medieval Islamic solution (that of the Andalusian Zahirite theologian Ibn Hazm) of a controversy to comprehend texts' ambivalence; on this view texts can be at once historical and pertinent for all times.

> [T]he Koran speaks of historical events, yet is not itself historical. It repeats past events, which it condenses and particularizes, yet is not itself an actually lived experience; it ruptures the human continuity of life, yet God does not enter temporality by a sustained or concerted act . . . In short, the Zahirite position adopts a view of the Koran that is absolutely circumstantial without at the same time making that worldliness dominate the actual sense of the text: all this is the ultimate avoidance of vulgar determinism in the Zahirite position . . .
>
> What Ibn Hazm does . . . is to view language as possessing two seemingly antithetical characteristics: that of a divinely ordained institution, unchanging, immutable, logical, rational, intelligible; and that of an instrument existing as pure contingency, as an institution signifying meanings anchored in specific utterances. It is exactly because the Zahirites see language in this double perspective that they reject reading techniques that reduce words and their meanings back to radicals from which (in Arabic at least) they may be seen grammatically to derive. Each utterance is its own occasion and as such is firmly anchored in the worldly context in which it is applied. And because the Koran, which is the paradigmatic case of divine-and-human language, is a text that incorporates speaking and writing, reading and telling, Zahirite interpretation itself accepts as inevitable not the separation between speech and writing, not the disjunction between a text and its circumstantiality, but rather their necessary interplay.[19]

Said also underlines the highly contextualized situation of the Koran, which is presented in terms of a speaker, God (through an angel), to an addressee, Muhammed, the Messenger. Thus, context is incorporated and emphasized in the text itself. All this reveals to Said what he is anxious to show: the importance of understanding the context and the role of the dialogical relationship in comprehending a message.

In one of Said's most powerful statements, the opening chapter of *The World, the Text, and the Critic* entitled "Secular Criticism", a distinction is made between two modes of belonging: *filiation* and *affiliation*. Although the terms are borrowed from the subtitle to an article by Michael Riffaterre,[20] the notion has deep roots in Arab-Islamic thought and history. The terms condense two conflicting ways of life, one based on kin loyalty and the other based on common conviction. Tribe versus religion, nationalism versus class, the unconscious versus consciousness – all are possible transformations of the two principles. One is given, the other is supposed to be chosen. Although Said does not appeal directly to Arab examples to elucidate the difference, I sense that he articulates ever-present tensions between two distinct modes in Arab culture.

Filiation corresponds to *'asabiya*, a notion of group solidarity based on kinship, i.e., blood ties. In other words, it is a relationship of solidarity derived from biological and therefore unconscious and non-voluntary elements. Opposed to *'asabiya* stands the "kinship" derived from spiritual ties and shared beliefs. Islam as religion displaces pre-Islamic (*jahili*) tribal *'asabiya* with a fellowship of conviction that is affiliative, with a volitional dimension present in it. Ibn Khaldun presents the leap from *'asabiya* to "Islam" as one from the domain of the instinctive to the domain of the deliberate.[21]

The Koran makes it amply clear that solidarity should not be based on kin brotherhood but on spiritual brotherhood:[22]

O believers, take not your fathers and brothers to be your friends, if they prefer unbelief to belief; whosoever of you takes them for friends, those – they are the evildoers.

Say: "If your fathers, your sons, your brothers, your wives, your clan, your possessions that you have gained, commerce you fear may slacken, dwellings you love – if these are dearer to you than God and His Messenger, and to struggle in His way, then wait till God brings His command; God guides not the people of the ungodly.

Repentence IX: 24

Thou shalt not find any people who believe in God and the Last Day who are loving to anyone who opposes God and His Messenger, not though they were their fathers, or their sons, or their brothers, or their clan.

The Disputer LVII: 22

The believers indeed are brothers; so set things right between your two brothers.

Apartments XLIX: 10

In Arab-Islamic history the tension between Arabism and Islamism, with the implications of subjected people seeking equality through the universal medium of Islam against the elitism derived from Arabian descent, is well-known. The counter-movement to Arabism known as *Shu'ubiyah* (belonging to non-Arab peoples) assumed a literary form, and its proponents "derided the Arab pretensions to intellectual superiority in poetry and literature".[23] *Shu'ubiyah* was often the reverse side of Arab chauvinism. Said's approach coincides with the lofty ideals of an early revolutionary Islam, whose goal was to shed narrow nationalisms and "tribal" attachment, not in order to deny the existence of the varieties of human cultures, but to knit bonds based on humane awareness.

The notions of filiation and affiliation are not mutually exclusive, as Said points out. Bonds of affiliation may be degraded into filiation. An adherent to a school, party, or faith may define its practices clannishly, just as a member born into a given group may choose to belong to it, not through filiation but through critical awareness: "We have in Auerbach an instance both of filiation with his natal culture and, because of exile, affiliation with it through critical consciousness and scholarly work."[24] The contrast between filiation and affiliation is extended to cover contemporary literature and criticism. Said hears in critics such as Lukács a call for substituting affiliation for alienation, a form of failed filiation as a result of loss of meaningful contact with one's production, including children:

> [O]nly class consciousness, itself an insurrectionary form of an attempt at affiliation, could possibly break through the antinomies and atomizations of reified existence in the modern capitalist world-order.
> What I am describing is the transition from a failed idea or possibility of filiation to a kind of compensatory order, that . . . provides men and women with a new form of relationship, which I have been calling affiliation, but which is also a new system.[25]

Said's understanding of filiation in opposition to affiliation corresponds to the opposition of nature versus culture, the given versus the man-made, *Gemeinschaft* versus *Gesellschaft*, the tribal order versus the Islamic order in its pristine form. But what is interesting is that among all these possible nominations, he has chosen the filiation/affiliation contrast. "Thus if a filial relationship was held together by natural bonds and natural forms of authority . . . the new affiliative relationship changes these bonds into what seem to be transpersonal forms – such as guild consciousness . . . The filiative scheme belongs to the realms of nature . . . whereas affiliation belongs exclusively to culture and society."[26]

When viewing religions not as dogmas but as cultural worldviews and civilizational modes, we discern differences in the metaphor of paternity and filiation. The antipathy towards filiation, mindless fidelity to kin, and to bonds expressed in terms of fathering and begetting, may be sensed in the transformation of metaphors of creation from carnal intercourse, as in most polytheistic religions, to those of creating by speech, as in the monotheistic religions. God created the universe through a verbal order, and He made Adam (Genesis 1–2; Koran XLI: 9–12 and III: 59, among others). The emphasis is on word and work, on pronouncing and making. This stands in contrast to deities who create through copulation, as in Greek mythology. But nowhere among the three religions is the metaphor of filiation rejected as forcefully as it is in Koranic discourse. In the Biblical discourse, both in the Old and the New Testaments, divinity and paternity do overlap at times. A number of passages ascribe children to God (Genesis 6: 24), and consider Him as the father of the king (Psalms 2: 7; 89: 26, II Samuel 17: 14; I Chronicles 17: 13) or of the people of Israel (Isaiah 9: 6; 63: 14–16; Jeremiah 3: 19; Hosea 1: 10).[27] Islam categorically rejects attributing fatherhood to God and specifically refuses the epithet of "Son of God" to Jesus, although Islam recognizes a dimension of divinity in Jesus. Muhammed's humanity is also emphatically insisted upon in Islam, and his relationship to God is seen in terms of a human addressee, an "interlocuteur valable" rather than a kinsperson. Said's position against filiation and his support for affiliation invoke resonances of the Islamic *Weltanschauung*. In Islam, needless to say, the humanity of the Prophet has been sanctified at times, and the bonds of affiliation turned into filiation, but this only confirms Said's position that the nature of the affiliative should spring from examining the existing relationships in a system, rather than depend on the labels.

Said's quest echoes such Islamic antipathies to filial metaphors because they are part of his culture, not so much by virtue of his filiation, since he is not a Muslim, but through affiliation. He does not thoughtlessly reproduce his culture; he strives to produce a new system that would correct not only the Zionist tribalism by which his people have been victimized, but also Arab parochialism. In that sense, Said, like Auerbach, affiliates himself to his culture. Said, though he clearly binds himself to his roots, is nevertheless able to articulate most eloquently critiques addressed to practices and blindnesses in his own cultures, the American and the Arab. He criticizes the American academy and Western political establishments, Arab leadership and fellow Arab scholars as well as his much admired mentors, Marx and Foucault, whose short-sightedness he has been willing to underline, showing the Orientalist slant of Marx, for example,[28] and the lack of recognition of anti-hegemonic potentialities in Foucault.[29] After all, affiliation is based on a critical consciousness, and when that is lost, it turns more or less automatically into filiation. Said consistently rejects filiation, even when to do so puts him squarely against his own mentors and people (American/Palestinian).

One should not presume that Said is using the Arabic heritage for display and in an eclectic manner. His insertion of Arab sources and visions in his work is critical and springs from a personal need to overcome identity cleavages, as well as from a professional need to destroy artificial cultural barriers and build affiliative alliances and meaningful correspondences among different traditions.

It would be an exaggeration to claim that Said has constructed a viable system to replace the critical disarray of Euro-centrism, but he has opened the door and pointed towards future directions. Said's most profound lesson is his fidelity to criticism. His *démarche* of articulating the voices of marginalized culture, including their intimate metaphors, into the mainstream of global cultural discourse is a first step in a journey of a thousand and one steps. His position recalls that of Shahrazad, who, although her ultimate victory over the forces of authorial might came after a thousand nights of creative work, already triumphed on the very first night when she convinced Shahrayar to enter into a dialogical relationship.

Notes

1 For an account of Said's background and education, see Dinitia Smith, "America's Profoundly Persuasive Palestinian", *Washington Report on Middle East Affairs* (May 1989), pp. 26–31.

2 See the following articles by Edward Said: "An Ideology of Difference", *Critical Inquiry*, 12 (Autumn 1985), pp. 38–58; "Identity, Negation and Violence", *New Left Review*, 171 (September/October 1988), pp. 46–60; "Representing the Colonized: Anthropology's Interlocutors", *Critical Inquiry*, 15 (Winter 1989), pp. 205–25.

3 Articles by Edward Said have been appearing regularly in major Arab reviews since the 1970s. Two of his books have been translated into Arabic: *Orientalism* and *Covering Islam*.

4 See Said, "Foucault and the Imagination of Power", in *Foucault: A Critical Reader*, edited by David Couzens Hoy (Oxford: Basil Blackwell, 1986), pp. 149–55.

5 Said, "Jane Austen and Empire", in *Raymond Williams*, edited by Terry Eagleton (Oxford: Polity Press, 1990), pp. 150–64.

6 Said, "Narrative, Geography and Interpretation", *New Left Review*, 180 (March/April 1990), pp. 81–97.

7 Said, *Yeats and Decolonization* (Derry: Field Day Theatre [A Field Day Pamphlet 15], 1988).

8 Said, *Joseph Conrad and the Fiction of Autobiography* (Cambridge, Mass.: Harvard University Press, 1966), p. 12.

9 Said, "Foucault and the Imagination of Power", pp. 149–50.

10 Ferial Ghazoul, "The Metaphors of Historiography: A Study of Ibn Khaldun's Historical Imagination", in *In Quest of Islamic Humanism*, edited by Arnold Green (Cairo: The American University in Cairo Press, 1984), pp. 48–61.

11 Ibn Khaldun, *The Muqaddimah*, trans. by Franz Rosenthal (Princeton: Princeton University Press, 1967), I, pp. 6–14.

12 Nasr Hamid Abu Zeid, *Mafhum al-nass* (The Concept of Text) (Cairo: General Book Organization, 1990), p. 11.

13 Said, "The Text as Practice and as Idea", *Modern Language Notes*, 88, no. 6 (Dec. 1973), pp. 1072–3.
14 Said, *The World, the Text, and the Critic* (Cambridge, Mass.: Harvard University Press, 1983), pp. 37–8. See also Nasr Hamid Abu Zeid, *Mafhum al-nass*, pp. 35–84.
15 Isma'il R. al-Faruqi, "Islam", in *Historical Atlas of the Religions of the World*, edited by Isma'il R. al-Faruqi and David E. Sopher (New York: Macmillan, 1974), pp. 246–7.
16 Said, *The World, the Text, and the Critic*, p. 36.
17 Ibid.
18 Karl Marx, *A Contribution to the Critique of Political Economy*, ed. M. Dobbs (New York: International Publishers, 1970), p. 217.
19 Said, *The World, the Text, and the Critic*, pp. 37–9.
20 Michael Riffaterre, "The Stylistic Approach to Literary History", *New Literary History*, II, no. 1 (Autumn 1970), p. 39.
21 Ibn Khaldun, *The Muqaddimah*, I, pp. 306–7
22 All Koranic citations in this study are from A. J. Arberry's translation, *The Koran Interpreted* (New York: Macmillan, 1955).
23 Philip Hitti, *History of the Arabs* (London: Macmillan, 1970), p. 402.
24 Said, *The World, the Text, and the Critic*, p. 16.
25 Ibid, p. 19.
26 Ibid, p. 20.
27 Isma'il Raji al-Faruqi, "Islam", p. 246.
28 Said, *Orientalism* (New York: Pantheon, 1978), pp. 153–6.
29 Said, "Foucault and the Imagination of Power", p. 154.

9

THE PALESTINIAN INTELLECTUAL AND THE LIBERATION OF THE ACADEMY

—

Barbara Harlow

It is no exaggeration to say that for the first time in our struggle against Zionism the West appears ready to hear our side of the story. Therefore we must tell it, we must stand in the international theater created out of our struggle against Zionism, and therefore we must diffuse our message dramatically.
Edward W. Said: *The Question of Palestine*

Edward Said's exemplary contribution to the advancement of intellectual work and academic endeavor in the United States is critically informed by his position as a practicing member of multiple constituencies, both literary-critical and political. His work and intellectual trajectory remind us that not only is the world reflected in literature, but that literature works in the world. I shall thus begin my contribution to this collection somewhat obliquely with an account of certain aspects of the Palestinian *intifada*. I shall then proceed in the same apparently oblique fashion to consider the career and some of the writings of the martyred Palestinian intellectual, Ghassan Kanafani.

My theme is the relationship of struggles for national liberation to intellectual work, including the role of academics within educational institutions. That this theme is of particular importance to understanding Edward Said's career should probably go without saying. Nevertheless, it needs repeating that Said's often isolated and in some ways inimitable example has to be situated on the broad terrain of intellectual life, not only in the West but in those places still under the heel of brutal, totalitarian regimes that violently suppress what we often think of under the anodyne – but, in the best of situations, still meaningful – term, "academic freedom." To this end, I have found the writings of Kanafani, another "Palestinian intellectual" writing from what has been constructed as the other side of the First/Third World divide, to be indispensable, for reasons that I trust will become obvious as the essay proceeds.

In June 1990 the Israeli government extended the existing closing orders for Palestinian universities in the Occupied Territories of the West Bank and Gaza Strip for another three months. Already, when that extension was implemented, the universities had been continuously closed for two and a half years, since the beginning of the *intifada*, or uprising, on December 9, 1987. The universities, according to the Israeli government and its military occupation authorities, functioned as mobilization and organizational sites for the popular Palestinian challenge to Israeli domination. But the argument had become specious, proven to be fallacious by the 30 months of the *intifada*, which sustained itself despite the continuous closure of the universities. The ostensible justification for Israel's flagrant denial of Palestinian academic freedom and the criminalization of Palestinian education, that it was necessary for the sake of "peace," was revealed as concealing a different agenda: the de-education of the Palestinian people living under Israeli occupation.

This date, December 9, 1987, cited now and commemorated as marking the onset of the *intifada*, does not signal a radical beginning or even a decisive departure for the historical trajectory of Palestinian resistance and its struggle for self-determination and self-representation. Rather it was a critical turning-point in, and continuation of, its recent history, punctuated by such dates as 1948 – the establishment of the state of Israel – and 1967 – the Israeli occupation of the West Bank and Gaza Strip. So, too, the military closure of Palestinian universities by Israeli occupation authorities does not betray a dramatic new policy or even any subtle change on the part of the government. Between 1974 and 1987, for example, prior to the *intifada*, Bir Zeit University, located just outside the West Bank town of Ramallah, was closed sixteen times for periods ranging from one to four months. Nonetheless, and despite the fact that the university did not enjoy a single "normal" academic year, Bir Zeit did graduate fourteen classes during that period. Despite, too, its ongoing closure throughout the *intifada*, Bir Zeit, like other Palestinian universities, has succeeded in continuing to educate and graduate Palestinian students. And in June 1990, as the result of an alternative, often clandestine, educational practice, a practice constantly threatened by the arrest, detention and deportation of faculty, administrators and students, approximately 80 students (albeit a significant decrease from the pre-*intifada* numbers of 250) did receive their degrees from Bir Zeit University.

However the beginnings of the *intifada* are dated, to whatever event its beginning is attributed, whether to the automobile "accident" in which an Israeli army vehicle hit the car of Palestinian workers from Gaza, killing four, or to the public dismissal by the Arab League summit that Fall of the question of Palestine from its agenda of priorities, the progressive development of the *intifada* from apparently spontaneous mass demonstrations to an organized and protracted popular uprising consolidated itself in the last weeks of 1987. The first of the *nida'at*, "calls" or communiqués, that would continue to organize the events of the *intifada* and articulate its slogans, goals and program, issued by the newly constituted Unified National Leadership of the Uprising (UNLU), appeared on January 8, 1988. Call No. 2, two days later, elaborated a projected reterritorialization of the West Bank and Gaza, a Palestinian redrawing of the political and cultural topography of Israeli occupation: "Let us close all streets to the occupation troops . . . Let the Palestinian stones fall upon the heads of the occupation troops and agents. Let Palestinian flags wave . . . Let us disobey the curfew orders . . ." (pp. 16–17). Call No. 3 appeared on January 18, 1988, and appealed to all sectors of the Palestinian population – shopkeepers, workers, students, taxi and bus drivers, doctors and health service person-nel, owners of medical-supply factories and pharmacies, owners of national capital, academics and professionals – to participate in the elaboration of a liberated topography. Students were summoned: "Let us teach them that their policy of closing educational institutions . . . will not benefit them . . . Let us mobilize the student masses from villages, camps and cities in the school of revolution and struggle" (p. 20). And academics, too, were enjoined to deploy their skills, position and training in rewriting the Palestinian historical narrative: "You should participate in the popular and national committees, as well as the specialized committees, and contribute effectively in the uprising. You can help by donating food and other aid, by your literary writing, by writing popular songs and slogans, by contributing to media campaigns, as well as organizing marches and sit-ins against the occupation policies" (pp. 21–2).

Education – students, faculty, institutions – was explicitly mobilized as an integral and functioning arm of the *intifada* program. Subsequent calls by the leadership in the coming months would elaborate the specific projects to be undertaken by teachers and students as well as the emergent general parameters of a concerted and sustained popular education. Education was itself written into the history and chronology of the *intifada* as days of academic solidarity, like those on behalf of prisoners, deportees, and families of the martyrs, were announced: "Monday, April 16th, is the day of solidarity with the educational institutions; attend them as a challenge to the closure decisions" (Call No. 13: April 12, 1988); "May 5th is a day for foiling the enemy's decision to close academic institutions. We shall go to these institutions from 9am till midday" (Call No. 15: April 30, 1988); and, as military pressure against intifadist students intensified, "June 15th is a general strike day for solidarity with detained students and supporting popular education" (Call No. 19: June 8, 1988). Concrete educational guidelines were delineated:

The United National Leadership has decided to challenge this racist occupa-tion law [closure of the schools and universities] by breaking the order. [We]

call on our students, teachers and educational institutions and administrations
to challenge this law in a unified way and in all places, by organizing the
educational process on a nationalist basis; whereby you can defeat the policy
of keeping our people ignorant. We also call on international institutions and
organizations to support our people's struggle to defeat this policy. (Call No.
9: March 2, 1988).

and

We call on all teachers to cooperate fully in the process of popular education
and to escalate their struggle to protest the occupation's measures, such as
depriving them of their salaries and continuing to close the academic
institutions. (Call No. 16: May 13, 1988)

and

All students and employees of educational institutions should attend these
institutions, and be committed to the study hours lasting until noon. Popular
education should be continued and consolidated. (Call No. 17: 22 May 1988)

and

We urge students, teachers and academic institutions, to continue education
and to compensate for lost school time on official holidays, while affirming
total adherence to the strike on full strike days and increasing popular
education to raise our students' academic level. (Call No. 19: June 8, 1988).

and six months into the *intifada*,

We urge those in charge of the universities and other educational institutions
to organize the academic life (Call No. 20: June 21, 1988).

The first issue of *Qadaya tarbawiya* (Educational Issues), distributed a
year later by one of the popular committees for education, described the by
then well-developed alternative popular education project: "*al-ta'lim al-
sha'bi* (popular education) is distinguished by the fact that it is practiced in
the circumstances of daily life (*ahya'*), not in regularized institutions," and
further, that it is "governed by democratic relations between teachers and
students" (p. 7).

A decade earlier, Edward Said, having traced for a United States academic
audience the century-long trajectory of the Zionist enterprise and its
colonizing transfer from Europe to the land of Palestine, had written with
optimistic confidence in *The Question of Palestine* of an apparent Western
readiness "to hear [the Palestinian] side of the story" (p. 232). Three years
later, in June 1982, the Israeli Defense Forces (with United States support)

invaded Lebanon and laid a summer-long siege to the western sector of its divided capital, Beirut. At the end of August, following extended negotiations and US promises of international protection for the civilians who remained behind, the PLO fighting forces under Yasir Arafat withdrew from Lebanon to be redispersed in other Arab countries from Tunisia to Yemen. A scant two weeks following the PLO departure from Lebanon, IDF forces entered West Beirut to oversee the massacre by Lebanese Christian Phalangists of several thousand Palestinians in the refugee camps of Sabra and Shatila. The Palestine Research Center was destroyed, and its entire historical archives were confiscated and removed to Israel. These records, which would later be part of a "prisoner exchange" arranged between the Israeli government and Palestinian representatives, documented part of the life-history of Palestine and became a site of political contest between opposing claims to the land and its history.

The PLO leadership in exile, meanwhile, riven into conflicted political and ideological factions, took up separate residences in Tunis and Damascus, to be reunified only at the "national unity" meeting in April 1987 of the Palestine National Council (PNC) held in Algiers. Before the PNC would meet again a year and a half later, the *intifada* initiatives in the Occupied Territories developed to change radically the existing spatialized historical – and hierarchical – configuration of exile and occupation that had characterized the Palestinian resistance struggle. From within the Occupied Territories, the Palestinian population collectively enacted Said's earlier dictum: " . . . we must stand in the international theater created out of our struggle against Zionism, and . . . we must diffuse our message dramatically" (p. 232). And on November 15, 1988, the PNC, at its nineteenth meeting held in Algiers, issued the Declaration of Independence for the State of Palestine.

In the early months of the *intifada*, while international press and TV camera crews were still allowed to work in relatively unrestricted conditions inside the Occupied Territories, a new image of the Palestinians, "the children of the stones," was disseminated to a Western public that had long been provided with an exclusive US-Israeli-sponsored rhetoric of the immanent threat posed to Western ethical values and physical safety by "Arab terrorists." The re-education of a US popular audience on the question of Palestine, a self-representing remaking by the Palestinians themselves of their traditional images as either refugees with UNRWA ration cards or Kalashnikov-carrying guerrillas, was undertaken from within the *intifada*. As Said pointed out in an interview with Bruce Robbins in early 1988:

> I think the best thing about the present moment is that a lot of people are taking note of the heroism of the Palestinians and their refusal to capitulate. And obviously their concerted and organized resistance, which is emerging in

an unprecedented way. And I think a part of this is that a lot of the media –
that is, the print media, the electronic media, and of course the radio – have
been reporting the events, which in and of themselves are impressive on their
own. (pp. 37–8).

As he reminded his readers parenthetically in "*Intifada* and Independence,"
"*intifada* is the only Arabic word to enter the vocabulary of twentieth-
century world politics" (p. 23).

The educational, cultural and political impact of the Palestinian *intifada*
on US academic discourse – and university activism – has been nearly as
alarming to US supporters of the state of Israel as has been the exemplary
popular *intifada* education in the Israeli-occupied territories to the military
authorities. Nor is the pro-Israeli project to foreclose that critical discursive
development within the US academy without analogy with the closure of
Palestinian universities in the Occupied Territories. The *AIPAC College
Guide*, published by the American Israel Public Action Committee in 1984
to counter the overwhelmingly indignant, even outraged, responses, both
popular and (less often) official, to the Israeli invasion of Lebanon and the
massacres in the Sabra and Shatila refugee camps, included blacklists of
individual scholars supporting Palestinian rights (such as Edward Said
himself), as well as a campus-by-campus review of over 100 US universities
which had held pro-Palestinian activities. The *AIPAC Guide* was followed
in 1988, in reaction to the *intifada* and its radically transforming impact on
public perceptions of the Palestinian struggle, by *Israel on Campus: Under
Fire*, published by the University Service Department of the American
Zionist Youth Foundation as a "kit" to assist in organizing campus
campaigns against a popular re-education of US academics, students and
intellectuals on the question of Palestine. Palestinian academic freedom,
however, represents not only open universities but the right for those same
universities to develop their own independent curricula and to select their
faculty. It also entails a liberation of US academic discourse.

> **Or take the American reaction to the militant Palestinian students in the
> Occupied Territories. These students have quite literally become the vanguard
> of struggle against the occupation, but they have paid a steep price in arrests,
> houses demolished, schools and universities closed. If this were happening
> almost anywhere else, there would be a solid phalanx of professors protesting
> the infringements on academic freedom. With the exception of the usual
> intrepid few, the opposite has been the case.**
>
> Edward Said, *After the Last Sky*

In an address to a conference on Palestinian academic freedom in the
Occupied Territories, held in Washington, DC in June 1990 by the Palestinian
Academic Freedom Network (PAFNET) as part of a new campaign in US
universities on behalf of Palestinian academic freedom, Edward Said argued
that, under the pressure of the *intifada*, the Israeli example has lost much of

its rhetorical gloss of "peace, security and democracy" to become a negative and brutal message. The Palestinian demand for self-determination and self-representation is instantiating itself in the very work of the *intifada*, from the "children of the stones" to the Unified National Leadership and the organized network of popular committees that are elaborating the infrastructural bases – medical, educational, agricultural, social security, legal – of a future Palestinian state. The intifadists are successfully retaking for themselves both projects of the term *representation*: *Darstellung*, or portrayal, and *Vertretung*, to stand or speak for. Reminding his largely student activist audience at the academic freedom conference, Arab and non-Arab alike, of a number of "facts," Said enjoined the diversity of listeners to assume a new and collective responsibility of their own to act upon the Palestinian lessons and critical example of the *intifada* within a US educational space.

It is still the case, Said insisted, that the US remains the only totally committed supporter of Israel in the world today, and that there continue to be, despite the work of the *intifada*, enormous gaps in knowledge about the question of Palestine; that the US relationship with Israel is its last remaining post-war commitment – whereas the *intifada* has provided the model for the global uprisings of the last two and one-half years; and that, indeed, in the United States the relationship between the universities as an institution, the dominant media, and the intellectual class is still so contained by US government interests as to ensure an "iron curtain" between Western and Arab cultures. Furthermore, Said went on, the only way to maintain these "facts" as constitutive of a US social and political reality and against a counter-representation of the issues is through "brutal censorship." That counter-representation, the self-representation of the Palestinian people, must, despite the existing attempts at coercion, be worked for in order to assure its popular endorsement. Said urged his audience: (1) to bring forth the human dimension of the Palestinian experience; (2) to associate (much as did Nelson Mandela in his televized "town meeting" in New York on June 21, 1990 when he refused to dissociate himself and the ANC from their "comrades in arms" Yasir Arafat and the PLO) "safe" and "unsafe" causes – Palestine, said Said, is an *and*, a conjunction; (3) to stop being silent, since there is always an alternative space in which to speak; (4) not to be dissuaded by "experts" and "authorities" whose interests are vested in maintaining an institution-ally credited and sanctioned ignorance; and, finally, not to be afraid.

For all the optimism concerning the West's apparent readiness to "hear the Palestinian side of the story" that he had evinced in *The Question of Palestine*, Said had nonetheless concluded the book's introduction with a rather more melancholic proviso:

> To explain one's sense of oneself as a Palestinian in this way is to feel embattled. To the West, which is where I live, to be a Palestinian is in political

terms to be an outlaw of sorts, or at any rate very much an outsider. But that
is a reality, and I mention it only as a way of indicating the peculiar loneliness
of my undertaking in this book. (p. xviii)

That undertaking, with its long-term goal of the liberation of the land of
Palestine, has discovered, indeed is elaborating, a new expanded context
that must include following the example of the Palestinian *intifada*, the
liberation of the US academy and a radical transformation of its critical
discourse.

**It is not enough to indicate who is to be held responsible and to stop there, it
must be explained why our position on this problem, a position that seems so
clear to us, has been accepted only by a minority, and this for merely tactical
reasons (as with the Eastern bloc and the neutralist countries), and why our
opponents' position, which to us appears so irresponsible, has in spite of
everything been accepted by the entire world.**
                               Abdallah Laroui, *The Crisis of the Arab Intellectual*

What Edward Said, writing in Palestinian exile in the United States and
from within its educational institutions, referred to as the "embattled . . .
loneliness of [the] undertaking" to represent to the West the question of
Palestine has its own concordant and intersecting history among Palestinian
intellectuals working in the Arab world. "The Slope" is an early story by
the Palestinian writer, critic and journalist Ghassan Kanafani. Written in
Beirut in 1961, and based on Kanafani's own experience as an instructor in
the UNRWA schools in Damascus, where his family eventually settled
following their exile from Palestine in 1948, the frame story tells of a
neophyte teacher's first day in a classroom:

He had spent the night before tossing and turning in his bed until morning
thinking about one thing: how hard it was for someone to stand up in front
of people . . . and for what? To teach them! Who do you think you are? he
asked himself. You've spent your miserable life without anyone teaching you
anything useful. Do you really think you have anything to teach others? You,
of all people, who have always believed that school was the last place where
a man learns about life? And now you are going to be a school teacher? (p. 1)

The school's principal curtly tells the teachers at their first meeting that
they must make do with the lack of resources and educational materials for
their students, after which Muhsin, the story's teacher, makes his uncertain
way to his classroom. Here the class is quickly taken over by one of the
pupils, a small child, unkempt and poorly dressed, but who has a story to
tell. It is the story of his father, a shoemaker who lives and works at the
foot of a hill below the splendid residence of a rich man. But the other
children do not applaud this story, demanding instead to hear the rest of it,
and the child goes on to improvise a conclusion, to his fellow pupils'

satisfaction: the death of his father. Muhsin is impressed and takes his new
student to the principal for further approbation of his storytelling ability.
But the principal, as it turns out, doesn't like the story he hears, and
recommends instead that the child be expelled from the school. Whereupon
Muhsin himself, now in league with his student, takes up his own version
of the continuation of the child's story. In the end:

> The principal looked again at Muhsin who was standing beside the child, one
> next to the other as if they were one. He shook his head several times without
> saying anything. Then he went back and sat down in his soft leather chair,
> and began to leaf through his papers looking from time to time out of the
> corner of his eye at Muhsin and the child. (p. 4)

Kanafani's story offers a tentative exemplum, some six years before the
establishment of an independent Palestinian liberation organization, of the
emergent parameters of an organized resistance movement. The hierarchical
structures of authority and authorship – of principal, teacher, student –
institutionalized in the school at the beginning of the story are radically
transformed through the critical telling and analytical re-telling of the story
of the child's father and his passive acquiescence in his own exploitation.
The frame story remakes the framed story, for if, at the "end" of the child's
tale-telling, his father remains at the bottom of the hill with the rich man
still firmly seated at the top, the analogous pyramidal structure of the frame
story is altered: officialdom in the person of the principal remains seated,
silent, before the nascent solidarity of the teacher and student who stand
now on the same ground to face him.[1]

In an interview just a few weeks before his assassination in July 1972,
Kanafani described his personal narrative as characteristic of the larger
Palestinian history: "I think that my story (*qissati*) reflects in the extreme a
traditional Palestinian background" (p. 136). Born in comfortable circumstances in Akka in 1936, he left his home and land with his family in the
fighting that surrounded the establishment of the state of Israel, a move
that he described in the same interview as not only geographical but
political, from middle class to lumpenproletariat. After periods of residence
in Lebanon and Syria, he taught school in Kuwait between 1956 and 1960,
when he was recruited by George Habash to return to Beirut and work
with the Arab Nationalist Movement. In 1966, at its founding, he joined
the Popular Front for the Liberation of Palestine (PFLP) and became the
first editor of its journal, *al-Hadaf*. A novelist, theorist, critic and journalist,
Kanafani was posthumously remembered in 1990 by colleagues such as
Faysal Darraj on the occasion of the 1000th issue of *al-Hadaf*; Darraj
acknowledged Kanafani's continuing influence over the journal's role of
providing a "written collective memory" (p. 5) of the Palestinian resistance.
The previous year, *al-Hadaf* had reprinted Kanafani's critique of the

resistance organization following the massive Arab defeat in the 1967 June War: "Thoughts on Change and the 'Blind Language'" ("Afkar 'an al-taghyir wa 'al-lugha al-'amya").

This critique was originally presented by Kanafani on March 11, 1968 as part of a public lecture series in Beirut that invited major Arab writers and intellectuals to consider the impact of the June 1967 defeat on Arab society and thought. As such, Kanafani's text can be located within the context of the enormous corpus of theoretical, historical, personal, and literary reassessments of the limited successes and multiple defeats and setbacks of recent Arab history that emerged in the immediate aftermath of the war, reassessments that continue today to characterize much of Arab cultural production. As Faysal Darraj has pointed out in "The Current State of Arab Culture":

> The June 1967 defeat was the most serious event in modern Arab history. Its significance and results surpassed those brought about by the establishment of Israel in 1948. Israel's establishment was an expression of the defeat of the Palestinian people and the impotence of the Arab regimes in a certain historical period when they were dependent on the colonial forces. But the June defeat was an expression of the defeat of the Arab revolution as a whole. (p. 26).

"Thoughts on Change and the 'Blind Language,'" however, distinguishes itself, in 1968 when it was written and again 20 years later, within this particular literary history by its materially-grounded critical analysis of the tendency to engage unreconstructed and tyrannical fetishization of "self-criticism" that only indulges a self-interest.

Ghassan Kanafani is best, perhaps exclusively, known to anglophone readers for his literary writings, the short stories and novels such as *Men in the Sun*, *Return to Haifa*, and *All That's Left for You*. Consistent with the international division of labor, in the cultural arena the metropolis has in recent years "discovered" the literary work of its former colonies. The importation of the "raw material" of poetry, fiction and even drama has in turn provided the resources for the theory factories of the West, where these materials are processed and transformed into consumable commodities for an elite audience – later to be re-exported to their places of origin. What is conscientiously neglected in this redistribution of goods is the critical and theoretical contribution from the "periphery" itself that would challenge the dominant paradigm of economic and cultural dependency.

While Kanafani's literary narratives, like even the early "The Slope," themselves elaborate a rigorous critique, on the basis of class and ethnicity, of distorted social and political relationships of power, he was himself a major critic, historian, journalist, and theorist of the Palestinian resistance until his assassination by the Israeli Mossad in a car-bomb explosion in

Beirut. Indeed, the last text written by Kanafani before his death and published posthumously, "On the Case of Abu Hamidu and Cultural 'Cooperation' with the Enemy," suggested the outlines of a radical analysis of, first, the role of gender within the revolutionary movement, and, second, the material conditions limiting the strategic relations between select representatives of the Israeli and Palestinian parties to the "Middle East conflict."

"Thoughts on Change and the 'Blind Language'" itself proposes a similarly critical reading of the Arab socio-political arena, and the essay's combined lexicon of political scientific terminology, such as "patriarchy" (qa'ida al-'ubuwa) and "party activism" (hizbiyya), and the more organic metaphorical terms such as "blind language" (al-lugha al-'amya') and the "circulation of blood" (al-dawra al-damawiyya), makes manifest the necessary and critical intersection in Kanafani's work of what has often been dichotomized into the cultural and the political. Contained in each of these apparently disparate but theoretically interconnected key terms is Kanafani's focus in the essay on the "younger generations" (like the child in "The Slope" – or, more presciently, the "children of the stones") in the Arab world and the possibilities for social and political renewal they represent.

That same commitment to a younger generation also informs his fictional works, where it is often the child who introduces the historicizing potential inherent in the dynamics of contradiction. In the opening pages of Men in the Sun (1962), for example, Abu Qais's son reminds his father of the difference between an educated critical analysis and the defeatism of religious resignation, just as in Return to Haifa (1969) the Palestinian child, Khaled/Dov, abandoned by his parents in their flight from Haifa in 1948 and now a recruit in the Israeli army, instructs his parents, when they find him again in 1967 on "returning" home following the "defeat" and the opening of the borders between Israel and the now Occupied Territories, in the lessons of secularism and the danger of too sectarian a definition of nationalism. So too, the pupil/storyteller in "The Slope" provided the liberatory example, both to his father and to his teacher, of refusing the finalities of historical and narrative closure. Like Edward Said's polemical concept of "affiliation," Kanafani's argument for the restoration of the "circulation of blood" in the Arab and Palestinian social and political corpus demands a radical restructuring of the patriarchal and authoritarian ties of hereditary filiation into more collective, "democratic" structures.

The projective historical narrative of defeat and still immanent renewal of the material and intellectual conditions of the Arab world in its immediate post-1967 phase, can be traced in Kanafani's analysis in "Thoughts on Change and the 'Blind Language'". It can be further located within the larger political debates of the period, the apogee perhaps of the struggles for national liberation throughout Africa, Asia, Latin America, and the Middle East that marked the end of territorial imperialism – the period of what Said has recently referred to as the "grand narratives of enlightenment and emancipation." The need, stressed by Kanafani, for an adequate assessment of the real material and political strengths of the "enemy," as well as of one's own concrete possibilities within historically determined circumstances, was likewise critical to the resistance agendas of "Third World" theorists such as Amilcar Cabral of Guinea-Bissau and Frantz Fanon, as was the debate between vanguardism and popular struggle in resistance organizations from Cuba, Nicaragua, and El Salvador to the Philippines and China. Kanafani's examination of the multiple contradictions, of greater and lesser magnitude, confronting the Arab world in the aftermath of the 1967 defeat responds critically to Mao Tse-tung's 1957 statement "On the Correct Handling of Contradictions among the People." And the essay's insistence on the vital importance of the party, of party formation and party activism, in creating and educating informed and responsible cadres as well as a popular democratic revolution, together with the critique of an overweening fetishization of the "leader," is not without its analogue in the work of Antonio Gramsci on revolution, the state, the intellectual and the people, and the role of the party, in other words, "the modern prince." The theoretical premises and specific historical analyses elaborated by Kanafani in "Thoughts on Change and the 'Blind Language'" thus firmly ground the essay in the political controversies of the time, in the Arab world in particular but in the international arena as well. Read now, two decades later, in the period of post- (or neo-) colonialism, with radical alterations in the conventional tripartite division of the globe into First, Second and Third Worlds, those same theoretical premises resonate once again, albeit within the new historical configuration of economic imperialism, "technological underdevelopment," and multinational capital – what Edward Soja has designated as our "postmodern geographies."

The dialectical and reciprocally informing relationship between narrative (*riwaya*) and criticism (*naqd*) that distinguishes "Thoughts on Change and the 'Blind Language'" disrupts each of the traditionally respective generic fields in which Kanafani wrote, as well as reworking the interactions between them, from the "literary," the short stories and novels, to the weekly newspaper commentaries on, and theoretical contributions to, the historically critical debates being staged within the resistance organization. Particularly crucial to his polemical analysis of the resistance was the consistent critique of the limitations of and the militant recalcitrance toward the task of criticism within both the ranks and the leadership of the organization. Each succeeding crisis within the movement articulated the conjunctural occasion for a review of its past and a remapping of its future trajectory.

Following Black September, for example, when King Hussein's Jordanian army massacred thousands of Palestinians and eventually expelled the PLO from Jordan, Kanafani, in an editorial on "The Resistance Facing a Fateful Decision . . . What Now?," called for a meeting of the PNC to discuss seriously the issues confronting the organization, and argued against a "prodigal sensitivity, so unjustifiably invested in, in particular toward the relationships among the groups of fedayeen, and between them and their friends, as if the massacre and the lessons of the massacre were less painful than collective criticism (*al-naqd al-rifaqi*) and self-criticism (*al-naqd al-dhati*)" (p. 3). The intellectuals, he had insisted a few months earlier in "The Battle of the Revolutionary Intellectuals," were crucial to the struggle, for it was they who organized its popular spontaneity, giving it coherence and direction, and it was this critique that Kanafani brought to the 1971 roundtable discussion on "The Palestinian Resistance in Its Current Situation" held in Lebanon to analyze the Palestinian mistakes in Jordan that led to Black September and the PLO's expulsion. The question of the internal organization of the PLO and "national unity," the structure of the organization's different, often mutually contradictory, relationships to the Arab nationalist movement, to the Jordanian nationalist movement, to the Jordanian regime or to the Jordanian people and the different sectors of that society, were prominant on the agenda. There was a real internal threat to the consistency and effectiveness of the self-critical analysis, Kanafani insisted, in the tendency to rely on "slogans" (*shi'arat*), including that of "self-criticism itself," proposed as if they were a "bewitching sorcery" (*sahar sahar*) (p. 161).

That slogans and rhetorical claims and assertions could be used in an historical revision of the Palestinian movement to substitute for analytical criticism was crucial to the last article, published posthumously, Kanafani wrote before his assassination: "On The Case of Abu Hamidu." Addressing himself to three apparently separate and discrete incidents, trivialized in their isolation from their historical context and analytical scrutiny, Kanafani raised again the urgent political questions for the resistance of its internal organization and its handling of external relationships. In 1971, following the PLO's move from Jordan to Lebanon, a young *fedai*, Abu Hamidu, was accused by their family of raping two sisters in a village in southern Lebanon. The two women were killed by their brother in the traditional act of revenge to restore family honor. Abu Hamidu was tried by the resistance and sentenced to death. Furthermore, the resistance was requested by the local inhabitants to leave their village. While being held in temporary quarters prior to his execution, Abu Hamidu was killed during an opportunisitc Israeli bombing raid across its borders against the now unsheltered guerrillas in Lebanon, a raid that killed many of the villagers as well.

For Kanafani, this so-called "incident" (*hadith*) was rather an issue, a case (*qadiya*) that required analysis of the multiple failures on the part of the resistance and its revolutionary program that the occurrence signalled: the failure, first of all, to maintain professional discipline within the ranks of its fighting forces; the failure, too, to address seriously and self-critically questions of gender and to re-educate its members in a socially progressive practice; and finally, the failure to establish effective and transformative working relations with the masses of the people. Rape (*ightisab*), according to Kanafani, is a political crime within the revolution and must be addressed as such, just as "crimes of honor" (*jara'im al-'ird*), like the brother's murder of his two sisters, are traditional (*taqlidi*) responses to "crimes of sexuality" (*jara'im al-jins*), the consequence of a coercive and repressive tradition maintained by "verbal terrorism" exemplified in the slogans of rape (*ightisab*), violation (*intihak*), and honor (*sharaf* and *'ird*) that the resistance itself had failed to overcome and transform.

At just about the same time that the Abu Hamidu case was unfolding in southern Lebanon, two Palestinian students appeared in a discussion (*al-tahawar*) with two Israeli students on a BBC television broadcast filmed in Cyprus. For Kanafani, this breach of the Arab boycott of Israel needed to be analyzed not in terms of a dogmatic or sectarian adherence to the boycott itself, but for its failure to address and come to terms with the political structures of the Western bourgeois media. According to Kanafani (who thus anticipated Edward Said's critique of a tendency on the part of the PLO apparatus to ignore the specific circumstances of the United States in presenting its case to the US government), media work in the West should be done through friends from within the Left movement who are positioned to provide progressive advice on the most appropriate circumstances for such work. On the other hand, in the case of Professor Finley, a foreign university professor in Beirut angrily accused of using a "Zionist source" in his curriculum, Kanafani challenged:

> what are we afraid of in such matters as these? Are we supposed to deny our educational right (and duty) with regard to the intellectual and scientific achievements on the part of individuals from the enemy, or even their use? What this issue conceals is our complacency with an educational system in our countries that is incapable of treating this topic seriously. (p. 17)

The promise once seen by Kanafani as offered by Lebanon has been forfeited, in the wake of civil war and the Israeli invasion, to sectarianism and the power struggles of ever more fragmented militias and their respective sponsors. On a more extended theoretical level, according to Faysal Darraj in "Arab Culture": "The essential character of the prevailing Arab culture is not manifested in political allegiance or a partisan position, but in a series of ideological stereotypes which fight the defeat from defeated positions" (p. 25). Since Kanafani's death, a new concatenation of dates has succeeded 1967 in the Arab historical narrative: 1973, 1975–6,

1982. Since December 1987, however, the calendar is no longer punctuated by decisive years, but projected through the continuation of the Palestinian *intifada* in the Occupied Territories: "In the first, second, third ... twentieth ... thirtieth month of the *intifada* ..."

The urgent strategic and theoretical issues raised by Ghassan Kanafani in his writing, then, issues of patriarchy, party, blind language, the circulation of blood, democracy, education, gender and sexuality, dialogue with the "other," are currently being re-submitted from within occupied Palestine to the challenge of new historical developments. In an article entitled "The *Intifada*: Political Creativity and Popular Memory," Faysal Darraj has, in response to these challenges of theory, practice and the demands of history, claimed that "the *intifada* does not deliver a theoretical speech, but is making out of its multiple practices the highest form of theoretical discourse." Darraj goes on to ask: "but if its practice of creative theory without articulating it, its practice of revolutionary theory, leaves to 'others' the task of translating practice into the realm of written theory, when will the practice write its theory?"

The urgency with which Kanafani's work continues to speak to the social and political issues of the Arab world, and the global context as well, raises still another question: if Ghassan Kanafani were alive today, are there not still those who would feel it necessary to assassinate him?

> [Palestine] is one issue on which, as you know, there is a left-right break in America, and there are still a few groups, a few people – like Chomsky or Alexander Cockburn – who are willing to raise it publicly. But most people tend to think that it is better left to the crazies. There are fewer hospitable places, and you end up publishing for a smaller audience. Ironically, you also become tokenized, so that whenever there is a hijacking or some such incident, I get phone calls from the media asking me to come along and comment. It's a very strange feeling to be seen as a kind of representative of terrorism.
>
> Edward Said, "On Palestinian Identity: A Conversation with Salman Rushdie"

> ... intellectual and scholarly work from the peripheries, done either by immigrants or by visitors, both of whom are generally anti-imperialist, is not simply the work of individuals, but mainly an extension into the metropolis of large scale mass movements ...
>
> ... far from these incursions being additions to or expansions of the mainstream culture, they are instead movements that struggle over the same area of experience, culture, history, and tradition hitherto commanded unilaterally by the metroplitan center ...
>
> Edward Said, "Third World Intellectuals and Metropolitan Culture"

Ghassan Kanafani, the "commando who never fired a gun" as one obituary described him, was violently assassinated in Beirut by a bomb planted in his car by the Israeli secret service. His twelve-year-old niece Lamees was killed along with him. He was assassinated, it would seem, for the weapon of criticism that he had so unflinchingly wielded. No less dangerous than armed struggle (which Kanafani nonetheless refused in his writings to reject) is a strategic critical theory that would arm the resistance with a radical secular analysis. Such an anlysis proposes the grounds for mobilizing popular and collective support, both in its exposure of rhetorical posturing and coercive slogans, and as part of its larger project of dismantling the exclusivist ideological bases of a state apparatus – in this case the state of Israel, but analogously as well, the United States academy aligned with international interests of political and economic reaction and neo-colonial domination.

But if Kanafani died violently at the hands of a state terror squad, intellectuals in the United States like Edward Said, who have sought to re-open the universities and academic discourse to a public and critical discussion of the Palestine question, its integral place in the disciplinary curriculum and its role in making US foreign policy, have been the targets of less physically violent but no less dangerous attempts at character assassination. "Professor of Terror," an article by Edward Alexander in *Commentary* called him, referring to Said's essay on "An Ideology of Difference" published in *Critical Inquiry*, an academic journal that was itself taken to task in the same article as suspiciously engaged in the "tautologies and absurdities in such notions as 'postmodern' and 'intertex-uality'" (p. 50). "Critical Inquiry" and theoretical critiques were presented as an integral part of the danger to a sedimented institutionalization of obsolete conversationist alignments. Emmanuel Sivan, by contrast, took a rather more tortuous approach than Alexander's direct invective in rhetor-ically conscripting Arab reviewers of *Orientalism* (whom Sivan would in every other respect disdain to acknowledge) to aid in his attack on Said, an attack that in the end relies on the very same identity politics that Sivan purports to critique: "The Arab reviewers are all the more saddened by the fact that it had seemed as though Said was *one of them*, a secularist and a modernist" (p. 23, emphasis added). Another article in *Tikkun* identified Said with "discourse and Palestinian rage." And in a written exchange in the pages of *Critical Inquiry*, four years after "An Ideology of Difference" was published, an exchange that drew on the same formulas of negotiation and recognition as prescribed by the Israeli government, Said was targeted and rejected as a politically and academically unacceptable participant in "dialogue" – either academic or political. As Edward Herman and Gerry O'Sullivan point out in The *"Terrorism" Industry*, this notable representa-tive in the United States of "Palestinian terror" is systematically excluded from government and media lists of consultants and "experts on terrorism."

In his address to the 1990 conference on Palestinian academic freedom, Said had encouraged his audience not to be intimidated by these duly recognized "experts" and "authorities" and their sanctioned efforts to discredit the Palestinian demand for self-determination and self-representa-tion. And as he wrote in the introduction to *Blaming the Victims*, whereas "supporters of Israel do two things when they write and organize: they reproduce the official party line on Israel, or they go after delinquents who threaten to disturb this idyll . . .," it is necessary for "critics and opponents of the Zionist lobby in civil society [to] take as their tasks first to decode the myths, then to present the record of facts in as neutral a way as possible" (p. 11). Like Ghassan Kanafani before him, Said insists on the critical role of the intellectual – in the US academy as in the Palestinian resistance – as secular critic and counter-archival historian. In *The Question of Palestine* he maintained that

> the task of criticism, or, to put it another way, the role of critical conscious-ness in such cases is to be able to make distinctions where at present there are none. To write critically about Zionism in Palestine has therefore never meant, and does not mean now, being anti-Semitic; conversely the struggle for Palestinian rights and self-determination does not mean support for the Saudi royal family, nor for the antiquated and repressive state structures of most of the Arab nations. (p. 59)

The task is not, according to Said, to reproduce for Palestine a replica of a millenarian and sectarian Zionist ideology of diaspora and return, but rather to elaborate, through an unrelenting critical process, a secular vision of popular struggle and collective liberation. "Better our wanderings, I sometimes think," Said wrote in *After the Last Sky*, "than the horrible clanging shutters of their return. The open secular element, and not the symmetry of redemption . . ." (p. 150). The historical and political question of Palestine becomes illustrative and informing, then, for the work of theory and theoretical inquiry. Indeed, as Said cautions, even in endorsing "Trav-eling Theory," "once an idea gains currency, because it is clearly effective and powerful, there is every likelihood that during its peregrinations it will be reduced, codified, and institutionalized" (p. 239).

In speaking to the "question of Palestine," Said argued that "one of the features of a small non-European people is that it is not wealthy in documents, or in histories, autobiographies, chronicles and the like. This is true of the Palestinians, and it accounts for the lack of a major authoritative text on Palestinian history" (pp. xii–xiii). But if the Palestinian story is still to be told in the West, the very conditions of that telling, the representation – its *Darstellung* and its *Vertretung* – of Palestine, will necessarily, as happened with the child's story in "The Slope," be part of its making.

. . . and I'd say that's the quintessential Palestinian worry, that we are always doing things that we would like to have done in Palestine, but couldn't. We are doing them somewhere else at the wrong time, causing a lot of trouble for others. That's got to be said too . . .
Edward Said, "The Voice of a Palestinian in Exile"

. . . Palestine is not an ordinary place . . .
Edward Said, *Blaming the Victims*

From *Beginnings*, published in 1975, if not from his first work on Joseph Conrad (1966), through *Orientalism* (1978), *The Question of Palestine* (1979), *Covering Islam* (1981), *The World, the Text, and the Critic* (1983), the semi-autobiographical *After the Last Sky* (1986), and the edited collection *Blaming the Victims* (1988), Edward Said has argued in his writing for the intersection of culture and politics and the radical import-ance of narrative and of history in the elaboration of a critical place, an oppositional knowledge, and an alternative archival space. Nor are these issues, as he himself maintained in *The Question of Palestine*, simply "academic questions, in other words, but questions that bear directly upon the lives of millions of people, upon states, upon the international order" (p. 46). Like Ghassan Kanafani's writings, which charted the political trajectory of the Palestinian resistance on the terrain of armed struggle until his own untimely death, marking the conjunctural crises, territorial dis-placements and their reworking in critical debate, Edward Said's textual corpus traces a larger political itinerary, from the culmination of the age of decolonization in the 1970s, through the emergent reconfigurations of a new global order at the turn of the decade of the 1990s. That new order was perhaps most dramatically enacted in the release of Nelson Mandela after 27 years of incarceration in a South African prison, together with the unbanning of the ANC, the SACP and the UDF, no less than in the precipitate collapse of the Berlin Wall and the reunification of the two Germanys. These events, however, augur still uncalculated national and international realignments, something like a "postmodern geography," but wrought now under renewed pressure on the center from within formerly peripheralized spaces and regions. The relocation of the Palestinian resist-ance from outside and exile to inside and the struggle against an anachron-istic military occupation is one part, locally specific but with manifold ramifications, of this remapping of the world order, a re-placing of Palestine in the international atlas, the political lexicon, and even the OED, and within the US academic disciplinary order. Not only "*intifada,*" but "occupation" too, have, for example, acquired nexus-building semantic determinations in identifying as common and intersecting otherwise disar-ticulated struggles and dichotomized political spaces. Chicanos in Texas, to take another "local" example, regularly refer to the state as the "occupied territory of Texas."[2]

With the dissolution, as Said maintains in "Third World Intellectuals and Metropolitan Culture," of "mass movements led by extraordinary leaders," together with the disintegration of the "grand narratives of enlightenment and emancipation" (p. 40) that had characterized the era of decolonization, a newly critical practice of confrontation is urgently enjoined. This practice, in its rethinking of language, culture and the nationalist project, can no longer be premised on the obsolete "narrative by which a continuity is established between Europe and its peripheral colonies" (p. 43). Said's

work, with its insistence on the historical narrative and at the same time –
theoretically and biographically – informed by the importance of space, the
struggle over the land and against military occupation, engages explicitly in
the project of a radical reconstruction, around the issue of geography, of
the ascendant linear narrative of history led masterfully from the center.
Colonialism and the national liberation struggles waged against its controlling influence articulate not just a temporal sequence, but a critical re-
elaboration of geopolitical spatial arrangements and the politics of place,
what Soja presents – even if with a residual Eurocentric bias – as the
"conjunction between periodization and spatialization" (p. 64). This politics of place must be critically decentered, further sited and re-read around
a rethinking of the history of nationalism, Said maintains, and located
institutionally as well as territorially.

In a controversial interview in early Fall 1989 with the Kuwaiti newspaper *al-Qabas*, nearly one year after the Declaration of Independence of
the State of Palestine for whose English translation Said was himself
principally responsible, and following hard upon another US State Department refusal to grant a diplomatic visa to PLO Chairman and Palestinian
president Yasir Arafat, a Palestinian intellectual in exile in the United States
issued a renewed call to the Palestinian resistance for self-criticism:

> Ignorance is not an excuse. The PLO has been participating in UN activities
> constantly since 1974. It has had the chance to study the state of affairs in the
> United States . . . The question I would like to pose is the following. When
> will the PLO try to use the resources that are available to it to deal with the
> United States in a serious and confrontational manner?

Said went on to insist that

> there are many institutions in this country, university cities, professional
> unions, and numerous community sectors which support us completely.
> However, they have never been mobilized, exploited, or asked to do anything.
> Everything is arranged between Tunis and Washington behind closed doors.
> They come here, leave, and that is the end of it. Our need for a Palestinian
> presence in the United States should be coordinated and studied accurately –
> an intelligent and resistive presence . . . otherwise we will not reap the
> rewards of our West Bank and Gaza Strip people's brave struggle. Their
> deaths will be useless.

The liberation of Palestine, "not an ordinary place," may well provide one
critical example, one crucial occasion, for the re-opening as well of the
United States university.

Notes

This essay owes much – and should probably owe more – to the rigorous critical reading given it by Aklilu Gebrewold.

1 While teaching this story as part of E316K, Introduction to Criticism, at the University of Texas at Austin in Spring 1990, a particularly relevant illustration of the continued force of its analytical critique was provided by UT president William Cunningham. Following a series of egregious racist incidents perpetrated by two campus fraternities, and the angry outcry and demonstrations led by the Black Student Alliance that followed, President Cunningham chose to address himself publicly to these issues. Despite the fact that his speech was announced only at the last minute on campus, students and some faculty against racism did gather at the West Mall, UT's restricted "free speech" area (a small, partially cordoned, area where "free speech" is permitted daily between 12 and 1 pm), to engage the president in a critical exchange on the question of campus racism. Daunted by the demand for a dialogue, and refusing to depart from his prepared remarks to engage with student interlocutors, Cunningham abruptly terminated his speech and withdrew to his office, from which he would later chastise the students for not respecting his right to "freedom of speech." It was not difficult for students who had read Kanafani's story to analyze the rhetorical subterfuges of President Cunningham's "presentation" of the issues. (See *The Daily Texan*, Monday, April 16, 1990).

2 I thank Gilberto Rivera of Chicanos Against Military Intervention in Latin America (CAMILA) for making this connection clear to me.

References

"Al-muqawama al-filastiniya fi wad'iha al-rahin" (The Palestinian Resistance in Its Current Situation), *Shu'un filastiniya*, 2 (1971).

Alexander, Edward, "Professor of Terror," *Commentary* (August 1989).

Darraj, Faysal, "Al-intifada: al-'ibda' al-siyassi, wa-l-dhakkira al-sha'biya" (The *Intifada*: Political Creativity and Popular Memory), *al-Hadaf*, 962 (June 11, 1989).

Darraj, Faysal, "The Current State of Arab Culture," *Democratic Palestine*, 33 (June 1989).

Darraj, Faysal, "Kaif yanthuru al-mubda'un ila 'al-Hadaf' fi adadiha al-alf" (How Arab writers view al-Hadaf at its 1000th issue), *al-Hadaf*, 1000 (February 25, 1990).

Griffin, Robert J., Daniel Boyarin and Jonathan Boyarin, "An Exchange on Edward Said and Difference," *Critical Inquiry*, 15 (Spring 1989).

Herman, Edward and Gerry O'Sullivan, *The "Terrorism" Industry: The Experts and Institutions That Shape Our View of Terror* (New York: Pantheon, 1989).

Kanafani, Ghassan, "Ma'raka al-muthaqafin al-thawriyin" (The Battle of the Revolutionary Intellectuals), *al-Hadaf*, 2/70 (Octoher 10, 1970).

Kanafani, Ghassan, "Al-muqawama amam ikhtiyariha al-masiri . . . madha alana?" (The Resistance Facing a Fateful Decision . . . What Now?), *al-Hadaf*, 2/85 (February 6, 1971).

Kanafani, Ghassan, "Hawl qadiya Abu Hamidu wa qadaya 'al-ta'amul' al-i'lami wa-l-thaqafi ma'a al-'aduw" (On The Case of Abu Hamidu and Cultural "Cooperation" with the Enemy), *Shu'un filastiniya*, 12 (1972).

Kanafani, Ghassan, "Ma'a shahid Ghassan Kanafani: hadith yunsharu li awal marra" (With the martyr Ghassan Kanafani: a conversation published for the first time), *Shu'un filastiniya*, 35 (1974).

Kanafani, Ghassan, "The Slope" in *Palestine's Children*, trans. Barbara Harlow (London: Heinemann, 1984).

Kanafani, Ghassan, "'Afkar 'an al-taghyir wa 'al-lugha al-'amya'" (Thoughts on Change and the "Blind Language"), *al-Hadaf*, 919–20 (July 17–24, 1988). English translation by Barbara Harlow and Nejd Yaziji, *ALIF*, 10 (1990).

Krupnick, Mark, "Edward Said: Discourse and Palestinian Rage," *Tikkun* (November–December 1989).

Laroui, Abdallah, *The Crisis of the Arab Intellectual: Traditionalism or Historicism?* (trans. Diarmid Cammell, Berkeley and Los Angeles: University of California Press, 1976).

No Voice is Louder than the Voice of the Uprising: Calls 1–47 of the Unified National Leadership of the Uprising in the Occupied Territories/State of Palestine (n.p.: Ibal Publishing Ltd., 1989).

Qadaya tarbawiya 1 (end of August [1989]).

Robbins, Bruce, "American Intellectuals and Middle East Politics: An Interview with Edward Said," *Social Text*, 19/20 (Fall 1988).

Said, Edward W., *The Question of Palestine* (New York: Times Books, 1979).

Said, Edward W., "Traveling Theory" in *The World, the Text, and the Critic* (Cambridge, Mass.: Harvard University Press, 1983).

Said, Edward W., "An Ideology of Difference," *Critical Inquiry*, 12 (Autumn 1985).

Said, Edward W., *After the Last Sky: Palestinian Lives* (New York: Pantheon Books, 1986).

Said, Edward W., "On Palestinian Identity: A Conversation with Salman Rushdie," *New Left Review*, 160 (November–December 1986).

Said, Edward W., "The Voice of a Palestinian in Exile," *Third Text*, 3/4 (1988).

Said, Edward W., "Intifada and Independence," *Social Text*, 22 (Spring 1989).

Said, Edward W., "Interview," *al-Qabas*, 7–8 October 1989. English translation in *al-Fajr*, February 5, 1990.

Said, Edward W., "Third World Intellectuals and Metropolitan Culture," *Raritan*, 11, 3 (Winter, 1990).

Said, Edward and Christopher Hitchens, (eds), *Blaming the Victims: Spurious Scholarship and the Palestinian Question* (London and New York: Verso, 1988).

Sivan, Emmanuel, "Edward Said and His Arab Reviewers," *The Jerusalem Quarterly*, 35 (Spring 1985).

Soja, Edward, *Postmodern Geographies: The Reassertion of Space in Critical Social Theory* (London and New York: Verso, 1989).

10

THEIR OWN WORDS?
AN ESSAY FOR EDWARD SAID

——

Partha Chatterjee

I

I will long remember the day I read *Orientalism*.[1] It must have been in
November or December of 1980. In India this season is classically called
Hemanta and assigned a slot between Autumn and Winter. In Calcutta,
where nothing classical remains untarnished, all that this means is a few
weeks of uncertain temperature when the rains have gone, the fans have
been switched off and people wait expectantly to take out their sweaters
and shawls. I remember the day because the house was being repainted and
everything was topsy-turvy. I sat on the floor of the room in which I usually
work, now emptied of its furniture, reading Edward Said whom I had never
read before. I read right through the day and, after the workmen had left
in the evening, well into the night. Now whenever I think of *Orientalism*,
the image comes back to me of an empty room with a red floor and bare
white walls, a familiar room suddenly made unfamiliar.

For me, child of a successful anti-colonial struggle, *Orientalism* was a
book which talked of things I felt I had known all along but had never
found the language to formulate with clarity. Like many great books, it
seemed to say for the first time what one had always wanted to say. The
force of the argument made its impact in the first few pages, and half-way
through the book I found my thoughts straying beyond the confines of
Said's discussion. I was struck by the way Orientalism was implicated in
the construction not only of the ideology of British colonialism which had
dominated India for two centuries, but also of the nationalism which was
my own heritage. Orientalist constructions of Indian civilization had been
avidly seized upon by the ideologues of Indian nationalism in order to
assert the glory and antiquity of a national past. So Indian nationalists had
implicitly accepted the colonialist critique of the Indian present: a society

fallen into barbarism and stagnation, incapable of progress or modernity. I then began to see how, by dividing the domain of culture into the material and the spiritual, anti-colonial nationalism could assert the superiority of the East's spiritual heritage, while formulating at the same time a project of reform and regeneration in order to match the material strength of the West.

This chain of thought that began with my reading of *Orientalism* led some five years later to a book on the construction of the political discourse of Indian nationalism.[2] Yet, even as I worked on the book, I was troubled by a new set of problems. I was troubled in particular by the ease with which sociological theories of nationalism were able to subsume the political forms of the new nation-states within certain "modular" types derived from Europe and the Americas. Even the brilliance of Benedict Anderson's analysis of the modes of imagination of national communities[3] seemed not only to gloss over, but in fact refuse to recognize any cultural forms of imagining the nation that had not already been worked out in the West. The contemporary politics of Asian and African nation-states had apparently cast such a pall of pessimism that the anti-colonial struggle itself seemed little more than an inauthentic manipulative strategy of nationalist elites.

This account of nationalism flies in the face of a whole mass of evidence on the continued legitimacy of nationalist claims to cultural autonomy and self-determination. More importantly, by directing its inquiry towards the domain of the institutional forms of the modern nation-state, it misses entirely the site where the nationalist imagination is most creative. The very separation of culture into the material and the spiritual domains affords nationalism an inner space over which it declares its sovereignty long before the political battle with colonial rule is fought out. It is this inner space where nationalism launches its project of cultural hegemony, a project that seeks to unify within the forms of a single overarching community a multiplicity of social groups. Language, literature and cultural production, education and religion, family and kin – these are the areas where the project takes shape and the legitimacy of nationalism as an anti-colonial movement is produced. The supposed spirituality of the nation's identity affects in turn the materiality of a whole set of institutions and practices where it is sought to enforce this identity.

The success as well as the limits of nationalism's project of power must then be tested on this ground, which it declares its own true province. The inquiry, in other words, has to be turned away, even if provisionally, from the political conflicts between colonial regimes and nationalist organizations to that contested site of discourse where the nationalist imagination must appropriate, suppress or exclude different voices in order to produce its own authoritative speech. In this essay, I will look at one aspect of this contestatory process – nationalism's construction of the "new woman".

Since my material will be a set of autobiographies, I hope this autobiographical introduction to my essay in tribute to Edward Said has not been entirely inappropriate.

II

If there is one theme that dominates the new literature which emerged in Bengal in the nineteenth century, it is change. Everything was changing: nothing was likely to remain the same any more. There were, of course, prolonged and bitter debates about how best to cope with all this change. But at bottom the assumption was shared that the force working to alter the very foundations of society was both overwhelming and alien: the source of change itself lay outside and beyond control. It is important to remember this when considering the emergence of a "modern" consciousness of the self under colonial conditions.

The question of the "new woman" was, like other contemporary social issues, formulated as a question of coping with change. But who was to do the coping? The most eminent literary figure in Bengal in the late nineteenth century, Bankimchandra Chattopadhyay (1838–94), wrote an essay in the early 1870s comparing the virtues and faults of women of an older age with those of women of modern times.[4] Bankim began by declaring that in all societies it was men who always laid down the ways in which women must behave. "Self-interested men are mindful of the improvement of women only to the extent that it furthers their self-interest: not for any other reason." There was, consequently, no confusion in Bankim's mind about the social agency in question when considering women's character. If the modern woman was different from her predecessors, this was the result of social policies pursued by men: men's attitudes and actions were on trial here.

Bankim then goes on to provide a list of the virtues and defects of the "new" woman compared with those of the "traditional". It is a familiar list, reproduced, embellished, and canonized in succeeding decades in the prodigious nationalist literature on women.[5] In the past, women were uneducated, and therefore they were coarse, vulgar, and quarrelsome. By comparison, modern women have more refined tastes. On the other hand, whereas before women were hard-working and strong, they were now lazy and fond of luxury, unmindful of housework, and prone to all sorts of illnesses. Further, in the olden days women were religious. They were faithful to their husbands, hospitable to guests, and charitable to the needy. They genuinely believed in the norms of right conduct. Today, if women do these things, they do so more because of fear of criticism than because they adhere to their *dharma*.

Bankim may have felt that despite his initial remarks about the responsibility of society's lawmakers, the essay was likely to be read as a criticism of women themselves, whether traditional or modern. In the subsequent issue of the journal in which the essay appeared, Bankim appended three letters, supposedly written by women in response to the article.[6] All three complained that women had been treated unfairly by the author. The first retaliated with a list of accusations against the educated male:

> All right, we are lazy. But what about you? . . . You work only because the English have tied you to the millstone . . . We have no bonds of religion, you say. And you? You are ever fearful of religion because it is like a noose around your neck: one end of the rope is held by the owner of the liquor-store and the other by the prostitute.

The second argued that the defects of the modern woman had only been produced by the "virtues" of the modern man:

> Yes, by your virtues, not by your faults. If only you had not loved us so much, we would not have had so many defects. We are lazy because you have made us so contented . . . We are unmindful of guests because we are so mindful of our husbands and children . . . And, finally, are we not afraid of religion? In truth, it is only because we are afraid of religion that we dare not tell you what we should. You are our only religion. We are so afraid of you that we have no fear of any other religion . . . If this is a crime against religion, then it is both your fault and your virtue. And if you do not mind being asked a question by this prattling female – "You are our teachers, we are your disciples: what religion do you teach us?" . . . Oh shame! Don't spread tales about your slaves!

The third correspondent offered to exchange places with the modern male: "Come indoors and take charge of the house. Let us go out to work. Slaves for seven hundred years, and still you pride yourselves on your masculinity! Aren't you ashamed?"

I mention this essay by Bankim at the very beginning of my discussion of women's writings about themselves not only to remind us that the hegemonic discourse which framed these writings – the discourse of anti-colonial nationalism – was at its core a male discourse, but also to point out the capacity of this discourse to appropriate discordant, marginal and critical voices. In Bankim's case, the device was self-irony. The strand of nationalist thinking which Bankim represented sought to create a national leadership in the image of ideal masculinity – strong, proud, just, wise, a protector of the righteous and a terror to the mischievous. Relentlessly, he poured scorn and ridicule on an educated elite which, he thought, was failing to live up to this ideal. Self-irony was the mode by which he could, as a member of this inadequate elite, expose to itself its own weaknesses, even by assuming the voices of its "others" – those of the illiterate, the poor and the "mad", and also those of women.[7] The form was used widely. Indeed, fiction and drama in late-nineteenth-century Bengal are full of instances of women from "respectable" families as well as from the urban poor using the rhetorical skills of "common" speech and the moral precepts of "common" sense to show up the pretentiousness and hypocrisy of the educated male. We must not overlook the hegemonic possibilities of this internalized critique: it could, up to a point, retain its own legitimacy and appropriate both feminine and popular ridicule simply by owning up to them.[8]

The question is: up to what point? Or rather, in which discursive field? within what sort of boundaries? We cannot find a historically nuanced answer to this question unless we think of the field of discourse as contentious, peopled by several subjects, several consciousnesses. We must think of discourse as situated within fields of power, not only constituting that field but also constituted by it. Dominance here cannot exhaust the claims to subjectivity, for even the dominated must always retain an aspect of autonomy. Otherwise, power would cease to be a relation: it would no longer be constituted by struggle.

If nationalist ideology in late-nineteenth-century Bengal legitimized the subjection of women under a new patriarchy, its history must have been a history of struggle still. The dificulty facing historians here is that by working from the conventional archives of political history, women only appear in the history of nationalism in a "contributive" role.[9] All one can assert is that women *also* took an active part in nationalist struggle, but one cannot identify any autonomous subjectivity of women and from that standpoint question the manner in which the hegemonic claims of nationalist culture were themselves fashioned.[10]

My argument is that because of the specific conditions of colonial society, this history is to be found less in the external domain of political conflict and more in the "inner" space of the middle-class home. Fortunately, there exists something of an archive for us to delve into. This is a series of autobiographies by educated women who wrote about their lives and their struggles in this eventful period of modern Indian history. I present here a reading of five such autobiographies, beginning with a woman who was born in the first decade of the nineteenth century and ending with one who reached middle age in the first decade of the twentieth.

The autobiography would seem to be obvious material for studying the emergence of "modern" forms of self-representation. Unfortunately, here too the colonial condition works to displace the points of application of the usual critical apparatus. Historians of Bengali literature conventionally agree that the modern forms of biography and autobiography made their appearance in Bengal sometime in the middle of the nineteenth century because of the emergence of a new concept of the "individual" among the English-educated elite.[11] Yet, despite the continued popularity of the genre, it is difficult to explain why, instead of exploring individuality and the inner workings of personality, the facts of social history and the development of new cultural norms for the collective life of the nation comprise the overwhelming bulk of the material in these life-stories. The first comprehensive social history of nineteenth-century Bengal was a biography of a social reformer,[12] while the foremost political leader of Bengal at the turn of the century entitled his autobiography *A Nation in Making*.[13] The "new individual", it would seem, could only represent the history of his life by inscribing it in the narrative of the nation.

Not unexpectedly, autobiographies of women have characteristics rather different from those of men. It is not simply that women's life-stories are concerned more with the domestic than with the public sphere, which is a feature often noticed in women's autobiographies of the modern period in all countries. Nor is it a particular characteristic that the self-discovery of female identity acknowledges "the real presence and recognition of another consciousness" and that "the disclosure of female self is linked to the identification of some 'other'."[14] In a fundamental sense, all identity has to be disclosed by establishing an alterity. Men's autobiographies, it seems to me, do the same: the difference lies in the discursive strategies employed. In the case of the women's autobiographies we are talking about, the most striking feature is the way in which the very theme of disclosure of self remains suppressed under a narrative of changing times, manners, customs, and values.

When the first autobiographies came to be written in the second half of the nineteenth century by men who had achieved eminence in the new public life of colonial Bengal, the most common title given to these works was the *ātmacarit*. While this was meant to stand as a literal translation of the English word "autobiography", it also carried, more significantly, an allusion to the entire body of *carita* literature in the classical and medieval eras in which the lives of kings and saints were recorded. *Buddhacarita* by Aśvaghosa and *Harsacarita* by Bāna are perhaps the most well-known examples of a whole genre of religious and secular hagiographic writings in Sanskrit, whereas the *Caitanyacaritāmrta* (1615) is the most distinguished of numerous *carit* writings in Bengali in the two centuries preceding the colonial age. While the more obvious hagiographic conventions were quickly abandoned in the new biographical literature of the nineteenth century, the idea of the *carit* as the life of an illustrious man, told either by himself or by others, clearly persisted even in its modern sense.

Women's life-stories were not given the status of *carit*. Of some twenty or so autobiographies I have seen of nineteenth-century Bengali women, not one is called an *ātmacarit*.[15] This, in fact, gives us a clue to the nature of women's autobiographical writings in this period: these were not simply variants on men's autobiographical writings but constituted a distinct literary genre. The most common name by which they were described was the *smrtikathā*: memoirs, or more accurately, stories from memory. What held these stories together in a single narrative was not the life-history of the narrator or the development of her "self", but rather the social history of the "times". The most commonly employed narrative device was the contrast: "In those days . . .", "Nowadays . . .". The stories told were those of everyday life in the "inner" part of the house inhabited by women, of rituals and celebrations, of births, deaths, and marriages, of the sudden interruptions of everyday routine by calamitous events, and, of course, of how everything was so different "nowadays". It is not surprising that the first systematic survey of women's autobiographical writings has treated this material principally as a source for reconstructing the social history of nineteenth-century Bengal,[16] and that the first book-length study of women's autobiographies has carried out this exercise much more elaborately.[17]

What made the narrative history of domestic life particularly suitable as a "feminine" literary genre was the belief, inculcated, needless to say, by male guardians of literary conventions, that this required little more than the retelling from memory of impressions left by direct personal experience. One did not have to have the imaginative power or stylistic flair of the poet or the novelist in order to tell one's *smrtikathā*: anyone could do it. The immediacy, directness, and indeed the very artlessness of the form was seen to make it appropriate for an authentic "feminine" literary voice. When Charulata, the heroine of Rabindranath Tagore's story "The Broken Nest" (later made into a film by Satyajit Ray), first tried her hand at writing, she began with an essay called "The August Clouds", but soon discovered that it read too much like another essay called "The July Moon" written by her brother-in-law Amal. She then proceeded to write about the Kali temple in the village in which she had lived as a child. Tagore approved of this change in Charu's style: "Although in the early part her writing was cluttered by the excessively ornamental style of Amal, it soon acquired a simplicity and charm of its own, filled as it now was with the richness of a rural idiom."[18]

The genre, in short, did not require the author to express her "self" or examine the development of her personality. It was not the telling of an exemplary life, not even of a life of any importance: to this day, it is useful to remember, there are fewer biographies of Bengali women than there are autobiographies. The genre only required the writer to tell her readers, mainly women from a younger generation, how the everyday lives of women had changed. This allowed the questions to be raised: how are we to cope with this change? in what ways must we change ourselves? These were, of course, the central questions of nationalist discourse. However, in this particular case, the discourse enabled a more specific question to be asked – and answered: how must women behave in these changing times?

To discover how educated women of the nineteenth century answered this question, we will now look at some of their own writings. We will listen to their own words, but we will also do well to remember that sovereignty over language, a tricky business under the best of circumstances, is doubly vitiated for those who were subordinated, at one and the same time, to colonialism as well as to a nationalist patriarchy.

III

Shanta Nag, who came from a generation of middle-class women whose mothers were already educated, tells the story of how she learnt to read the alphabet. It was sometime around the turn of the century. Her mother, she says, would sit across the table teaching her elder brother and she would stand beside her, silently watching the proceedings. In a few months, without anybody suspecting it, she had learnt to read the first two books of the Bengali primer. The only difficulty was that in order to read she had to hold the book upside down.[19] Of course, by her time the education of women had become normal practice in middle-class homes in Bengal, and she herself would have learnt the alphabet and gone to school as a matter of routine. But the sense of acquiring a skill that was really meant for somebody else seems to have stayed with these early generations of educated women.

Nowhere is this more poignant than in the story of Rassundari Debi (1809–1900).[20] For her learning to read and write was nothing less than a life-long struggle. She had been born into a wealthy landed family; the village school was located in one of the buildings on the estate. When she was eight, her uncle sent her to this school where, for the next two years, she sat every day on the floor, the only girl in a roomful of boys, and was taught the Bengali alphabet, some arithmetic, and some Persian (which had still not been replaced by English as the language of bureaucracy). The teacher was an English woman.[21] Rassundari does not tell us this, but we know from other sources that her schooling took place during that brief spell in the early nineteenth century when Christian missionary women attempted to educate Indian girls, first in schools and then in their homes.[22] The attempt had to be given up rather quickly because the idea of women being exposed to Christian influences seemed far too threatening to the men of their families, and it was only in the latter half of the century when Indians themselves began to open schools for women and to produce what was considered a suitable modern educational literature in Bengali that the practice of middle-class girls going to school would become legitimate.

In the meantime, Rassundari's education came to an abrupt halt at the age of ten when the building in which her school was housed was destroyed in a fire.[23] It is doubtful how far her education would have progressed in any case, because at the age of twelve, in accordance with the prevailing custom, she was given in marriage.

From then on, her life was completely enclosed by the daily performance of her household duties. After the death of her mother-in-law a few years later, she had to take on the entire burden of running the house. She cooked three times a day for about thirty members of the household, and gave birth to twelve children, of whom seven died in her lifetime. Her responsibilities in the family would not allow her to go anywhere. Even when she did visit her husband's relatives on weddings and other ritual occasions, she would be accompanied on the boat by two guards, two maids, and ten or fifteen other people. "Like a prisoner on parole", she would have to return in a couple of days. Rassundari particularly lamented her failure to visit her mother before she died:

> I tried in so many ways to go and see my mother, but I was not fated to do so. This is not a matter of small regret to me. O Lord, why did you give birth to me as a human being? Compared to all the birds and beasts and other inferior creatures in this world, it is a rare privilege to be granted a human birth. And yet, despite this privilege, I have failed grievously in my duty. Why was I born a woman? Shame on my life! . . . If I had been my mother's son and known of her imminent death, no matter where I happened to be, I would have flown to her side like a bird. Alas, I am only a bird in a cage.[24]

Had this been all there was to Rassundari's life, it would have been no different from those of thousands of other women in upper-caste landed families in early nineteenth-century Bengal, and we would have had no opportunity to read about it in her own words. Fortunately, she nursed a secret dream. She was always a very devout woman, and sometime in her late youth she had a longing to read the religious epics and the lives of the great saints. She did not so much as dare look at even a piece of paper that had been written on, for fear of adverse comments, but every day, she tells us, she would pray to her god: "O Lord, give me learning, so that I can read books . . . If you do not reach me, who will?"[25] And yet she did not know how this impossible feat would be accomplished.

The way was shown to her in a dream:

> One day, in my sleep, I dreamt I had opened a copy of the *Caitanya-bhāgavat* and was reading it. As soon as I woke up, my body and mind were filled with delight. I closed my eyes and again thought of the dream, and realised what a precious gift I had received . . . I said to myself, "How remarkable! I have never seen a copy of the *Caitanya-bhāgavat* and would not recognise it even if I saw one. And yet, there I was reading it in my dream." . . . Every day I had asked the Almighty, "Teach me to read. I want to read books." The Almighty had not taught me to read, but had now given me the power to read books in my dream. I was delighted and thanked the Almighty.[26]

Rassundari, however, was to be blessed even more generously. That very day, while she was busy in the kitchen, her husband came in looking for their eldest son and said to him, "This is my *Caitanya-bhāgavat*. Keep it here somewhere. I'll send for it later." Rassundari waited until no one was around, removed a page of the unbound manuscript and hid it in her room. Later, she tried to read it and discovered that so many years after her brief period of schooling she could not recognize most of the letters. She then stole a page on which her son had practised his alphabets, and for months thereafter, whenever she was alone, she would compare the two pieces of paper and, painfully, and in absolute secrecy, teach herself to read.

Over the next couple of years, she worked her way through the *Caitanya-bhāgavat*. No one in the household knew of her accomplishment, except a few trusted maids. But Rassundari had perceived the existence of a whole new world which still seemed out of her reach.

> My mind seemed to have acquired six hands. With two of them, it wanted to do all the work of the household so that no one, young or old, could find fault with me. With two others, it sought to draw my children close to my heart. And with the last two, it reached out for the moon . . . Has anyone held the moon in her hands? . . . And yet, my mind would not be convinced: it yearned to read the *purāna*.[27]

Rassundari gathered up courage and shared her secret with her widowed sisters-in-law. To her surprise, not only did they not reprimand her, but in fact eagerly conspired to start a secret reading circle, arranging to procure books from the outer quarters of the house and setting up an elaborate warning system so as not to be discovered.[28]

In time, when her sons were grown up, it was no longer necessary to keep up the secrecy. In any case, the times had also changed and men of her son's generation looked upon the education of women as a virtue. It was with the assistance of her sons that Rassundari learnt to read the printed book and later on to write.[29]

Rassundari thought of her achievement as a divine gift. In fact, her testimony is quite unique in the collection we are looking at for the utterly sincere way in which it tells the story of a life shaped entirely by the inscrutable whims and fancies of a divine power, including the dreams and miraculous coincidences in which that power revealed its presence. It could well be a fragment, paraphrased in the prose of the nineteenth century, from the devotional literature of an earlier era. All subjectivity is attributed here to a divine agency, and Rassundari recounts her toil and sorrow – "the burden of three lives thrust into one"[30] – only as the story of a fate assigned to her. I should also mention that she notes with great satisfaction the good fortune of women younger than her, for "the Lord of the Universe has now made new rules for everything. Women today do not have to suffer . . . Nowadays parents take great care to educate their daughters. I feel very pleased when I see this."[31]

Before we leave Rassundari to move on to the life-histories of women whose beliefs were shaped more directly by the sensibilities of this "modern" world, we must note the way in which her story was given a place in the autobiographical literature of Bengal. When her book was published in the early decades of this century, it was introduced with two forewords – one by the dramatist Jyotirindranath Tagore and the other by the pioneering historian of Bengali literature, Dineshchandra Sen. Jyotirindranath saw in her writing "a simple and unselfconscious charm" and noted in particular the fact that "it was her thirst for religious knowledge which drove her to learn to read and write."[32]

Dineshchandra saw in it "a true portrait of the traditional Hindu woman", "the original picture of the long-suffering, compassionate Bengali woman". He remarked on the tendency in modern literature to focus on woman exclusively as the subject of romantic love, which produced, he says, a very incomplete picture of the Hindu woman who was, after all, also a mother, daughter, sister, sister-in-law, daughter-in-law, and mistress of the household and "had to earn credit in all of these roles before she would be praised by society." Rassundari's life was a model of such traditional virtues.[33] Of course, the social norms within which she led her life were often oppressive, but those were the undesirable aspects of tradition which had to be reformed.

Nationalists of the twentieth century saw in Rassundari's story only a confirmation of their construction of the true essence of Indian womanhood: self-sacrificing, compassionate, spiritual, and possessing great resources of emotional strength drawn from personal faith and devotion. This essence, they thought, needed to be recovered from the morass of bigotry and superstition into which tradition had fallen; to accomplish this end reform and education were required. What they did not recognize was that Rassundari's struggle emanated from a consciousness that was yet uncolonized by the Enlightenment. She submitted to, as well as resisted, a patriarchy that was pre-modern: her strategies of resistance also sprang out of traditions that far pre-dated the advent of "women's eudcation" as an agenda of nationalist reform. Above all, it did not require the intervention of nationalist male reformers to set Rassundari's consciousness into motion.[34] Indeed, in her time the nationalist project had not even begun. Only later did nationalism appropriate her story into its own pre-history.

If I might stay with this transitional period a little longer, I would like to introduce here the story of Saradasundari Debi (1819–1907).[35] Saradasundari was married at the age of nine into one of the most prominent families of colonial Calcutta. Ramkamal Sen, her father-in-law, was a close associate of English traders and officials. Although very much an advocate of Western education, he was also concerned with the preservation of religious orthodoxy. Saradasundari's husband had been educated into the new world, and every night, in the secrecy of their bedroom, he would teach her to read and write.[36] She, however, became a widow when she was still a young woman, and later in her life, although she could still read, she had lost her ability to write. The account we read was dictated by her to a younger male relative.

The story she tells us is one of suffering – the suffering of a widow with small children surrounded by male relatives intent on defrauding her of her property. Her main responsibility in the world was towards her children – giving her sons a good education and arranging for the marriage of her daughters. Whenever she could, she sought to escape the sufferings of the world by going on pilgrimage. She too was a devout woman, and the happiest episodes in the story that she tells occur in her journeys away from home.

Once again, hers was a life that might have been led by numerous other upper-caste women of her time. What prompted her amanuensis to get Saradasundari's story recorded in print was the fact that her son Keshab-chandra Sen was one of the most charismatic leaders of the religious reform movement in Bengal in the second half of the nineteenth century. It is as the life-history of Keshab's mother that Saradasundari's autobiography found a place in the archives of Bengali literature.[37] And it is in this respect that her account reveals traces of the struggle inside urban homes caught in the vortex of cultural reform. Unlike Rassundari, Saradasundari is much more self-conscious about her religiosity. She talks about her joy and fulfilment in the many pilgrimages she made in her life, and yet she talks about them with a sense of guilt:

> I felt then that I was being virtuous. I would not feel the same way now. I was a little childish then. Even now, I go on pilgrimages, but not to earn religious merit. I go only out of love, in the same way that I have love for my children and those who are my own. But I do not believe that I will gain salvation by going on pilgrimages . . . I had this obsession for religion and a strong urge to see the holy places. Even now I perform many kinds of worship, but all from the same feeling [of love]. I believe in my heart that there is only one God and unless I worship Him I will never be liberated. I cannot say with certainty that people never achieve liberation if they worship the deities with form [sākār], but I do know that they achieve it if they worship the formless God [nirākār] and that my own liberation depends upon His grace.[38]

Those who know the social history of Bengal in this period will immediately hear in these words resonances of the contentious debate between monotheistic Brahmo reformers and the defenders of Hindu orthodoxy. Living in an orthodox family, and yet the proud mother of a son celebrated for his radical religious views, Saradasundari was clearly caught in a conflict that was not of her own making. She had, therefore, to speak in two voices – one recalling with gratitude and joy her visits to the great Vaishnav temples of India and her miraculous visions of the deity, the other asserting her role as Keshab Sen's mother. It would be presumptuous on our part to declare one of the two as her true voice: what was true was her struggle to make both voices her own.

> I had to suffer a great deal because [Keshab] became a Brahmo. I had to bear with much insult . . . and ill treatment. There was not a day when I did not cry . . . There were times when even I thought that Keshab was doing wrong. I do not think so any more . . . I sought advice from my *guru*. He told me, "If your son accepts this new religion, he will become a great man. People will flock to him. Don't worry about this any more." I was calmed by his words.[39]

It should not be surprising for us that for this early generation of women from the new middle class of Bengal, the presence of society and religion as a set of regulatory practices appeared in the immediacy of family and kin relations converging upon the home. So too the presence of new currents in the outside world, including the presence of the West itself, appeared in the person of a male family member, usually the husband or a son. The great conflicts over social reform in a public domain peopled exclusively by males were thus transmitted into the lives of women inside their homes. Women, consequently, had to devise strategies to cope with the new demands made upon their loyalties and their desires. If Saradasundari seems painfully torn between a conventional devotion which gave her solace in an oppressive world and a rational religion preached by her radical son, we have another testimony which suggests a resolution of this dilemma. Significantly, it involves a woman who was able to escape the daily surveillance of the extended family and live a life with her modernist husband, as it were, outside the reaches of "society".

IV

Kailasbasini Debi (1830–95)[40] was the wife of Kishorichand Mitra, a prominent figure among the social reformers of the mid-nineteenth century. Kishorichand was an employee of the East India Company and held important administrative positions in the district towns of Bengal and Bihar. For several years of her married life, therefore, Kailasbasini lived alone with her husband, away from home in company bungalows and houseboats. Her husband taught her to read and write Bengali and some English as well. Later when he settled down in Calcutta, Kishorichand built a garden-house in the outskirts of the city where Kailasbasini would often live with her husband and daughter.

In marked contrast to the other stories we have heard so far, Kailasbasini talks of her married life as happy. She looked from a critical distance at the traditional life of the family she had left behind, but which was always waiting for her out there. She was horrified by the unhygienic and degrading conditions in which women in traditional homes were confined at childbirth[41] and regretted that other women she knew did not have the benefits of enlightened teaching which her husband had given her.[42] She was quite conscious of the way in which her husband had assiduously molded her thoughts and beliefs, and was grateful for it. Most of these views were rationalist, in the way in which rationalist arguments were used in the nineteenth century to supply instrumental justifications for traditional beliefs and customs. Thus, Kailasbasini says, echoing her husband, that the reason why widows are traditionally restricted to a hard life devoid of luxury is to make them unattractive to men, so that they do not become objects of their lust. The reason why meat-eating is regarded as polluting is because India is a warm country in which meat is bad for the health. The reason for idolatry lies in the need to provide a practical religion for ignorant people who find it difficult to conceive of an abstract formless God.[43]

There is no question that Kailasbasini saw herself as both more fortunate than and superior to other women around her. She was happy in the formative company of her enlightened husband. When he was away on tour, she tells us with a stunning simile, she spent her time "like Robinson Crusoe, eating, sleeping, reading, sewing, teaching my daughter and writing this journal."[44]

And yet, even for someone so free from the rigors of customary regulation and so happily enveloped by an entirely new conjugal tutelage, Kailasbasini required strategies to protect herself against the consequences of her husband's reformist projects:

> I do not believe in the rituals of Hindu orthodoxy, but I follow all of them. For I know that if I relax my hold, my husband will give up the Hindu religion altogether. My closest relatives are Hindus and I can never abandon them. For this reason, I scrupulously follow all the rules of the Hindu religion.
>
> I have this great fear that no one will accept food from my hands. That would be a shame worse than death. As it is, my husband eats out [without observing ritual regulations]: if I too join him, it would be a calamity.
>
> . . . Since I follow the Hindu rules, I have no problems, no matter what my husband does. That is the religion of the Bengalis, which is why those who are clever do not believe in it. But I never say this to my husband, although I know it would please him to no end if he heard it from me.[45]

I wish to suggest that we have here a moment where a strategy worked out within the space of the emergent nationalist middle-class home anticipated the form of a more general strategy which political nationalism would later attempt to use to create the solidarity of cultural communities compatible with the requirements of the modern state. A neat separation between a private domain of diverse individuals residing in bourgeois patriarchal families and a public domain inhabited by homogeneous citizens was not available to Indian nationalism. The rational-bureaucratic form of the modern state brought to India by the colonial power was premised precisely upon the denial of citizenship to colonized Indians. The strategy, therefore, had to use another distinction – between the spiritual or the inner, on the one hand, and the material or the outer, on the other. The latter was a ground surrendered to the colonial power; the former was where nationalism began to fashion its claims to hegemony. Kailasbasini, speaking from within this emergent middle-class home, is not telling us that religious beliefs and practices are private matters and that what is important for the life of the nation is the public behaviour of its citizens. On the contrary, she has discovered that the practices of the outside world which men have to get used to are in the end inconsequential, since what truly matters in the life of the nation are practices in the inner space of community life. Here it is the duty of women to hold fast to the religious practices of the community; even "private" beliefs are of no consequence. Her strategy mirrors a crucial move in the cultural politics of nationalism.

The home, I suggest, was not a complementary but rather the original site on which the hegemonic project of nationalism was launched. It is this which made women from the new middle class in nineteenth-century India active agents in the nationalist project – complicit in the framing of its hegemonic strategies as much as they were resistant to them because of their subordination under the new forms of patriarchy.

To return to Kailasbasini: the apparent stability of the manner in which she chose to reconcile the conflicting demands on her loyalty was undoubtedly made possible by the fortuitous distance between her conjugal home and the effective centre of her social life. The situation was to be repeated in the cases of many middle-class families of the Bengali diaspora that spread out into the cities and towns of northern India with the expansion of colonial administration in the second half of the nineteenth century. But in her case at least, the fragility of an individual solution worked out in the peripheries of society was exposed rather tragically. In 1873, when Kailasbasini was in her early forties, her husband died.

> ... I took the name "widow". When I hear that name, it is as though lightning strikes my heart. O Lord, why have you given me this name? How long am I to live with it? I will not be able to bear the suffering. I hope this name soon vanishes into dust. What a terrible name! My heart trembles at its very sound.[46]

Those are the last words in Kailasbasini's diary. As far as we know, she never wrote again.[47]

The project of cultural reform which nationalist ideology placed on the agenda in the second half of the nineteenth century did, however, provide the resources for women to turn personal misfortune into a new social identity. This becomes clear in the story of Prasannamayi Debi (1857–1939).[48] Born in an upper-caste landed family, Prasannamayi was married at the age of ten to a husband who turned out to be mentally deranged. After she had made two brief visits to her in-laws, her father refused to send her back, and from the age of 14 Prasannamayi lived with her parents and brothers. Her father was committed to the cause of reform and arranged not only to give the best possible education to his sons, many of whom were later to reach positions of eminence in their respective professions, but also to educate his daughter at home.

From a very young age, Prasannamayi showed signs of literary talent. Given her father's literary and musical interests, the family was part of a cultural circle that included some of the most prominent literary figures of the time. Prasannamayi was not only allowed to listen to these discussions but encouraged to take an active part in them. Often she would read out her own poetry in these distinguished gatherings. Even as a young woman, her writings began to be published regularly in major literary magazines and soon she came out with her own books of poems. Indeed, she became quite a celebrity as a woman who had overcome a personal tragedy caused by the retrograde custom of hypergamous child marriage to make a name for herself as a writer. Protected and encouraged by a circle of male relatives and friends which, in the late nineteenth century, was now far more self-assured about its cultural project, Prasannamayi became an exemplary figure, standing for all the virtues claimed on behalf of the "new woman".

We know about the tragedy of Prasannamayi's marriage from other sources:[49] she herself tells us absolutely nothing about it. In 91 pages of detailed description of domestic life in her childhood and youth and of dozens of relatives and acquaintances, she does not once mention her husband. All that she says about her experience of married life is that when she first arrived at her in-laws, dressed in the new fashion with petticoat and jacket and surrounded by rumours about her ability to read and write, she was regarded with great curiosity as "the English bride" [mem bau]. When she innocently made a display of her accomplishments, including a demonstration on the concertina, she was rebuked by her mother-in-law.[50] She allows herself only one comment on the custom of hypergamous kulin marriage of which she was a victim: "avaricious kulin parents," she says, "in their desire to preserve the reputation of their lineages, did not consider the uncertain consequences of giving their daughters in marriages of this sort, although many of these incompatible marriages led to much unhappiness. But it was difficult suddenly to break with a social custom."[51] She mentions the fact that several other women in her family had suffered because of such marriages, but then adds: "It is best that this unfortunate history remains unknown to the public."[52]

There is only one place where Prasannamayi slips from her objective narrative of social history to allow us a glimpse into the domain where women in her situation had to wage the struggle for identity and recognition. This occurs when she talks of Indumati, the widowed daughter of the reformer Ramtanu Lahiri. "This remarkable woman," she says, "was born only to teach the world the duty of love, to demonstrate that the purpose of human life is not indulgence but sacrifice – the sacrifice of the pleasures and desires of youth to the cause of service to others." But she also knew Indumati as a friend, and in their friendship both found the means to forget the immediate world:

> I cannot explain now how wonderful it was to forget ourselves completely. From morning to evening and then late into the night, we would talk, and time would fly past us. This was no political conspiracy, nor was it a discussion on some scientific problem. It was only the dream-like imagination and the pain of unfulfilled desire of two people inexperienced in the ways of the world. All the feelings and scenes that went into the making of this imagined world were products of our minds, bearing no relationship at all to the world of phenomenal things.[53]

Apart from this brief slippage, the rest of Prasannamayi's story is a model of nationalist social history written from the standpoint of the "new woman". She is critical of the irrationality and superstititiousness of many religious beliefs and customs.[54] She is horrified by the excesses of caste discrimination and is hopeful that the extreme rigidities of the system would be gradually weakened. "All must join in bringing about the welfare of the nation. We cannot live separately any more. All must join in worshipping the Mother."[55] She is grateful to her father, her brothers, and their circle of friends for the guidance and encouragement they gave her in fashioning a completely new role as a woman with an identity in public life. Her view on contemporary history was entirely one of the legitimacy of reform and national progress. On the other hand, she bemoans the fact that English education was leading to so much superficial aping of Western manners and the negligence of what was good in tradition: "Young people today can recite by heart the names of [Admiral] Nelson's ancestors but do not know the names of their own grandparents."[56] And she affirms without question the essential identity of woman as faithful wife and exemplary mother:

> My mother, Srimati Magnamayi Debi, was very patriotic. Her love for her country was without comparison. Every grain of Indian sand was to her like a speck of gold . . . Her immediate deity was her husband. Always abiding by

the commands of her husband, she built her life according to an ideal and taught her children to follow that ideal.[57]

If we are to take a linear view of history as progress, then our journey which began with Rassundari in the early decades of the nineteenth century has reached its fulfilment with Prasannamayi at its close. For in Prasannamayi, the nationalist idea of the "new woman" as a hegemonic construct would seem to have been actualized: her struggle has been completely encapsulated in the project to produce the nation – everything else is erased from public memory.

V

If I stop my culling of these archives at this point, the principal course of the narrative will have thus described a linear movement. Needless to say, this is not an accident. I have deliberately chosen and arranged the four texts in such a way as to produce exactly that effect. My object was to trace through these supposedly self-revelatory texts the genealogy of the nationalist construct of the "new woman". I could, of course, have read the same texts in the opposite direction, against the grain, as texts that show the marks of resistance to a hegemonizing discourse: I have, even in this account, pointed out several of these marks. But I wish to retain up to this point the smooth linearity of my story, if only to emphasize once more the powers of a hegemonizing nationalism to take in its stride a whole range of dissenting voices.

We have therefore a linear narrative. The nationalist will read this as a movement from bondage to emancipation; the feminist critic of nationalism will read it as a movement from one kind of bondage to another. In order now to mess up the picture and forestall both of these closures, I will continue my story a little further and consider the autobiography of Binodini.[58]

Binodini (1863–1941) was perhaps the most celebrated actress on the Calcutta stage in the last decades of the nineteenth century. The position of the professional actress was itself a creation of the newly educated, middle-class culture, supplying a need produced by the requirements of the new public theater modelled along European lines. Yet it was a need that was difficult to fulfil within the norms of respectability laid down for women. The solution devised by the early generation of theater producers was to recruit young women from among the city's prostitutes and train them in the modern techniques of the dramatic arts. It became a remarkable educative project in itself, producing women schooled in the language and sensibilities of a modernist literati, who learned to think of themselves as professional artists and yet were excluded from respectable social life by the stigma of immoral living. Binodini's life as a professional actress was produced by these contradictions of the new world of middle-class cultural production.

She was brought into the theater at the age of ten; when she was eighteen, she was at the peak of her career; at 23, she decided to leave the stage. The autobiography she wrote and published at 49 describes the 13 years of her professional life as a historical sequence of events, but everything before and after exists as though in a zone of timelessness. As a child, she was brought up in a Calcutta slum, in a household bereft of adult males. In her autobiography, she talks about the environment of the slum with consider-able distaste, remembering herself as a child looking upon her neighbours "with fear and surprise" and hoping she would never have to face such contempt.[59] She had been told of her marriage at the age of five or six, and there was a boy in the neighbourhood whom others referred to as her husband.[60] Whether this might have become a significant event in her life can only be speculated upon, because everything changed when her mother agreed to give her to the theater as a child actress on a monthly salary.

For a girl of 11 or 12 years old, training to become a professional actress was hard work. But then again, being in the theater was also like living in a large family: that is where one belonged. Binodini saw her identity as an actress entirely in terms of her place within this family of artistes. She submitted to its rules, did all that was required of her with dedication, and brought fame and popularity to the theaters she worked for. It is only when we locate this collective site where she grounded her identity and into which she poured out her feelings of loyalty – the extended family transposed on to the artificially constructed world of the middle-class professional theater which to her was the very real surrogate for society itself – that we begin to see the significance of the central theme of Binodini's autobiography: betrayal.

Binodini had been driven by the belief that the shame of being a woman of ill-repute would be removed by her dedication and accomplishments as an artist. Indeed, her acceptance of a position of concubine to various wealthy patrons seemed to her to be justified by the greater cause of art. She desperately needed to believe in the solidarity and well-being of her surrogate family, for it was only there that she could lead a life of worth and dignity. When her theater company faced a crisis, she even agreed, at considerable personal risk, to become the mistress of a wealthy businessman who was prepared to finance the founding of a new theater only if he could have in exchange the famous Miss Binodini. She was led to believe that her "brothers and sisters" in the company would express their gratitude to her by naming their new theater after her. When this did not happen, she felt betrayed.[61] This was the first of a series of betrayals with which Binodini marks out for us the story of her life.

Trained in the language and sensibilities of the new middle-class culture,

Binodini, we can well imagine, felt an intense desire to believe in the emancipatory claims made on behalf of the "new woman". Her life in the theatre had introduced her to Greek tragedy and Shakespeare, to the new humanism of Michael Madhusudan Dutt, Bankimchandra and Dinabandhu Mitra, and to the fervently nationalist representations by Girishchandra Ghosh of Hindu mythology and religious history. When she realized that she could only be transformed to fulfil the cultural needs of a class claiming to represent the nation but not given the place of respectability which the class had set aside for its own women, she learnt not to believe any more:

> Ever since I was thrust into the affairs of the world in my adolescence, I have learnt not to trust. The responsibility for this lies with my teachers, my social position and myself. But what is the use of apportioning blame? The distrust remains . . . How deeply rooted it is in my heart will become clear from the events of my life . . . And it is impossible to uproot it! I realise that faith is the basis of peace, but where is that faith?[62]

Something, Binodini felt, had been promised to her in return for her dedication to the ideals and disciplines she had been taught. If the enlightened virtues of respectable womanhood meant conformity to a new set of disciplinary rules, she was prepared to conform. Yet respectability was denied to her. She had a daughter whom she wanted to send to school: no school would have her. When the daughter died, she felt she had been betrayed once more.[63]

In late middle age, when she decided to write down the story of her life "to blacken white sheets of paper with the stigma of my heart",[64] she asked her teacher Girishchandra Ghosh to write a foreword to her book. Girish did, but Binodini did not like what her teacher wrote. Girish in fact sought to apply the classic appropriating strategy, pointing out "the great moral lesson in the insignificant life of an ordinary prostitute . . . On reading this autobiography, the pride of the pious will be curbed, the self-righteous will feel humble, and the sinner will find peace." He went on to comment on "the aspersions" cast by Binodini on the guardians of society: "Rather than emphasising the didactic aspects of her art, she has tried to tell her own story. The concealing of the personal which is the essence of the technique of writing an autobiography has been compromised." Girish recognized that Binodini had her reasons to feel bitter, "but such bitter words are best left out of one's own life-story. For the reader whose sympathy [Binodini] must expect will refuse to give it when he encounters such harshness."[65]

Binodini, as I said, was not satisfied with this foreword and insisted that her teacher and the greatest actor on the Calcutta stage write "a true account" of all that had happened. The revised version never came, because a few months later Girish Ghosh died. To Binodini, this was another betrayal: "My teacher had told me, 'I will write the foreword before I die.'

... But it was not in my fate ... By leaving the foreword unfinished, my teacher taught me once more that all that one wishes in life is not fulfilled."[66]

The most heart-breaking betrayal, however, came in Binodini's attempt to build a life of her own outside the theater. For 30 years, from about the time she left the stage, she lived with a gentleman from one of the wealthiest and most respected families in the city. She put into this relationship all her feelings of loyalty and devotion and felt free, loved, respected, and cared for. What she did not realize was the inevitable fragility of the arrangement, because individual patronage, no matter how sincere, could hardly overcome the boundaries of a newly constructed world of the dominant which could only claim to speak on her behalf but never recognize her as its constituent part. Lying on his deathbed, the worthy gentleman made her a promise: "If I have devotion and faith in God, if I have been born in a virtuous family, you will never have to beg for protection." Death, however, rendered him powerless to fulfil his promise. His family, one can guess, did not feel in the least bit obliged to recognize an embarrassing relationship. Binodini was betrayed once more.

Ignoring the advice and admonitions of all her teachers, therefore, Binodini in turn felt that she was under no obligation to hide her deep-rooted scepticism about the verities of customary belief and convention. Determined to tell "her own story", she violated every canon of the feminine *smrtikathā* and wrote down what amounted to her indictment of respectable society in the form of a series of letters addressed to her deceased lover. Perhaps her very marginality enabled her to assert this autonomy over her own words. With bitter irony, she wrote in her preface to the book:

> Hindu men and women, I take it, believe with complete sincerity in heaven and hell, in birth and rebirth ... Although he [her lover] is no longer on earth, he must be in heaven, from where he can see all that has happened to me and can feel the pain in my heart – if, that is, the Hindu religion is true and the gods are true; if, that is, birth and rebirth are true.[67]

Before we close our narrative of the nationalist transition, therefore, we need to remind ourselves of Binodini's story. For it tells us once more that the story of nationalist emancipation is also a story of betrayal. Necessarily so. Because it could only confer freedom by imposing at the same time a whole set of new controls, it could only define a cultural identity for the nation by excluding many from its fold, and it could only grant the dignity of citizenship to some because the others always needed to be represented; they could not be allowed to speak for themselves. Binodini reminds us once more that the relations between the people and the nation, the nation and the state, relations which nationalism claims to have resolved once and

for all, continue to be contested and are therefore open to negotiation all
over again.

VI

Having written this nicely inconclusive last sentence, I am struck by doubt.
The sentence promises further episodes in the story of women and nationalism, and I feel I have succeeded in avoiding a closure. Have I?

In a recent article,[68] Edward Said has spoken of "an incipient and
unresolved tension" in the contest "between stable identity as it is rendered
by such affirmative agencies as nationality, education, tradition, language,
and religion, on the one hand, and all sorts of marginal, alienated or . . .
anti-systemic forces on the other." This tension, he says, "produces a
frightening consolidation of patriotism, assertions of cultural superiority,
mechanisms of control, whose power and ineluctability reinforce . . . the
logic of identity."[69]

Said is thinking of "the cruel, insensate, shameful violence" that has
taken place so often in the name of patriotic affirmation of identity in the
Middle East. I am thinking of the equally shameful violence that has
become virtually endemic in India in the matter of political relations
between Hindus and Muslims, or in more recent years, between Hindus
and Sikhs. I therefore find myself in agreement with Said when he says:
". . . it must be incumbent upon even those of us who support nationalist
struggle in an age of unrestrained nationalist expression to have at our
disposal some decent measure of intellectual refusal, negation and
scepticism."[70]

But then he says: "It is at precisely that nexus of committed participation
and intellectual commitment that we should situate ourselves to ask *how
much* identity, *how much* positive consolidation, *how much* administered
approbation we are willing to tolerate in the name of our cause, our
culture, our state."[71] And here I begin once again to have doubts. Are we
still trying to sort out that old liberal problem of "good nationalism" versus
"bad nationalism"? Must it be our argument that a little bit of identity and
positive consolidation and administered approbation is all for the good,
but beyond a certain point they are intolerable? I have to think twice before
I vote for this one, because it was not very long ago that I argued
vociferously against the posing of this kind of liberal paradox.[72]

One of the ways of avoiding the paradox is to question and reproblema-
tize the all too easy identification, claimed by every nationalist state
ideology, of the state with the nation and the nation with the people. As an
act of intellectual scepticism, this might well involve risks that are more
than intellectual. But speaking now only of effects in the intellectual
domain, one important effect will be, I think, the somewhat startling

discovery that the most powerful and authentic historical achievements of anti-colonial nationalism were often won outside the political battlefield and well before the actual contest for political power was settled. This discovery will open up once more the question of who led and who followed, and of when it all began. It will introduce, in short, an agenda to rewrite the history of nationalism with different actors and a different chronology. It will also demonstrate that the culturally creative forms of anti-colonial nationalism seeking to establish a zone of hegemony outside the intervention of the colonial state cannot be covered by the "modular" forms of nationalism produced in Europe or the Americas.

What is crucial, however, is for us to be able to show the many risky moments in this narrative of anti-colonial nationalism, the alternative sequences that were suppressed, the marks of resistance which people sought to erase. Much intellectual work of dissent in post-colonial countries is today performing precisely this task. It is arguing that the history of the transition from colonial to post-colonial regimes is highly problematical, that the promise of national emancipation was fulfilled, if not fraudently, then certainly by the forcible marginalization of many who were supposed to have shared in the fruits of liberation. Indeed, the opening up of the whole problematic of the national project within and outside the domain of the state makes it possible for us now to make the radical suggestion that the cultural history of nationalism, shaped through its struggle with colonialism, contained many possibilities of authentic, creative, and plural development of social identities which were violently disrupted by the political history of the post-colonial state seeking to replicate the modular forms of the modern nation-state. We too, like Binodini, have to tell a story of betrayal.

My doubts are about the effectiveness of this critique. Having to survive in a world pulverized by the concentrated violence of the Gulf War, I cannot, I am afraid, share Said's easy optimism in "scholarship and politics from a world viewpoint, past domination, toward community."[73] It is the very biculturalism of intellectuals in post-colonial countries – a necessary biculturalism which they have to work hard to acquire – which enables them to see through the sham and hypocrisy of today's myths of global cooperation. For us, it is hard to imagine a plausible state of the world in which our relation to the dominant structures of scholarship and politics will be anything other than adversarial.

It would be dishonest, therefore, to claim that the critique of nationalism is straightforward. Rather, the more realistic tactic is not to underestimate nationalism's capacity to appropriate, with varying degrees of risk and varying degrees of success, dissenting and marginal voices. I must, for the sake of truthfulness, note here that Binodini today is an honoured name in the public history Bengali theater. Her life as a story of struggle and betrayal is a popular subject for plays and films, and the official liberality of the new domain of the state does not allow any judgement of sexual morality to affect the esteem accorded to her as an artist.

In the new public domain of the state, yes. In the ethical domain of the community? Doubtful. Only a few weeks ago, I came across a brief letter in a Calcutta daily which will remain etched in my memory for a long time. A leading actress of yesteryear, now in her seventies and honoured with several state awards, was complaining about an article on a deceased actor in the newspaper, in which she had been mentioned as his "close friend and companion". "There is only one truth I know," she wrote. "I am the wife of the late Nirmalendu Lahiri and I bore four of his children. I do not know any other truth about our relationship."[74]

The ethical domain of nationalism remains very much a contested terrain, not least because its political success was so massive and thoroughgoing, but also because its ideological bases remain so much a site of struggle – even today.

Notes

I began writing this essay in the Spring of 1990 when I was teaching at the New School for Social Research, New York. An earlier version was presented at the New York Academy of Sciences and at Princeton University. I am grateful to Nirmalya Acharya, Talal Asad, Sibaji Bandyopadhyaya, Dipesh Chakrabarty, Tapati Guha-thakurta, U. Kalpagam, Debes Roy, Ranabir Samaddar, Asok Sen, Michael Sprinker, Kamala Visweswaran and Judy Walkowitz for reading and commenting on the earlier version.

1 Edward W. Said, *Orientalism* (London: Routledge and Kegan Paul, 1978).

2 Partha Chatteriee, *Nationalist Thought and the Colonial World* (London: Zed Books, 1985).

3 *Imagined Communities: Reflections on the Origins and Spread of Nationalism* (London: Verso, 1983).

4 "Prācīnā ebam nabīnā", *Bankim-racanābalī*, ed. Jogeshchandra Bagal, 2 (Calcutta: Sahitya Samsad, 1954), pp. 249–56. All translations from Bengali sources used in this essay are mine.

5 I have discussed the genealogy of the nationalist construct of the "new woman" in "Colonialism, Nationalism and Colonialized Women: The Contest in India", *American Ethnologist*, 16, 4 (November 1989), pp. 622–33, and "The Nationalist Resolution of the Women's Ouestion" in Kumkum Sangari and Sudesh Vaid, eds., *Recasting Women: Essays in Colonial History* (New Delhi: Kali for Women, 1989; New Brunswick. NJ: Rutgers University Press, 1990), pp. 233–53.

6 "Tin rakam", *Bankim-racanābalī*, 2, pp. 254–6.

7 Sudipta Kaviraj has analysed the use of self-irony in Bankim's writings in "Bankimchandra and the Making of Nationalist Consciousness: I. Signs of Madness: II. The Self-Ironical Tradition", Occasional Papers 108 and 109, Centre for Studies in Social Sciences, Calcutta, 1989.

8 That every such critique and its subsequent appropriation also sows the seeds of instability in the field of discourse goes without saying. Bankim, for instance, as Sibaji Bandyopadhyaya has reminded me, has to cover the risk of his

statement about universal male dominance by asserting the ethical truth, independent of male actions, of the virtue of wifely devotion. The contradiction is only barely concealed.

9 "... this generally signifies an addition of women into the framework of conventional history ... In this sense, with a few exceptions, the women worked within boundaries laid down by men. The history uncovered in this way is a 'contributive' history," Kumari Jayawardena, *Feminism and Nationalism in the Third World* (London: Zed Books, 1986), pp. 260–1.

10 This same problematic is at the center of Edward Said's work since *Orientalism*, which has been criticized for hypostasizing an omnipotent Western imperial discourse that left no space for indigenous resistance. Said's recent essays (some of which I discuss at the end of this paper) take up this question in detail, showing how the relations between colonizer and colonized, domination and resistance, are infinitely mediated and frequently contingent.

11 This is the central argument of the most systematic study of the biographical genre in Bengali literature: Debipada Bhattacharya, *Bāmlā carit sāhitya* (Calcutta: Dey's, 1982).

12 Sibnath Sastri, *Rāmtanu lāhidī o tatkālīn baṅgasamāi* (first ed. 1904), in *Śibnāth racanāsamgraha* (Calcutta: Saksharata Prakashan, 1979).

13 Surendranath Banerjea, *A Nation in Making: Being the Reminiscences of Fifty Years of Public Life* (Bombay: Oxford University Press, 1966; first ed. 1925).

14 This is how Mary Mason identifies the difference between women's autobiographies and those of men. Mary G. Mason, "The Other Voice: Autobiographies of Women Writers", in James Olney, ed., *Autobiography: Essays Theoretical and Critical* (Princeton. NJ: Princeton University Press. 1980), pp. 207–35.

15 I should qualify this statement a little bit. There are no women's autobiographies that are called *ātmacarit*, but I have seen, for the nineteenth century, two biographies of women which are called *carit*. Of these, *Kumudinī-carit* (1868) is the life of a Brahmo woman presented as a devout and exemplary, almost saintly, figure. The other, *Lakṣīmanīcarit* (1877) is an account by a husband of his deceased wife.

16 Srabashi Ghosh, " 'Birds in a Cage': Changes in Bengali Social Life as Recorded in Autobiographies by Women", *Economic and Political Weekly: Review of Women's Studies* (October 1986), pp. WS88–96.

17 Malavika Karlekar, *Voices from Within: Early Personal Narratives of Bengali Women* (Delhi: Oxford University Press, 1991). The recent publication of this work makes it unnecessary for me to talk at length about the social-historical location of these autobiographical texts.

18 Rabindranath Thakur, "Nastanīd", *Rabīndra racanābalī*, 7 (Calcutta: Government of West Bengal, 1962), pp. 433–4.

19 Shanta Nag, *Pūrbasmrti* (Calcutta: Papyrus, 1983; first ed. 1970), p. 16.

20 Rassundari Dasi, *Āmār jīban* (Calcutta: De Book Store, 1987; first ed. 1876).

21 Ibid., pp. 5–6.

22 See Ghulam Murshid, *Reluctant Debutante: Response of Bengali Women to Modernization. 1849–1905* (Rajshahi: Rajshahi University Press, 1983); and Meredith Borthwick, *The Changing Role of Women in Bengal, 1849–1905* (Princeton, N. J: Princeton University Press. 1984).

23 *Āmār jīban*, p. 14.

24 Ibid., pp. 38–9.

25 Ibid., pp. 32, 41.

26 Ibid., p. 41.

27 Ibid., p. 56.

28 Ibid., pp. 57–8.
29 Ibid., pp. 63–6.
30 Ibid., p. 97.
31 Ibid., p. 109.
32 Jyotirindranath Tagore, "Bhūmikā" in ibid., p. v.
33 Dineshchandra Sen, "Grantha paricay" in ibid., pp. vii–xiii.
34 Conventional history has it that Bengali women in general were illiterate before the period of social reform in the middle of the nineteenth century. We have some evidence, however, that this was not necessarily the case. See, for instance, Poromesh Acharya, *Bāmlār deśaja śikṣādhārā*, 1 (Calcutta: Anushtup, 1989). Even upper-caste women, for whom the prohibitions on reading and writing were likely to have been the most stringent, sometimes managed to escape them. Prasannamayi Debi, whose autobiography we will discuss later in this essay, mentions that several women from an earlier generation in her village were literate and one even ran a school where she taught both male and female children. *Pūrbba kathā*, p. 81.
35 Jogendralal Khastagir, ed., *Keśabjananī debī sāradāsundarīr ātmakathā* (first ed. 1913) in *Eksan* (Autumn 1983), pp. 1–52.
36 Ibid., p. 4.
37 Being an "as-told-to" account, this is not, strictly speaking, an autobiography, although that is how it is titled. It is clearly directed towards satisfying the curiosity of Keshab Sen's followers and admirers. Saradasundari herself seems quite conscious of the role she is expected to play; but she also resists. I am grateful to Kamala Visweswaran for alerting me to the need to make this point.
38 Ibid., p. 17.
39 Ibid., pp. 33–4.
40 Kailasbasini Debi, *Janaikā grhabadhur dāyerī* (first ed. 1952) in *Eksan* (Autumn 1981), pp. 7–48.
41 Ibid., p. 11.
42 Ibid., p. 44.
43 Ibid., pp. 42–3.
44 Ibid., p. 21.
45 Ibid., p. 32.
46 Ibid., p. 45.
47 This Kailasbasini is not to be confused with the Kailasbasini Debi (Gupta), who wrote the well-known early tracts on women's education, *Hindu mahilādiger hīnābasthā* (1863), and *Hindu abalākuler bidyābhyās o tāhār samunnati* (1865).
48 Prasannamayi Debi, *Pūrbba kathā*, ed. Nirmalya Acharya (Calcutta: Subarnarekha, 1982; first ed. 1917).
49 Nirmalya Acharya, "Grantha-pariciti" in ibid., pp. 99–104.
50 *Pūrbba kathā*, p. 44.
51 Ibid., p. 37.
52 Ibid., p. 89.
53 Ibid., p. 55.
54 For instance, the annual pilgrimage for a bath in the Ganga which often led to numerous deaths in boat disasters; ibid., p. 34.
55 Ibid., p. 71.
56 Ibid., p. 51.
57 Ibid., p. 14.
58 Binodini Dasi, *Āmār kathā o anyānya racanā*, eds. Soumitra Chattopadhyay and Nirmalya Acharya (Calcutta: Subarnarekha, 1987; first ed. 1912).
59 Ibid., pp. 17–18.

60 Ibid., pp. 16, 78.
61 Ibid., pp. 38–45.
62 Ibid., p. 13.
63 Ibid., p. 62.
64 Ibid., p. 64.
65 Girishchandra Ghosh, "Baṅga-raṅgālaye Srīmatī Binodinī" in ibid., pp. 135–44.
66 Binodini Dasi, ibid., p. 8.
67 Ibid., p. 3.
68 "Identity, Negation and Violence", *New Left Review*, 171 (September–October 1988), pp. 46–60.
69 Ibid., p. 56.
70 Ibid., p. 60.
71 Ibid.
72 See my "A Response to Taylor's Modes of Civil Society", *Public Culture*, 3, 1 (Fall 1990), pp. 119–32.
73 Edward W. Said, "Third World Intellectuals and Metropolitan Culture", *Raritan*, (Winter, 1990), pp. 27–50.
74 Sarajubala Debi, letter to the Editor, *Anandabazar Patrika* (February 1991).

INTERVIEW WITH EDWARD SAID

—

Jennifer Wicke and Michael Sprinker

JW: Edward, could you tell us about Cairo and its strategic importance for you culturally, politically, both in your child-hood development and also as a kind of pivot of your metropolitan thought?

EWS: Working backwards rather than starting with my early years there, certainly Cairo has always seemed to be the great alternative city for someone like myself who spent a lot of time in big Western cities, especially New York, but also London and Paris. But lurking in the background is this figure of a gigantic and, at least from my point of view, undigested, metropolitan presence in the eastern Mediterranean which I think I first became conscious of as a kind of antipode to Alexandria. Both in literature and in my own biography, Alexandria had been the place where one went for a window to Europe, given the presence there of foreign communities, great numbers of Greeks, French, Italians, Armenians, and Jews. So powerfully did they impress me as populations who existed principally in Alexandria, that even today I find it quite amazing that there are Greeks in Greece, Italians in Italy, and so on. And of course Alexandria is in literary terms a city with much more resonance in the West than Cairo. Yet I never felt very comfortable with Alexandria. It just didn't strike me as having the kind of spirit and sporty, irregular coherence somehow that Cairo did. So there was this sense of Cairo as an alternative, *my* alternative.

And then Cairo, in my prolonged thinking about it, breaks down into two cities. One the ancient city, the city of the sphinx and the pyramids and that whole pharoanic dimension highlighted by modern Western interest in Egypt, especially in the period from Sadat on. Sadat deliberately stressed this aspect by exporting the King Tut exhibition to the US, thereby splitting off ancient Egypt in a certain sense, and making Egypt a commodity for mass Western attention in a new way. But then there is the other city which, I note again, was undigested as a whole, nondescript and incoherent for outsiders, except that it was very, very factual in my thought as housing Islamic, Arab, African, anti-colonial experiences, parts of which have never been truly accessible to the West. Yet even within that city, you could separate off the colonial city from its main body, and get a much smaller, more specialized locale made up of sites, for example, like the island on which I grew up, Zamalek, an essentially European enclave where families like my own lived: Levantine, colonial, minority, privileged. And then there are other sections of Cairo, like Garden City, where the embassies were located, where the British embassy was the focus of the central controlling power that was considered to be the counter-balance to the palace during the years of the British occupation from the 1880s until 1952. The British ambassador was the great figure of this site – the high commissioner whose embodiment was Lord Cromer along with all those people who opposed the Egyptian nationalist movement. But of course there was always Arab Islamic Cairo, teeming with all sorts of cultural riches on the everyday level in districts like Gamaliya, Shubra, Bulaq, Ataba, Bab el Louk.

Another thing that I became aware of fairly recently, say within the last 15 years, was the sense of a very powerful current of thought located in Cairo in which the whole question of Egyptian cultural identity, transmitted historically, was formulated. There is a literature on this topic that I also came to know a relatively short time ago. One of the important figures in this discourse is Hussein Fawzi, a geographer who was later rector (I think) of the University of Alexandria. Anwar Abdel Malik makes very ingenious use of Fawzi in *Egypt's Military Society*. I also got a book the other day by an Egyptian parliamentarian called Milad Hanna, in which he too develops the notion of an Egyptian personality and Egyptian culture as a separate thing from the Egypt known to the West, and the work of many coherently discrete centuries. A tremendous emphasis is placed upon the cultural integrity and distinctiveness of Egyptian culture and of Egypt itself as a phenomenon, altogether separate from the Arab environment. Some of the rhetoric is partly a xenophobic reaction to the

Arabism of the Nasser period, Nasser being the leader who appeared to have introduced Egypt into the Arab world as its focal point. So there is a retreat from this in the literature I'm referring to, but that isn't all there is to it.

To go back to the early years of my awareness of Cairo: I grew up there, spending a large part of my youth in the place but strangely not as an Egyptian. I certainly never felt myself to be Egyptian, which is one of the perverse things about the city, that it allows you to be there as an alien and yet not feel injuriously discriminated against in any way, nor to feel the hostility of what might have been a culturally xenophobic, deeply enclosed and secret personality. I never felt *that*, but at the same time I also always felt that I wasn't *of* the place. Not because I wasn't in fact, but because in Cairo one felt the presence of a very complex urban and cultural system, which was what you would give the names of Cairo or Egypt to. I never belonged to it, even though I was, and remain, close to it. This is quite special. I've always been interested in how that system is inscribed in the language, in the Cairo version of the Egyptian dialect. It emerges in films and later in television drama, radio, journalistic writing and even the popular literature of the place, with which I became acquainted over the years.

What I am really trying to say is that there is a peculiar paradox in a city at once a great metropolitan center, a great alternative site (1) to the powerful contained interests of the metropolitan West in the Orient and (2) to Alexandria, the Levantine city par excellence; and yet, most impressively, Cairo is a city that doesn't force upon you some sort of already-existing totality. In other words, there's a certain relaxation in the idea of Cairo — at least the way I've gradually grasped it — which makes it possible for all manner of identities to exist unhurriedly within this whole. The idea is an indistinct one but you can actually experience it. All kinds of histories, narratives, and presences intersect, coexist in what I suggest is a "natural" way. For me that defines the pleasurably urban — not Paris, the vigorously planned city as an Imperial Center, nor London, with its carefully displayed monumentality, but rather a city providing a relaxed interchange between various incomplete, partially destroyed histories that still exist and partially do not, competed over, contested, but somehow existing in this rather, in my view, fascinating way. Cairo has come to symbolize for me, therefore, a much more attractive form of the way in which we can look at history, not necessarily to look at it as

something neatly manageable by categories or by the inclusive-
ness of systems and totalizing processes, but rather through the
inventory that can be reconstructed. Cairo requires a certain
effort of reconstruction. I'll give you a further example here.

When I was in Cairo recently, I was doing a piece on the
great belly dancer Tahia Carioca. One of the things I wanted
to do was to get documentation for writing the article. I
wanted to have pictures. So where would I get pictures? Now
the woman herself, Tahia Carioca, was recently divorced. Her
last husband, who was 30 years younger than she, left her, and
in the process took all her property. She lives in a little
apartment by herself, and apparently he took all of her films,
all her prints, as well as all her pictures. She has nothing. So I
went to the central cinema archives in downtown Cairo with a
film-maker friend of mine, a Lebanese woman who makes
documentaries. The experience that I am about to narrate
could only happen in Cairo. We went there together, and we
walked into this apartment in an office building in downtown
Cairo, which is about a block from where my father's office
used to be, and I said, well, I'm looking for documentation on
the films of Tahia Carioca – I was told by Tahia herself that
she made 190 films – a lot of films! – and discover that literally
nothing is left of that record in any printed source. I earlier
had called the place and asked for what stuff might be available
at the archive, and the woman who had put together something
for me had gone to visit a friend in the hospital but the file was
locked in her drawer, so I couldn't get it. So I said, "Well,
surely there must be a bigger file from which all these things
came." The man there said I was welcome to look at the
library, so we walked down to it. They have a library which is
roughly the size of mine here, and my guide said, "Here they
are. There are the books." I said, "How can I find out what
films she made?" He said, "What do you mean, like a list?" I
said, "No, a catalogue with a bibliography of films." He said
he wouldn't know and so he asked a lady who seemed to be
the librarian. I said to her, "Have you got a list of films?" She
said, "Films of what?" I said films, for example, like Tahia's
famous *Le'bet il sit*. She said, "No, no we don't do it that
way." I said, "Well what way do you do it?" She said, "We
have a list of films that are made in Egypt." "Fine," I said,
"could we have that?" She said, "We only go up to 1927,"
and gave me this volume. It's arranged in a completely
haphazard way. And then I turned to the man, who seemed to
know who I was (the man who had been leading me round),

and said, "What do you do?" He said, "I'm a film critic and I work here." "Do you have any pictures?" He replied, "Yes, I think I do have a picture of Tahia." He said he was doing a study on the Mahfouz novels that had been turned into films. So he goes into his office and pulls out a sheaf of pictures, about 60 or so, and we start leafing through them, and we finally find one. She apparently made a film based on one of Mahfouz's middle period novels, so he had her picture in his drawer. I said, "What's the name of the film?" He didn't really know. He turned the picture over and there were some notes on the back – presumably including the film's name – but he couldn't read his own handwriting. And he said he'd find out for me. I said, "When was the film made?" But again he didn't know.

What I felt was a sense of routine muddlement and also of utter nonchalance. How could it be that he didn't know any of the things I was inquiring about? But this is the situation people live in. If you really want to resurrect and reconstruct Cairo's history, you probably could. The proof is that the woman who was with me, the Lebanese lady who was very upset that I didn't get what I wanted, actually went back to the archive and spent a day, quite generously, to help me. She compiled a list of some 80 or 90 of Tahia's films and just gave them to me. It was all done by hand. There are no computers. But much of it is there and even though it isn't, you actually *feel* that it's all there. The question is how to recover it, and that is more or less an individual quest, because the social and the collective enterprise of compiling, let's say, an official history of Egyptian film, which until recently was the central cinematic experience of the whole Arab world, is just not done. It couldn't happen. That infrastructure and organization doesn't exist. What exists instead are these individual enterprises which are allied to each other, undertaken for different reasons but sharing common interests.

JW: There is a kind of entropy but with no sense of loss.

EWS: Yes, no sense of loss. I feel the loss because I'm coming from here and I have a deadline and all that sort of thing, but in the economy of the city, that's not the way it works.

JW: What about collectivity, political collectivity, for example?

EWS: There are all kinds of interconnecting and interlocking and sometimes, I suppose, competing collectivities. Of course many are the ones that are based on syndicates. Egypt, after all, is modern, and Cairo is a very modern city in many respects, much more highly developed than anywhere else in the Arab world. There is a developed sense of syndical groups and interests – the cinema people, the writer's groups, the lawyers and then on down through the various vocational and artisanal groups: some of them have a millenium of history behind them. Cutting across them are the new Islamic groups with their own infrastructure, their own economy, their own political and social organizations, education etc. And then you have the state groups, the official institutes and establishments, say, the people's assembly and the ruling party with its congress. And then I suppose you have at the local level the groups that exist in quarters in Cairo which have attained an identity that is in some instances hundreds of years old. The area of Khan el Khalili, etc. One of the people whom I know quite well in Egypt now is a novelist called Gamal al-Ghitani, who is a younger disciple of Mahfouz. Like Mahfouz, he writes about one district of Cairo called Gamaliya in such works as *Zayni Barakat*. There is a whole literature and consciousness of the area which is itself a collectivity – the coffee houses and the shoemaker and the brassmaker – a vocational artisanal community. All these exist and they function. How they function all together I have no idea, but they do and you can see they work in the economy of the city. Of course, dominating the whole thing is not only the Azhar and Sayidna Hussein, but also such harsher patterns as those provided by the connection between the state and its dependency upon the embassies, the Western powers. You have the imperial dependency relationship, and then you have this vast and complex honeycomb of connections that exist in Cairo on the local and regional level. And then intersecting with them, the Islamic and official parties of opposition as well as the various Sufi brotherhoods. It's an extraordinary thing to contemplate.

The thing that is slightly more difficult for me is the language, Arabic, particularly spoken Arabic. For me – this may be a distortion on my part because I first heard that language before in a sense becoming literate, being able to read it – the language of Cairo, which is a spoken dialect, is quite unique to Cairo. It is extremely eloquent, very concise, clear. It is totally different from any other Arab dialect. And in a certain sense it is a kind of *lingua franca*, because the radio, to a certain degree the largely colloquial radio of talk shows, the television, film above all, which went through all the Arab world, are all in this dialect. That suggests to me a certain common currency which is then itself connected to the hieratic language of the Koran and the state religion, Islam. The Cairo dialect is also connected to a classical Arabic literary history, and then more particularly to the tradition of Egypt itself, which has its own literary tradition, its own great writers, its own canon, particularly in the modern period. It was very important for me emotionally when Mahfouz won the Nobel Prize. He's one of the summits of this complex urban configuration which is Cairo and which played a tremendous role, not only in the Arab world, but in my own excavations of modern culture.

JW: To stay on the subect of Cairo, could you talk about the autobiographical novel you are writing about your youth?

EWS: I've been thinking about it as a memoir, and I've just recently signed a contract to produce it. But what it is exactly is something I really can't talk about now. It's a text that I think exists only in performance and not something I can easily describe. But it would certainly be an attempt to connect, well I'll tell you, the, shall we say, the imaginary and fictional resonances. A lot is based on the following: in much of my childhood there was in a certain sense, an unknowing, a kind of unself-conscious participation without knowing too much, for all kinds of reasons that have to do with my schooling and my family, the restrictions, the sense of belonging and a little series of compartments that led me into the colonial avenues and finally brought me to this country. There was a constant narrowing from the English system into the Western cultural orbit. Part of what I am trying to do now is to go back and to open up the things that I didn't know then, to see if I can do that, since I can only do it through speculation and memory and imagination. The interesting thing about this project is that the discipline that I've imposed on myself as I write the book is that I don't want it to be a book that reads back into those years a political awareness or political program that I have now, if you see what I mean. I don't want to do that. I want to try and do the Cairo-Jerusalem-Beirut axis, which is the one I grew up in, in a pre-political way in which all the political realities of the present nevertheless are somehow there in a figured or implicit form, held in suspension.

MS: Could you talk about your sense of Nasserism in your youth? How acute was that?

EWS: Nasserism as such was to me a later development. Nasser came to power after I left Egypt to go to boarding-school in the US, and therefore I always saw Nasserism through an optic that was at one remove from the society. My family remained in Egypt well after 1952, but, for example, the revolution of 1952 took place while I was here in this country, so that Nasser was always somebody I apprehended through his speeches, through reading about his exploits in the Western media. He was of course universally condemned, deplored here. My experience of Nasserism was one which you might say was already mediated and slightly distanced by a political ideology, which in a certain sense Nasser brought. That is what Nasser in fact introduced, not only into the lives of people in the Middle East but in my own life. Looking back, it's fascinating to me to think through my own relation to the early years of Nasserism, say from 1953 to 1960, which were the last years that I went to Egypt as a sometime resident because I never went there between 1960 and 1975. For that whole period of time, 15 years, I just never set foot in the country.

During the years from 1955 to 1960, Nasser introduced the nationalization laws – these directly affected my family's business. One of the announced targets of Nasser's "Arab socialism" was the foreign merchant class to which my father belonged and of which he was a great pillar. Nasser introduced a kind of anxiety, a fear, that of course I absorbed simply from being around my father. His worry was that new restrictions were being proposed on trade, commerce, and finance, all of which my father was deeply involved in. And I, in an unnatural and highly emotional way, magnified this into a crisis of the whole society. But one of the interesting things that has happened over the last 30 years, beginning in earnest during the late 1970s and more noticeably now in the last couple of years, when I have gone back to Egypt, is the extent to which I have been able to dissolve that artificial sense of a society in crisis, and see how Nasser and Egypt meshed in other interesting ways.

There's now a whole literature in Egypt about Nasser's secret police, which I saw as threatening exclusively me in a way that made me feel helpless. I felt like a rather passive and isolated victim, the subject of Nasser's repression. But I had not yet begun to discover how many friends of mine had been in jail. One of my closest friends, to whom I dedicated *The Question of Palestine*, was killed in 1960 or 1961. He was a member of the Communist Party, and was beaten to death by Nasser's secret police. So it is a very complex relationship in which there is a great deal of back and forth between myself and Cairo, you might say, as the center of Egypt under Nasser. I was relatively unaware of what was really going on. I then saw Nasser – though one admired him as a great Arab leader

– through the prism of my family's interest; now I see that there was a kind of neurosis there which I couldn't deal with. I either worried about the fortunes of my immediate family, or I created this kind of superhuman figure, a figure of Arab nationalism and its defiance of the West and of imperialism, neither of which is absolutely accurate of course. The reality was that Nasser was in constant tension with his own society, and that I never saw until much later.

JW: It was embedded in your own history.

EWS: Yes. But not for me to deal with.

MS: To continue with similar concerns, but on a quite different terrain. You just talked now about growing up in the Arab world in a very peculiar position.

EWS: Yes, in a cocoon.

MS: And you came to the United States and have spent the majority of your life here. You went to Princeton, Harvard and became as Western as one could imagine, mastering Western culture, in my view in a quite extraordinary way. Western humanism, to give it a convenient label, has been tremendously important to you intellectually. In your work, particularly over the last decade, you've been extremely critical of Orientalism, of ethnography, and yet, not really critical in the same way of, say, Auerbach, Lukács, Blackmur, and Adorno. All of these people, although they were not directly involved in the orientalist project, nevertheless were part of the discourse of Western humanism, which is part and parcel of that same project.

EWS: Every one of the people you mention – with the possible exception of Lukács, about whom I know less, I mean about his views on the non-Western world – in every one of them I could locate for you a place in their texts, in which they are ethnocentric to a fault. In the piece I wrote about Blackmur, I've singled out his rather, I thought, jejune reflections on the Third World. He was, after all, on a mission to the Third World from the Rockefeller Foundation. This was in the days of John Foster Dulles, the Cold War, so the influence of the disabling context there is almost total. Similarly with Auerbach. I translated one of his last essays, "Philology and *Weltliteratur*," precisely because it seemed to me to be so interesting a reflection on his own work, but also so pessimistic about the onset of all these new languages and cultures, most of them non-European, that he had nothing to say about, except that they seemed to frighten him in some way. He had no concept that they might in fact betoken a new level of cultural activity, let's say in the Third World, that was not previously there.

MS: Even though he spent the Second World War in Istanbul.

EWS: There was no discernible connection between Auerbach and Istanbul at all; his entire attitude while there seems to have been one of nostalgia for the West, which gave him the spirit to sit down and write this great saving work of Western humanism, *Mimesis*. So I'm very conscious of that. But, the way I would put it is, that what I have seen myself as trying – perhaps in a rather sentimental way, but it's very conscious, or it has become very conscious in recent years – as in a certain sense, trying to, first of all expose the lapses and the ethnocentric soft spots. But in some way, because I admire the effort nevertheless, somehow to extend their work into areas that interest me. In other words, I'm not exactly answering them, but I'm extending their work into areas they avoid by adopting some of their modes of examination, their attention to texts, their *care*, which I think is the central factor here. It's a kind of scrupulosity, which I suppose you could call humanism. If you pare down that label and relieve it of the unpleasantly triumphalist freight that is carried with it, you are left with something that I think is very much worth saving. The one place where I feel a tremendous lack on my part, through ignorance, is in failing to make as many connections as I'd have liked between the Western humanists and comparable figures in the non-European world.

However, I began to do that in a recent piece that I wrote . . . I may have sent it to you, called "The Voyage In." All the figures considered in that essay were writing in the Western tradition, you know, but the first two, C. L. R. James and George Antonious, are people for whom the West is something that you could in fact have a positive relationship with. But for a later generation, the relationship is inevitably one of hostility. But nevertheless there is a sense in these earlier figures of understanding what the West is all about. In that sense, I'm beginning to draw out patterns from my peculiar background, not so much my ethnic background, but the non-Euoprean background.

One of the reasons that I've been trying to do that has to do with an eagerness to complete work inaugurated by Auerbach, Adorno et al. that I consider to be incomplete by virtue of its ethnocentrism and lack of interest in the part of the world where I grew up. So there is an attempt to claim attention there. But also this moves a little bit into an evolved position about orientalism, because I've become very aware of how some of the work I've done, especially *Orientalism*, but also

Covering Islam, has seemed to some not very careful readers
to be proposing a kind of indiscriminate conflict between East
and West, between Islam and Christianity, between the culture
of the West and the culture of the Third World – a set of total
oppositions. I've always been taken as in fact proposing that
kind of scenario; many of my hostile critics have argued that
this is *really* what I'm saying, that I'm really arguing for a
resurgence of nativism and that I am to be blamed to a certain
degree for the rise of Islamic fundamentalism, and so on and
so forth.

MS: This is what you call in the imperialism lectures, "The Politics
of Blame." You yourself are being blamed for the politics of
blame.

EWS: One has to be aware of the way in which certain feelings that
you have don't really become clear intellectually until later.
They don't provide an intellectual track for you to follow until
really much later. For example, Du Bois says that it's very
important for a black man in white America to be absolutely
scrupulous in discriminating between those aspects of white
culture and white civilization that are the enemy, and those
that one can align oneself with, draw positive things from, etc.
That's really what, in a certain sense, my attitude has been to
people such as the ones we've been talking about. Instead of
saying that all of them are on one side and all of us are on the
other, there may be another mode that can come into play at a
level of intellectual and cultural discrimination and elaboration
that establishes a different relationship from the purely adversarial or oppositional one.

MS: You call this "The Politics of Secular Interpretation."

EWS: Yes, precisely.

JW: Could you say what you intend by this concept?

EWS: To go back to the earlier formation which I've given a history
of in the third lecture on imperialism. The opposition to
imperialism is of course the emergence of nationalism. Nationalism is many, many things. Obviously one aspect of it is a
reactive phenomenon. It's an assertion of identity, where the
problematics of identity are supposed to carry the whole wave
of the culture and of political work, which is the case in the
early phases of nationalist struggle against European colonialism. You could see it in the Algerian case, in the Malaysian
case, in the Philippine case. You could see it in various aspects
of the Arab world, and certainly in the Caribbean. There is an
emphasis upon forging a self-identity as a nation or a people
that resists but has its own integrity (as in Césaire's *négritude*).

But it does seem to me that despite essential virtues there are great limitations to that intellectually as well as politically. The limitations have to do with the fetishization of the national identity. The national identity becomes not only a fetish, but is also turned into a kind of idol, in the Baconian sense – an idol of the cave, and of the tribe. That, it seems to me, then produces, pulls along with it, the rise of what I would call a kind of desperate religious sentiment. This is not everything about the rise of fundamentalism, for example, in the Islamic world, the Christian world, or the Jewish world, but it's an important constituent here.

JW: As opposed to what?

EWS: The notion of secularism. This goes back to actual living human beings. Men and women produce their own history, and therefore it must be possible to interpret that history in secular terms, under which religions are seen, you might say as a token of submerged feelings of identity, of tribal solidarity, 'asabiyyah, in Ibn Khaldun's phrase. But religion has its limits in the secular world. Possibilities are extremely curtailed by the presence of other communities. For example, when you assert an identity, one identity is always going to infringe on others that also exist in the same or continuous spaces. For me the symbol of that, in the Arab world, is the problem that has been postponed from generation to generation: the problem of the national minorities. Not only the Palestinians, whose denied presence of course proved to be one of the major failures of the Zionist movement, but also the problems with the Jews as a national community to which the Palestinians are only beginning now to try to provide answers in this larger Islamic context. But also there are the many obvious problems with the place of Armenians, Kurds, Christians, Egyptian Copts. The status of all of these groups is extraordinarily inflamed. Therefore, to address such issues, it seems to me that you need a secular and humane vision, one based on the idea of human history not being the result of divine intervention but a much slower process than the politics of identity usually allow. To fight around the slogans provided by nationalist, religious, or cultural identity is a much quicker thing, the formations easier to coalesce around: embattled identities that create traditions for themselves going back to the crusades, or going back to the Phoenician period or going back to the Hellenistic period. I'm actually citing cases of social and religious minorities in the Arab world, where this rhetoric of impossibly early (usually imagined) pedigrees is extremely heated, as opposed to secular interpretation which argues for historical discrimination and for a certain kind of deliberate scholarship. It implies a certain interpretive sophistication. Above all, it argues, and this is the point, for the potential of a community that is political, cultural, intellectual, and is not geographically and homogeneously defined.

At the basis of all this is the extraordinary power and yet the extraordinary failures of the geographical model for human politics. Because what does it produce? The geographical model produces, for example, the kind of thing described in Paul Carter's *The Road to Botany Bay*, which shows how whole entities were fashioned by acts of naming and geographical charting: his example is Captain Cook and Australia. That's realy a large part of the history of colonialism. This in turn gives rise to embattled, emergent resistance movements which then in turn, and here's the tragedy of nationalism, fall into homogenized unities, imagined communities. They successfully recapture the geographical identities charted by the imperialists. In the Arab world, for example, the Sykes-Picot agreement of 1916 is the basis for all the national states today – Iraq, Syria, Lebanon, Jordan, Palestine – and for all their "little" nationalisms. These then became reified, stable entities, and on them is built the usually repressive apparatus of the national security, one-party state. Therefore, one has to get beyond geography to these other communities which are trans-national which, you might say, are based upon an ideal of secular interpretation and secular work. Obviously I'm not suggesting that everybody has to become a literary critic; that'a a silly idea. But one does have to give a certain attention to the rather dense fabric of secular life, which can't be herded under the rubric of national identity or can't be made entirely to respond to this phony idea of a paranoid frontier separating "us" from "them" – which is a repetition of the old sort of orientalist model where you say that all orientals are the same. Correlatively, we now have this reactive occidentalism, some people saying the West is monolithically the same, opposed to us, degraded, secular, bad, etc. The politics of secular interpretation proposes a way of dealing with that problem, a way of avoiding the pitfalls of nationalism I've just outlined, by discriminating between the different "Easts" and "Wests," how differently they were made, maintained, and so on.

JW: To carry on in the same vein. How do you feel about Gayatri Spivak's negative response to the question, "Can the subaltern speak?"

EWS: I have heard her speak a lot about this. She's reacting to the idea that the subaltern can be *made* to speak and thus becomes a kind of new token in the repertoire of dominant discourses.

JW: That certainly happens.

EWS: Of course. It's a real possibility. But her position does seem to me to dismiss or not to take seriously enough the various, and in many ways quite unconnected, appearances of groups from Subaltern Studies to various attempts at interpretive political communities in the Middle East, Latin America, Africa, and the Caribbean. For example, certain wings of the Egyptian opposition strike me as very interesting in this respect; they mix Marxism with nativism, with a kind of international sense of Marxist or post-Marxist discourse in the West. Or think of similar efforts in the Caribbean. It seems to me C. L. R. James exactly indicts this notion that the subalterns are always puppets and marionettes who make their speech the same way as the West.

James, while we're on this subject, is really the progenitor of a great amount of quite interesting and quite independent Caribbean literature. The same is true of the African-American opposition movement or the feminist movement in this country. Both have produced, of course, parrots and mimics and all the rest of it, but they have also produced quite important alternative discourses, which perforce overlap with dominant discourses. This by no means invalidates their strength and independence. The same is true in Africa in the work of various novelists. I don't mean the kind of thing that has gone on about not speaking in a Western language, that to preserve your identity you have to speak in the native language. I'm referring to philosophers, various African ethnologists and ethnographers, and of course the numerous political movements that are not about simply enthroning an idol of the past created largely by the West. They are after some new configurations, some new political process. You can find this in India, you can certainly find it in Japan. It does seem to me that the fear, which is real enough, that the subaltern could be just another form of imperialism does not take enough into account the presence of a genuinely impressive alternative to this outcome, for which in the last two or three years the *intifada* has become a symbol.

MS: What you're really arguing for is a kind of internationalism?

EWS: That's too indiscriminate a word. Let's say that these new processes take place in a generally international context. In other words, one can't locate what one is talking about in only

one context or in an absolutely new and pure space. The force
of the phenomenon that I am talking about is that it takes
place in many different places, and I suppose those places
taken all together could be considered international. But I think
it still has very deep roots in a local and national situation.

JW: So the politics you are recommending is not a cradle of
universal values?

EWS: No, not at all. I think talk of "universal values" tends to
produce a sentimentalism that exactly takes us back to the
early days of comparative literature. Woodbury, for instance,
the first professor of comparative literature in this country at
Columbia in 1892, goes on about congresses of gentlemen
scholars, jurists who survey (I think I'm quoting more or less
exactly) the scene with a kind of superior detachment, with a
general all-encompassing love for all of humanity. Utter nonsense. That's not what I'm talking about.

MS: Let's take the question out of the context of comparative
literature and give two examples of internationalism: one, the
moment of international socialism, from the end of the nineteenth century and Marx through a certain point in Lenin, let's
say up through the mid-twenties; and the second, a genuine
international moment and one that surely everything you've
said is determined or is made possible by. This is the moment
of decolonization, which was genuinely international and
remains so up to the present. How would you now situate
yourself, the kind of work you do, and the kind of work you
think would be valuable to pursue, in relation to that political
project, which is after all ongoing?

EWS: The point is that decolonization, as I talk about it, is really
two moments. The first moment was, you might say, the
exhaustion of the classical empires after World War II.
Obviously it begins earlier than that, around the period shortly
after World War I, and it continues and climaxes in the
ceremonies, as I call them, of leave-taking and independence.
Of course, the most famous one is midnight August 15, 1947.
That is a great moment about which one can feel a certain
amount of nostalgia. But the other moment is much more
problematic. It's not really over, because the struggle over
empire continues in other regions of the world and into the
present: Ireland, South Africa, Palestine. That is to say, the
drama of decolonization is supposed to culminate in independence, and indeed it did in certain places. But in others it
didn't; it continued. Algeria is one of the examples which
continues the struggle to be free, now taking alarmingly

retrograde forms. In the early 60s so too were Viet Nam, Palestine, Cuba, all of the Portuguese colonies of Africa; and then there was the reappearance of a kind of resurgent colonial contest in those parts of the American empire or continuous to America such as Chile, Nicaragua, etc. There the process seems to continue in surprising ways, not only in actual colonial conflicts but also in the whole drama or spectacle of neocolonialism and dependency, the IMF, the debt trap, etc. So that's the problem. It's the continuation of the colonization process which has not been contained by the moment of decolonization. That's what interests me, number one.

At the same time, in the decolonized world, and even in the world that is proceeding in its efforts towards liberation, there remains what I call the dialectic of independence and liberation. That is to say the dynamic of nationalism unfulfilled by real liberation, a dynamic whose clear goal is national independence in the form of a conventional or semi-conventional state with a whole new pathology of power. The pathology of power in a state like Iran is very different from that in a state like Iraq, from a state like Malaysia, very different from the Philippines, and so on and so forth. Eqbal Ahmad is one of the few people who has tried to talk about this in a systematic way. But as against that, I think the project that continues is that which appears in hints in Fanon, and is figured here and there but not systematically in the works of Cabral, or James. One ought to be able to talk more interestingly about what we were saying earlier, to make more precise the interpretations of various political and intellectual communities where the issue is not independence but liberation, a completely different thing. What Fanon calls the conversion, the transformation, of national consciousness into political and social consciousness, hasn't yet taken place. It's an unfinished project, and that's where I think my work has begun.

For me, the most urgent locus for this problematic is the Palestinian question. During the history of my own direct political involvement, we went from the goal of one secular democratic state, to the immense transformation that in November 1988 took place in Algiers, in which I participated. We turned ourselves from a liberation movement into an independence movement. We talked about two states, an Israeli state and a Palestinian state. Now the principal political struggle concerns the price of having willingly committed ourselves to national independence. It's the tragedy, the irony, the paradox of all anti-imperial or decolonizing struggles that independence is the stage through which you must try to pass: for us independence is the only alternative to the continued horrors of the Israeli occupation, whose goal is the extermination of a Palestinian national identity. Therefore, the question for me is: how much of a price are we going to pay for this independence – if we can get it at all – and how many of the goals of liberation will we abandon? I don't at all mean "liberating" Israel, or the whole of Palestine; I'm talking about ourselves as a movement, as a people. How much of a price are we going to pay in deferred liberation? This involves very concrete problems. What are you going to do about, for example, the three million Palestinians who are not from the West Bank in the diaspora. What formula do we have for that? What is the price we're going to pay in political compromises with our neighbors, Jordan, Israel, Syria, Egypt, etc.? And with the super-partner of them all, the United States? This, after all, is a moment which is dominated by the United States, particularly with the defection of the USSR internationally. Many of us compare Gorbachev with Sadat. By the way, that's not just Alexander Cockburn's notion; it's an idea he got from the Arab context where the exit of the Soviet Union (never a wonderful or even helpful ally) made things worse.

JW: Because you referred to it earlier, can you talk more about the *intifada*?

EWS: Let's begin with the way that the *intifada* has been commodified and presented on American television. Consider the recent statements of Thomas Friedman that it is essentially a series of discrete acts of throwing stones, of firebombing, etc. In fact, it's not a series of discrete acts. It can't be understood that way. It is the creation of a political entity for which the stones are a symbol. The creation of an alternative force which you can't turn off and on. Shamir says, "We will allow elections if the violence is stopped." To suggest that the *intifada*, I mean the model, is the stone thrower who can be prevented from doing that implies either that there's some behind-the-scenes manipulator of the struggle or that it's just a series of blind acts without any basis in any social actuality which is producing these live acts. Therefore, Shamir and others say, you should stop, because we're going to offer you a kind of sop, which is to give you elections so long as of course we retain control through occupation. My interpretation of this is that we should present the *intifada* as an alternative, an emergent formation, by which on the simplest level Palestinians under occupation have decided to declare their independence from the occupation by providing different, not so much models, but different forms for their lives which they themselves administer, develop and have in fact created.

JW: It's an entire cultural movement.

EWS: Exactly. It's a cultural movement which says that we are not going to cooperate, we can't any longer live under the occupation, and therefore we must provide for ourselves. Since they have closed the schools, we provide our own schools. They've made health care difficult through the imposition of taxes on the hospitals, so we provide our own health service. One of the aspects of the Israeli system of laws designed to humiliate and punish the Palestinian economy has been to regulate agriculture so that you couldn't plant trees, you couldn't plant fruits, you couldn't dig wells, etc., without the permits, which the Israeli administration either never gave, or made it difficult to obtain. So what has happened is that now with the expropriation of land, with a domination of the network of settlements defended by the Israeli army, there is the possibility for the Palestinians to provide an agricultural alternative to that one. That is to say, the use, for example, of private gardens and houses and the creation of a food delivery service through the collectivization of the bakeries, and the use of children to deliver food in a new pattern that can't easily be dominated by the Israeli military. But it's still very limited.

JW: This new network escapes regulation.

EWS: Right. And the same has happened of course in places on the West Bank, which have become in effect liberated zones. The Israeli army has now discovered that it is not possible to enter these places without severe losses. What they have done with the border police is to bring in people who patrol through outbursts of violence. The border police, in a kind of orgy of destruction, kill as many people as they possibly can. But that still, to my way of reading it, proves the existence of these liberated zones, which for a while were free of Israeli occupation. So the upshot is really quite remarkable. We can observe it through telecommunications, through the implements of instant communication which Palestinians have begun to master. There's the whole rural Palestinian world, certainly, but there's also the presence of a complete system of fax machines and telephones controlled by American corporations but not completely dominated by them. One of the great achievements of the Palestinian revolution has been its mastery of this network of communication. It is quite remarkable. It functioned all through the siege of Beirut. All of these situations, which are supposedly dominated by an Israeli siege, have been completely pierced. It's an unprecedented communication network.

So all of this then we can actually watch. In a concrete way we see this new state emerging. What we Palestinians are saying is that we are already practicing our liberation and self-determination. We declared a state; the state is already there. We don't want, we don't need the recognition of others, although we have gotten 80 or 90 recognitions from other states. So the question now, the way we look at it, is not whether the *intifada* is going to stop or not, because it's irreversible. It's a process that has already taken us very far in a direction of self-consciousness, independence, and national liberation. The question is, when are the others going to catch up with us, whether that's going to happen or not. The great problem is that the Gulf crisis set us all back a number of years. There was poor leadership and incredible incompetence. Now the situation is very dark indeed.

MS: There were two things that occurred to me while you were talking. Let me ask the more local one first. You spoke about telecommunication. You've written about this very eloquently, about the control of the media and the way independence struggles in the Third World, particularly the Iranian Revolution, but also Palestinians, are represented in the American media, or the "culture industry." But everything that you just said a moment ago shows that to be a half truth. The Adornian notion of a totally deominated and dominating system of mass cultural production is only the apparatus of the media, and that can be mobilized in an entirely different way.

EWS: One of the great choruses that you find in the media, indeed produced by the Israeli propaganda apparatus, is that a lot of this is happening *because of* the presence of television. They blame television. That's why Kissinger advised that the one way of stopping the *intifada* was not to let the media in – total nonsense.

JW: Taking up that thread, what would be your attitude now towards the, let's not call it the culture industry, let's just talk about the possibilities of mass communication, etc. Where are the places to intervene? How do you present a counter-narrative, another story, another side of events?

EWS: One of the failures of Left writing on the media – it is not only true of Adorno and Horkheimer, but of all the major, shall we say, critiques of domination including the marxism of Althusser and of Fred Jameson – is that there's a kind of fascination with the techniques of domination. Foucault ultimately becomes the scribe of domination. In other words, the imagination of Arab people is really an account of the victories of the power dominating them. The site of resistance is eliminated. As opposed to that, I would say people like Gramsci and Raymond Williams take a much less systematic view. I feel much closer to the latter.

First of all, there's a sense of the fragility of the achievement of the culture industry or the dominating apparatus. After all, just as it was put there, it can also be dismantled or evaded or used to different purposes. There's nothing inevitable or even necessary about it; it's there, it can be taken apart. Second, no matter how dominating an apparatus is, it cannot dominate everything. That, it seems to me, is the central definition of the social process. So what Chomsky says is partly wrong. He sees all information controlled by media that are tied in not only with corporations, but with the military-industrial complex and, indeed, with the government and complicit intellectuals in this country. This analysis is insufficient. There are endless opportunities for intervention (including his own considerable efforts) and transformation that occur within this society. You don't always need to begin at the beginning, that's the point. You could take advantage of the over-development of this dominated apparatus and intervene strategically at certain moments. For example, in the case of the Palestinians where the picture that's presented is incomplete, you can try and complete it, or you can take advantage of the deep contradictions in the society. Such a process would produce somebody like myself, who is a committed Palestinian nationalist on the one hand, and yet through education and certain kinds of intellectual affiliations, a member of the elite. The conjunction of these two makes it possible for me to appear on television to intervene in the ways that I've tried to do. I'm not saying it's the whole story or that it's made tremendously important changes, but at least you get the sense that you are able to combat the domination and to alter the situation and give yourself and others hope.

The most important thing, from my point of view, has been the absence of a master theory for this. It seems to me that's been the great problem with Marxism, or proletarian internationalism. It seems to me that the attempt to invent or devise a discourse that is adequate in its universal contours and detailed power to the new forces of the media or the new social forces outside Europe has not met with great success. It seems to me to have missed a lot of the contradictions, a lot of the untidiness of the moment, etc., many of them due to nationalism, about which Marx had virtually nothing to say. In the conflict between the hedgehog and the fox, the fox in a certain sense is more interesting. The need for a relatively more unbuttoned, unfixed, and mobile mode of proceeding – that's why the Deleuzian idea of the nomadic is so interesting – is to me a much more useful and liberating instrument. Much of what we are talking about is essentially unhoused. You might say the real conflict is between the unhoused and the housed. I don't see the need for a master discourse or a theorization of the whole.

MS: If I could press you on that just a bit. You are absolutely right about the first moment of Marxist theory. It came too soon and too much has changed in the interim. On the other hand, and this is why I stress the notion of internationalism, given the strength of the opposition, of global capitalism – Grenada was one instance, but Cuba, Nicaragua and Viet Nam are others – these individual local struggles simply cannot on their own be sustained, or at least they have failed to do many of the things that they promised. All of these countries are economic wrecks. The reason is that they have not been able to link up in some kind of counter-federation to the Euro-American imperium. Clearly, any Palestinian state will face the same kind of massive opposition, which will try to strangle it in the cradle, so to speak.

EWS: Except that the Palestinian issue has already built into it by virtue of the existence of important diaspora communities, both Palestinian and Jewish, an international dimension which connects with South Africa, Nicaragua, etc. Much of the interesting work in the last decade has been the mapping of these networks of connection, of Palestine to Nicaragua for instance. So you already have a kind of blueprint of connections made which could furnish a network for connections to others.

One has of course to reckon (speaking only of the United States) with the presence of localized interests that specialize in single issues and thus, paradoxically, reflect the dominant discourse of division of labor in their counter-strategies. The Nicaraguan or the pro-Sandinista, anti-Contra support is specialized into that, the Salvadorans into another, the South Africans another. We need to find ways that connect these political groups to each other in this society: this cannot be put off. Palestine is very important in this respect, partly because

Palestine is always the one that's denied, for various reasons, and also the common factor. You notice that people can talk about Nicaragua and South Africa, but find it very hard to include Palestine. The moment you start pushing, Palestine turns out to be the case that's considered transgressive and slightly messy. And that's why I think an early intellectual effort is very important.

There is a connection in terms of arms trade and counter-insurgency theories, etc., between the Contras, the Saudi Arabians and the Israelis – that whole connection and the Iran-Contra affair, which wasn't really looked at very carefully. It's not only that there is this massive actuality, but there's also the important theoretical and intellectual perspective which we need to flesh out through what I would call a kind of globalism in the study of texts. This is why, for example, I have very little interest, except residually, in the notion of the national literature, English literature, French literature, and so on. All of these specialities in which professionally we're engaged, whether we like it or not, don't interest me very much any longer, any more than the interest that I have today in things like history and anthropology etc. is an interest in those fields as fields, but is rather an interest in the connections between them. So that intellectual effort, speaking only for myself, is the direct result of an existential and historical experience in which we Palestinians have been punished by provincialism and the isolation imposed upon us originally by imperialism, but by this very society, which says that you're specialized, you must become "an area expert." All that entire ideology of separation and exclusion and difference etc. – the task is to fight it. But you can't fight it on one level and be shy or tactful on the others. It's got to be fought on all the fronts. That's where I think we are right now.

MS: What you seem to be saying now, and have also articulated elsewhere, is that because imperialism has constructed and produced so much of the world as we know it, a kind of worldliness is in fact the only viable intellectual, political, or personal rejoinder.

EWS: But here's where I think it's been very important to have some live connection with an ongoing political movement. When I talk about worldliness, I don't just mean a kind of cosmopolitanism or intellectual tourism. I'm talking about the kind of omnicompetent interest which a lot of us have that is anchored in a real struggle and a real social movement. We are interested in a lot of different things. We can't be confined by our identities as professional scholars of, say, English literature in the nineteenth century. Nobody's happy with that, but the alternative isn't to just get interested in more things.

JW: Many of our colleagues are perfectly happy with just this narrow professional identity.

EWS: I think that's passing. The idea that you can sort of dip in and read *The Nation* and the *New York Review of Books*, and then you listen to a little Mozart, and then you riffle through a volume of Cage's scores. That's not what we are talking about. What has been very important for me, providing a kind of discipline, is the sense of a community and a movement in progress to which I am committed and in which I am implicated. You take all the attacks that brand you, in my case as a terrorist or a kind of delinquent, as a criminal, etc. You pay a price, in other words. But also it imposes upon me some sense of responsibility to a community which is not a specialized group.

For my part, the greatest, most admired worldliness, is that of the great comparatists, the Auerbachs and the Spitzers of an earlier generation, or the Frankfurt critical theorists, people like Horkheimer and Adorno. Especially Adorno, who could really talk about anything, everything. There was this kind of vocabulary of attention to high culture, mass culture, etc. Of course, it was limited by ethnocentrism, as I said earlier, but by and large they broke the disciplinary constraints. Still, they never, it seems to me, confronted seriously the problem of audience, audience viewed as a political and, you might say, human community. Not an ideal or idealized community. In the case of Adorno, some communities he simply took for granted have simply disappeared, can't possibly exist any longer.

MS: Clearly Adorno gave up on the possibility of any kind of political struggle. Once you do that, I think you're saying, then you've given up the real game.

EWS: You've given up the real game, which is communication with actual people and communities. Partly this is also true of two intellectuals whose work I've learned from a great deal and been friendly with in all kinds of ways: Jameson and Chomsky. Chomsky's loneliness and his self-imposed marginalization have derived from his unwillingness, for whatever reason, to be involved in the messy political details of a back-and-forth movement with a community. In the case of Jameson, there has been a sense in which his community is essentially the community of philosophical theorists, or liberated theorists, which gives a very restricted view. Of course both Chomsky and Jameson are very open to solicitations from the political world, and they are very generous people, but their fundamental connection is not to an ongoing political movement. But maybe I'm being too critical of them.

MS: To move on to a related question. You will recall when *Beginnings* came out in 1975, there was a whole issue of *Diacritics* devoted to it, including a long interview with you. At that time, you drew a line between your academic intellectual life, which *Beginnings* and the book on Conrad represented, and the political life which you were simultaneously leading. You yourself said something to the effect "It's like I'm two separate people." It seems clear that in the last decade this is increasingly not the case. That is to say, you have begun to integrate these two distinct identities in a much tighter and more immediate way. What is your current understanding, first, of your career in the university in relation to your political life or your political activism, and second, of the way this relationship can or should be negotiated by other university intellectuals who maintain political commitments demanding time, energy, and often certain personal risks?

EWS: I'm not sure that any one can negotiate all the things one does. I wouldn't now talk about a separation as I did in 1976. There I was much more conscious of being a professional scholar of literature in a department which seemed to, not exactly impinge on me, but to demand certain things from me. I don't feel that anymore. And in what I've been writing since *Orientalism*, I've felt that there is a kind of traffic that I've allowed myself between overtly political and cultural, intellectual, and specialized work that makes possible, you might say, a zone which I've existed in without worrying about whether I am really an academic or really a political partisan. Those divisions don't seem to be that interesting anymore. What I've since allowed myself to do, partly because of the pressure of time – I'm growing older, I don't have as much energy as I used to have, and there are more demands on my time – is to be guided by certain things that seem to attract me and let myself go with them. For example, my recent interest in music, on which in the past 5 or 6 years I've written quite a lot.

This comes back to your question about mass culture versus elite culture. One of the failures of Adorno, as I read him, is that he thought elite culture was disappearing into mass culture, whereas in fact today one can still witness a very lively concert life based almost entirely on classical music, which as an elite institution has a very powerful social presence in contemporary life. And it's not based upon new music, but on a curatorial interest in the past. That's something to be accounted for. It's a vestige, if you like, but it's still there, and it has a presence, in spite of Adorno's predictions at the end of *The Philosophy of New Music* that this music was going to remain unheard. In fact, we've never had a greater multiplication of classical music, in records but also in concerts and in many interesting types of performance.

All I'm trying to say is that one is provided, largely because of New York, with a panorama of intellectual opportunities for intervention. I've pursued my interventionist bent without trying to theorize or explain or predict it in any way by saying, now that I've written my Conrad book I'll now write my Marx, and from my Marx I should then write the Husserl book, and so on. Instead of following that sequential trajectory, I think I've kept to the idea of trying to do all of these things contrapuntally, given the constant presence in my life of my ongoing Palestinian obligation and political commitment. I've stopped being able to calculate the pros and cons of what I do. I just don't have time to do it any more. Maybe that's some form of carelessness.

JW: Could you talk more about the importance of music? I know for you personally it's of great moment, as a musician and as somebody who cares about it. But I'm curious about how you would situate the music that you write about and perform yourself, the classical tradition. Does this constitute an autonomous realm of artistic production that doesn't in a sense suffer from the inscription of, let's say, ideology and politics?

EWS: It does. I'm right in the middle of these problems and therefore perhaps not well-positioned to say something from a large perspective. I'm writing the Wellek lectures that I'm giving at Irvine in a month. In them I try to – they're called *Musical Elaborations* – survey those things that are of particular interest to me. Again and again they converge on the public and the private – the public, in an Adornian sense with all of its processes of power and accreditation and authority and orthodoxy; and the private, which is the position of the listener or the amateur or the subjective consumer of music, like myself. I wouldn't call it an autonomous realm, but I certainly think one can talk about it as having a kind of relatively autonomous identity.

What I've picked for analysis are, first of all, the performance occasion itself, which I talk about as an extreme occasion, but an occasion with a temporality and a locale that are quite marked in the social life of the West, especially the late capitalist West. The second lecture is an attempt to account for that whole dimension within music that goes, you might say, from the technical transgressive of the *diabolus in musica*, forbidden intervals for example, to large questions of morality and aesthetics which culminate in the work of Wagner and Strauss, and perhaps ultimately link up with the question of Paul de Man – that is, of the complicity between music, ideology, and social space. The third lecture is a study of melody as an important aspect of identity in classical music, the contours of the individual melody. My point of departure is the *Contre Sainte-Beuve*, in which Proust says that he can tell the *air de chanson* of each writer. He uses the element of melody to identify the style and the particular signature of every artist: thus each has his own melody. And I then say, well, what about looking at that in terms of composers – the melody of the composer. I was very impressed by the work of the English musicologist Wilfred Mellers, who wrote two books, *Bach and the Dance of God*, and *Beethoven and the Song of God* – both attempt to do a kind of musicological analysis of an overpoweringly present theme in the structure, but also in the melody of their work. I'm interested in melody, first of all, on the level of the listener's being imprinted by the composer's identity and then seeing how far that can go into the question of solitude, since composing is a solitary act, into the question of the public profile of the composer. Rather than talk about all of music, I've tried simply to carve out of this long and largely silent experience of musical awareness that I have, to carve out interesting topics that might enable me to talk about music in social and political, but above all in aesthetic, terms.

The main problem I have and don't have any answer to, is that it's strange that, for example, the music of my own Arab and Islamic tradition means relatively little to me as I write this book. I've never been interested in or compelled by it as something to study, although I know it well and have always listened to it. The same is roughly true of popular music. Popular culture means absolutely nothing to me except as it surrounds me. I obviously don't accept all the hideously limited and silly remarks made about it by Adorno, but I must say it doesn't speak to me in quite the same way that it would to you or to my children. I'm very conservative that way.

MS: It's a kind of block, in short. This is somewhat unfair, but one might say that the great Western classical musical tradition is for you an unproblematic refuge of greatness. You could say, of course, that these *are* great figures, but one might also say, following some of your earlier remarks, that, for example, African popular music is much more global, combining all these strands. It might seem to speak to some, but it falls on deaf ears here.

EWS: I don't know about deaf ears.

MS: You yourself don't listen to reggae and rock, but they are the great popular political music of our time, in the West anyway.

EWS: I've read a great deal about it, but it's not what I first want to listen to when I listen to music. Perhaps what I'm really writing about is the persistence of this Western classical tradition, and maybe failing in the end to be successful at it. I'm really quite nervous about what I'm doing. It's all very well to write an individual article about a concert that one has heard, or an opera that one has attended, but it's a different thing to put it in this relatively abstract frame that I've called "musical elaboration." But I see it all as part of what Gramsci calls the elaboration of civil society. The social plays a certain role. Nobody would ever deny that rock culture has taken over and in a way is much more interesting intellectually to somebody of my own perspective, but nevertheless it seems to me that there is this kind of strange, maybe neolithic formation that I call classical music in which the great figures are people like Glenn Gould and Toscanini, whose work has really attempted to assert the presence of this tradition, while in other ways, reaching out from it to the questions of mass society, technology, communications, radio programs.

MS: Let's shift our focus somewhat. What do you think now of the scene in not just academic, but general cultural criticism, of literary criticism, to keep it within that realm? Where do you think it's going? What do you think is important that's being done? What do you think are the kinds of things that haven't been done that should be done, etc.? You've asked this question of me enough times, so I'm going to ask it of you.

EWS: The reason I ask you the question is I really needed to know, because I haven't followed it as systematically as either of you has. I simply lost interest in literary theory about ten years ago. It just doesn't strike me as something that I have needed to be up on, on a day by day basis, or as something that is of interest to me in what I'm doing on a given day.

MS: But you do see yourself as intervening in that arena in a very
      powerful way. We aren't the only ones who have been affected
      by this. There are literally hundreds of people who are doing
      the type of work you have recommended in your own critical
      practice.

EWS: That has to do with a personal relationship perhaps, with
      accidents. I've been very conscious, for example, of not want-
      ing to impose myself on students in the way in which people
      like de Man and other members of the (now defunct) Yale
      School have done, to become part of a school, to formalize
      what it is that I do in teachable ways or anything like that. I've
      always thought of my teaching, which I do all the time with
      great excitement and nervousness, as actually performing acts
      of analysis or reading or interpretation, rather than providing
      students with methodologies that they can go out and apply to
      situations. In other words, I think of myself as providing
      opportunities for students and friends, rather than encoding
      insights in some way that can make them useful tools later on.
      I just don't seem to be able to do that.

      I'm impressed, to get back to the question about criticism,
      I'm impressed by the extent, and I don't understand the reason
      for it, by the extent to which there seem to be fads and waves.
      Deconstruction, for example, seems now to be completely
      exhausted. I don't see anybody doing anything interesting as a
      deconstructionist. I watched with some interest and eagerness
      the emergence of something called the New Historicism, its
      peak and its now apparent sliding into an orthodoxy of some
      sort, where people feel they have to repeat the words "New
      Historicism." I still don't quite know what it is. I think of the
      debates that go on in places like *Diacritics* and *MLN*, in
      Cultural Critique, the minnesota review, etc. My attention is
      not commanded by them. I don't really know, and I'm finding
      that I'm in such a scramble most of the time to keep my head
      above water to answer the deadlines, to meet the commitments,
      etc., that I've simply lost interest in anything that is meta-
      critical.

      What really compels my attention outside the doctrinal
      boundaries of "lit crit," which I don't read any more, are
      interesting, daring, novel attempts to do something from an
      historical point of view, across discursive lines in often trans-
      gressive ways, in ways that try to connect politically and
      intellectually with other interventions. I've been very interested
      for the last couple of years, although I haven't written about
      it, in feminism as one of the sites where those things happen,

because there isn't really a unitary feminist discourse as yet. It's still very much going through various phases, independence and separatism, various kinds of meta-historical, meta-theoretical ventures. The work of Joan Scott, for example, is very interesting to me. It's a form of contestation which I find invigorating and amazing. But to say that out of it one can derive a particular position strikes me as quite false and quite wrong.

It seems to me that whereas, say, ten years ago I might eagerly look forward to a new book by somebody at Cornell on literary theory and semiotics, now I'm much more likely to be interested in a work emerging out of concern with African history, or, for example, a book that I just read recently by Helen Callaway, *Gender, Culture and Empire*, which deals with the role of European women in Nigeria, and raises the question of imperialism and feminism. Or Jean Franco's new book on Latin American women, *Plotting Women*. That sort of thing is not programmable.

JW: Sort of theorists without portfolio.

EWS: Even the word theory suggests something to me that . . .

MS: You would want to abandon that?

EWS: Yes I would. I just feel that's a guild designation now that has produced a jargon I find hopelessly tiresome.

MS: What you were saying just now was that the horizon of literature, and therefore literary criticism, is not the literary text, literary analysis and formal poetics, etc., but is something wider – culture, history, society. It seems to me you said, "I don't want to have a position." But that is your position, and that has implications.

EWS: Well it's not strictly speaking my position. It comes as a strange paradox or, at least for me, an unsolvable riddle. That is to say, I am of the rather strong persuasion that all texts – and the texts that interest me the most are the ones that are most this way – all texts are mixed in some way. This whole notion of a hybrid text, of writers like García Marquez and Salman Rushdie, the issues of exile and immigration, crossing of boundaries – all of that tremendously interests me for obvious existential and political reasons, but also because it strikes me as one of the major contributions of late twentieth-century culture. There are certain figures who are most important to me, renegade figures, people like Genet, a man who in his own society was an outcast and outlaw, but who transformed this marginality into, I wouldn't say a vocation, because that is something much more deliberate than it was, but a kind of passionate attachment to other peoples, other than friends, whom he lives with and then later quite consciously betrays. There is evidence for this political poetics in his play, *Les Paravents*. It's also marvelously the case in his book *Le Captif amoureux*, which has just been translated into English. I tried to focus on this aspect of Genet in a recent issue of *Grand Street*. Those are the phenomena that deeply interest me, the people who were able to go from one side to the other, and then come back.

On the other hand, I'm not one of those who believes that the way to proceed is to find an alternative canon to the great literary masterpieces. I have this strange attachment, again it's a residual or vestigial consciousness, to what I consider in a kind of dumb way "great art." It seems to me that works like *Moby-Dick* or *Mansfield Park* or *Gulliver's Travels* are autonomous literary texts and need to be understood and studied that way. I haven't at all given that idea up. For me these works first of all represent a kind of private experience of pleasure in reading and reflection. That's really what I'm finally discovering. In other words, they represent certain hours of private enjoyment, you might say, that have been companions of my intellectual and aesthetic attention for a long time; they are favorites, in a word.

MS: Let me try to tease something out of that and see where it goes. In your current massive project on culture and imperialism, a lot of your reading and analysis centers on the great nineteenth-century novel and its passage into the high modernist tradition in English . . .

EWS: And French. There are parts which you haven't seen which deal with the French novel and then culminate in the early works of Gide and all of Camus. I read them against the colonial background of North Africa and the Levant and that whole group of adventure novels, exotic quests, etc. Then I trace them out further into the literature of resistance in the poetry of Abd el Qadir, the great Algerian warrior of the nineteenth century. I refer to him in passing, but I continue through the work of the early Algerian historians and the attempts to reconstruct the history of the Maghreb. These sections of the book are just notes, but they are part of a picture, as are extended analyses of music. The idea is to present as much as I can of a full portrait of nineteenth-century culture as it bears on empire.

JW: One specifically literary question that one might ask is the following. You use imperialism as a very important new optic through which not merely to read these texts, but to measure their importance, their cultural power, their reach, etc. Does that happen because these are great texts, because of their genius, their linguistic finesse, or any other way you want to term it?

EWS: Well, that's an interesting question. That certainly happens in some instances inadvertently. The references to Antigua in *Mansfield Park* are a very important part of the book. I'm sure if you were to look at more focused English writings on the West Indies – there is a great literature in the late eighteenth and early nineteenth centuries that represents the West Indian interests in England – you would find a much more noticeable presence of an articulated imperial attention, one much more noticeable than that in *Mansfield Park*. But to come back to the question of the masterpieces: they're the ones which would be in the common area of examination and investigation of people to whom in the first instance this work is addressed, that is, other students of literature and culture. So in that respect there's the question of availability. Nobody in this group has *not* read Dickens' *Bleack House* or *Mansfield Park*.

Second, the origin or source of their authority. That's the point, too, that they are a part of a canon. I'm very interested in showing the connection between their authoritative presence in the metropolitan culture of Western Europe and America. Making the connection between the authority in the metropolis and their contribution to the persistence of the imperial attitude and the need of imperialism itself is not an attempt to indict them, but to show how, in an almost passive way, because of their magisterial metropolitan achievements, they conferred upon the keeping of territories and subject peoples a dubious privilege of subordination.

Third, they're also symptomatic. They strike me as a symptom that supports the argument I'm making, that there is no dissent, not even in the canon which is supposed to represent, as Lenin and Hobson talk about it, "higher" ideas and higher values, as distinct from the rather base attitudes in the business of imperialism itself. It is a kind of continuity which I'm interested in. In other words, you could trace a line from the actions, from the profits, from the nefarious practices of imperialism in the colonies to the very structure of the novel, to a certain kind of spectacle, or a certain kind of ethnographic, historical, scientific writing. The point then would be that these works do not provide a refuge from the worldliness of the imperial attitude, but in fact confirm it.

And fourth, it seems to me that there's an act here of rebellion against these works which I have read, and which played a very important role in the formation of my consciousness, my aesthetic, intellectual, professional consciousness, as a student of Western literature and culture. I'm reading them now in a way that I never read them before. But more importantly, I'm reading them now in conjunction with the whole process of resistance to them which exists in the Third World, and which I'm also talking about in what was the third of my lectures on imperialism but is now the third section of my book, *Culture and Imperialism*. In other words, to read them by themselves is not what I am doing. I'm trying to read them contrapuntally against this movement of dissent and resistance that takes place from the very beginning of imperialism. Of course that's a story we don't really know because, as Barbara Harlow has suggested, not nearly enough work has been done on those connections.

JW: This is a devil's advocate question. Is it possible that such a strategy can become very schematic in the sense that reading Camus with Fanon is going to presuppose that Fanon's rewriting has the legitimacy, the strength of subsequent histories of decolonization, etc.? I'm not saying this to say, "Let's try to salvage these works," but to ask, "Does it exhaust them?"

EWS: No it doesn't exhaust them.

JW: Is Dickens somehow evacuated because we can read his texts as active interlocutors in the imperialist project? Then does everything else disappear?

EWS: No, no not at all. That's the point I'm trying to make. Perhaps I'm not making it well. I don't think that at all. Precisely because I give attention to these texts which are "masterpieces," my interest in them is *for themselves*. There is an intrinsic interest in them, a kind of richness in them. These are great writers, and because of that fact they are able to comprehend a situation which allows them to be interesting even to the point of view of an oppositional analysis. But it doesn't exhaust the works. The works remain interesting nevertheless. In a certain sense they are interesting and powerful becuase *they are* interesting and powerful works, not just because they are available to this particular analysis. But the fact is that the analysis has never been done before.

In my imperialism book, I survey the whole, rather peculiar history of important cultural criticism, including that of Raymond Williams himself, who simply never looked at that connection at all, though it is absolutely there. But does it in the end indict the archive as one that is "nothing but" imperialism? Of course this is what people said about *Orientalism*, that I was really attacking all the orientalists for everything they did. That's a total distortion of my argument. I'm saying that one of the reasons lesser Orientalists were able to do what they did in narrow political terms was partly because they had behind them, not only the resource of a tradition and great social power, but also because the work was interesting in and of itself. For example, Jones or Massignon or Lane, or any of those early scholars, are themselves interesting. They are not simply cartoons lurking beneath the surface. I'm not saying that their surface and aesthetic achievement constitute a kind of camouflage for a Colonel Blimp or some ridiculous French general lurking underneath. I think it's important to be able to see the two working together in some way; obviously Bernard Lewis can't see it and never will.

MS: But how would you respond to a West Indian friend of mine who said once of Proust, that this novel is simply a kind of decadent, private experience that does not speak to him, to his cultural formation.

EWS: That's true of Achebe's response to Conrad. He said, well, people study Conrad, but Conrad is just a racist. No matter how clever a writer he is, however good at depicting local color, in the end his political attitudes are despicable to me as a black man. That's another version of the same argument. But they're not that to me. There's no reason for me to perform acts of amputation on myself, intellectual, spiritual, or aesthetic, simply because in the experience of other people from the Third World, a black novelist from Nigeria like Achebe or your West Indian friend, can make my Proust or Conrad into someone who is only despicable. I can share in feelings of alienation, and extremely severe critique, but I can't fully accept the dismissal of these writers; because they have meant a great deal to me and indeed play a role intellectually and aesthetically in the cultural life of the world in which we live.

MS: But only in certain sectors.

EWS: That's true.

MS: Your project suggests not only that one understand the Western tradition in a new way, but that there are all these other cultural traditions, which are in principle equally rich, equally valuable in this slightly peculiar conjuncture we are in. In the *New York Times* last Wednesday, there was an article about teaching the sitar and there were all these egregious screeds from neoconservatives . . .

EWS: They called me three or four times to be interviewed for that article and I never responded.

MS: And what was said was that they – you, Achebe, the Left – haven't shown us anything to substitute for the Western canon. I think that's nonsense.

EWS: Yes, like Saul Bellow (I think) asking, "Where is the African Tolstoy?" That's the other side of it which is also very egregious. I'm not sure that it's necessary to find another object to study. There are other cultural experiences which may not be as rich – this is where we have to accept the tragic or the ironic other side of what we are talking about. It may in fact be the case that, having happened in Paris in the late nineteenth and early twentieth century, Proust may not have to happen again. And too, it may not be necessary to look again for a gigantic novel of memory and nostalgia. This may lay upon us the obligation to look for other sources of experience which are not codified and not codifiable in that form. That's all I'm saying. That doesn't bother me. When a student says to me, well, you're reading Gide's *Immoralist*, why don't we instead read an Algerian novel of that time? My reply is that there was no Algerian novel at that time, any more than at the time that Mahler wrote his symphonies there was a Trinidadian symphonic tradition. It's the adversarial juxtaposition in this ludicrous way that makes the whole enterprise almost comic; that is what I'm rejecting.

MS: It would be possible and legitimate to say that, for instance, Proust happened, but also that there are other things happening now and they are of equal urgency and therefore we may not want to read Proust or Conrad.

EWS: That's something else. Equal urgency is where I might disagree with you. You're posing a theoretical question for which I don't think there's an answer. I am saying that practically, for me, given my particular interest and project, which is very limited I'll grant you, it is urgent for me to read Proust or whoever it is that I'm talking about in this book, who exists within Western culture at a particular moment. That by no means imposes an obligation on anybody else to do the same thing. Somebody who may wish in fact to take up the question, is it necessary to read Proust at all? – it may not be necessary. I'm not saying that it is. It's a private decision on my part to do this, given a certain public and historical reality which is urgent for me, which includes anti-colonialism and anti-imperialism. I don't really know how to extend this into a general program of intellectual attachment. That's my problem. Maybe it's a lack of perspective on my part. Maybe it's a lack of capacity to formulate theoretical models for study and for investigation that I don't feel I have the time for now.

JW: To choose another site in this same problematic. The censoriousness in a certain strand of feminism, American feminism, that would say, "Well, it's just all sexism in the canon and why read it?" To perform this act of excision is ludicrously inadequate. Moreover, to move back to Third World considerations, a figure like García Marquez is not going through this agony about, "Let's substitute all of the canonical figures for Third World writers." It simply doesn't enter into his mode of literary production. It's a peculiar liberal idea of one-to-one substitution and correspondence. It seems to me that involves real political and theoretical consequences.

EWS: I'm very interested in Third World literature. In many of the gestures made by writers, but not all certainly, there's a quite conscious effort to re-do and re-absorb the canon in some way. Conrad is one of the dominating figures of Africanist discourses that Christopher Miller talks about. That strikes me as really interesting, because it's not just dislodging one and putting in another one, but is really an act of engagement with it and doing something quite different than just substituting for and displacing it. There are various kinds of projects of writing back, revising, re-appropriating.

JW: Somebody like N'gugi will say, as he did recently at Yale, "I think my new novel is very interesting because I've tried to make the narrative structure more akin to . . ." Then he listed a host of people he's been reading.

EWS: Sometimes the prescriptive and programmatic imperatives of a particular methodological vision strike me again as not exhausting all the possibilities of what one does and what it's possible to do in fact. That's why I'm very uncomfortable with these rather rigorous and I think in the end nativist sentiments. The idea that you shouldn't read Proust because nothing in it answers to you, that could be a false characterization, not so much of Proust but of you. Maybe the three of us are too cosmopolitan.

MS: I think that is in fact part of it. What you've said again and again is that this is the cultural tradition into which . . .

EWS: In which I find myself right now.

MS: I can't be other than what I am, you might say. But the point is that there are lots of people in the world who *are* other than all of us. A lot of them now are students, people from the subcontinent, from Africa, etc., who come to the United States to be educated. They are forced to do very traditional English lit or comp lit, but then what they say is, "I want to write on post-colonial fiction." But presumably you would say "yes" to that, or would you?

EWS: I don't know: I wonder about that. What I'm interested in having students do, who come with those kinds of concerns and those kinds of backgrounds and imperatives, is to say what it is that the academic situation at Columbia or Stony Brook or Yale, whatever the university happens to be, what it is that is presented to you. And if what is presented to you is in fact a canonical or traditional method, and you are supposed to take all of that in, then the initial process is to understand not so much how that works, but where it comes from. It's perfectly okay to study the curriculum, not by simply reading all the authors in order to fulfill the requirements, but to study it critically and to understand the place of all these things in the procedures of scholarly interpretation and how that has attached itself to various political and ideological formations in the larger society. This dissertation by Gauri Viswanathan, an Indian student of mine, was brilliant precisely because of that. She took as a point of departure the presence of an English curriculum in Indian schools and then tried to discover its archeology. That seems to be the issue that presents itself to a student of the Third World coming here. If you change these sides, if you have done the work here, gotten a PhD and gone through the obstacle course, then you go back to a place like Egypt or the West Indies or India and you're equipped with a professional degree in English from an American or English university. One of the most prevalent and pathetic things of all is to see that precisely the student who was here looking for ways of studying his or her own literature will go back there and be forced by the system there to become the very model of an English professor in America.

MS: The kind of courses that we're talking about, the ones we ourselves want to teach, are unthinkable in most of these countries.

EWS: In Egypt I noticed that the curriculum of Cairo University, which is a fascinating agglomerate of Islamic and Arab nationalists, of left-wing and quasi-colonialist attitudes, is all presided over in its content and its procedures by Saintsbury. It's very disheartening, although a lot of the professors I spoke to were aware of it and interested in making changes.

MS: In a conversation I had with Ranajit Guha the other day, one of the first things he asked me was "How old are you?" I said,

"I'm thirty-nine." He said, "Aah!" I said I'd written to him because I am a great admirer of his work, and he replied that if I were ten years older I wouldn't be saying that. No one of that generation reads him; he can't speak to the people of his own generation.

EWS: Yes it *is* a generational thing.

MS: But those curricula and the people who perpetuate them are still very much in place.

EWS: They have become completely reified, and one can sympathize with the dissatisfaction of students who come here from the Third World looking for ways out. But I'm not sure that the way out is simply by mechanical substitution of post-colonial fiction for nineteenth-century fiction.

JW: And isn't that romanticizing anyway? Then they're taking in what is their own literature somehow. It just defaces the institution.

EWS: Totally. It makes a laughing matter out of it, or a shadow figure out of it.

JW: What strikes me strongly, and disagree with this if you think it's not the case, about so much of your literary critical work is the question of narrative and how strongly that impinges on the entire structure of your thought. Not to the exclusion of poetry, but you have concentrated more on narrative. Also, you questioned, and in my view rightly so, the attitudes of those like Lyotard who have elevated to a theoretical paradigm the loss of narratives. I just wondered how you would comment on the prominence of this category in your own thinking.

EWS: It's really a direct product of the Palestinian experience, and my sense of my own past — I'm sure it's equally true of most Palestinians, even most Arabs and other Third World people who historically were forced to submit to master narratives — that the array of master narratives which are those of the European odyssey have been so extraordinarily dominant. Perhaps in my case it's exaggerated in importance because I was so much a product of the colonial system, but it has played a fantastic cultural role in our lives, so that one of the things I've tried to do is to reconstruct that narrative problem with all of its power and strength and to show its socio-political prevalence throughout. And then having done that, beginning to think of alternatives to it. Not just counter-narratives in the case, for example, of the Palestinian reconstruction of identity after 1948, which has always interested me, and the beginnings of the Palestinian political position which has been the acquisition of the permission to narrate and that whole business.

But also, and I'm at an early stage in this, the interest in anti-narrative strategies of one sort or another.

For example, my interest now in popular culture, so far as I'm interested in it, in the Arab world. This whole excavation of Egyptian cinema that I spoke about earlier is part of that. I haven't gone very far in it because I've been so occupied with the other one, which is really very much a kind of cataloguing and noting of effects. You're absolutely right the way you put it: it's almost crowded out every other kind of interest. I think that Lyotard played a very important role at one point when he first published *The Postmodern Condition*, precisely because everything seemed to be ruled out in favor of what he calls "competence" and "performability." It struck me as simply not the case. I was very interested in the anti-narrative, the anti-linear, in the notion of consecutiveness of efforts, and opposed to that, the whole question of lingering and noting certain areas of experience. At that moment I came to be terribly interested in the work of John Berger, *Another Way of Telling*, in that whole defense against these master narratives and the air of administrative competence that they brought. It may have in a rather artificial way pushed out other interests, but I have not had much time to develop them. Poetry, for example.

JW: I didn't mean to say there was an imbalance, but your interest in narrative is not along the lines of Fred Jameson, who takes Narrative with a capital "N" as the core human experience and looks with enormous nostalgia at what he sees as a diminishment of narrative. It seems to me you look for intersections and renarrativizations.

EWS: Right. That sort of thing rather than the grand narrative, in which I simply don't believe. I think it's very hard for First-World intellectuals to understand the suspicion with which Third-World intellectuals take the question of narrative as in the case, say, of the narrative provided by Western Marxism. Even on the notion of Western Marxism itself, I am critical of Perry Anderson's implicit premise that Western Marxism is the norm by which one judges the progress or failure of Marxism as a whole. I'm not sure that that's the case. There's Marxism in the Third World, for example, which is an interesting story quite removed from the major avenues of the West. Paul Buhle makes the point, actually, in the C. L. R. James book. Western Marxism in Perry's sense excludes Marxism in the Caribbean, which is itself phenomenally interesting and has been politically and theoretically productive. But in Perry's account, Fanon is not to be found and neither is Walter Rodney. The great figures in Africa and Asia, the communist movement of Bengal, for example, are blithely ignored. I'm just not sure that the world historical importance Perry gives to the Western Marxist trajectory is the one I would want to keep with me, although of course I admire it, and Perry Anderson, very much.

MS: I sympathize with that. I was going to ask you a question about Marxism specifically, not just in light of what we said.

EWS: Waiting until the end for the most difficult questions.

MS: All of the things we've been talking about, in a way, have focused on the contradictory or at least tensional points in your work. They've all been in and around questions of something called "the Western tradition" as opposed to all kinds of other things that are going on, either at the same time or not, and which may impinge or may not. In the case of Marx, for example, you have drawn attention to the colossal blindness of Marx himself to things outside of Europe, the essays on India, the notion of an Asiatic mode of production, and so on.

EWS: Right. Nationalism. He didn't understand that at all.

MS: At the same time, one of the epigraphs to *Orientalism* is taken from *The Eighteenth Brumaire*. You have specifically said, not only today, but on other occasions, "I've never said I'm a Marxist." You didn't say, "I'm not a Marxist," but, "I've never said I am a Marxist," which is fair enough. What are the specific political and theoretical reservations that you have about Marxism in particular? One of the things you just said is, "Marxism is clearly not just a Western phenomenon"; it's been tremendously rich and productive in revolutionary movements all over the world. And yet, it seems to me, you've always drawn back from ever making that kind of political and theoretical commitment to Marxism. I'm wondering how you would try to negotiate that problematic.

EWS: First of all, Marxism, in so far as it is an orthodoxy, an ontology, even an epistemology, strikes me as extraordinarily insufficient. The protestations or the affirmations of belonging or not belonging to a Marxist tradition seem to me to be interesting only if they are connected to a practice, which in turn is connected to a political movement. Most of my interaction in the United States with Marxism has been academic. It's hard for me to take it seriously, except as an academic pursuit of one sort or another. But I've never indulged in anti-Marxism either. I may have been critical about certain of Marx's pronouncements, but I've never been an anti-

Communist; in fact, I've denounced anti-Communism as a rhetorical and ideological ploy. But Marxism has nonetheless always struck me as more limiting than enabling in the current intellectual, cultural, political conjuncture.

MS: Do you think that is true within the Palestinian movement?

EWS: I think it is especially true in the Palestinian movement.

MS: Can you talk about that?

EWS: For example, take the Popular Front, which declares itself a Marxist movement. In so far as the rhetoric, the analyses, even the organizational practices of the PFLP could be described as anything, they certainly could not be described as a Marxist party. They could be described in other ways, but those of a classical Marxist party they are not. Its analyses are not Marxist. They are essentially insurrectionary and Blanquist, dispiriting to the organization of the PFLP and also "the masses," whom they seem to address. They have no popular base, never did. Not in Oman or in Lebanon nor, to the best of my ability to judge it, now on the West Bank and in Gaza. They have a certain constituency, but the mass party in the Palestinian movement, the mass party in which the majority of the peasantry is to be found, is Fatah, which is not a Marxist party. It is a nationalist party. So, in the Third World revolutionary scene, it is usually the Marxist party which is the party of the minority, and is at some distance from the grass roots of the movement, that is to say, the critical mass which makes the movement into a revolutionary force on the ground.

MS: That's an important discrimination which I would like you to talk about, because clearly what you said is not true of El Salvador, for example. The guerrilla movement there is and has been Marxist from the outset.

EWS: In the Arab world there isn't – and I was very very interested in this about 15 or 16 years ago when I studied it – in the whole history – again, there are all kinds of personal limitations here which I must admit to at the outset – but in the whole history of Marxist organization, theory, discourse, and even practice in the Middle East, there seems to be no convincing evidence of a Marxism that went beyond Russian Marxism of the twenties and thirties. There has been some presence of those Marxist currents that interest us in the West, the Marxism of early and middle Lukács, the Marxism of Gramsci, later Althusser – although Althusser is a special case, because at a certain moment in the sixties there was a certain Althusserian element in the Arab world, which imported Althusserianism as a superstructural addition, a fact to be taken account of in the rhetoric of Arab Marxism. But by and large, the development of Western Marxism was not reflected in Arab Marxism. There is, rather, a reaching out to the experiments and the ideas and the gestures of orthodox and unorthodox Russian Marxism of the twenties and thirties, which would include Stalinism and Trotskyism. The Marxist parties were essentially Moscow-oriented. To the best of my ability to judge it, the development of a theoretical Marxism in the Arab world did not seem to meet adequately the challenges of imperialism, the formation of a nationalist elite, the failure of the nationalist revolution, etc. – all the problems that we now face, including Zionism itself. And the interesting and effective, such as they were, efforts were limited to dealing with these other problems that didn't come from within the Marxist tradition. That's played an important role in my own energies.

I've been much more conscious, because of my own particular background, with all of its limitations and drawbacks, of the failures, of the lack of reach, in the Marxist tradition. That leaves, nevertheless, a great deal there to be interested in, for example, the whole notion of class consciousness, the labor theory of value, certain attitudes towards race, and the analysis of domination, etc., which come out of the Marxist tradition. But for me it's much less than it is for you a coherent doctrine. For me it's a series of gestures, sometimes recuperated by parties, sometimes not. Sometimes by experience, sometimes not. Sometimes by theory, sometimes not. It is very difficult for me to identify with Marxism. You say what are you identifying with. I can't identify with a Marxist party here. I can't identify with a Marxist rhetoric here, or a discourse, and the same is true in the Arab world. So in my own experience there is this strange gap. It would therefore be presumptuous for me to say, well, I identify with the Marxism of Lukács, or the Marxism of Adorno. They all strike me as interesting, perhaps historically important texts, but no more than that.

And yet, just to conclude, I've also been very much conscious of Marxism and have tried my best to deal with it in a very vigorous way. I have been conscious of the anti-Marxist gestures of some of the philosophers and theoreticians who interest me, such as Foucault, who is at times hysterically anti-Marxist. I'm aware as well of the anti-Marxism and anti-Communism of most of the American intelligentsia. But in the main, I find myself to a certain degree in sympathy with Chomsky's position, a kind of anarcho-syndicalist position,

which has great romantic appeal. Like Chomsky, I am sus-
picious of Bolshevism and have a general fear of dogmatic and
orthodox consensus. Perhaps I'm too interested in alternatives
which, it seems to me, Marxism has foreclosed. What I'm
really trying to say is that the rhetorical and discursive accounts
in Marxism, the accounts that are given by Marxists in this
setting we are discussing, strike me often as less interesting
than other theoretical and political possibilities that are not
comprehended by those statements. I just think intellectually
and politically in this country we're capable of a much more
active and more effective role without trying ourselves to
fetishize ideas about what Marxism is or could be. It seems to
me that there are, given the peculiar structure of an immigrant
society such as this, which has nevertheless transformed itself
into a society of domination, of class, and of privilege with
astonishing kinds of economic and social imbalances and
distortions – in this society there's more scope for an intellectual project that isn't so circumscribed.

MS: Would you say that the movement, particularly in the *intifada*
and I suppose before, has become, even though the PLO is not
a Marxist party, nonetheless, would you say that the Palestinian national movement is a class-based movement?

EWS: Yes to some degree, and I'm distressed now, because of the
configurations of the international and regional contacts, of
the extent to which, at least outside the Occupied Territories,
the movement is dominated by class interests that are not at all
progressive. There is a tremendous confluence of the high
Palestinian bourgeoisie in the PLO, and with it an ideological
dependency upon the United States viewed as the private
fiefdom of whichever administration happens to be in office.
There are all kinds of negative things that we can go into in
greater detail; they distress me a great deal. On the other hand,
you simply can't overlook the fact that Fatah is the most
powerful force. Of course, it's probably not as strong intellectually and in leadership – in which the Communist Party,
Democratic Front, Popular Front, and the Islamic movements
all participate. It seems to me, however, that the idea of a
unified leadership is the solution. Some kind of coalition for
the purposes of insurrection. But in the final analysis, once you
move into action, then there are other considerations, other
tactics, that have to come into play.

Gramsci's essay, "The Revolution against Capital," a reading of the October Revolution, suggests that the revolution
didn't follow what Marx had predicted, but was in some

respects a creative departure from, a reaction against, following through all of those things Marx said about the class struggle. I think that kind of superceding is always true, which of course is one of the reasons why Gramsci is such a problem, not only in Western Marxism, but in Italian Marxism too.

JW: It surprised me in your recent writing how favorable you were to Deleuze and Guattari's notion of a politics of dissent that comes out of things like urban movements, student squatters, etc. Taking that together with what one might call your voluntarism of attention – which is a word that you privilege in literary critical terms and I think translate into the political sphere – how would you position yourself now?

EWS: Yes, I'm not happy with that formulation. I was just anxious to get to some kind of conclusion quickly, but in fact I would prefer to have a much more open conclusion. It's really a statement of where one could find possibilities for alliances. It derives from a certain despair, really for the most part of finding allies for what I'm interested in doing in the traditional places. My stress upon the informal, the unconventional, the unplaced, is a shorthand for saying one must look elsewhere than in the rituals and performances of conventional metropolitan intellectuals.

JW: This isn't a recommendation for a kind of micro-politics?

EWS: Not at all. The more I've looked at that sort of thing, the more it strikes me as a spinning of wheels. To end on a kind of self-critical note, I seem to be in a position of saying about various critical or political projects, well, they're doing this right, but they aren't doing that part right. I don't want to seem to go through ticking off what's good and what's bad. I'm just simply registering reactions to things that you're asking about. I'm really much less than perhaps I give the impression, much less certain about what I'm doing and my whole enterprise as I see it now, with this work on culture and imperialism and on music. I'm often concerned that I'm simply dipping into certain formations, certain moments of culture and political experience, and I really do view what I am doing as a suggestion for others to help in, or provide me with ways in which I might go. The one thing I want to resist is the idea of a finished project, or one that can be put coherently into a new language or a new theoretical mode. I feel very strongly about that; it's not what I'm interested in; that's what I want to get away from.

      If I ever get around to it, what I may be doing in a few years from now is a book on intellectuals. It would be an attempt to talk about this different style, rather than the one which has characterized the intellectual specialist, the policy-maker, or the formulator of new disciplines. What is the word that Peirce uses? Some notion of *abduction*, generalizing from the known facts. A hypothesis of the new situation, projecting forward. I suppose it also is an admission of the fact that I still feel, even with regard to the Palestinian movement, and certainly in the context in America in which I find myself – I still feel, finally, somehow misplaced. I don't feel that I really have found or can ever find a solid, unchanging mode in which to work. For me it's too shifting. That's a tremendous limitation, but one I'll have to live with.

Note

This interview was conducted with Edward Said by Jennifer Wicke and Michael Sprinker in the Spring of 1989, and edited and somewhat modified in the Summer of 1991.

INDEX